Twice Forgotten

Twice Forgotten

AFRICAN AMERICANS and the KOREAN WAR

An Oral History

DAVID P. CLINE

The University of North Carolina Press

CHAPEL HILL

Designed by Jamison Cockerham
Set in Arno Pro, Scala Sans, Cassino, and Irby
by Tseng Information Systems, Inc.

Jacket photograph by Private 1st Class Charles Fabiszak, US Army,
NARA File no. 111-SC-358355, Department of Defense HD-SN-99-03053

Manufactured in the United States of America

The University of North Carolina Press has been a member
of the Green Press Initiative since 2003.

LIBRARY OF CONGRESS CATALOGING-IN-PUBLICATION DATA
Names: Cline, David P., 1969– author.
Title: Twice forgotten : African Americans and the
Korean War, an oral history / David P. Cline.
Description: Chapel Hill : The University of North Carolina Press,
[2021] | Includes bibliographical references and index.
Identifiers: LCCN 2021030605 | ISBN 9781469664538
(cloth ; alk. paper) | ISBN 9781469664545 (ebook)
Subjects: LCSH: Korean War, 1950–1953 — Participation, African American. |
Korean War, 1950–1953 — African American. | Korean War, 1950–1953 — Personal
narratives, American. | African American veterans — Social conditions —
20th century. | BISAC: HISTORY / African American & Black | HISTORY /
Military / Korean War | LCGFT: Oral histories. | Personal narratives.
Classification: LCC DS919 .C55 2021 | DDC 951.904/2 — dc23
LC record available at https://lccn.loc.gov/2021030605

A note on language: Throughout this book, the terms "Black" and "African American"
are used interchangeably to describe Americans of African descent. Additionally,
some narrators use words such as "negro" or "colored" that were in use during the time
period they are discussing. The N-word, in its entirety, also appears a number of times
in the interviews. In every instance, it is being used by an African American person
quoting the hateful, demeaning, and terroristic language used against them by whites.
While I understand encountering this word may be difficult for some readers, in order
not to silence the narrators or blunt the intent and impact of the language they were
subjected to, I have elected to reproduce the word without intervention. — DPC

For

Larry Hogan, Ernie Shaw, Julius Becton, Charles Berry,

and all those who answered the call.

Thank you for your inspiration.

Contents

PART III **The Battles Continue**

A section of illustrations follows page 109

The Fight of Their Lives

At the time that Charles Bussey was born in Bakersfield, California, in 1921, to be Black in America meant to be in a constant state of warfare. Growing up "in a bigoted town taught me some hard lessons," he recalled, but it also taught him how to fight for himself. Perhaps more important, it also taught him the need to recover quickly before the next fight began, good training for leading troops into battle as commander of the segregated 77th Engineer Combat Company during the Korean War. "Growing up as I did, helped prepare me for being a company commander in combat."[1]

Although the history of the Black freedom struggle is as long as the history of African Americans in America, there are within it, as historian Adriane Lentz-Smith has put it in documenting the contributions of Black soldiers, "certain moments [that] emerge as particularly formative or even transformative."[2] She points to World War I as one of those moments, but the argument can fairly be extended to all US wars, African American participation in which created highly visible stepping-stones along a path to freedom. From the Revolutionary War forward, African Americans recognized military service and times of war as unique opportunities to both participate in citizenship and to apply pressure for a greater piece of the same. These wars, moments of national crisis and international vulnerability, emerge as fissures in the hard shell of the American racial order, times when African Americans were able to gain incrementally greater freedoms while exposing their ordeal on a global stage.

The desegregation of the military and the participation of African Americans leading up to and during the Korean War were key components of and building blocks for the long civil rights movement. By taking a moment to ride along on the shoulders of Black soldiers and sailors in the pages that follow, we shall see that the desegregation of the military took longer than most accounts have acknowledged. When desegregation finally arrived, it came as the result of a series of combined forces: the continuous and constant willingness of African Americans to take up the burden of armed service in a racially unjust military in order both to claim a piece of the American democratic promise and to force that democracy to include them at last; a sustained campaign of pressure from African American civil rights activists and organizations, from the Black press, and from ordinary citizens; the actions of President Harry S. Truman and the executive branch in pushing civil rights broadly, calling specifically for the desegregation of the military and directly pressuring the branches of the US Armed Forces; and the Korean War itself, the particular needs of which forced those branches that had lagged behind to scrap strict segregation.

African American participation in the armed forces, although its form differed within each war and historical period, served as a means to leverage new freedoms from a country that had long promised but failed to deliver them. At the same time, military service exposed African Americans to new ways of experiencing democracy, which in turn slowly led to increased demands for individual and collective access to that democracy. The pathbreaking service of the Tuskegee Airmen and other Black veterans of the world wars, for example, did not lead directly to America's mass civil rights protests of midcentury nor to the civil rights legislation finally created in the 1960s, but it did bequeath a legacy of experience and tactics that would remain at the center of the movement as it came into full blossom.[3]

In the stories that follow you will find painful segregation, pathbreaking but still sometimes painful desegregation, and childhood, family, training, war, and prisoner stories full of pathos and grit and sorrow and otherworldly forbearance. In other words, you will hear the voices of survivors. You may not hear the words "civil rights" mentioned often — indeed, they were just joining the national lexicon during the years of the Korean War — but make no mistake about it, this is a civil rights story. This is a story of people fighting to be recognized as people, as full human beings with all rights and privileges thereof and, not to put too fine a point on it, willing to sacrifice themselves to achieve it. Truman may have been a paternalistic integrationist and the armed forces under his command grudging and halting in their move toward equality, to say the least, and the bloody yawp of battle's incessant need for more bodies the true reason that the races finally mixed, but it did happen. And it did make a difference that eventually led to greater change. Although the "police action" in Korea has at long last finally been officially acknowledged as the war that it was, its nickname, the Forgotten War, still remains sadly appropriate. But the men and women from twenty-two nations and from many backgrounds who served do not deserve that same fate. And especially those African Americans who served and who fought, not one war, but many, deserve to have their voices join the chorus of those who called for freedom. The African American veterans of the Korean War era do not deserve the fate of being twice forgotten.

The Korean War broke out just more than seventy years ago, at a time that the issue of the unequal opportunities and treatment America afforded its Black citizens was coming to a peak, playing out in greatly increased civil rights activism, occasional racial violence, and ever louder demands from the Black community and progressive politicians that the systemic oppression of African Americans be dismantled with haste. The armed services, which had long exiled Blacks to a few menial positions and nearly always in segregated Jim Crow circumstances, would be the testing ground for policy reform, especially after President Truman ordered the desegregation of the military by executive order in 1948. Desegregation of the military, however, did not quickly follow Truman's order, nor did it come easily, playing out instead in fits and starts over the course of the Korean conflict.

It is worth saying a few words here about the difference between "desegregation" and "integration," terms which are often mistakenly used interchangeably. They are far from the same thing. Since segregation is the separation of people according to a characteristic, in this case race, desegregation is the elimination of that practice. The mixing of people on the basis of race, whether by legal or social means, is integration. As we shall see, at times the military employed all three of these practices: segregation, desegregation, and integration. Truman's order, however, was simply a call for the abandonment of the arbitrary separation of troops by race, or segregation. Integration, rules mandating a policy of the inclusion of diverse races, usually according to a typical minimum or maximum percentage of the whole, would come later. There is also often a colloquial understanding that "integration" means equal distribution and equal treatment, and although this is often the ideal sought, that is not the strict definition, nor is it often realized. That's what someone like Lemuel Hines, a Marine Corps veteran, means when he says, in chapter 5, "I don't use the word integration no way, because it's no such thing [really]." According to the definition of "integration," when units in Korea desegregated from strict racial separation and replaced that by having a single African American soldier in a white army unit, say, that was—strictly speaking—integration, but was that individual still isolated? In all likelihood. Was that individual still denied equality of treatment? Well, that depended.

In 1962, the Reverend Martin Luther King Jr. attempted to parse this rhetoric by way of declaring desegregation merely the means to the ultimate end of true integration. At a church conference in Nashville that November, King declared that segregation "represents a system that is prohibitive" in that it denies equal access but that desegregation is "eliminative and negative, for it simply removes these legal and social prohibitions." Integration, on the other hand, "is creative, . . . and therefore more profound and far reaching than desegregation. Integration is the positive acceptance of desegregation and the welcomed participation of Negroes into the total range of human activities. Integration is genuine intergroup, interpersonal doing. Desegregation then, rightly, is only a short-range goal. Integration is the ultimate goal of our national community." He continued that a desegregated society that is not integrated is a society "where men are physically desegrated and spiritually segregated, where elbows are together and hearts apart," leaving us with "a stagnant equality of sameness rather than a constructive quality of oneness."[4] Desegregation, though, would be the necessary first step.

Popular culture provides an interesting, if troubling, example. The television show *M*A*S*H*, which portrayed a fictional mobile army surgical hospital on the frontlines in Korea, aired from 1972 to 1983, and was based on the 1970 film, which was based on the 1968 novel *M*A*S*H*, by Richard Hooker. The character of Dr. Oliver Wendell "Spearchucker" Jones appears in all three, and while his middle name was changed to Harmon in the film and televised versions, his nickname, a common racial insult, remained intact. The character is described as having gone to "some jerkwater colored college" before going on to medical school and then getting drafted by the Eagles as "the best fullback in pro ball since Nagurski." Jones, also a collegiate javelin champion, which is supposedly the source of his offensive nickname, is then drafted by the army and sent to an evacuation hospital in Korea as a neurosurgeon. While Hooker's intention may have been to lampoon American race relations, in addition to skewering army life — and in fact the novel is filled with ethnic nicknames for other characters — the language he employs is far from subtle. Jones is described repeatedly as "a nigra" and through such phrases as "darkness at noon" and "that big animal." In the television series, his full name is rarely mentioned, and at one point his doctor roommates joke about selling him. But in all three versions of the story he is also portrayed as a top surgeon in one of medicine's most notoriously difficult specialties and as a key component of a desegregated medical unit. Jones himself acknowledges some of the trickier workings of the desegregated army: It is not just overt racists he's wary of because "there are so many phonies around. The worst are the types who knock themselves out to show you that your color doesn't make any difference. They are part of the black man's burden too."[5]

Without the war, the desegregation of the military would have likely come in time as the armed forces came under greater political and ideological pressure, both internally from the African American community and externally from the perceived Cold War pressure from allies and enemies alike to live up to its promise for freedom and equality for all. The Korean War, though, was the catalyst for immediate change, bolstered both by military leaders' dissatisfaction with the performance of its segregated troops and by the urgent need for increased manpower during a time of war.[6] The desegregation of the military's four branches during the more than three years the Korean War lasted also both influenced and in turn was influenced by the burgeoning civil rights movement. Black veterans returned to the United States having experienced new freedoms, however slight, and transformed those experiences into demands for equality at home.

In a number of ways, the integration of the armed forces and the participation of African American soldiers and sailors during the Korean War brought the simmering Civil Rights Movement to the boiling point. African Americans in the early and mid-twentieth century fought daily skirmishes for their own civil rights, and they fought it on many fronts: in fair housing, fair employment, equal treatment under the law, nonsegregated accommodations, and the list goes on and on. If the long civil rights movement was a war, and it certainly had all the trappings of one—precise tactics, mythic generals, a heroic mass of enlisted "soldiers," decisive moments, and grinding daily fighting—then military desegregation, and the Korean War that enabled it, was one of its great battles. The Korean War itself, as experienced by those African Americans who served during it, advanced the cause of civil rights and forged a path forward into civilian life. It was a crucial stepping-stone between the important inroads made during World War II and the civil rights legislation of the 1950s and 1960s, beginning with *Brown v. Board of Education* just after the Korean War.

The example of successful desegregation and, eventually, some level of integration provided by the armed forces, and the "conversion" to racial reconciliation experienced by individuals through exposure to those of another race, created a precedent that would be followed in desegregating schools, transportation, and other hallmarks of American life in the decade to come. As one Black editorialist predicted in 1951, "An even larger number of white men will during and after this war serve as a leaven in many American communities—as spearheads in the movement toward a real and sound interracial unity."[7]

Those African Americans who returned from the Korean War, having tested limited new freedoms and citizenship rights, later translated these newly tested definitions of manhood and womanhood and equality abroad into civil rights activism at home. Many returning Black veterans and their supporters sought to answer, in the real world, the question, posed by a fictional North Korean officer in the contemporary war film *Steel Helmet* (1951), "Black boy, why you fight this war . . . you can't even sit in the front of the bus?"[8] These veterans demanded far more than bus seats and contributed in a wide variety of ways to the dismantling of Jim Crow.

The war, of course, brought with it a great cost. From the time the Utah-sized nation of Korea descended into civil war on June 25, 1950, to the signing of an armistice on July 27, 1953, an estimated 36,000 Americans and 415,000 South Koreans had been killed and 105,000 Americans and 429,000 South Koreans wounded. Somewhere around 1.5 million North Koreans and Chinese also lay dead, with untold numbers wounded. African Americans participated in the Korean War and supported it from home in great numbers. Nearly 100,000

Black soldiers and sailors were on active duty when the war began, and by the time a cease-fire was called, 600,000 African Americans had participated and around 5,000 had lost their lives.[9]

Perhaps the best-known story of African American participation in the Korean War is that of the army's all-Black 24th Infantry Regiment, known as the Buffalo Soldiers. By the time it was disbanded in 1951, the Deuce Four had acquired one of the longest records of unrelieved service on the front lines, often holding positions while white units retreated past them. But it had also earned a troubled and troubling reputation back home as the result of accusations of disorder and cowardice and multiple courts-martial. Although the men of the Deuce Four were eventually shown to have been no more susceptible to retreat than their white counterparts while fighting under worse conditions, the story of the 24th Infantry Regiment has sometimes threatened to obscure the contributions of other segregated African American units in Korea, and certainly that of individual African Americans who served. In the US Army alone, three infantry divisions—the 25th, the 2nd, and the 3rd—each had all-Black infantry regiments. The army also had five artillery and one tank battalions, a ranger company, an engineer company, and support units, all segregated. Especially in the army, segregated units remained long after it is commonly thought that they were disbanded, and desegregation when it occurred was far from a wholesale process of equal racial distribution. Much more common was the distribution of one or two African Americans at a time into formerly all-white units.

Then there are also the stories of the air force, navy, Marine Corps, and National Guard units, each with their own nuances and trajectories, which are highlighted in the pages that follow by those who endured them. The bigger story of race in Korea, however, may be the integrated and barely integrated units that were far more common than segregated units, especially as the war ground on, and the fact that soldiers and sailors returned from Korea to an America still very much fractured by the divisions of race and structures and limitations of de facto and de jure segregation.

John B. Jackson, a Black veteran of an army mortar company, recalled that he "realized sometime through training that we were fighting for democracy for a people I had never heard of. And I looked back and I said, 'Jackson, wait a minute, you're going to Korea to fight for democracy and when you left Houston, Texas, you were segregated, you did not have the word "democracy" [in your vocabulary].' And I was angered about this because President Truman is sending me over there but yet I knew that if I ever got back to Texas I would still come back to that same undemocratic system."[10] His words, spoken fifty years after the end of the war, echoed that of a prescient *Chicago Defender* columnist who half a century earlier predicted that Black soldiers, who were then experiencing military success in the first weeks of the Korean War, would "whip back the Communist onslaught with their blood — some with [their] lives — only to return home to find it's still open warfare on the extension of American rights to all citizens regardless of race."[11] African Americans at all levels of society and leadership, however, refused to let this stand, even though the fight would be long and grueling. Indeed, it was a struggle that had been going on for hundreds of years by the time the Korean peninsula descended into war. And so this is very much a story of rights and of perseverance as well.

James Forman, a director of the Student Nonviolent Coordinating Committee and a speaker at the March on Washington in 1963 and the author of 1968's call for reparations, the "Black Manifesto," was one of the more contentious and important voices of the modern civil rights movement. But already in 1947, when enlisting in a segregated US Air Force at the age of eighteen, he had a commitment to the struggle *and* a sophisticated understanding of the forms that struggle itself actually takes. In his later autobiography, he recalled his reaction to finding out, during training, that the technical schooling that had been used as bait for African American recruits would not actually be available to most of them:

> We felt double-crossed by the Armed Forces. It was a special kind
> of anger, caused this time by outrageous hypocrisy and the feeling
> of having been taken. I had accepted the contradictions of entering a
> segregated Air Force, the way I "accepted" other kinds of segregation —
> in the sense of deciding not to fight them every time they came up. This
> "acceptance" was, I think, an answer to the question, how does a person
> survive psychologically in a society of all-pervasive racism? To fight it
> every time, all of the time, is to commit a kind of suicide. Even people
> who are challenging racism as a full-time job find there are certain things
> they accommodate because those experiences do not raise major issues.
> Such phenomena vary, according to the conscious of a person and the
> stage of a struggle. But while I worked to find my definitions of the
> larger struggle, and how to wage it, life in the Air Force continued to
> press down with its daily insults — above all, its hypocrisy and double-
> dealing. I began to see the Armed Forces in broader terms, too, as a
> dehumanizing machine which destroys thought and creativity in order
> to preserve the economic system and the political myths of the United
> States. I decided that we should not commit suicide on a mass basis; we
> should save most of our energy for an organized struggle.[12]

This is an important passage, and an important distinction between kinds of resistance. Tolerance for the time being, in sacrifice to a larger goal as part of a strategy, is not actually acceptance. In fact, it is not only cunning but speaks of a great inner strength. Jackie Robinson showed the same when his manager Branch Rickey struck a deal with him before drafting him as the first African

American major league baseball player in the modern era—if Robinson could hold his tongue, and his fists, for two years, to turn the other cheek, at the end of that time he could unleash with a vengeance. Some active-duty military and veterans could do that, some could not. Struggle, resistance, takes many forms.

That's why this is not a traditional book of military history, focused on battles and strategies in the field. This is a book about the multiple strategies of resistance and creating change, and as such, it requires reading hard against the grain of military history to get at the social and cultural stories lurking within and so see the civil rights story there. This book also fights against the grain of civil rights history to illuminate the military story there. When I started this project, an unbelievable twenty years ago now, I was green as could be, but I also thought that the history of military desegregation and African Americans' Korean War–time experiences must be an integral part of the civil rights story. After all, Truman called for desegregation, it happened during the war, desegregation was a major goal of the civil rights movement, the war ended in 1953, and the Montgomery Bus Boycott was in 1955. Obviously, it's not quite that simple, but the path that is absolutely there was missing from most of the standard civil rights movement historiography. Also unbelievably, not much scholarship has pushed this idea forward in those intervening years, years in which I became less green and perhaps a little more knowledgeable. And still I am convinced that what happened in the military between World War II and Vietnam is an important part, a crucial part, of the African American freedom struggle and civil rights history and that we can only learn it and appreciate it by putting battles and military strategy mostly to the side and listening, deeply listening, to the experiences of those who lived them. And it does take deep listening—and reading against the grain and between the lines—because much of what is said in these pages about race and struggle and freedom is said very subtly. It is said in the manner of those who know the truth of a situation—Jim Crow—so well that it seems to call for little explication. A few words can carry a cargo load of meaning and weight. Part of what we hear is what Forman was getting at above, that the struggle to just survive was so all consuming that going to battle daily against racism was inconceivable if the goal was to stay alive to someday fight an organized and tactical battle against inequality and win.

In the chapters that follow we will hear directly from those who lived this history, starting with how conditions were before Executive Order 9981, then moving into the experiences of enlistment, training, and service, before taking some time to look at how these experiences influenced and were translated into calls for action in postwar civilian life. At times it will feel like a war story, at times it will feel like a struggle for civil rights, and often it will feel like a civil rights story taking place within the covers of a war story, which is exactly what it is. Let's listen.

Introduction

The Segregated Military and the Journey toward Change

You've heard that there's no atheists in foxholes? There are no bigots. You want somebody! They could be polka dot and you get to love him. You get to love him. He gets to look out for you. You get to look out for him and all of that shit dies. It just dies.

JOHN CANNON, lieutenant colonel, US Army, retired

African Americans have participated in all of America's wars, from the colonial militias during the American Revolution to World War II, and for nearly as long as Blacks have served, African Americans have called for their equal participation in a desegregated military. Why then, when it was finally achieved, did it come about when and how it did?

The segregated military had its institutional roots in the Civil War. Eager to participate in the project of securing their own liberation, African Americans served in four distinguished but segregated regiments in the Union army, regiments that Reconstruction era legislation then made permanent and protected by law.[1] Although service conditions were mandated to be equal to those of white soldiers, the units would remain separate. The several thousand soldiers in the four regiments acquitted themselves well again during the Spanish-American War of 1898, and their reputation for discipline and high morale became a source of Black pride nationally. However, the white public, already sensing the implications of what a truly equal military meant for the larger society, grew increasingly hostile to Black servicemen, and the US Army and state militias responded by reversing some of the improvements originally offered to Blacks during Reconstruction. Between 1890 and the 1910s, the army rolled back its policies of equal treatment and pay for its Black soldiers, and state militias that had desegregated under federal order in 1867 once again resegregated Blacks or banned them from service altogether.[2] Violent public episodes resulted, as local whites turned against Black servicemen in their midst, occasionally with devastating results. In one famous incident in Brownsville, Texas, in August 1906, the white mayor and a number of prominent white community members responded with outrage to the news that Black soldiers from the 25th Infantry, stationed at nearby Fort Brown, had run amuck in the town's streets, firing rifles indiscriminately and killing one white man and wounding another. The Black soldiers and their white commanders, however, insisted that the men had been peacefully sleeping in their barracks, and when the mayor and his allies produced spent rifle shells from the streets, they asserted that the shells had been planted. Believing the townspeople, President Theodore Roosevelt dishonorably discharged all 167 servicemen and barred them from future service, and the specter of Brownsville — and "the murderous potential of Negroes with guns"—would be raised frequently in subsequent years by those who would see African Americans dismissed from the US Armed Forces or their roles diminished. Never mind that years later it would be revealed that the rifle shells had indeed been planted and the men of the 25th framed by white citizens of Brownsville who had wanted them out of town.[3] The Black press closely covered the Brownsville events, and the *Chicago Defender*, a premier nationally distributed black newspaper, ran an editorial declaring that the army had "not a shred of evidence to sustain the ground for punitive action." In fact, almost seventy years later after a sustained campaign to exonerate the troops, the army cleared the records of all 167 soldiers and declared the discharges to have been a "gross injustice."[4]

As the conditions for Blacks worsened in both military and civilian life, African American activist organizations, including the National Association for the Advancement of Colored People (NAACP) and the National Urban League, increased their focus on military service as a means both to participate in the nation and as way to crack open the door leading to greater freedom and equality. African Americans recognized that the US Army was the largest single employer of Blacks in the country and that it trained many of its employees in the South and transported others from the South. As such, African American inclusion in army training meant that the army would inevitably run into and oppose Jim Crow. A significant goal of Black activists in the early decades of the twentieth century, therefore, was not just to change the Jim Crow military but to force the military to challenge and end Jim Crow itself in the United States of America.

It was no surprise, then, that when the United States declared war on Germany in 1917, the NAACP and other organizations encouraged Black Americans to enlist as a means of achieving greater equality and economic advantage. Citing emancipation from slavery as a glorious result of Blacks' participation in the Civil War, W. E. B. Du Bois, editor of the NAACP journal *Crisis*, added that in the twenty years since the end of the Spanish-American War, "despite many setbacks, we have doubled or quadrupled our accumulated wealth."[5] He argued that further military involvement would help Blacks realize even greater successes. But a combination of white citizens' pushback and army recalcitrance stymied such predictions until many years later, especially after violence involving Black soldiers, again from the 24th Infantry, broke out in Houston in August 1917.

As part of the growing war effort, the army had begun construction of Camp Logan on the outskirts of Houston and had sent the 3rd Battalion of the 24th Infantry from its base in New Mexico to guard the construction efforts. Houston's white population and even the construction workers resented their Black servicemen's presence, and the men were subjected to local Jim Crow laws and daily humiliations and abuse. As a relative of one of the soldiers recalled more than a hundred years later, "They sent these soldiers into the most hostile environment imaginable."[6] The tension reached a crisis on August 23 after a Black soldier was arrested for allegedly interfering with the arrest of a Black woman. A rumor suddenly broke that a white mob was en route to the camp. As a precautionary measure following the arrest, the soldiers had been ordered to turn over their weapons. And up to that point, the men had been torn, with some peacefully surrendering their weapons, while others, moved to tears while testifying to near constant harassment and assault, refused. As historian Adriane Lentz-Smith explains, "Turning over their rifles meant betraying their manhood, betraying themselves, and betraying each other." But when the false rumor of the encroaching white mob rushed through the camp, the soldiers' anger at being "treated like dogs" by white Houstonians boiled over, and they responded en masse, marching east into the city and, over the next two hours, battling with white police and citizens. Four Black soldiers and sixteen white civilians, including five policemen, died. In the aftermath, three courts-martial were held in San Antonio to try 118 indicted soldiers. In the first, the largest murder trial in US history, 64 Black soldiers were tried, and 13 were eventually put to death by hanging. Witnesses from Houston, who regularly referred to the accused as "n——s," failed to identify a single soldier who had fired a fatal shot.[7]

Before the violence in Houston, the US Army had been considering creating sixteen new all-Black regiments. These plans were now scrapped out of a stated fear that Blacks and whites training in the same areas would lead to a "national calamity."[8] Yet the Selective Service Act of May 1917 never mentioned race, and over the next two years 367,410 African Americans were inducted into the army. What to do with them? The army's solution was to drastically limit opportunities for Blacks, consigning most to noncombat labor and support positions. Almost 90 percent of African Americans who served during World War I did so in unskilled or semiskilled support roles, with little or no formal military training.[9] The army didn't stop there, attempting to decrease permanently the potential combat role of Black soldiers in future conflicts. And its attitude toward its Black troops can be seen in the inspector general of the army's final report on the Houston affair: "The tendency of the negro soldier, with fire arms in his possession, unless he is properly handled by officers who know his racial characteristics, is to become arrogant, overbearing, and abusive, and a menace to the community in which he happens to be stationed."[10]

During World War I the US Army deliberately excluded the four traditional Black combat regiments from service in Europe, instead exiling them to remote garrisons, supposedly in order to prevent further violence between Black soldiers and white civilians. The 25th Infantry drew guard duty in the Hawaiian and Philippine Islands, and the 24th Infantry patrolled remote outposts in the American Southwest along the border with Mexico. This was the first major conflict since the Civil War from which these proud troops were excluded.

Finally bowing to pressure from the NAACP and a Black community that was investing heavily in war bonds, the army established two Black divisions, the 92nd and 93rd Infantries, with a total strength of four thousand men, and sent them into battle in France. The 92nd, under US command, had a troubled record; however, the 93rd, drawn primarily from state militias, fared better since, rather than being directed by prejudiced white American officers, they were assigned to French command. The French treated them as they did native French soldiers, with the same training and weaponry and little reported racial intolerance. Three of the four regiments comprising the 93rd received France's top award for a military unit, the Croix de Guerre.[11]

Following World War I, African American leaders on the home front were well aware that white racism had severely limited Blacks' chances for advancement through military service. Reflecting back in the pages of *Crisis* in 1925, Du Bois claimed that "Negro haters entrenched in the Army" had conducted "a concerted campaign of slander" that supported the notion of Blacks innate inferiority as soldiers and their incapability as leaders.[12] His earlier optimism now gave way to his fears that such prejudice would keep African Americans from advancing through the armed forces and would severely limit them again in any future conflicts.

After the war, the US Army drastically reduced overall troop strength, and the Black regiments were similarly downsized, with the number of Black servicemen falling from a wartime high of 404,000, or 11 percent of army manpower, to a low of 3,640 active-duty Black personnel in August 1939, accounting for about 1.5 percent of enlisted men and functionally decommissioning the

Black regiments.[13] The 24th Infantry survived, but by 1922 it had been reduced to 828 men, who primarily performed housekeeping and construction work at Fort Benning, Georgia, and were mostly untrained for and unprepared for battle. Even so, the army, especially during the Great Depression, could provide a steady job, and a small number of African Americans continued to enlist.

Black soldiers who returned to civilian life after World War I, and those who had supported them at home, were profoundly disappointed that white supremacist policies determined the wartime treatment of Black soldiers and prevented their further advancement. Many African Americans had at first enthusiastically supported the war effort in the hopes that military participation would, as it had during the Civil War, open a place for Black advancement. So it was that when war clouds once again loomed on the horizon, many Blacks joined Du Bois in feeling less than enthusiastic about supporting or joining the military. Indeed, this overtly political issue played out in the pages of Black newspapers when opponents of Franklin Delano Roosevelt took out full-page advertisements to highlight the humiliations suffered by Blacks in the military under Roosevelt. Such public pressure could prove effective. The very same day that an advertisement in the *Baltimore Afro-American* focused on the plight of the highest-ranking Black man in the military, Col. Benjamin O. Davis, who had seen a hundred white colonels promoted ahead of him, Roosevelt suddenly promoted Davis to general and appointed William H. Hastie, a former civil rights attorney and the nation's first Black federal judge, to the War Department's new Office of the Civilian Aide on Negro Affairs.[14] But these appointments were token efforts, belying any serious institutional change in the army's treatment of its African American servicemen.[15]

Further domestic pressure came from the March on Washington movement, promoted by Brotherhood of Sleeping Car Porters' president A. Phillip Randolph and activist Bayard Rustin. Beginning in 1933, Randolph and Rustin began organizing lower- and middle-class African Americans, preparing them to march en masse on the government in Washington, DC, to demand the integration of the military and greater employment opportunities for Blacks. In September 1940, Randolph led a delegation of Black leaders, including Walter White of the NAACP and T. Arnold Hill of the National Urban League, to meet with President Roosevelt to demand an immediate end to segregation in the armed forces. However, the White House responded with an official statement, affirming that "the policy of the War Department is not to intermingle colored and white enlisted personnel in the same regimental organizations."[16]

Seeking to bring more pressure on Roosevelt, Rustin and Randolph announced a mass protest march in the capital, scheduled for July 1941. With participation predicted at over a hundred thousand marchers, the march led President Roosevelt, a week before the event was to occur, to issue Executive

Order 1802, creating the first Fair Employment Practices Committee. Pressing their advantage, Randolph and his colleagues demanded that nondiscrimination policies apply to federal domestic employment as well. Receiving this concession, Randolph agreed to cancel the march, although he kept the March on Washington movement organization functioning, partly in order to monitor the government's delivery of its promises. This proved slow in coming, even as the Japanese bombing of Pearl Harbor brought the United States into World War II in December 1941.

African American women were, from the start, equally involved in demanding an equal part of military service. Mary McLeod Bethune, a contemporary of Randolph's and like him a tireless activist for Black advancement, also worked on behalf of a desegregated military for both men and women. President of the National Association of Colored Women from 1924 to 1928, she founded the National Congress of Negro Women in 1935 and in 1936 she accepted President Roosevelt's appointment to the post of administrative assistant for Negro affairs. She became president of the NAACP in 1940 and campaigned for African American participation in World War II. She actively recruited African American women for the Women's Auxiliary Army Corps, including Dovey Johnson Roundtree, who after her WAAC service, beginning in 1942, would go onto become a lawyer and represent other Black WAACs in antidiscrimination cases in the 1950s.[17]

Army leadership continued to assert that Blacks were unsuited to combat and to relegate them primarily to segregated labor units. Although the Selective Service Act mandated that "there shall be no discrimination against any person on account of race or color," Secretary of War Henry L. Stimson, who believed that African Americans lacked the intelligence to handle modern weapons or the skills to be officers, had stated in 1940 that he would not support the act because of Blacks' poor combat skills and behavior.[18] "I saw the same thing happen twenty-three years ago," he said, "when Woodrow Wilson yielded to the same sort of demand and appointed colored officers, and the poor fellows made perfect fools of themselves. One at least of the Divisions behaved very badly. The others were turned into labor battalions."[19] The US Army instituted a cap on Black inductions and enlistments to 10.6 percent, just enough to staff its racially segregated support units. It even failed to fill those slots, however, neglecting to induct Black draftees, rejecting five out of every ten Black applicants due to supposed poor health or illiteracy, and postponing inductions of African Americans on the grounds that insufficient segregated training facilities prevented their incorporation. Not one African American was called up from the draft issued after the Japanese attack at Pearl Harbor.[20] Secretary of War Stimson later admitted that the army had instituted "rigid requirements for literacy mainly to keep down the number of colored troops."[21]

Segregation, indeed, outright racism, often ruled at stateside training camps, even well outside the South. At some camps, commanders banned the possession of African American newspapers; Black officers were banned from socializing with whites at Selfridge Field, Michigan; and at an army base in Pennsylvania, white officers issued an order that "any association between colored soldiers and white women, whether voluntary or not, would be considered rape ... [a]nd the penalty would be death."[22] The American Red Cross, at the army's request, kept segregated blood banks up to the Korean War.

Military leaders refused to take responsibility for these racist policies. Communist agitators and the African American press, which the armed forces considered to be both subversive and inflammatory, were blamed for Black discontent, although some military investigations pointed at least some blame at the system of racial segregation itself. Writing to First Lady Eleanor Roosevelt in July 1943, Civilian Aide on Negro Affairs Hastie criticized the Black press but acknowledged that, "there is room for great improvement in our handling of the Negro in the Army."[23]

During the last days of World War II racial progress in several distinct areas created the atmosphere for change out of which demands for an integrated military would at last emerge. In the military itself, a few professionals risked desegregating facilities and, in some rare cases, combat units. On the home front, civil rights activists applied pressure from both within and outside of the military, often by publicizing racial inequities and violence in the services. Perhaps the most important contributing factor, however, was how the war itself made Americans rethink their ideas about race and relations between Blacks and whites. According to historians Sherie Mershon and Steven Schlossman, World War II was a watershed moment in which Americans generally experienced a shift in how they viewed the relationship between ethnic and racial diversity and a unified American nation. The Nazi atrocities in Germany and, to some extent, the race riots that swept the American nation around this time prompted some to question discrimination and redefine national identity in broader terms. As Mershon and Schlossman assert, "Although few whites advocated complete racial equality, the idea that reducing racial discrimination would serve the national interest was more widely accepted and more frequently discussed during the war years than it had been at any time in the recent past."[24]

The postwar military also began to reconsider its racial policies for a purely practical reason: efficiency. In order to best use those troops available to them, including Black troops, military commanders were forced to consider how segregation, racial conflict, and even racial violence negatively contributed to the armed forces' efficiency. For these pragmatic rather than idealistic reasons, some military leaders began to adopt racial policies that were consistent with those fostered by civil rights proponents, and thus Black participation in the war and Black civil rights efforts became more mutually supportive as the war progressed. African Americans exercised their demands for greater democracy based, in part, on their participation in the war effort, and Black protest grew in step with the progress of the war. Membership in the NAACP, for example, exploded from 50,000 in 1940 to 450,000 six years later, including 15,000 Black servicemen. Perhaps a chief factor in this growth and the most visible program to combine elements of Black protest with support for the war was the so-called Double V Campaign, instituted by a number of Black newspapers and organizations and calling for victory on two fronts — over totalitarianism abroad and over racial inequality at home. As an editorial in the *Atlantic World* put it, "[The] slogan of the First World War was: 'drop all grievances and pull together to make the world safe for democracy.' . . . Wiser and more determined now . . . the Negro is saying that giving up his grievances should be accompanied by [whites] giving up discriminations against him."[25] The editorial board of the *Baltimore Afro-American* added, in a piece aptly titled "Still Cannon Fodder": "We've been fighting our county's wars since 1775, always getting a slap on the back when the fighting begins and a kick in the pants when it's over. One hundred and sixty-five years is a long time, long enough to win a square deal."[26]

The Double V Campaign, created by the *Pittsburgh Courier* in February 1942, drew its name and inspiration from a 1941 letter to the editor written by James G. Thompson, a cafeteria worker at a company doing defense contracting. Thompson wrote, "The V for victory sign is being displayed prominently in all so-called democratic countries, which are fighting for victory. . . . Let we colored Americans adopt the double V for a double victory. The first V for victory over our enemies from without, the second V for victory over our enemies from within. For surely those who perpetuate these ugly prejudices here are seeking to destroy our democratic form of government just as surely as the Axis forces."[27]

Led by the Black press, the Double V Campaign was essentially a public relations effort that encouraged Black people to support the war and included such things as posters, pins, songs, and even Double V hairstyles. In exchange for this support, African Americans demanded advances in civil rights. Black newspapers brought attention to cases of Black servicemen unfairly tried or convicted, as well as to episodes of unethical or illegal discrimination against Black troops, and decried the conversion of Black combat troops to support units, calling for more Blacks to experience combat. Supporters believed not only that African Americans now had an ideal bargaining position, using their war support and the American ideal to leverage greater freedoms, but also that if the nation did not deliver, the outcome would be dire. As one Black corporal warned, "A new Negro will return from the war — a bitter Negro if he is disappointed again. He will have been taught to kill, to suffer, to die for something he believes in, and he will live by these rules to gain his personal rights."[28]

Despite armed forces leadership's deep distrust of the Black press, which it considered to be fomenting divisiveness, its relationship with African American newspapers and the communities they represented nonetheless slowly began to thaw, and the US Army and the civilian Office of War Information began to work with Black journalists in 1942 and 1943. On a somewhat parallel track, William H. Hasti saw his job as the War Department's Civilian Aide on Negro Affairs as monitoring military racial policies and pushing for reform; as early as 1941, before the United States even entered the war, Hastie blamed segregation itself for poor performance and morale among African American service members and recommended immediate experiments with integrated troops. The army brass's reception, however, was less than warm, Hastie's reports and suggestions gained no traction, he was left out of important decision making, and he soon resigned in protest that segregation remained entrenched. The path Hastie forged, however, would be followed directly to desegregation. Attorney Truman Gibson, who replaced Hastie, pursued many of his predecessor's goals but in a less inflammatory style. Downplaying his ties with civil rights organizations and choosing not to issue his own plans for policy reform, Gibson instead worked largely behind the scenes. Not only did he earn the respect and approval of armed services leaders as well as some enmity from the Black community, but he also won the ear of the president. Gibson's steady pressure on both President Truman and the military brass beginning in 1943 was in large part to thank for the president's eventual military desegregation order.

Before then, however, the slight progress Blacks in the military enjoyed during the last days of World War II continued into the postwar period as the US government and the various branches of the armed forces examined the future role of Black troops. The US Navy led off, abolishing some racially restrictive policies in February 1946: Blacks were no longer restricted to menial service roles, they could serve on combat ships, and all navy housing and other communal facilities were desegregated. However, the navy maintained quotas stipulating that Black personnel could never constitute more than 10 percent of the manpower on any ship or in any station, and it kept the Steward Branch segregated and restricted to Black and Asian personnel.[29] The US Air Force staked out a less progressive position. Although arguing that complete desegregation would best benefit the force by having each job filled by the most qualified person regardless of race, the air force nevertheless failed to stipulate a timeline toward that goal, resulting in stalemate and a continuation of the status quo. While certainly limited, these changes represented the leading edge of the armed services' postwar racial change. The army and the marines proved far more recalcitrant when it came to affording African Americans greater opportunities in their branches.

The postwar army recommitted itself to segregation despite its own studies revealing that interracial units performed effectively and that white officers at all levels had overwhelmingly positive experiences working with Black troops. Surveys also found that white enlisted men were much more likely to have positive feelings about serving with Black soldiers if they had actually worked together, demonstrating that fear rather than real-world experience was the factor most limiting change. The army, however, suppressed many of these findings, largely maintaining the status quo and modifying its racial policies only slightly.[30] Furthermore, the so-called Gillem Board, under Lt. Gen. Alvan Gillem Jr., recommended in February 1946 that the army retain its wartime 10 percent quota as a way to ensure that the number of Blacks would at least not drop precipitously and advocated ongoing training in racial sensitivity throughout the branch. The board's report, Circular 124, was adopted in April 1946, and its most progressive assertion was that manpower in future wars should be used to its maximum potential "without regard to antecedents or race."[31] This ambiguous and vague wording committed the army to very little; still, it was enough to cause consternation among a number of army leaders who felt that the Gillem Board was proposing eventual desegregation and thus had gone too far. Backlash from commanders on the ground meant that in the years immediately following the official adoption of Circular 124, few of its policies were ever implemented, and those that were—including attempts to recruit Black officers and to incorporate Black artillery and infantry units into previously all white divisions—were soon abandoned. To add fuel to the fire, in response to high Black reenlistments immediately following the war, the army suspended new African American enlistments during 1946 and 1947, increased the stringency of entrance standards for Blacks, and divvied up Black personnel among its various commands. This resulted in a decrease in the number of African Americans in the army from 16 percent in 1946 to 9 percent, below quota levels, by mid-1947.

The situation in the Marine Corps was even worse. The corps created a fixed rather than proportional quota for Black participation and then reduced even that small number, ensuring that the number of Blacks serving in the Marine Corps would never top 2 percent of the total. Moreover, the Marine Corps maintained segregation by assigning African American marines either to the segregated Steward Branch or to combat support or service posts.[32]

African American organizations responded loudly to Circular 124. An NAACP spokesman castigated the army for not going far enough, describing the new policy as trying to "dilute Jim Crow," rather than eliminate it, "by presenting it on a smaller scale," and the *Pittsburgh Courier* concluded that the policy represented no serious change of heart on racial segregation.[33] Many African

Americans were especially upset by the continued use of racial quotas, and no matter how far the military might go in addressing other aspects of racial inequality, the armed forces' insistence on quotas would subject them to continued pressure from civil rights advocates. This pressure was brought into the nation's courts in 1946 when a young Black would-be enlistee sued the secretary of war and a Pittsburgh-based recruiting officer for refusing to allow him to enlist.[34]

As the war proceeded with segregation intact and little concrete evidence of racial advancement, the morale of African American soldiers and public perceptions of the war effort within the Black community both suffered. Racial tensions rose and sometimes climaxed in incidents of racial violence, most often in southern states.[35]

Even with the influence of civil rights organizations, some shift in white attitudes toward racial inequities, and a growing emphasis on the need for racial equality in the armed forces — based both on ideals of freedom and on strict efficiency — the individual branches wavered, largely due to internal resistance to reorganizing the racial structures within the military. Change, when it did come, would issue not from within the armed services but from outside, with the intervention of the president himself. And much of what would prompt that change would come from the streets and the horrendous state of US race relations, where Black lives — especially the lives of Black soldiers and veterans — had come to matter very little.

Truman Listens: The President Takes on the Military

As Black soldiers and citizens fought for an equal share of democracy from the Civil War forward, their efforts — even their very presence — was to those intent on sustaining white supremacy an egregious affront. The threat of African American equality was met with a war of terror, the result of which was untold violence, often in the form of lynching. As one nonprofit justice organization has reported in a comprehensive accounting of over 4,400 lynchings, "No one was more at risk of experiencing violence and targeted racial terror than Black veterans who had proven their valor and courage as soldiers. Because of their military service, Black veterans were seen as a particular threat to Jim Crow and racial subordination."[36]

At Fort Benning in April 1941 a Black soldier was lynched in the woods, a crime that remains unsolved, and a Black private was shot dead by a military policeman; additional incidents occurred in 1943 in El Paso, Texas, and, in 1944, in Camp Claiborne, Louisiana, Camp Shenango, Pennsylvania, Camp Stewart,

Georgia, and March Field and Camp San Luis Obispo, California. Racial violence was rife within society at large; in 1943 alone, there were 242 so-called race riots in forty-eight cities. Although the violence did not always involve military personnel, a number of the incidents were attributed to wartime migration both inside and outside the South, as well as from the white supremacist response to increasing numbers of Black soldiers stationed at military bases in southern towns.[37]

What the media or white America saw as a Black riot was often simply an action of resistance on the part of African American soldiers and citizens, fighting mistreatment and racial subjugation. In other cases, it was indeed the explosive release of steam built up under the relentless, demeaning pressure of Jim Crow harassment. The poet Langston Hughes coined the phrase "Jim Crow shock" and likened it to the "shell shock," or post-traumatic stress, suffered by GIs after combat. Commenting on an incident in which a Black GI, recently returned from a year in the South Pacific, struck a white officer at a southern camp, Hughes conjectured that the soldier was experiencing "segregation fatigue which, to a sensitive Negro, can be just as damaging as days of heavy air bombardment. To fight for one's country for months . . . then come home and be subjected to the irritations and humiliations of Southern Jim Crowism, Dixie scorn, the back seats if any in buses, is enough — I should think — to easily drive a sensitive patriotic colored American soldier NUTS. The best of psychiatric care," Hughes continued, one surmises with his tongue only partly in cheek, "should be given them to prevent their developing discrimination-neuroses as a result of Jim Crow. Southern whites . . . who suffer from color domination complexes should also be treated by psychiatric methods."[38]

Hughes could be forgiven his gallows humor, for the reality of humiliations and violence at the hands of resentful whites was quite stark and quite real. So-called bus incidents were particularly common as African Americans traveling on Jim Crow buses and trains came in contact with whites attempting to enforce segregation, legally or otherwise. The sight of Black veterans in uniform, and the accompanying respect that military clothing and bearing usually demand, was too much for some whites.[39] For their part, African Americans nearly universally found being segregated dehumanizing and, as one Black newspaper editorialist put it, hardly any of us . . . have escaped this ugly form of arrogant racism."[40] One such bus incident led to the court-martial of Jackie Robinson, soon to be known nationally as a baseball star and racial barrier breaker.[41] During another incident in Fayetteville, North Carolina, in 1941, white military police (MPs) used billy clubs to pacify a group of Blacks returning from leave on a segregated bus, and the resulting violence left one African American and one white soldier dead and several more of both races injured.[42] In 1945, white MPs again assaulted a Black service member, this time a sailor on his way by train from a California naval base to Florida. As the *Chicago Defender* reported it, placing the blame firmly on the army, the two "prejudiced-crazed and power-drunk" MPs, "apparently encouraged by a harsh Army jim crow policy which has permitted almost everything in the book, . . . viciously assaulted" Woodrow Reed outside of Mobile, Alabama.[43]

In 1947, pacifist and activist Bayard Rustin helped to organize the Journey of Reconciliation, an effort to highlight the inhumanity of Jim Crow by testing a 1946 federal decision that had banned discrimination on interstate transportation. Nine whites and nine Blacks boarded buses and traveled across the country, suffering beatings and arrests. As Rustin himself later recalled, buses were an important target at the time, partly because of their use by soldiers just returned from World War II. "You will also remember," he recounted, "that 1946 was a crucial period, because many Blacks who had been in the army were returning home from Europe. There were many incidents in which these Black soldiers — having been abroad and exposed to fighting for freedom — were not going to come back to the United States on their way home and be segregated in transportation."[44] Rustin and some of his colleagues were arrested and spent thirty days on a chain gang, gaining much publicity for the incipient civil rights movement as well as for the plight of African American soldiers who had just risked their lives at war.

Bus incidents and other episodes of racial violence and persecution were at last being routinely covered not just by the Black press but by the mainstream white media, which had begun paying greater attention during the wave of racial violence in 1943. This elevated media attention made more whites aware of Black dissatisfaction with the cultural and legal status quo, and this awareness increased as the war progressed, with *Life* magazine declaring in 1944 that "America's No. 1 social problem" was racial strife.[45] National unity was paramount during wartime, and fixing racial discrimination could be promoted as a way to keep the peace and draw the country together. The quest for national unity contributed to a new nationalism that subjugated individual racial, ethnic, and religious identities to a larger, and purportedly internally peaceful and consistent, American identity.

Pointedly, discrimination against Blacks was seen in the light of Nazi theories of racial superiority and the atrocities that accompanied them. More and more, whites came to see that Jim Crow racial policies were inconsistent with the goals of the war and contributed to social division at a time when national cohesion was deemed necessary to the war effort. Black newspapers even more explicitly pointed out the similarities between America's racism and Hitler's fascism, describing "jim crow streetcars for Jews" in Poland, where "first Germany robs the Jews of property, jobs, and schooling and then insists that they are inferior as a race and diseased," and concluding, "How much like our dear old Southland this sounds."[46] Social science also contributed to the conversation, most notably Gunnar Myrdal's landmark work *American Dilemma* (1944), the most penetrating discussion of American race relations yet published. The fifteen-hundred-page volume detailed the false promise of liberty and equality that had still not been fully extended to African Americans. "White prejudice and discrimination," Myrdal wrote, "keep the Negro low in standards of living, health, education, manners, and morals. This, in its turn, gives support to white prejudice. White prejudice and Negro standards thus mutually 'cause' each other."[47]

As the Black press had done earlier, the white media now promoted the idea that the US racial situation was, simply put, embarrassing. With the world looking on, some white Americans felt that they had to get their own house in order. In other words, as the war progressed, an increasing number of whites came to see the war in the same terms as those defined by the Double V Campaign. A 1943 editorial in the *Nation* typified this viewpoint: "It is time for us to clear our minds and hearts of the contradictions that are rotting our moral position and are undermining our purpose. We cannot fight fascism abroad while turning a blind eye to fascism at home."[48]

The most infamous bus incident, though only one of many, was that of Isaac Woodard Jr., an event that led directly to Truman's order for military desegregation. Sergeant Woodard, who had served honorably in a labor battalion in the Asia-Pacific Theater, was beaten and blinded by sheriffs in South Carolina in 1946 while traveling by Greyhound bus to his home in North Carolina just hours after being discharged from the army at Camp Gordon in Augusta, Georgia. When the bus stopped at a rest area just outside of Augusta, Woodard asked to use the bathroom, enraging the bus driver, who alerted police in Batesburg, South Carolina. They pulled Woodard from the bus, into an alleyway, and beat him so severely with nightsticks that he lost his sight permanently. They then arrested and charging him with disorderly conduct.

Woodard's blinding was the last straw for President Harry Truman. Truman Gibson, the civilian aide on Negro affairs, recalled a meeting at the Oval Office with Truman and several aides; the president was visibly rattled and vividly described the Woodard assault. "This shit has to stop," Gibson remembered the president saying.[49] On another occasion the president again invoked the Woodard beating, proclaiming, "When a mayor and a City Marshal can take a Negro Sergeant off a bus in South Carolina, beat him up and put out one of his eyes, and nothing is done about it . . . I am going to try to remedy it."[50] Looking back on this period a few years after the Korean War, Truman would recall that "my very stomach turned when I learned that Negro soldiers just back from overseas were being dumped out of Army trucks in Mississippi and beaten. . . . Whatever my inclinations as a native of Missouri might have been, as President I know this is bad. I shall fight to end evils like this."[51]

Harry S. Truman, a social conservative from a Jim Crow state, was an unlikely civil rights advocate. Truman's racially segregated upbringing in Missouri and his general agreement with the status quo did not mark him out as an activist for social change. His views about the inferiority of African Americans are clearly recognized today as racist beliefs, and yet he managed to separate these ideological views from his feelings about segregation, which he considered immoral and antithetical to the American purpose. During his ten-year US Senate career, beginning in 1934, Truman regularly supported pro–civil rights legislation. And during his difficult reelection battle in Missouri in 1940, Truman realized and embraced the powerful role that Black support could have for his political success.

After succeeding to the presidency following Roosevelt's death in 1945, Truman realized that he would again face a tough reelection battle, this time in a national contest, and he knew he would need the African American vote. He was also aware of the pressure from A. Philip Randolph and others to desegregate the military, including an effort in November 1945, in collaboration with the NAACP, the National Medical Association, and the National Negro Publishers' association, to pressure the Veterans Administration to desegregate its hospitals.[52]

His moral commitment to legal equality, spurred in part by his abhorrence of the wave of anti-Black violence in the South in the immediate postwar years, combined with political efficacy propelled Truman to create the first national survey of civil rights needs *and* eventually to issue the executive order to desegregate the US Armed Forces.[53]

After meeting about racial incidents in September 1946 with the newly formed National Emergency Committee against Mob Violence, whose members included the NAACP's Walter White and former first lady Eleanor Roosevelt, Truman convened a new President's Committee on Civil Rights to investigate race relations and recommend civil rights measures. Seen by some as a tactic to delay actual reform, the committee was in fact crucial, charged with figuring out "how State, Federal, and local governments [can] implement the guarantees of personal freedoms embodied in the Constitution" by suggesting "more adequate and effective means and procedures for the protection of the civil rights of the people of the United States."[54] The president thus mandated a civil rights agenda that would lead directly to the desegregation of the military, and to substantial societal reforms.

Truman later recalled that he established the President's Committee on Civil Rights "with a feeling of urgency. No sooner were we finished with the war than racial and religious intolerance began to appear and threaten the very things we had fought for."[55] Of course, these threats did not actually appear suddenly but had been ever present. Nevertheless, Truman's new sensitivity to them was essential to motivating the committee, whose 1947 report, *To Secure These Rights*, was published in book form and was widely read both inside and outside government and the military. It set forth an agenda for civil rights policy reform that would be followed for years to come.

Around the same time, in November 1946, Truman established an Advisory Commission on Universal Training to look at the issue of segregation in the military and in other areas of American life. It was at a meeting of this committee that Truman Gibson recalled the president turning to him and saying, "I've been mulling over this issue of segregation. . . . I'm going to take the bull by the horns. I'm going to help your people." He then told the committee members that he was going to desegregate the US Armed Forces by executive order.[56]

Truman seems to have become a true believer, but his interest in the rights of African Americans was also politically savvy; facing a tough reelection campaign, deep factional divisions within his own Democratic Party, and likely defeat by the Republican opponent, Thomas E. Dewey, Truman turned to the increasingly powerful Black electorate for support. He was under particular pressure from the African American community to address segregation in the armed forces, especially by another campaign led by A. Philip Randolph, who had earlier pressured President Roosevelt into using Black troops, and by Congressman Adam Powell, who early in July filibustered the congressional draft bill and added an amendment to desegregate the military. Randolph, along with Black minister Grant Reynolds, formed yet another pressure organization in 1948, the Committee Against Jim Crow in Military Service and Training. Promising that the persistence of a segregated military would lead directly to African American draft resistance, Randolph told Congress that "Negroes are in no mood to shoulder a gun for democracy abroad so long as they are denied democracy here at home."[57]

Leading a group of mostly northern Democrats who supported Black voting rights and military desegregation, Truman faced challenges from southern conservatives, who split off to form the pro-segregation, anti–civil rights Dixiecrats (formally the States' Rights Democratic Party) under Strom Thurmond, and from Henry Wallace and others on the far left who favored accommodation with the Soviet Union. Key to retaining control of the Democratic Party and establishing a winning campaign strategy, Truman courted the Black vote in part by acquiescing to demands to integrate the armed forces, which he did by bypassing Congress and issuing Executive Order 9981 on July 26, 1948. This and other overtures to African American voters may have given Truman the slight margin he needed to eke out a victory in the presidential election.

Truman may have gotten some help from the sports world as well: Jackie Robinson, who had served stateside in the army during World War II, re-integrated Major League Baseball when he joined the Brooklyn Dodgers on April 15, 1947. His Dodgers coach, Branch Rickey, had first signed Robinson on November 1, 1945, to play for the Montreal Royals, a Dodgers farm team. A few months later, on January 29, 1946, Rickey also signed Negro Leagues pitcher Johnny Wright to the Royals. Wright was also a veteran of the US Navy, having served several years during the war years and distinguishing himself on the mound for the Great Lakes Naval Station's all-Black team and for the Brooklyn Naval Air Base team. Although Wright did not make it the majors, his Royals teammate Robinson did, and Robinson was followed by Larry Doby, who debuted with the Cleveland Indians on July 5, 1947. Like Wright, Doby had served in the US Navy, enlisting in 1943 and getting his discharge in 1946. He also played on the all-Black team at Great Lakes Naval Station before serving at a number of bases around the United States and then overseas in the Pacific theater during the war. While stationed in Hawaii, he befriended major leaguer, navy man, and future Indians teammate Mickey Vernon. In October of 1948, Doby, who was only in his second year in Cleveland, and fellow Indians pitcher and former Negro Leagues great Satchell Paige made history when they reached the World Series. The navy veteran helped hoist the World Series trophy for Cleveland on October 9, 1948, just three months after Truman's executive order.

Truman's language was carefully selected and did not use the terms "desegregation" or "desegregate," nor did it stipulate a timeline. Instead, he wrote, "It is hereby declared to be the policy of the President that there be equality of treatment and opportunity for all persons in the armed services without regard to race, color, religion, or national origin. This policy shall be put into effect as rapidly as possible, with due regard to the time required to effectuate any necessary changes without impairing effectiveness or morale."[58] His language was purposeful and carefully selected not to alarm, especially those in the South. However, his intent was clear: military desegregation was on the way.

In the days immediately following Truman's order, response was somewhat restrained; the *New York Times* reported that "Military Equality Is Demanded," and the *Los Angeles Times* stated that Truman had "ordered a drive against discrimination in the armed forces." The *LA Times* further speculated that Truman's "action may be ascribed not to any deep devotion to constitutional principles which he has just discovered, but [to] an effort to catch the minority votes in the big cities of the North."[59] The Black press, however, made no mistake about the importance of what Truman had done despite, or maybe because of, Truman's careful sidestepping of specific language about desegregation. It took a far different and far more celebratory approach, deploying its largest font sizes on blazing headlines. The *Chicago Defender* boisterously announced that Truman had "Wipe[d] Out Segregation in [the] Armed Forces," that the "Army Order Means No Segregation," and even that Truman had personally "Wipe[d] Out Jim Crow." On the front page of its July 31, 1950, issue, it recommended that readers "SAVE this PAPER it marks HISTORY."[60] The order had made Truman, according to Roy Wilkins of the NAACP, "the darling of the Negroes."[61]

Most African American activists, however, recognized immediately that Truman's order had not gone far enough, and they pushed for actual and immediate desegregation rather than simply encouragement for such to occur at an unstated future time. Randolph, as head of the League for Nonviolent Civil Disobedience against Military Segregation, dismissed the order as "meaningless" and continued to encourage Blacks to boycott service in the armed forces unless segregation in the army and navy was ended by August 30, 1950.[62] Lester Granger, director of the National Urban League, also pressured the president to desegregate the military quickly and in early September 1950 presented a "seven-point plan to end discrimination against minority groups in the armed services" to Defense Secretary James Forrestal. The plan called for restudying the Gillem report, immediately deploying experimental integrated units, and ending racial quotas.[63]

Truman responded to this pressure by establishing the President's Committee on Equality of Treatment in the Armed Services to plan and work with the military to effect timely integration and naming Granger as one of the five, later seven, members. The committee became known as the Fahy Committee after its chair, former solicitor general Charles H. Fahy, and, in addition to Granger, included John Sengstacke, publisher of the *Chicago Defender*. Sengstacke's newspaper, not surprisingly, embraced the new committee and Truman's efforts, saying that they indicated that those involved understood that "Jim Crow has got to go."[64] Mollified, A. Philip Randolph withdrew his support of the military boycott and publicly supported Truman's efforts.

But not all African American activists were convinced that Truman was doing enough. The League for Nonviolent Civil Disobedience against Military Desegregation, which Randolph had helped to found but which he formally left after Truman's order, vowed to press on until the elimination of segregation and discrimination in the US Army had been ultimately achieved.[65] And an organization called the Campaign to Resist Military Segregation continued to press the boycott. One of its members, James Peck, wrote in an editorial that he had ceased paying income tax until the military was desegregated and castigated Randolph for "play[ing] into the hands of President Truman, who, by his meaningless order, hoped to undermine the civil disobedience movement." Peck and others pledged to keep the pressure on.[66] Pressure came from elsewhere as well, and African American support of the war effort was far from universal. Among the Black newspapers, the *Pittsburgh Courier* was perhaps the most critical of

Truman, and the *Afro-American* consistently called for quick action on integration of the services rather than more palliative words and vague deadlines.[67]

Among other critics of Truman's approach was the actor and singer Paul Robeson and the members of the National Civil Rights Congress, a coalition organization founded in 1946 to unite three groups with ties to the Communist Party USA. Robeson refused to support the idea that Black participation in the military would advance the cause of African Americans in general and was also opposed to African Americans participating in what he saw as colonial intervention in Asia. Speaking at the Congress of the Partisans of World Peace in Paris in April 1949, Robeson was quoted as saying, "We colonial people have contributed to the building of the United States and are determined to share in its wealth. We denounce the policy of the United States government, which is similar to Hitler and Goebbels.... It is unthinkable that American Negroes would go to war on behalf of those who have oppressed us for generations against a country [the Soviet Union] which in one generation has raised our people to the full dignity of mankind."[68] Robeson joined the National Civil Rights Congress in 1951 in presenting copies of its manifesto on American racism, "We Charge Genocide," to representatives of the United Nations.

These protests were still to come in November 1948, however, when Truman's appeals to African Americans turned the tide of the election and put him into the presidency. As one letter writer to a Black newspaper put it, "I vowed if Mr. Truman continued to stick to his civil rights recommendations throughout his campaign, I would vote for him since he was the first President to come out for equal rights to all people. The colored people of this country are much more intelligent than many of the leading white people think they are. If they had the same privileges in Georgia that they do in California, they would not abuse their privileges. They are just human beings with dark skin, and as a general thing they have the same feelings, hopes, and desires that other people have."[69]

Promising greater equality in the military—motivated perhaps in part by political expediency and without strong military support—was one thing, but implementing it was another. The very next day after Truman issued the order, Gen. Omar Bradley resisted in the pages of the *Washington Post*, claiming that "the Army is not out to make any social reforms." Bradley pledged that the army would change its policy of segregation only "when the Nation as a whole changes it."[70] Hanson W. Baldwin, military editor at the *New York Times*, jumped to support Bradley, declaring, "It is extremely dangerous nonsense to try to make the Army other than one thing—a fighting machine." Although Bradley later recanted and claimed to have been misquoted, his words of resistance had set a tone that many in army leadership would adhere to for years.[71] Truman and the army brass found themselves in a standoff.

When the Fahy Committee, Truman's committee charged with monitoring compliance with his order, suggested that the racial quota system be dropped and that all-Black units be disbanded and their personnel integrated into formerly all-white units, Secretary General of the Army Gordon Gray flat out refused to comply. Pressured by the president personally, Gray eventually agreed to a compromise in January 1950, adopting Special Regulation 600-629-1, which called for "Negro manpower [to be] utilized in accordance with [its] skills and qualifications" and assigned without regard to race. Two months later, the army suspended use of its racially based quota system but reserved the right to return to a race-based system if it found the new criteria—based on physical, mental, and psychological characteristics—to be inferior. Even so, the army regarded its new racial procedures to be nothing more than experiments, and as the interviews in the following chapters bear out, the military, to varying degrees, retained segregation until at least a year into the Korean War, and in some cases much longer.

Indeed, initial desegregation occurred in complete piecemeal fashion: practiced in one way here, in another there, not at all in a third place. Curtis James Morrow, for example, was raised in the de facto segregated North and trained in an integrated training camp before being sent to Korea. There he found himself assigned to a unit and noticed that the soldiers in his truck were all also African Americans while the white soldiers were lined up behind different trucks, the first signal that his military experience had gone from integrated to segregated. "We had gone through basic training alongside white soldiers and had been together up to this point. . . . Being separated at such a time was unnerving. What was Whitey up to?" Morrow's suspicion can be easily understood; the army had done little to earn the trust of its African American soldiers, and its inconsistent racial policies just emphasized the point. Morrow's unit, the 24th Infantry Regiment Combat Team of the 25th Division is known as the last all-Black unit in the US Army, and finally dissolved by the end of September 1951, with its troops dispersed into other desegregated or integrated units.[72] In truth, individual exceptions remained for most of the war and the army, by its own admission, was still establishing Jim Crow units through the spring of 1952. So, let us turn now to the story of the military's inconsistent responses and how these played out on the ground in Korea and eventually led to the desegregation of America's military. We will start by looking first at Black Americans' experiences in joining the military, traveling to assignments, and going through training.

Stateside

1

Crossing Jim Crow
Enlisting and Traveling
to Boot Camp

Joining the military could mean a number of new experiences for African Ameri-
can soldiers and sailors, especially when it came to crossing the lines of Jim Crow.
For many, their first experiences of novel racial laws and customs took place on
the trains and buses that conveyed them to training camps. For those reared
in the South, the experience of enlisting in the military and traveling across the
country for training might mean leaving behind some of the trappings of seg-
regation; however, this wasn't always as comforting or welcome as one might
expect. The North and West offered up unfamiliar encounters that could be any-
thing from disorienting to downright frightening. For those going the opposite
direction who had been reared with fewer legal restrictions, the experience could
provoke a range of emotions from shock to anger. As one editorialist wrote in the
Chicago Defender newspaper in 1952, "To be ordered out of a seat on a train
or bus or street car and forced into a separate segregated section simply because
of the color of your skin is one of the most humiliating experiences in the life of
a colored citizen."[1]

Soldiers and sailors using civilian transportation, as they often did when
traveling to and from bases, were exposed to the varieties and vagaries of local
laws and customs. In one 1953 incident in Columbus, South Carolina, two full
years before Rosa Parks made her famous stand against the segregated buses
of Montgomery, Alabama, a Black soldier sat next to a white female on a pub-
lic bus, causing the bus driver to call in local police. However, the other African
American soldiers on board collectively resisted, refusing to turn over one of their
number, and so the police officers arrested all forty-eight of them.[2] *The many*
humiliations inherent in Jim Crow could quickly escalate into outright violence
and the so-called bus incidents that profoundly influenced Truman's decision to
issue his executive order actually occurred on all manner of conveyances and
continued to take place after the executive order had been issued. Violent as-

saults of veterans and soldiers traveling in uniform indeed continued long after the military had largely desegregated, with such events continuing throughout the 1950s and into the 1960s. Retired US Air Force lieutenant Thomas Williams testified before a 1954 congressional committee investigating interstate travel that he had received ill treatment from both civilian police and the military. Police officers in Alabama, he said, told him, "You're lucky we didn't beat your brains in for refusing to move back behind the white folks. Now we're pretty fair because if a white man had insisted on sitting back with the cullud folks, we'd a beat his brains in just as quick." Williams, at the time a pilot in training at Craig Air Force Base in Alabama, was arrested—in defiance of federal law outlawing segregation on interstate transport—on his way from Florida back to Alabama when he refused to sit in the segregated section of a Coastal Stages bus.[3] The military was not typically quick to defend its own if the accused was Black and in some cases added to the victimization; Williams reported that he was ultimately relieved of his air force duty for "his persistent temerity in protesting such un-American treatment."[4]

The excerpts below deal with a variety of such experiences but begin by exploring why African Americans enlisted in the first place, given that they would likely serve in segregated units. The segregated military—before and for some time after Truman's executive order—severely curtailed African Americans' chances for advancement, available duties, and indeed civil rights. Why join? Why did African Americans participate in the military? The variety of answers together paint a common picture: although the military was racially segregated and offered only small measures of equality and opportunity, it was still preferable to what one could often find on the home front. As Ike Gardner from Lynch, Kentucky, recalls, "I enlisted in the army because I didn't want to go in the coal mines." An African American serving on a navy vessel might sleep in segregated quarters and be allowed only to be a cook, or a Women's Army Corps (WAC) member might have to train and sleep separately, but he or she could earn a paycheck and eat three meals a day. Eddie Wright, raised in a sharecropping family, adds, "Everything I did in the military was better than what I experienced in the fields in Georgia." James Wiggins, also from Georgia and who served with the 24th Infantry Regiment in Korea, had never seen a milk carton before his basic training. "And also that is when I took my first shower," he adds, "because being from Augusta in the South, we had that #10 washtub that we took our bath in."[5] African Americans weren't just escaping poverty in the military; even though it was segregated, the Jim Crow military itself rarely presented the true threats that made up daily life in the South. Bill Peterson remembers, "I think I said, 'I'd rather go to Korea, because at least you issue me a rifle and I'm allowed to use it. Now, if I went to Biloxi, Mississippi, it might be used on me.'"[6]

For those Korean War veterans whose service first came during World War II, the situation then was even more acute, but the answers to the question "Why serve?" were quite the same. Although the service was segregated and offered Blacks few choices and little equality, it still offered steady pay, a possible pension, job training, the chance to leave a life dominated by poverty and cruel discrimination, and, importantly, the opportunity to participate in a deeply symbolic aspect of American life, even if in a limited way. As we will see, enlistment during World War II could be a patriotic act or part of the cultural tide of the moment, but it could also stem from dissatisfaction. Serviceman James Gilliam may have enlisted on a sudden whim out of anger that he was held back from job advancement while a less hardworking white colleague was promoted, but that situation symbolized the deep inequalities of the status quo. Gilliam's decision to quit his job was as much an act of defiance and agency as it was a fit of pique.

Enlisting

JAMES H. GILLIAM SR., WILMINGTON, DELAWARE

I'm James H. Gilliam Sr. I was born in Baltimore in 1920, which means that I'm eighty-five years of age as of August the 6th. I remember Pearl Harbor vividly, [learning about it] over the radio and [in] the paper. And the interesting thing about that, I don't get the feeling that that incident, as important as it is to history, I don't really get the feeling that it impacted the people of color community to the same degree that it affected the Caucasian community. Because it was at that time you had a real segregated military force. I think the Black community kind of felt this rejection very keenly. But that was pretty much the pattern of life at that time. The only branch of service where you had what I would call a reasonable chance of [Black people] advancing was the army, [where] there was some breakthroughs after World War I. At that time [in the navy,] I was not aware of any [Black] people outside of the mess department. And if you got a promotion, you might go to the top of the enlisted ranks by acting right and acting good. Certainly nothing in the Marine Corps. And also, at that time, you had the United States Army Air Force.

Interestingly enough, I was not drafted into the military. I went there as a result of a fit of anger about my treatment with the Old Age and Survivors Insurance, which is now a key part of the Social Security Administration. [I worked] in the insurance division there [with a white guy,] and he was taking all the credit and getting all the promotions. And interestingly enough, what was happening was brought to the conscious level [for me] by a young white worker from West Virginia who looked at me and said, "Jim, why are you helping this guy to look good? Let him go for himself." She had a real impact on me. And when I stopped doing things [for him], the overall supervisor called me over to his desk and he said, "You're not being cooperative. You have no team spirit." So I told him to go to hell. I got so annoyed, when I went out to lunch, I just went right over to the recruiting station and joined the army.

It was around that time there was some ripples going about this group in Tuskegee becoming regular army people, and to promote that, they had a road interview team. I was still in college, and this interview team came to Morgan College and interviewed those people who indicated an interest in becoming affiliated with a unit like that. I was one of the people selected, but I never went beyond that point simply because they discovered I was color-blind, you know. But they offered me an opportunity to still become an officer.

James H. Gilliam Sr.
Captain, 365th Regiment, 92nd Infantry Division
US Army
Interviewed by Thomas Healy, October 16, 2006, Wilmington, DE
James H. Gilliam Sr. Collection (AFC/2001/001/48906), Veterans
     History Project, American Folklife Center, Library of Congress

JULIUS W. BECTON JR., SPRINGFIELD, VIRGINIA

[I am] Julius W. Becton Jr., retired lieutenant general. [I] was in the 2nd Infantry Division, 3rd Battalion, 9th Infantry. Started in Saint Louis and we were the first major unit to go to Korea.

I grew up in suburban Philadelphia in a Main Line place called Bryn Mawr. [I] attended Lower Merion High School, played football, was fairly active in school, an integrated [high] school. In 1942, Hap Arnold, who was the chief of staff for the Army Air Corps, visited our school because he had graduated from there many years earlier. [Arnold] was giving us a long song and dance about joining the Army Air Corps, "win your silver wings and gold bars." Well, about September of '43, the football [team] almost en masse went down to take the battery examination. On the 28th of December 1943, six of us joined the Army Air Corps enlisted reserves to win our silver wings of a pilot and gold bars of a 2nd lieutenant. We finished school, graduated in June, and in July went on active duty. I might add that none of us ever became commissioned pilots. That's how I got started.

Going on active duty in July of '44, I went to Biloxi, Mississippi. A great place for a young Black from suburban Philadelphia to go in 1944? I wasn't igno-rant of what happened in the South because my parents were from Virginia and

North Carolina and we would travel to down to Carolina country. It was the Old South. So I knew about segregation, I knew about Jim Crow, I knew about what you could or could not do. The military basically—if the base was in the northern place, you were treated like anyone else off base. If the base was in the southern part, you were treated like they do down there. So in Mississippi, we knew where we could go, where we could not go, walk or not walk, the water fountain, what bathroom you could use or not use. It was very clear. On the base, it was strictly segregated; the Blacks were off to themselves.

In our Black area, we had a small service club which used to close at nine at night. One Saturday evening, the security guard, who was always white, was there and he wanted to go home early—he had a date or something—so about 8:30 p.m. he started saying, "Time to close, time to get out." Apparently we were not moving fast enough to the door, so he took his carbine off his shoulder and he had a magazine in the carbine and he pulled back on the receiver, which puts a round into the chamber. And then we really did move. He made a mistake; he was so impressed with the fact that we were moving so fast that he pulled it back a second time. And nothing came out, which meant that [he] had an empty magazine, nothing in the chamber, and he was bluffing. Well, he got a lesson that night. Nice story. He got beat up. Well, we didn't kill him, but he would never forget that.

The other story I tell [about Biloxi was about when] two of us went into town on a pass. Another young Black, George Barber from Pittsburgh, [and I] were walking down a street in front of [the] stores. And we heard a large noise and turned around and there was a large pickup and [we] heard someone say, "There are two of them." These guys drove that truck right down the street on the pavement. I guess they tried to run over us. We flattened against the building, they went by, and they were laughing. We ran as fast as we could back to Keesler Field, never to go back to Biloxi until we transferred out.

If I were to fast-forward about the thirty-five years, the next time I was in Biloxi was 1982. I had flown into the international airport in my own plane since I was a lieutenant general with aircraft capabilities. I was met by the deputy adjutant general. I was escorted with a motorcycle escort to a hotel where I was speaking to reserve component officers. I walked up onto the platform [with a] standing ovation, and I couldn't help remarking, "My, how things have changed."

Julius W. Becton Jr.
Lieutenant general, 542nd Heavy Construction Company; 369th
Infantry Regiment, 93rd Infantry Division; K Company and
L Company, 9th Infantry Regiment; 101st Airborne Division

US Army Air Forces/Corps
Interviewed by Kate Ellis and Stephen Smith, February 2003, Springfield, VA
American RadioWorks, Minnesota Public Radio

JOHNNIE GIVIAN, JACKSONVILLE, NORTH CAROLINA

My name is Johnnie Givian. I was born in a little tiny place located directly south of Selma, Alabama, about seventy-nine miles. And this place was a junction more than [it was] a town or city. It was called Mempa, Alabama, and we was raised on a farm. My mother was like a sharecropper to someone else that had the farm, and we were raised there. There was thirteen of us, and myself, I'm one of the latter three out of that thirteen, the third one from the last. A lot of things about my mother and my father happened before I was born, but by the time I was able to remember well, my father wasn't there. I heard a lot of different tales about how he left or how they got along and everything. I never knew him, but I knew my mother until the day she died, in 1946, probably about April or May. I was in Atlanta, Georgia, and I was very young. My mother had passed away a little over nine or ten months earlier, and that left me as a family with seven siblings that was living there [on the farm]. And then I had two sisters there in Atlanta and I was living with one of them. I had done stopped going to school because of the conditions, the need [for me to work]. And my sister had a couple children and I was trying to help her and that didn't last but about a couple months though. I had a big hurt on me because I'd just lost my mother. Didn't know where my daddy was so I was kind of like loose out there. The boys that I knew [in Atlanta,] they was getting in trouble, and I was trying to get out [from] around them. I wanted to make something of my life and I just didn't want to go to jail, and I was afraid that [I would] because they were getting in trouble and if I hung with them, then I felt that I'd be in trouble [too] and I was worried.

A friend of mine and I was talking one day, and we agreed that we'd go get in the military. Nothing about the Marine Corps, [but] we agreed and we got together and went down to the post office in Atlanta, Georgia, 'cause that's where the recruiting officer was at that time. And all I knew really was navy and army, you know, I didn't know about this thing called the Marine Corps. So I went in and I sat down and went before the navy board and I took the test. And they told me that I had passed to go into the navy but it will be almost a year before I would go [because of quotas]. And I didn't want [that], I wanted to get out of Atlanta [and] to get away from these people that I knew. I just wanted to get somewhere where I felt safe.

Coming back down the hall, there was a marine standing in the door, and he called us in and he said, "Don't you young men want to go in the Marine

Corps?" And he literally just about had to let me know what the Marine Corps was all about, showing me all these big pictures and everything. I was excited and I was glad to go, [but] I said, "I can't go in the Marine Corps, I just was accepted by the navy [and] they said they was gonna put me on a list and when they get a[n] opening, they were gonna call me." I didn't want to, you know, violate the law again. And he said, "Let me tell you, you ain't gonna be in no trouble if you pass these tests. Then I can send you away in the next two weeks." So I got excited and I sat down and took the test. I passed the written tests, there were two of them.

He told me, "The recruiting officer is gonna be in [in an hour], and if he passes you then you can go in the Marine Corps." He had guaranteed me that he would send me in the Marine Corps in ten days. [But] I was too small—I didn't weigh enough for their weight test—[and] I was too short for their height [requirement] because back then the Marine Corps had restrictions on whether you were tall enough. Before I left, he said, "You're too light, you're gonna have to do something [about your weight]. I want you to get yourself four pounds of bananas. Before you come back here, you eat them."

I went down and I bought the four pounds of bananas and I ate them, but I didn't eat the peelings. I was all excited—went down to the lobby of the post office and waited about an hour [until] this sergeant was in. So I come back up and he juggled around, and I'm sure that he put his toe on the scales, and I passed.

The man that was with me, he passed, so we was supposed to leave in ten days in this Marine Corps. I saw all this stuff and I got so excited, big trucks and guns, everything. And the only thing [that] was holding us back [were] the birth certificate[s]. I didn't have a birth certificate, and the man that was with me didn't have one, but his mother had a birth certificate. Mine was down there lost in Alabama somewhere. So [the officer] told me that if I didn't have a birth certificate I had to [have the endorsement of] my next of kin, which was my sister, so I went home and got her to sign a document that I was of age and everything, and I took it back and they put me on a schedule to leave in ten days. [My friend] couldn't leave because his mother wouldn't give him the birth certificate and wouldn't sign him in there. So that's how it come about me getting into the Marine Corps. I was so excited about the Marine Corps because it was so exciting to see all the things [that] was going on. I already know about the navy ships and stuff, you know, but I didn't know too much about the Marine Corps.

Johnnie Givian
Corporal, unit unknown
US Marine Corps
Interviewed August 17, 2005, Jacksonville, NC

FRED ASH, JACKSONVILLE, NORTH CAROLINA

My name is Fred Ash and . . . I was born in Mississippi, a little town called Delisle. It's a French town. My whole family lived mostly with my grandmother, my mother's mother. We were very, very poor actually, but we were sort of wealthy [too] because we had livestock. And at the age of twelve or thirteen, I think I was what I would [call] a professional ox driver. My parents had two yokes of oxen. Oxen was powerful animals, more so than mules and horses. And we'd use them for plowing, for cleaning up new ground, and whatever else that was necessary. And salaries was very low. For a yoke of oxen and a driver, the salary was only about $2.00, $2.50 a day. I dropped out in about the eighth grade, but after I got in the Marine Corps, I finished my education, I went on to complete the twelfth grade.

Actually, the way I started off [in the military,] I was working at the Gulfport Naval Base. And I got into it with a foreman—he claimed I disobeyed him. I had already put my age up in order to get a job. See, I was only sixteen years old, and you're supposed to be seventeen in order to work out there. He said, "Well, I tell you what, if you don't go back to work [when] I instruct you to go back to work, I'll have you drafted into the military." [So] I started in the Marine Corps in 1945, but I was too young. So I stayed in what they called Zero Platoon, 'cause they was about to send me back home, and I didn't wanna go back home. I wanted to stay and become a marine, and that was really the way that it started out that I got in the Marine Corps. I was called up at the age of seventeen, and when I got to Camp Shelby, instead of me coming back like the rest of my comrades did, they picked me out of a group and sent me on to Montford Point. After I got signed up, I caught a bus from Gulfport to Jackson, [then] got a train ticket to . . . Atlanta, and then from Atlanta to Wilmington. Then they put us on a bus into Jacksonville and from Jacksonville into Montford Point.

During the time I came in, you had two types of servicemen, you had Afro-American and you had the white. But now it's not like that, everybody's all one, and that's the way I think it should have been anyway. Because any time a man is risking his life, the only life that he'll ever have, other than the one in heaven, he should be accepted.

Fred Ash
Master sergeant, 7th Marine Division
US Marine Corps
Interviewed December 17, 2004, Jacksonville, NC

JAMES H. LACY, CHICAGO, ILLINOIS

[I enlisted to] get away from home. [My] father was a homebuilder. [He had a] very good [job with] E. A. Lacy & Sons, that's the company, construction company. Men and [his] sons worked for him, [but] payday, the men get paid, not the sons! [My] three brothers [and I] worked after school and weekends, when [the] men were off with families. [I] got tired of working and [having] no money in [my] pocket. [That's the reason] why I left home. When [you're] seventeen, parents have to sign [the enlistment form. I] told them I would run away, [so] they signed it.

All I knew was I was getting away from home, that slavery. And I did. The army was a good place for me. [My] education [got] interrupted early, so every chance [I got] I would go to night school. When in Japan, I enlisted in night school and started taking courses in typing. Other guys were going to bars. The company commander heard about this, [and] he said, "I like what you're doing and like to help people help themselves." He sent me to soldiers' university for weapons repair. After that he sent me to supply school in Osaka, [where I] stayed in a lovely hotel.

[The] school for supply [had both] Black and white [soldiers enrolled]. After school, I went back to segregated units. Weapons school was the same way. [Even] after I was back in the States and was reclassified, I had to take tests again, and my score was pretty high, [and I was] sent to administrative school. [I] lived in Headquarters Detachment II, in Fort Riley, Kansas, which was all colored. Detachment I was all-white . . . [and it] was on the hill [in a] big block building, everything in one building, sleeping, office, kitchen — [a] lovely place. Detachment II [was] down on the riverbed and made of wood houses, long houses, and [a] mess hall on the end. [We] would have to get mess kits and go down to the end. A big flood washed all our houses, everything away. [So they] moved Detachment I away to a better place and put us up on the hill, still all colored.

But in school, it was all mixed. Then I was assigned to Intelligence G2 in [a] big office and all races worked together, but when we left there [at night we] went back to segregated units. [That was] 1951. President [Truman] started integration in 1948, [but my] whole time in the service, till discharge, I was always in segregated units. Although I worked with the guys in Fort Riley, the living conditions were different. [But I] didn't know any better; [I] was used to that. When I went to administrative school, it was mixed and you had to stay at the school and it was mixed. I was a corporal and had a field commission, got my stripes in the war, so I was more or less in charge. I was over some whites and Blacks. We got along very good. I would give orders and leave them alone.

James H. Lacy
Corporal, 24th Infantry Regiment, 25th Division
US Army
Interviewed by Stephen Smith and Gerald Early, January 8, 2003, Chicago, IL
American RadioWorks, Minnesota Public Radio

CLENTELL JACKSON, APPLE VALLEY, MINNESOTA

I was born in Minneapolis, Minnesota, General Hospital, 1929. I went to vocational [school]. I was going to go to North [High] but all my buddies were going to vocational and I wanted to go where they were going. 'Course we lived over north at that time. There were only certain areas where Blacks could move back in those days: North Minneapolis and South Minneapolis, 31st Avenue, there were Blacks there, and Franklin and Cedar, that's where I used to live. It's all built up there now, all changed.

I don't know how to put this, but [my buddies and I enlisted because] we were scared, to tell the truth, because the cops were picking up everybody. There was a [white] girl that was fooling around with a lot of guys, and she started naming a lot of guys, and she just come up with any name. I don't even know the girl, but she gave my name out as well as the other guys. There was about six of us that went into the service at the same time, and we were perfectly innocent, but our word wouldn't hold for anything, it wouldn't carry no weight. I don't know who the girl is, to this day, I don't know who this girl is. They say she lived in those huts over between 8th Avenue and 6th Avenue North and between Aldrich and Lyndale Place, where they put up those Quonset huts. This was years ago, that was an all-Black area, but after they put up the huts, everybody moved into them.

The [police] were picking up everyone. Every name she called, they would pick them up. I was about seventeen, and I told my mom we were going skating over in Saint Paul, I forget the name of the arena, but we went over there and all that time we were over there they were going from house to house looking for us. We came home, snuck into the house, and that next day we went down and enlisted. And once Uncle Sam had us, the cops couldn't do anything, we were home free. Now, we're innocent, but our word didn't hold no weight at all.

[My parents] never told me, but I don't think my ma wanted me to go [into the service]. But my dad said, "Well, if it keeps him out of jail, let him go." Because they were hard on young Black kids at that time, really hard on us. It was rough in school and everything else. You couldn't concentrate in school. I remember, I was good in math, and we had a test [in] beginner's algebra. I got the highest mark in the class and the teacher, he was prejudiced, and he gave me a D. All the students—white and Black—were so surprised because I was the best student in the room and he gave me a D. And I only got one or two wrong. Those were the hardships we had to go through.

Clentell Jackson
Technical sergeant, 25th Infantry Regiment, 24th Infantry Division
US Army
Interviewed by Tina Tennessen, September 10, 2002, Apple Valley, MN
American RadioWorks, Minnesota Public Radio

JESSIE BROWN, HARVEY, ILLINOIS

[I'm] Jessie Brown. I live in Harvey, Illinois, seven miles south of the city limits of Chicago. I was in the 25th Infantry Division, 24th Regiment, 2nd Battalion, in Korea. I come from [an] army family: father in World War I, three brothers in World War II, and three of us in the Korean War.

I volunteered, regular army, [at] nineteen years old. [There was] not much else to do, [and me and] five other teenagers wanted to go into the military, so we signed up together. We rode out that afternoon. And [they] put me in charge of the guys, and we took a bus trip from our hometown, Hayti, Missouri, where I lived with my father, into Saint Louis. I was in charge of meal tickets and it made me very proud to be in charge for a couple guys. Got into Saint Louis that night and they processed us and we went to bed, and from then on we were inducted into the military. From there we went to Fort Knox, Kentucky, and took our basic there. Then we were separated [because] from Fort Knox, my friends were shipped out to other places. One of them went to Germany. I went to Camp Hood, Texas, from Fort Knox. I was inducted into [the] 73rd Engineer Combat Battalion.

That was a horrible experience because we had to do all the work and all the training. We were infantrymen and engineers. They came up and said they had [a] shipment of guys going out, volunteer[s] to go to Far East Command, and asked who wanted to go. [Now at] that time I was such a crack soldier that [even though] I had only been there seven months, they wanted to promote me from private to sergeant. I understood the military because I listened to my father and all my brothers in such a way that they didn't have to teach me, I already knew it. My lieutenant said, "You want to go overseas?" and I said, "Yeah, I'll go," 'cause I wanted to travel. So I turned down my rank of sergeant and [transferred to the 24th and] went overseas to Japan, and it was a great experience.

I was enjoying the army so good. I knew of racism because of where I was born. I experienced it there because we only had white officers. But they were nice, the ones we had in the 24th. Very nice people.

Jessie Brown
Private 1st class, Company 2, 2nd Battalion, 24th Regiment, 25th Division
US Army
Interviewed by Stephen Smith, January 7, 2003, Chicago, IL
American RadioWorks, Minnesota Public Radio

JOHN CONYERS, WASHINGTON, DC

[In] 1943 was the first race riot [in Detroit]. I was graduating from the eighth grade. And my father had gone down to Hughes, Hatcher, and Suffern to get a suit and apparently didn't know anything about the riot. Somehow there was a navy soldier involved at Belle Isle—the Belle Isle Bridge that goes into the island of Belle Isle. And they were pulling people off the streetcars, beating them up severely, injuring them permanently. There were a lot of deaths, and we were so terrified because we didn't have an automobile, so we knew he had to take the streetcar. And it was coming in over the radio, you know, this riot. And finally my father showed up, and somehow he had managed to escape the people that were beating up everybody.

The same week I graduated from Northwestern High School [in Detroit], I got a job at Lincoln Motors. And it was funny, jobs were hard to find. You remember [Congressman] Charlie Rangel joined the army because when he graduated from high school he couldn't get a job in New York City. Now, you know, you'd say, "I know it was bad if that's what was happening." But my father called up Nelson "Jack" Edwards, who was the union leader at Lincoln Motors, part of Ford. I got a job inspecting the motor blocks as they came off the line and I was going to school nights, getting ready to go to college, going to Cass Technical High School. And there were all different operations around me. There was this one short, heavyset African American gentleman—he wore a big rubber apron because he would shoot the water into the motor block to make sure it was waterproof—and we'd talk. I remember one day [we had] this conversation [and] it cut me like a knife. He said, "I see you reading all the time." I said, "Yeah, I'm getting ready to go to Wayne University. I'm going to go to law school." He looked at me and he said, "You know how many times I've heard that kind of talk?" He said, "People come here and they never leave. I'm one of them." He said, "That's what I thought I was going to do, and then I got a family and then the kids came," and his voice trailed off. And that hit me, you know— maybe I'm not going to make it, maybe I'll be just like all these other guys with some long story or tale of what happened, what went wrong. But it created a resolve. I said, "I'm not ever going to let anything stop me from doing this. I've got to do it." And I remember him and that three-minute conversation as clearly as if it had happened yesterday.

[But] I was in a National Guard unit, [the] 1279th Combat Engineers, that was activated [in 1950]. Well, [in 1948] a fellow named Harry Woods, who was another Northwestern graduate, came over, and he told me, "John, I'm in the 1279th Combat Engineers National Guard of Michigan. You should get in that because you are busy in school and you're working at Lincoln Motors Local 900." I said, "Fine." So I joined the reserves and we used to meet, I think it was, once a month at the old Michigan Central Station. [But] my studies got heavier and heavier and so I came to Captain Homer Matthews, who lived on Hartford, who had been in World War II and was a captain in the reserves, and I said, "Captain"—he was captain of A Company—"I don't have time." He said, "Fine, Conyers, I'll tell you what you can do. We'll put you on leave or we can just give you a discharge outright." I said, "Put me on leave." [But] I got this letter—it said: "August 19, 1950. Report. You have been activated."

And so I sauntered down to the old train station building there off of Michigan Avenue and told my commanding officer that there has been a mistake here, that I'm not going with this unit and I had told all of my friends that I was in school full time. So I said, "Goodbye, fellas. Too bad you guys got to go." And that's another thing that I will [always] remember, what he told me. I came in and, you know, [said,] "It's too bad about what's happening." He said, "Conyers, [unless] you want to be the first person court-martialed in the 1279th you will get over there and get your gear, 'cause you're going with us." I said, "But, but, but—." He said, "But nothing! I was in World War II and I'm going and you're going with us." And boy, when everybody heard I had to go, they had the biggest laugh. "Conyers, I thought you weren't going. Ah-ha-ha. You gotta go, too!" And everything [I got] was mismatched and oversized. I had only [the] things that was left.

[The National Guard] was desegregated, but . . . because most of the people were from Detroit, there were a few whites in it, but not many. It was mostly a Black unit. The furthest I had ever gone [before] was to Chicago or maybe to Lansing, [and now] we're going to Fort Lewis, Washington. And this train was the slowest-moving train I've ever rode in my life—you go through every town and you stop. And I couldn't believe [it,] "This is America, man." I'm looking, saying, "Wow," and these guys were playing cards and having fun and I was just wowed to this whole notion that "this is America," which I had never seen before.

John Conyers
US representative, 13th District of Michigan

Michigan National Guard, 2nd lieutenant, 1279th Combat Engineers
US Army
Interviewed by Renee Poussaint, August 20, 2007, Washington, DC
National Visionary Leadership Project
Interviewed by Louis Jones, September 19, 2003, Detroit, MI
Detroit Oral History Project

First Experiences of Jim Crow:
Comparisons with World War II

Some of those African Americans who saw service in Korea were veterans of World War II and could contrast their experiences in the later war with those they had been through a decade earlier. Here William Cooke, of Dorchester, Massachusetts, recalls experiencing Jim Crow for the first time during his World War II training, and Ernest Shaw discusses the opportunities for advancement that serving, especially as an officer, could bring him. Shaw had a college education and earlier service as an enlisted man in World War II, but serving in ROTC (Reserve Officers' Training Corps) and reenlisting after the war allowed him to earn an officer's pay and approach his goal of buying a pickup truck and becoming an agricultural agent in his home state of Texas, a goal he later accomplished.

For many northern Black recruits, the trip to basic training camp was their first experience of life in the segregated states. Although they had often experienced bias at home, they had not faced the overt racial restrictions of the Jim Crow South. In contrast, southern Blacks were often equally shocked to face integrated transportation to their camps and to interact with whites in new surprising new ways.

BERTRAN F. WALLACE, DAYTONA BEACH, FLORIDA

[I am an] eighty-four-year-old GI who served in World War II and the Korean War, and I want to share with you a story. In World War II, I served as an enlisted man in a segregated army. Those of you, perhaps, who are not familiar with [the] segregated army, that meant in America that you were either Caucasian or you were considered a Negro. That was the word that was used at that time. And so I served with a Negro outfit in World War II [and] in the Korean War as an officer in Ko-jedo [Prison Camp].

[After World War II, I went] to Columbia to get my graduate degree. And while I was living in New York in 1949, I was commissioned as a 2nd lieutenant, as a staff specialist based upon my graphic arts career. I was assigned to the 1150th ARSU, which was a school in New York City. I think our first place was on 42nd Street, then we moved to 44th Street. Truman had integrated the military prior to that, so the unit that I was assigned to was integrated. I never felt that I was segregated, because the 1150th ARSU school was all integrated.

However, when I reported for my first meeting, there was a lieutenant colonel [who] asked me when I walked in with my uniform on, with my gold bars, "What the hell are you doing here?" That was his question to me. And so I responded as I normally do when questions are asked like that. I came back, I guess, rather sharply and said, "Because I belong here." Well, following that, about two weeks later, I received a telex from the governor [that] said either you transfer to military police or resign your commission. Either or. I could not understand this other than the colonel must have said that I did not belong to this staff specialist group that consisted of people who were editors in the news, in the media. And yet I was a staff specialist. That's what I was commissioned on. And I had my degree from Lincoln, and I had my graduate work from Columbia, and I was working for the newspaper. So I was very qualified. I was told by my lawyer in New York at that time that I could have sued the federal government for denying me and for sending me that telex. Well, because I believe in my country and because I believe that whatever I accomplish, that I must merit that, that I wasn't going to use the law at that time to fight my problems. I accepted the transfer.

I really didn't want to be a military police officer. That was because of my World War II experience as an enlisted man. I transferred from the school to what they call the 33rd Military Police Battalion, and there was one company, Company D [I think], was all Black. And the other three companies, A, B, and C, were all white. This is now the Korean War. Since Truman had indicated that we were integrated, we were integrated, but still segregated, because my company was all Black. Which meant there were no other [Black] officers or enlisted personnel in Company A, B, and C. Because the powers that be — and I'm going to refer to my blue-eyed brother as the power broker and the powers that be — the powers that be was making the decisions, so therefore they made the decision that Company D would be Black. And there was a Captain Silver, who was a very fair-complected young man, I don't know whether he was Hispanic, but he was a light-skinned man of color [and he] was our company commander. Needless to say, we won every damn thing. Company D was the best company in the battalion. Because we knew that we were segregated, we wanted to prove to others that we were the best. And we were the best.

Now, the Korean War was in effect, and there was a need for MP officers. The outfit that we were assigned to [was] put on alert, then off alert, called to active duty. You're either put on alert, or you're off alert. You're on alert. You're off alert. And at that time I got tired of being put on alert and off alert. So I volunteered for the Korean War. Second Lieutenant Wallace, 0973449. So I had gone from 17030092, which is an enlisted [man,] to an officer, which would be 0973449.

And when I reported to Fort Jay, which is on Governor's Island in New York, I indicated on my application that I could best serve my country in the 1st Army Area or the 6th Army Area, that I felt that I could not serve my country very well in [the South].

Now, I didn't specify [but] I had grown up in the South, and I just couldn't handle prejudice very well. I discovered that when I was overseas in North Africa and Italy when I felt free. And I had a difficult time handl[ing] that. So when I reported, I indicated that. Well, I didn't know until four or five years later in my career that the provost marshal, who happened to be from Utah and a member of the faith that is in Utah, had written in my report that I was unfit to be an officer and that I needed to enroll in a course of Americanization. Because I indicated I could best serve my country in the 1st and 6th Army, which meant that I should be able to serve my country anywhere. And it said to me that this gentleman was very prejudiced in his thinking, where I was being very honest, because I felt free. I did not handle prejudice very well. I still don't handle it very well because I think that all human beings are equal in the eyesight of God. That's my strength, and that's my belief.

So I was assigned to MP school in Georgia. There was a lot of problems there that I encountered with officers, prejudice. I finished ninth in my class out of eighty-eight officers. And then all of us were given assignments to go overseas.

Bertran F. Wallace
Major, Battalion and Prisoner of War (POW) Command, 743rd
   Military Police Detachment, Military Police Corps
US Army
Interviewed by Brenda Breter and Jason Caros, April 9, 2007, Daytona Beach, FL
Bertran F. Wallace Collection (AFC/2001/001/01649), Veterans History
   Project, American Folklife Center, Library of Congress

WILLIAM COOKE, DORCHESTER, MASSACHUSETTS

We didn't have any problems [with living conditions on base] during the Korean service. It wasn't a problem. If you had asked me about World War II, it was a different story. It changed a lot, changed a whole lot. I'll tell you an incident [from] World War II. Just off the base, I went to a little place to eat a sandwich, and a fellow at the little hotdog stand came and wrapped it all up. I unwrapped it. He told me I can't eat it there. I said, "I bought it here," and he said, "Well, you can't eat it here." So I ate it. And by the time I got through eating it, well here comes the MPs. The sergeant got out and he looked at me and he said, "What's wrong, Captain?" I says, "Nothing wrong. I bought a sandwich and I ate it. And that's all there was to it." So he says, "So what do I do now?" I said, "I'm going

to salute, you're going to return the salute, and you go on about your business."
So that's what he did.

What the story was, if [the hotdog vendor] had just said, "I got an officer here, a captain," they would have sent a man of equivalent rank or higher. And if they'd sent a man of equivalent rank, I would have asked his date of rank. And if I had a couple of days ahead of him, I would have told *him* to salute and go on about his business, too. But I know what he must have said—he said, "I got trouble with a *boy*." That's what he said. That was in Missouri, Camp Robinson. That was during World War II, so a lot of things changed since then, see, because then you weren't supposed to sit up there where the whites sat, you weren't supposed to sit there.

[I remember] another occasion during World War II—I was just a shaved tail then—I was going off the post. I got on this bus, and there was no seats in the rear. The only seat was by this little white girl, white woman. The other jokers were standing up and I just went and sat down. So the bus driver, he kept on driving until we got off the post, then he stopped his bus. He said, "Lieutenant, you can't sit there." I said, "Why not?" He said, "You gotta go to the rear." I said, "There ain't no seats back there." [He said,] "Well, you can't sit there." I said, "Well, I ain't gonna move." So he says, "If you don't move, this bus ain't going to move. We're going to stay right here." So that's when I got hassled by *my people*. Because my people started with, ". . . That's the worst part about these people from the North that come down here and make it hard on us." So I looked around and I gotta go back to the complaints of my people! So I said to the bus driver, "Open the door." And I got off and I got a cab and I went into town. But that's what we went through as soldiers in the white man's army fighting the white man's war.

William Cooke
Captain, 272nd Field Artillery, Massachusetts National Guard
US Army
Interviewed by David P. Cline, October 23, 2002, Dorchester, MA
American RadioWorks, Minnesota Public Radio

ERNEST K. SHAW, HOUSTON, TEXAS

I'm Ernest K. Shaw, county agent emeritus through the Texas A&M system. I'm a native of Terrell, Texas. I'm seventy-six years old. I was with the 7th Division, 31st Regiment, 1st Battalion, Able Company, 3rd Platoon, as platoon leader.

[I enlisted] after graduating from high school, May 15, 1944. Put my age up in order to enter the service. [I enlisted] with a good friend, his name was Norman

Lincoln. We were going from my school to downtown to deliver something. We thought, we're out of high school, so what next? The war, World War II, was on, and so we said, why not join the army? Of course we did that, put our names down, Local Board Number 1 in Terrell, Texas.

Fortunately, or unfortunately, the war was winding down and they were not drafting and you couldn't volunteer. So I had to forgo service at that time. That fall I went to Shorter[-Flipper] College, a small African American college, named after [Henry Ossian] Flipper, the first African American to receive a commission from West Point. The school is named Shorter-Flipper-Curry in Little Rock, Arkansas. Stayed there September to April, and we were called in even though we had put our age up to get in. Chances are I could have missed the war altogether, but I was delighted that they called me in. My mother sent me the note that the Local Board One was seeking my whereabouts. I came back to Terrell and then Dallas and that's where I put my hand up and swore to protect my country and carry forth its mandates.

That's the first time I was in an environment that was totally unsegregated 'cause we moved into the main building of the bus station. From there we went to Fort Sam Houston in San Antonio and went through normal processing. Went from San Antonio to Sheppard Field, Texas, and Sheppard Field was part of [the army] air corps at that time, became part of [the] air force in 1947. Went through basic training in Sheppard Field, then was shipped to Clovis, New Mexico, with the army air corps.

[Basic training] was segregated and five weeks' duration. Following basic training, normally [they] send you to different bases to do different things. Fortunately that year of college was beneficial [and] made a significant difference, even in a so-called segregated situation. I made a reasonably high score on the AGCT [army general classification test]. Rather than doing normal activities that African American recruits were doing, I was given a job as clerk. I became "Clerk Non-Typist 055" and stayed there for three to four months, then volunteered to go to . . . Manila with the 13th Air Force and stayed till November of '46. While there, we were at a place called Clark, and . . . I was able to move up from private, to PFC [private 1st class], to corporal, to buck sergeant. It wasn't that I was that smart, but most of the veterans were getting out and moving on. The vacancies were there. I also went to school and took courses in music appreciation and boxing. It was a delightful experience. Manila is a beautiful city. "Pearl of the Orient," that's what it was called. I stayed there and came back to Texas and was discharged in November of '46. During that time, I had a chance to see the world from a different perspective. Even though I had gone over in the bottom of a ship, [when] we came back we were all together, Black and white, on the ship from Manila to San Francisco. Of course, [after] San Francisco we were segregated [again]. I remember we came from California, to Denver, Colorado, and we had to take our places where it was official and legal to be. That put me back home to Terrell, Texas.

I had grown up in that environment. My father was a farmer. We had no buses in my hometown of Terrell. Really, [segregation] didn't exist for me. We were pretty socialized and acculturated to do what we were expected to do with the right attitude and be as comfortable as we could be [where] we found ourselves.

My brother had gone to World War II, too. When I arrived home, my dad was quite concerned about what I had experienced in World War II. When I had gotten to the Philippines, even though the war was over, the results were there, were physical. He thought, I don't know what it was like for you boys, but you're home now. We'll have to see [how you handle] the expectations here, and if you find that difficult, maybe I can help you move on to another place where you might be more comfortable. Knowing my dad, he was saying, get on or get off. So I started writing to colleges. I wrote to Wilberforce in Ohio, Prairie View, and Tuskegee — they said, if you're willing to sleep in the attic, come on. So I took the chance of going to Tuskegee in Alabama, and I *did* sleep in the attic.

I joined the ROTC with no intention of going back to the service because I'm not really gung ho, but they paid a little addendum for being in the service and I had no source of income besides my GI bill. So I decided to join the advanced ROTC, which enabled me to earn some additional money and I would be commissioned as a 2nd lieutenant in two years rather than four years. I took the plunge, and that went well. I learned a tremendous amount of knowledge in the ROTC; they taught courses in leadership and organization and tactics, things a person needs to know: discipline, trusting, sharing, and conceptualizing. Made me a better-rounded person.

[I] had no conscious awareness of [Truman's executive order in 1948]. I do know that in '48 we had a football game in Columbus, Georgia, and one Strom Thurmond had broken from the Democratic convention and set up a meeting in Charleston. We knew about that and knew there was some unrest. But being a student, we just knew that something was not right. What was not right was the African American community up in arms wanting more opportunity. And they were being restricted.

In '48 I was a junior in Tuskegee, and we would have to ride [at] the back of the train, but having grown up where I did, it was okay. We did what was expected of us by the law. I was a Christian person, Methodist. My parents taught me [that] things are probably going to get better but until they do you keep going with the right spirit. When Truman signed the order, things started to change for me. When I went to Fort Eustas, summer of '50, normally [I] would have to ride. I took the train. Following what I knew what was right, I knew that we should be able to eat in the diner. I asked if I had to sit in a place [that] had a circumscribed thing around it, and [the] conductor said, "No, if you prefer to sit out there, be my guest." My wife has a saying, "Education is the art of learning, and if you want to be educated, ask a teacher." I had a right to be out there based on the law, and the man knew the law and permitted me to be out there.

When I arrived in Saint Louis, we came back into the southern area where it was legally segregated because of *Plessy v. Ferguson*. That law, passed in 1896 in New Orleans, brought about legal segregation of the races, particularly in the South. So when I got back to Virginia, it was Saturday, and I'm a 2nd lieutenant. Conductor came and asked me if I wanted to move. And I said, "No." He said, "A lot of your people are getting on board, you can get on that coach if you choose." It was a local coach. I said, "I'm fine," and used the whole seat comfortably and rode until an Anglo lieutenant go on and we chatted all the way there. It was okay. We did what was expected, and so it went.

In 1949, I was sent to Fort Hood after two years of ROTC. Fort Hood was one of largest camps in the country. [I] was sent there even though I'm [a] native Texan because the 4th Army area is made up of four states of Texas, Louisiana, Oklahoma, [and] New Mexico. I was commissioned at Fort Hood in the summer of 1949 with a 2nd lieutenant's rank. I felt fine [going back in]. I had spent all my money. I had my college degree but no money. I was glad to be in the corps and to get the commission. I went on a short tour of duty over at Fort Eustis, Virginia, in the summer of '49 or '50 with the expectation of learning skills but also saving some money to buy a truck so I could become a county [agricultural] agent.

The war [in Korea] started when I was in Virginia at Fort Eustis on the James River. Having gone to the summer program, I saw the opportunity it afforded me to be in a different lifestyle than I had experienced as an enlisted man in World War II because I had become an officer. I went down the James River and saw how officers lived and how they were given privileges and opportunities. I said, "This is awesome, this is a rare opportunity."

Ernest K. Shaw
First lieutenant, 7th Division, 31st Regiment, 1st Battalion
US Army
Interviewed by David P. Cline, January 10, 2003, Houston, TX
American RadioWorks, Minnesota Public Radio

CALVIN ELIJAH BROWN, NEW BERN, NORTH CAROLINA

I'm Calvin Elijah Brown. I was born at Lake Charles, Louisiana, May 14, 1928. And I went to school and [lived with] my mother and my stepfather and my two siblings. At the death of my mother in 1942, I was raised by my cousin and his wife. And World War II was going on. And I worked at an air base, and I drove a truck. And at seventeen, I joined the coast guard, in 1945. And I went overseas to San Juan, Cuba, Hispaniola, Saint Thomas, Virgin Islands. I was a mess attendant, or steward's mate, if you will.

Well, the coast guard did not discriminate, as far as I could see. Now, mess attendants, or steward's mates, were strictly relegated to Blacks in the navy at that time, but in the coast guard, white boys or Black boys could both be steward's mates, or cooks, or whatever. And that was the difference. The coast guard made sure that they had a proper ratio in each branch of the service. But there was no discrimination, according to a job that was to be filled in the coast guard. And I was an officers' person. I made officers' beds. And they wanted to send me to cooking school, but I just simply told them that I did not want to go, because I didn't think I had the ability to learn how to cook for a bunch of men. But they said, "Oh, we can teach you." Well, it was almost time for me to get out, anyway. So I told them, "No, I'll just go home."

And in 1947, in April, we came back to the States, and the ship I was on, the Coast Guard cutter *Spruce*, which was a buoy tender, was decommissioned in Charleston, South Carolina. I went back to Lake Charles, Louisiana. Well, I was eighteen years of age then, and I fooled around, drew my mustering out pay, and I think I got a job doing construction work, something of the kind. But anyway, I passed the marine recruiting station, and I saw this guy with this beautiful dress blue uniform on, and, "Hey," I said, "Gee, that's a sharp looking outfit there!" A couple of people that I knew were already marines. And on that poster that year, I think Uncle Sam [was saying]: "I challenge you to become a United States marine." I looked at the poster and said, "Well, I'm gonna try to be a marine." So I went in, and I signed up, and he sent my papers to New Orleans. On the 24th day of July, 1946, I joined the United States Marine Corps, and I came here to Montford Point to be trained. My drill instructor was Corporal Howard Meyer at that time. He and his assistant, Corporal Allen, made sure that I got the word, so to say.

Calvin Elijah Brown
Sergeant, unit unknown
US Marine Corps
Interviewed May 17, 2004, New Bern, NC
Montford Point Marines Project
Copyright © 2006 Randall Library, University of North Carolina at Wilmington

First Experiences of Jim Crow:
Traveling to Boot Camp

*Although Capt. William Cooke recalled above that Jim Crow had largely disap-
peared on base by the time of the Korean War, many other soldiers recalled battling segregation both on and off base. For many, these experiences came as they
traveled across the country, leaving their familiar home regions and entering new
territory on their way to training or to ship out for overseas. Here Larry Hogan
and Dorothy Boyd recall incidents of encountering a racially segregated restaurant. Unlike Cooke's encounter on an army base, Hogan's experience happened
on a street corner in the nation's capital while he was on his way to Korea. For
Boyd, who had grown up in Massachusetts, her time at an air force base in Alabama introduced her to the rigors of Jim Crow. Her response was typical of many
northern-raised African Americans who had little experience of or patience for
the arbitrary racial restrictions they encountered. Such incidents were endemic
around southern training camps, where local white citizens and Black military
personnel clashed in various ways.*

*Interstate travel, at the time leading up to and during the Korean War, had
been desegregated in 1946 by federal order, yet many African Americans during this time recall having to travel in segregated buses and train cars and even
having to switch from one car or seat to another when the vehicle entered an
area governed by Jim Crow. We begin with the story of James Meredith, who
after his time in the air force would famously go on to desegregate the University
of Mississippi in 1962 under the protection of the federal government, a campaign he said he began to deal a blow against Jim Crow. Meredith also began
a solo 220-mile March against Fear from Tennessee to Mississippi in 1966 but
was shot by a white gunman on just the second day. Others took up the march,
around fifteen thousand in total, making it the largest civil rights demonstration
in Mississippi at the time.*

JAMES MEREDITH, JACKSON, MISSISSIPPI

You see, I graduated high school in Florida, and that was three years after Harry
Truman had signed the desegregation order. But the order was for each branch
of the military to submit a plan, a proposal, for desegregating the military in
their own deliberate speed. And the air force was the first to submit it, and the
air force had been approved while I was a senior in high school. They hadn't
started [yet,] but they had approved it. And in order to go into the desegregated
air force you had to go north because you could not exist in the desegregated air
force from the South, you could still only go to the segregated air force. Okay?
So I went to Detroit and volunteered and went to Sampson Air Force Base,

New York, in the Geneva area. They had established a boot camp for Blacks and whites to go to boot camp together. I was in the first group, and I finished boot camp, and I went to New Mexico Western College. This was the first time that the Black and white [personnel] had gone to technical training school together in the air force.

James Meredith
Staff sergeant, unit unknown
US Air Force
Interviewed by Renee Poussaint, June 27, 2006, Jackson, MS
National Visionary Leadership Project, Library of Congress

LARRY "LEN" LOCKLEY, SPRINGFIELD, MASSACHUSETTS

My name's Larry Lockley, from Springfield, Massachusetts. I'm seventy years old. I grew up in Springfield. I went to elementary and high school here. I got out of high school in 1950, June, and the Korean War started at the same time, and they were picking up guys, they were drafting guys, and I didn't have a job, didn't know what I was going to do. Some of my buddies got drafted, people were going left and right, so I thought why not? I went in the service January 5, 1951. I knew what I wanted to do—I always felt that I would go in the navy, even when I was a kid. My mother was from Virginia, Norfolk, . . . and she had talked about the navy and the water. I loved the water. We're in a landlocked area around here in Springfield, and she took my sister and my cousins and me to Boston so we could see the ocean, way back there. And I loved the ocean. I was glad to go [even though] it kind of put me back from a lot of things I wanted to do in my life.

I went to Great Lakes, Illinois, for boot camp, went with one other African American fellow from Springfield [and] thirty-five other white candidates. Most of them were fellows that I'd known, Italian fellows from the South End, and we rode on a train to Great Lakes, Illinois. [On the train to camp,] we hooked up with a company of another thirty-seven or so people, predominantly white, and one Black fellow from the South, [Charlie]. But the fellows I was with, they kind of told Charlie and me that, because they were northern fellows too and weren't into the whole of issue of what segregation was about, they said, "We have your back," if anything came up. And nothing really did that I can remember.

We had liberty after we finished boot camp, [but] Chicago was segregated in '51 and [there were] certain places you could not go. I remember Minsky's Burlesque Show, we couldn't go in there, and downtown was segregated to a certain extent. I finished corpsman school and was sent to Chelsea Naval Hospital in

Boston. And Boston at that time was really all right. Because it was [in] the 1st Naval District and there were a lot of navy people there and the issues of racism weren't as prevalent as they came to be in later years. There weren't too many Black corpsmen up there, but on the base it was great.

One incident that I had [though], a fella got shot, an African American fellow got shot in Boston, and the service tradition is that you try to send someone home with the body that's close in rank and the same nationality. This fellow was from Texas: Marshall, Texas. I didn't know him [but] I was elected. I got on a train in Boston, changed trains in Missouri, which was racist, had to lay over there. [When I went] to a movie, had to take a Black cab to the movie and then come back and make sure the body's transferred. And I got to Texarkana, Texas, and Marshall, a little stop there. The conductor [came] and I said, "Well, I have a ticket to ride back here." And he said, "No, here I'll tell you where to ride." So that was my first real indoctrination into what [segregation] was about.

And from [Boston] we transferred to Norfolk, Virginia. And another fellow was a [private] 1st class, he was from Boston, John Canazaro, and we met because we were both going down [to Norfolk]. We were assigned to the *Lake Champlain*, a C839 aircraft carrier [that] was recommissioned. So we were bunked and we met with our group. Out of twenty-something people, I was the only Black in the group, but guys in my group were really great, and we got along fine. And a couple of fellows I hooked up with and became really good friends. We became a tight-knit group.

There was a ferry between Norfolk and Portsmouth where the ship was coming out of mothballs. And on this ship, it was really funny, people would be sitting in the bathroom [with] open doors, the workmen and everything, reading the paper or whatever, but when you got off the ship, there were segregated bathrooms on the dock. Then when we went from Norfolk to Portsmouth, there was only one Black place in town to hang out in [in] Norfolk and the same thing in Portsmouth, but taking the ferry back and forth, there were separate waiting rooms. Also, I remember one time, I forgot, we were coming up from Norfolk. Canazaro always had a car. And we stopped on Route 13 to get something to eat. And I went in, and they said we can't serve you. This is probably in '52. And I said, "What do you mean, you can't serve me?" And I just went on out, and said, "The heck with it!" I remember one time that happened.

Larry "Len" Lockley, PhD
Hospital corpsman 2nd class, USS Lake Champlain
US Navy
Interviewed by David P. Cline, October 29, 2002, Springfield, MA
American RadioWorks, Minnesota Public Radio

[I trained in] Fort Howard, California. It was an integrated unit, the first one that they had after President Truman signed that executive order to integrate the armed forces. It was very challenging, and I was fortunate that I was put in a leadership position.

I became a squad leader, so there was no problem there. I had white soldiers [under my command but had] no problems. [Everything was] integrated. Mess hall was integrated, the sleeping quarters, the classrooms. It was [a] very new experience [having grown up in Texas].

I'll tell you the truth, when we first traveled from Houston to Los Angeles by train and we had to eat together, it was kind of frightful to open that dining room and see all those white soldiers sitting there. It was kind of shocking, but one of the cooks there, he used to say, "Go on man, go on and sit down, you're in the army now, don't act like you're different." So I guess that kind of helped me a bit. . . . Right, that was another experience, too, to be in the same quarters with white people. But I got along real well with them, I had no problems. I did what I was supposed to do, I followed my orders, and in fact I did especially well and it paid off. I was selected as soldier of the month six weeks [after] I was there. They sent me to San Francisco for the weekend, and they gave me a pass to go to the movies, and I got another pass to pick up some groceries and things, extra food. So I really enjoyed it.

Billy J. Baines
Corporal, 24th Infantry Regiment, 25th Division
US Army
Interviewed by David P. Cline, January 10, 2003, Houston, TX
American RadioWorks, Minnesota Public Radio

MANUAL "MANNY" TEXEIRAS, BOSTON, MASSACHUSETTS

This is what the average person doesn't realize that servicemen go through. Norfolk [Virginia] was segregated at the time. I saw guys get on the bus wounded and all messed up, and they had to go to the back. We used to fight with the civilians taking the bus onto the base all the time. They'd call the police on us and they'd say, "We don't care what you are, go to the back." But finally they said if you don't leave the servicemen alone, we won't let you on the base.

Manual "Manny" Texeiras
Seaman, USS Mindoro
US Navy
Interviewed by David P. Cline, October 22, 2002, Dorchester, MA
American RadioWorks, Minnesota Public Radio

CHARLES EARNEST BERRY, PORTLAND, OREGON

I was raised here [in Chattanooga, but] I didn't graduate from Howard [High School] until later [because] I went into the service [in] 1946. And then in the service I completed my education and got a GED through Howard. Well, the reason I joined the service was that as a youngster I used to see the soldiers over at Fort Arthur. And they'd come in on Saturdays, and they'd have a lot of fun. And I liked their dress. And then here in Chattanooga, the only employment that you really had was working in a hotel or some type of menial work, and I wanted something better. And I had a girlfriend and I wanted to get married, but I wanted something where we could have a nice home and a car and maybe a couple dollars in the bank.

So one day I got off work and I saw this sign says, "The US Army Wants You." So, I told my sister, and so we told Mama and got all the paperwork done, and so I joined the service. I was seventeen, [so] my mother had to sign. But when she signed the papers she didn't really read them, because she didn't know I was going till my sister told her where I was. But after she started getting the allotment checks, she didn't care!

I left Chattanooga by Greyhound and went to Fort Benning, Georgia. The bus arrived into Fort Benning, Georgia, at the bus station there, you know, you had segregation there. And they called you that old southern name. And we had to get in the back of the bus to go to the fort, catching the bus to go into Fort Benning. So just before the bus got ready to pull out, the driver said, "One of you has to get off," so this white soldier could ride. So a fight [developed] from that, and he didn't ride. And so once we got into Fort Benning, they checked us in and read us the riot act. And that was my first experience with the military, which I thought was kind of funny because I was used to segregation in the first place, but it was not in such a harsh form.

Fort Benning was quite an experience. It was just a holding company till they ship you out to your basic training. And the next morning I think was very comical. This guy [comes and] all of a sudden I wind up on the floor! I was on the top bunk, and he says, "Get up! It's time to go to reveille!" I looked out the window and it ain't even daylight. And I curled back and went back to sleep. And all of a sudden I wind up on the floor. And the problem was, I hit the guy. I had a temper. And that's when I was introduced to a six by six. That means [you have to dig] a hole six feet wide and six feet long and six feet deep.

Charles Earnest Berry
Master sergeant, 24th Infantry Regiment, 25th Infantry Division
US Army
Interviewed by Michael Willie, February 13, 2003, Chattanooga, TN
Charles Earnest Berry Collection (AFC/2001/001/05950), Veterans
*   History Project, American Folklife Center, Library of Congress*

HARRY TOWNSEND, SILVER SPRING, MARYLAND

My name is Harry Townsend, my rank now is colonel. I was with the Triple Nickle[s] [555th Parachute Infantry Battalion, during World War II] and I was with the Headquarters [Battery], 25th Infantry Division, in Korea from July of 1951 to June of 1952. [The 25th Infantry Division] was an integrated division that had a segregated regiment in it, the 24th Infantry. They had some [segregated] artillery units there [too,] but the biggest unit that was segregated was the 24th Infantry Regiment. I was in headquarters of the 25th [as] a liaison. [I was a] pilot and an artillery spotter and also a helicopter pilot. I was flying the spotter planes and the helicopter for the command at HQ.

My father died when I was very young, but my uncles were all in World War II. One was in the navy and several of them were in the army and they were in the segregated army. I always wanted to be a soldier and in my high school yearbook it said that I wanted to be a soldier: "Harry Wheatlan Townsend. Hobby: Military Tactics." Yeah, so even back then. I was always interested in flying and in 1948 I bought an airplane with some people and got my pilot's license and trained others, so I knew how to fly. I built model airplanes when I was small. I tried to join the air force in World War II, but my eyes, they wouldn't let you wear glasses at that time. Now, but not then.

Before I [enlisted and] got in, I was a member of what they called [the] Citizens Military Corps. That was a unit that . . . trained people to be officers who couldn't go to college. It was like ROTC, but it was a civilian [group] and you go to summer [training] camp. I went to summer camp in Fort Howard, Maryland. That was stopped in 1940 because the war started.

Everything was segregated in the army when I went in. The world was segregated. I grew up in Philadelphia. It was segregated in Philadelphia, but it wasn't segregated by edict, that you *had* to be segregated. So it was difficult because even after we left Fort Henry, when we were going down to Fort McClellan riding in the trains, and when we'd go through towns they'd pull the curtain so they wouldn't see African American troops on there. And [enlisted men] couldn't go to the dining car. [As] an officer, if I was riding on a train on official duty and I had to use the dining car, they had one section on the dining car in the trains in the South and it had one curtain on a table that they'd put around you. If I were doing a duty, taking a body someplace for the military, you know, you were segregated. If you had a group of people and some of them were white, they'd separate you on the train.

[There were] four different Black fighting units and they had their artillery battalions with them, so those were the battalions you'd be assigned to if you were a combat soldier. They had engineers and quartermasters and support troops. But the policy was that you did not arm Black soldiers. When I was with the OCS [Officer Candidate School] and went to Europe, rather than being assigned to an infantry unit I was assigned to an engineer unit and I didn't know the first thing about being an engineer. They wanted me to be a platoon leader in a dump truck company, and then I was [in] a firefighting platoon.

[In 1948, when Truman signed the executive order,] I was with the 3rd Battalion of the 505th [Division,] 82nd Infantry Regiment. We really integrated the army just a little bit before Truman's order came out because General [James] Gavin decided that's what he was going to do. In November of 1947, General Gavin decided that [since the] Triple Nickle was attached to his division, rather than have a separate unit, he said, "Well, they're part of the unit, they're part of the airborne, they're part of my command, so I'm going to make them the 3rd Battalion of the 505th." I think [General Gavin] was a straight military man. He had been in combat, and he understood that a commander had a certain leadership quality and a loyalty to his troops in combat and that in combat you needed to fight for one cause. You were all fighting together and dying together, and he didn't have the stomach to continue with the segregation.

I thought Truman had a lot of guts doing it and I was quite surprised because he was a captain in the artillery in the military in World War I and he said that "enough is enough. People are fighting and dying for their country, then they should enjoy integration." I had gotten a regular army commission by then. I was on a competitive tour, and they [...] I thought getting [integration] would help. Integration, if you could be part of it, would add to the unity. As long as you were segregated you would be denied privileges, you could be denied access to supplies, you could get people in leadership positions who didn't like you and would do things that would get you killed. For example, there was [a] general order ... [that] you couldn't put a stockade or a POW camp within medium artillery distance [of] the front lines because the prisoners would get killed, but ... the commander of the 92nd Division signed an order that stockades for Black soldiers would be within that artillery range. He just didn't like the idea, leading Black troops. He was a segregationist.

So when they changed in the military [with Truman's initial order] it was quite a disappointment when I first went to Fort Henry in Virginia and got off the train with all the draftees and they took us to their barracks around 11:30 at night, and when they . . . saw me they said, "Well you can't stay here." I was the only [Black person] in the whole barracks. And they took me across the post and put me in a barracks by myself, I was alone in the barracks. They processed me there and then sent me down to Fort McClellan.

Harry Townsend
Colonel, Headquarters, 25th Infantry Division
US Army
Interviewed by Stephen Smith, March 7, 2003, Silver Spring, MD
American RadioWorks, Minnesota Public Radio

LAURENCE "LARRY" HOGAN, BOSTON, MASSACHUSETTS

I'm Sergeant 1st Class Larry Hogan, and I live here in Boston. I served in Korea with the 7th Infantry Division, 31st Infantry Regiment, Love Company. I spent ten months and twenty-nine days on the line in Korea. From 1952 until the last day, January 27, 1953, all through the armistice, all through the talks they were having. Did all the fighting up and down the line, so most of my time was in combat.

I volunteered for the infantry. One of the things about the infantry — some people can be a doctor, some people can be a lawyer, nurse, policeman — any of those jobs I wouldn't take on a bet, not my thing. But at that time I could do [the infantry]. I was psyched for that. Knowing that you're going into the infantry and knowing what you're going to do made it a little easier for me psychologically. One of the reasons was that you got ten thousand dollars if you got killed, your family got that, and ten thousand dollars back then was a lot of money. You got a pension, an allotment came home to my mother and sisters, that was good. I got paid about seventy-eight dollars a month for my rank, the lowest rank, but when I went into combat I got another fifty a month. So I was becoming a millionaire there in my own right!

My experiences in Korea, in a way, were better than some of the experiences I had here. Because in the States, people perform, you know, they go into their act to justify whatever they're doing. Everybody's got a horror story from the States. But if you talk to the guys from the 24th who fought [in Korea], they got a worse horror story, 'cause they were under the gun and they were getting left there. I mean that was life and death. Here, it was a lot of fighting, it wasn't life and death. But it was harassment, you know, it was just a lot of things that were going on.

It wasn't too bad in Fort Dix, [New Jersey]. But when I left to go to Korea, I went down to Washington, DC, because I wanted to see the capital. A guy gave me a ride in a Cadillac, picked me up right there on the West Side Highway with my duffel bag. In those days you could hitch. We used to do that after the Second World War. You would see soldiers, sailors. We got into Baltimore late at night. He had to get a hamburger, and I couldn't get a hamburger.

So the next day he left me off, and I remember being right in Washington, and one of the buildings up there has got "Equal Justice under the Law" [written on the front of it]. I forget which, the Treasury? But one of the buildings there. And I'm looking at the building, and I'm going over there [to Korea] to fight. I looked at the capitol. Never saw [it] before, it was my first time really leaving New York to go somewhere, and I said I'm gonna see the capitol before I go to Seattle, where I'm supposed to go to.

I wanted to get a hamburger. I would have done it in New York, you know. And I'm waiting and waiting, and the guy's waiting on everybody, and I'm starving and I say, "You know, can't I get a hamburger?" And he says, "We don't serve niggers here." And in those days you carried your whole issue, your two pair of pants, your this, your that, everything was in the duffel bag, everything you own. Plus you got your records, your shot records, you traveled like that. And I took the duffel bag, and I threw the duffel bag through the window. I said, "Look, all I want is something to eat," and I knew if I did this, I'm going to jail. And if you [get taken] to Fort McNair that was on the air force post, and the air force *eats*.

They call the MPs. The MPs come and took me to Fort McNair in Washington. They had really good food. I had a bed, a private room, something like that. And a colonel came down and talked to me. And I told the colonel what had happened, and he said, "Jeesh," you know. I mean I got my orders and everything, and I got a good record as a soldier.

And I told him, I said, "Can you believe this? I'm getting' ready to go over there to fight?" "You're shippin' out, you're goin'," he said. "Do you have any money?" "Nah, I don't have any money." They gave me the government chits, they gave me $150 and put me on a train and I went across the country on the Milwaukee Road, and then on the Union Pacific to Chicago. I had a beautiful ride across the country on the train. And that's an individual incident that happened to me, but I'm sure things like that happened to people.

Laurence "Larry" Hogan
Sergeant 1st class, 31st Infantry Regiment, 7th Infantry Division
US Army
Interviewed by David P. Cline, October 25, 2002, Boston, MA
American RadioWorks, Minnesota Public Radio

DOROTHY M. (PHILLIPS) BOYD,
DORCHESTER, MASSACHUSETTS

I'm Dorothy M. Boyd, served as Phillips, born September 25, 1932. I'm the commander of this post, [William E. Carter American Legion Post, Mattapan, Massachusetts]. [I'm the] second female commander. I was in the air force during the Korean conflict. My mother had five sons in the service. I went into the air force because I was tired of ironing those army pants! I served at the time they were integrating male/female, Black and white. We were the guinea pigs. Went thirteen weeks for basic training, and from there [I was] sent to different bases [for specific training]. Mine was communications. From San Antonio, I went to Cheyenne [Wyoming] for [communications] school, graduated in the top ten of my class.

We were the first class that came under integration. We would go into town and it was a mess. In my estimation they had more segregation and racial problems on base, and to have to go off base and deal with it too keeps you from wanting to go off the base and deal with all the foolishness.

In Montgomery [Alabama], I went into Woolworth's—the furthest south I'd ever been [before] was Philadelphia. [I was] waiting for someone to wait on me, [but] every time the person would come and walk past me. After five minutes, I said to the girl, I said, "Excuse me, when are you planning to take my order?" She said, "We don't take niggers' orders. You'll have to go to the other side, and they'll wait on you over there."

I said, "Okay. This is sad." I said, 'You mean to tell me I put this uniform on to protect your ass"—that's just the way I said it to her—"for you to tell me something like that. I don't think so." So I got up and was heading out the door and this lady came and said, "Oh Miss, that was so rude of her." And I said, "She can't help it, she's doing what she was told to do, but I don't have to take it."

I said, "I think that's really sad." I don't know how I'm going to last down here. My mother sent me a letter and I said, "I have to answer your letter because the next one they might have to hang on the tree next to me." I couldn't keep my mouth shut. I came home [after my three years of service] because they wanted to send me to Kentucky and I said, "No, I'm not going back south, I'm going home."

Dorothy M. (Phillips) Boyd
Airman basic, WAF
US Air Force
Interviewed by David P. Cline, October 20, 2002, Mattapan, MA
American RadioWorks, Minnesota Public Radio

Stanley Perry Stone, born March 28, 1928. [I was in the] 3rd Army Division, 41st Signal Construction Battalion, Fort Rucker, Alabama, [from] November 25, 1950, to November 25, 1952. I found out I was drafted two weeks before induction. So I was given a two-week notice. [I was] nineteen. I [did not] want to go into the military due to the fact that there was a lot of segregation going on in the South, in the military, and I wasn't born and raised in segregated conditions, so I didn't think I really wanted to serve under those conditions. Before I was drafted, my mother and father tried to get a deferment, but there was nothing going on, I had to go.

So I left [Minneapolis] November 25, from the Milwaukee Depot, to Fort Riley, Kansas, the processing center. There are three forts there: Funston, Forsyth, and Fort Riley. When we pulled in there at night, there was a big troop train parked there, these were soldiers on their way to Korea. I stayed in the processing center for about three weeks. After that, we were called out every day, after reveille, and after each mealtime, and orders were being read, and they picked out seven of us who were Black and segregated us right there. They called our names out and asked us to step forward, and the seven of us stepped forward. That's the way the segregation began. [We] were all from Minnesota, one from Saint Paul. I didn't see any other Black soldiers at that particular area.

The next day we were put on a train on our way to Camp Rucker, Alabama. The move orders were given to me; I was head of the six soldiers. I had all the paperwork for them, [and] I noticed that behind our names there were asterisks, which indicated we were colored. The military police took us to the train station. We had meal tickets and fare. We were put on a train with just three coaches on it. We were on our way to Fort Rucker, Alabama, and we didn't have any meals on the way. We were supposed to stop during that travel, [but] traveling through the South, we were not allowed to get off the train and go and eat in white establishments, so we had to stay on it.

I think it was about a ten-hour ride. It was an open car, like a caboose on the end, an old converted cattle car, that we were in. We were sitting right next to the engine, the tinderbox. It was all wood, and the steam was coming in through the windows and cinders on the floor, it was terrible. So cold, raining, conditions were terrible.

When we arrived . . . in Alabama the next day, we were met by more MPs and army personnel, [and] we were taken to Fort Rucker. When we got there, it was cold, rainy, and damp, everything was disorganized. They gave us some bedding. We met the white officer, who was the CO, company commander. He noticed we hadn't used any of our meal tickets up, so they served us food right away.

Stanley Perry Stone
Corporal, 41st Signal Construction Battalion, 3rd Army Division
US Army
Interviewed by Tina Tennessen, August 19, 2002, Minneapolis, MN
American RadioWorks, Minnesota Public Radio

2

Life in the Barracks

Experiences in Segregated and Integrated Training Camps and Schools

For most new recruits, the transformation from civilian to military life began with basic training. Training camp experiences varied widely from branch to branch, camp to camp, and year to year, especially with regards to race in the years around Truman's order. Some camps integrated right away, but even then, desegregation certainly did not always equate to equal treatment, with some veterans recounting horror stories of racial intimidation and violence. Many other camps, especially in the army, delayed integration far into the Korean War, although unofficial army policy had, by June 1950, supposedly abolished segregated basic training.

On the ground, the individual camp commander established the rules at most training camps, and whether or how desegregation would be implemented was no different. Some camps attempted to integrate soldiers barrack by barrack, some bunk by bunk, some immediately after Truman's order in 1948, some not at all. This occurred despite the issuance, as early as 1944, of a War Department memorandum forbidding base segregation on the basis of race.[1] Exacerbating the situation was that many Black soldiers and sailors were trained in facilities located in the Jim Crow South; indeed, Gen. Dwight D. Eisenhower issued a 1947 directive, in direct violation of Gillem report recommendations, that all Black army inductees, enlistees, and reenlistees be trained in South Carolina at Fort Jackson, whereas whites could be trained at various army camps throughout the country, including at four camps in states without de jure segregation.[2]

The oral histories that follow establish that African American veterans underwent a vast range of experiences—integrated, segregated, desegregated, and somewhere in the confused middle—throughout the country before and during the war. Even more than the contemporaneous Black newspaper cover-

age, which revealed much, these excerpts expose the whims of policies not fol-
lowed, the exceptions to the rule, and the realities of racism and segregation in
the armed forces even after segregation was supposedly prohibited. Racism, of
course, could never quite be eradicated.

Training Camps before Executive Order 9981

The following excerpts from veterans who served in both wars establish the base
conditions of training experienced by many African Americans in the World
War II era and how those conditions changed over time. In many cases, despite
growing pressure for racial change culminating in Truman's order, that change
was scarcely noticeable. Most revealing here, however, is how individual each
experience could be, even under the umbrella of racial policies. Jack Brice, for
example, was trained in segregated circumstances for the navy during World
War II, served each day in an integrated unit on board ship, but had to return to
segregated quarters to sleep each night. During his army training for the Korean
War, he was plucked from officer training to play football rather than fight. He
wouldn't be the only one.

RUTHERFORD VINCENT "JACK" BRICE, ATLANTA, GEORGIA

I guess I have [had] an interesting up-and-down kind of a career. By that I mean
I served as an enlisted man, an NCO [noncommissioned officer], and an officer. See, when I enlisted in the navy in 1942 I was seventeen. And during World
War II I served in the navy during [a] time . . . that the military was segregated.
And except for the Black NCOs and officers that were assigned to the Diesel
Training Center at Hampton Institute in Virginia, there were no military occupation specialties that included Blacks. I was one of the fortunate 143 experimental Blacks that were sent to aviation machinist mates school. Initially I went
to [Great Lakes near] Chicago to become a sailor, then shortly afterwards was
sent to Memphis Naval Air Training Station in Memphis, Tennessee.

I remember the first day that we arrived there they gave us a mattress cover
to go and pick up all of our clothing. As we were walking along with these big
mattress covers over our backs with the clothing in it, the white troops were
marching along saying, "Cotton pickers." They were teasing us. We didn't think
it was funny at all, as a matter of fact. I think out of the one hundred and forty-
three it was something like forty of us that completed the school. And I have no
clue where most of them went. I think I saw one or two afterwards during that
whole war. I was sent to Syracuse University, first college campus I was ever on.
I was still a little boy and I was taught to be a supercharger specialist. They were

putting an airplane into the fleet [at] Alameda, California, a F4U Corsair. It could turn inside of a Zero, the airplane that the Japanese had, and they thought that was quite impressive. And it had a supercharger that made it a lot faster. So, at any rate, I finished that school and was then sent to Alameda to join the Carrier Area Service Unit 14. And it was a part of the fleet that included the *Intrepid*. So during that war, I was in Guam, Saipan, Leyte [Gulf], and Guadalcanal all with that fleet that was going through the Pacific.

As I said, [at] the time it was a segregated navy service. And it was interesting; I'd go in the daytime during duty times and work with my [integrated] crew because I was a specialist in that area. And then I had to go to the forward part of the ship out of the hangar deck to speak with my compadres, so to speak, the guys that were the cooks, bakers, and steward's mates. Some were Black and some were Filipinos. But the quarters were separate, completely. Then you'd go back to do your duties wherever you were assigned.

I left the navy in 1945, beginning of 1946. They were letting people out who had finished a certain amount. The war for all practical purposes was over. I had signed a chit, staying in the reserves, to go to college. I went to Morgan State College, now University. [I decided to enlist in the army] and I had to resign the reserve in the navy to take the commission in the army . . . on the 6th of June [because I] graduated on the 6th of June, 1950. It was commencement day as well as commission day. The 16th of June, 1950, I was sent to Fort Benning to the associate officer's basic course, and to the infantry school, and to jump school, and ranger school.

So at any rate, on the 16th of June '50, I went to Fort Benning, and on the 26th—I'm in infantry—on the 26th of June the Korean [War] broke out. My class consisted of the infantry class from West Point, all of them, [who] for the most part went to Korea immediately. The general that was school troops commander at Fort Benning at the time was going to be in some way in charge of a training center at Fort Knox, Kentucky. And when we got our assignments, because I had played football—I was a minor all-American running back—my name was not on the list to go to Korea, it was on the list to go to Fort Knox, Kentucky, [as] assistant athletic officer in special services at Fort Knox. And I just could not believe this. I'm an infantry officer, airborne trained, the whole bit, and I just thought that was the sickest thing in the world. When I got there I went to the general's office, and he said, "You've been assigned to play football and coach my backfield." In [fact,] Whitey Ford basically had the same kind of situation as a pitcher on that [camp's baseball] team. This general just pulled together all the athletes he could. He was a freak in that regard. And he was looking out for his career, you know. So, we won the 2nd Army championship. We beat the Quantico marines in the championship. I came back to Fort Knox in January, and in February I had my orders to go to Korea. I had served my purpose.

Rutherford Vincent "Jack" Brice
Captain, 1st Battalion, 23rd Infantry Regiment, 2nd Infantry Division
US Army
Interviewed by Frederick Wallace, April 22, 2003, Atlanta, GA
Rutherford Vincent Brice Collection (AFC/2001/001/05397), Veterans
    History Project, American Folklife Center, Library of Congress

FRED ASH, JACKSONVILLE, NORTH CAROLINA`

When we got in to Montford Point, a marine guard came on the bus, and he was giving orders and asking names and so forth and so on. And to us everything was funny, so he ordered us to stop laughing. And it was sort of a hard thing to do, 'cause, you know, I had never really had no one order me around or talk to me like that nowhere unless I said something back to them. So anyway, when we got inside the building, he came up again and was talking to us, and he asked us certain things, like where we were from and how old we were and why did we come in the Marine Corps and all this. Anyway, I was somewhat of a wise bird, you know, and I kept on wising off to the guy, and it made him mad. So he told me to turn around and face the wall. We were standing in the hallway, about ten or fifteen of us, so he told me to face the wall, told me to get up close to the wall. I was still laughing, you know, the next thing I know he had bumped my head up against the concrete wall and right away I had a [bruise], and I hadn't been at Montford Point forty-five minutes. But that stopped the laughing.

The rated [officers] was white, like sergeants and corporals, but the PFCs and privates was Black. And mostly what went on was they, the whites, would [give] one order, and then one of these Afro-Americans would hear this, so he'd come right behind the white NCO and jump on you for the same thing. So actually you got two chewings out, because the Afro-American would copy behind him and do the same thing. My Afro-American drill sergeant, he was a PFC ... from Louisiana, big, tall, heavyset, about 6′ 7″, weighed about two hundred and some pounds, but he didn't look like he had an ounce of fat on him. He was well built.

My first liberty after I got out of boot camp was in Jacksonville, and ... you'd leave the camp [on] a bus to the bus station, and the bus station was divided. You had a section for Blacks, and you had a section for whites. And if you was going to the base you could get on a bus that you sit anywhere you wanted on the bus, but if you was going, say, to Wilmington, Kinston, or New Bern, you got your tickets and you went to the back of the bus, even if you was in a uniform.

And downtown Jacksonville, there was a divided line there right where the train station is. They had MPs that would constantly patrol that area, and they would keep the whites on the upper side of the tracks, and they would direct the Blacks across the track. Up until you got to the railroad tracks the streets was paved, but then after you passed that, it was all dirt.

After we got out of boot camp, we went to an organization at Montford Point called H and S Company, where you did guard duty and whatever else that they had to do. At that time, we really wasn't allowed over at Main Side [of Camp Lejeune]. Main Side was, well, a section for mostly whites. I went one time . . . on a trash run — they had these fifty-five-gallon drums that you'd make about three or four trips a day [to] every section wherever they had them at and empty them in a dump truck — and you even didn't eat over there. When you would take a break for lunch, you'd come back to Montford Point. . . . While we were over there, we'd always knock off in time to get back to our camp, to Montford Point, to get our lunch or dinner, whatever it was. And they would tell us that we couldn't eat over at Main Side or in the mess halls over there because we had to eat where they drew our rations. That's what they told us. But to me it, it, it didn't make sense. And then . . . if you would go over there they'd look at you like you were something from outer space anyway. And they give us the name, Camp Montford Point [would be called] Monkey Point, . . . [by] some of the whites. [But] I so rejoiced over being a marine it, it didn't matter too much.

Fred Ash
Master sergeant, 7th Marine Division
US Marine Corps
Interviewed December 17, 2004, Jacksonville, NC
Montford Point Marines Project
Copyright © 2006 Randall Library, University of North Carolina at Wilmington

JOHNNIE GIVIAN, JACKSONVILLE, NORTH CAROLINA

In 1947, they was trying to cut back on the military, so I signed up to get out because I just felt like somebody was choking me all the time. And I got out of the Marine Corps and I went back to Atlanta and I was looking for a job, and I saw the same stuff. [And] if you got out then you had to get in the reserves. I think I stayed out thirty days and came back [into] the reserves. I met my wife and she just kept on insisting that I stay [in the marines,] but that was after 1949.

When I came back [into the regular marines,] I came right back to Montford Point and Montford Point hadn't changed no kind of way. The only difference was that when I got out of the Marine Corps I was labeled as a steward [and when] I went back [into the marines] they put me in what we called the motor transport, AAA Motor Transport Company, and that's [a] Black [company] there at Montford Point. They put up a sign that they was looking for people to go on a detachment, leave Montford Point and go somewhere else for a certain length of time. And my name appeared on there to go to [Camp Pendleton in] California. I was happy about that 'cause I had heard a lot of good stuff about California. We got on a train one day and rode out there, and they put us in a barrack, fifty-two of us. Everything out there was white, the whole base was except us now as a unit. We was the Montford Point Detachment Unit, I believe it was. But they put us in one wing in the corner of that barracks — ... it's the oldest building out there, [the] Hughes Building. We was on one wing and ..., [when we] went to the mess hall to eat they had an area roped off for us. We'd go in there, they were segregated. They weren't as nasty as some of the people around down in [the South,] but they was segregated. We had to go to the furthest row. We couldn't go up there and eat [anywhere]. We just had to eat in that one place where they had it roped off and the same way in the barracks sleeping. The theater was roped off at a certain area where we would go. [That] was in Camp Pendleton, California, and I stayed there about seven or eight months. I pretty well stayed out of trouble, you know, because I minded my business, I didn't try to be something that I know I wasn't.

I volunteered to go to Guam ... and I stayed there about eighteen months. They was starting to integrate the Marine Corps [then]. There was a lot of negotiating going on with the president and everybody, and when I got to Guam they was in the early stage of integrating. And we were put in the barracks with everybody else. I was in the fire department over there [which was] about half and half white and Black. And we had scraps here and there but nothing major ... the Blacks and the whites were coming together.

[When] the Korean War started, the unit I was with over there, they were sent back to the States. So I came back to the States, and when I got back to Camp Lejeune [in North Carolina,] I found a lot of racial [prejudice still remained] in the marines. I stopped at Pendleton, left there, and come back to Camp Lejeune and everybody [had] the same racial [prejudice.] You run into it, you run into it. You know, you get out there now and get too close, you run into, but see back then you would run into it [all the time].

Johnnie Givian
Corporal, unit unknown
US Marine Corps
Interviewed August 17, 2005, Jacksonville, NC
Montford Point Marines Project
Copyright © 2006 Randall Library, University of North Carolina at Wilmington

My name is Fannie Keyes Coleman. I was born in Oriental, North Carolina, and that's down east, as we call it, east of New Bern. I was [from] a family of ten, six boys and four girls. Our father worked at a sawmill, and my mother was a housewife, as well as she worked in the fields to help to support the family. I went to [school in] Oriental first and then to high school in Pamlico County in Bayboro, North Carolina. And from there, I went to nursing school in Wilmington, North Carolina, Community Hospital. It was a school of nursing for Blacks. The way I got there, I was in New Bern visiting [and I] went to an outdoor toilet. And there was ads all over, newspapers all over: go to school, this, that, and the other. So I told my parents, I found the school I want. I want to go to Wilmington, I want to become a nurse. So they sent me to Wilmington. They had to get a bus from Oriental to New Bern and from New Bern to Wilmington in order for me to enter nursing school.

Nursing school was from '48 to '51, and it was a three-year program, and you only got one week out of a year for vacation 'cause you get from books to practice right there in the nursing school. So for that reason, you could not just take off and leave. They would give us a week off each year out of the three years that I was there. In my class, there were thirty-eight, and they came from various parts of North Carolina [and a] few from as far away as South Carolina. And there was just nurses, just all girls. We had our own dormitory [with] our own house mother, and from there, we could walk over to the hospital to begin our training. From day one, you start with the book. And then, from the book, you went to practice. From there I had to go to Richmond and Norfolk, Virginia, for affiliation in pediatrics, had to go to Tuskegee, Alabama, for affiliation in psychiatric nursing. And then, after that, of course, you had to go to Raleigh to take your state board to become an RN [registered nurse].

The way I really learned about [Montford Point] was the general or commanding officer would allow a bus to [come to] Wilmington to pick the student nurses up [for dances]. We were on [the] south side [and] we were not allowed on the north side because there were "ladies" over there; that part of Wilmington was not what they wanted us exposed to. So when we got ready to get on our buses, the Black girls, the Black city ladies, girls, got on one bus, and we were allowed to get on our bus. The city girls, ladies, were not allowed to ride on the same bus, [and] we were not allowed to ride with the so-called city girls. They [would] call your name off like a roll call, you got on your bus, you were seated, and then they would drive us over here.

When we got to Montford Point, we were parked at the building that we were going [to], which is still standing. I think it's their gym, now. We were allowed to go in, be seated, and then they had bands, big-name bands here at Montford Point . . . I think Louis Armstrong was one of them. Maybe Count Basie, I'm not sure. But they were name bands that we hear records of today. Then, we would go in there as the music began to play. Of course, the young marines would come and pick the lady that they wanted to dance with. We could dance with any marine. We could get in a group with the city girls, but once we finished, then we were called off, got back on our bus, and we were taken back to Wilmington to the nurses' home.

As a young female, [this was my] first exposure to a whole building of young men, and they were willing and ready to dance with you. Once you got one and he decided you were his partner for the night, every dance that came on, either slow or fast, that was your date for the night. And with that, of course, give me your name, give me your address. They could write to us [but] could not visit except a certain time at our dormitory. But [we were] like I said, a group of young girls, first time away from home, being exposed to a whole building of young men. It was exciting.

When you're getting ready to leave, you're holding hands, you're laughing, you're throwing kisses 'cause there was no contact, throwing kisses and saying, "I'll see you again." This type [of] thing. It was just such a good feeling. And on the way back to Wilmington, everybody was laughing and talking and singing until we got back to the nurses' home, then we had to be quiet, had to be counted to go in for the night. Well, to me, coming from a small town, from a very sheltered family, this was like a whole new world. And being on a Marine Corps base and dealing with predominantly Black [marines,] that opened up a whole new world, a whole new look on life to me as to whether it should remain this way or what was happening.

Fannie Keyes Coleman
Nurse, unit unknown
US Marine Corps
Interviewed August 17, 2005, Jacksonville, NC
Montford Point Marines Project
Copyright © 2006 Randall Library, University of North Carolina at Wilmington

THOMAS E. CORK SR., LOUISVILLE, KENTUCKY

I remember about [the marine base at] Montford Point, [there was a] very small town, Jacksonville, right there, and I became the age I thought I could go into a bar. They had a bar out at Jacksonville. They called it the Black and Tan—now, you can figure out what that was about. The white marines be on one side being served, and the Black marines be on the other side. The only thing separating us was the bar in between us. During the early part of the evening, we stayed on our side, but late at night, we would switch sides, to a point. We could mix and mingle with those guys during this bar time. And then, after that, they'd go back on their side. The other problem I had there was getting back to the base. You go on liberty and you had to be careful getting back because the buses were segregated. There were only so many marines could ride that bus at one time. There was seats on the back of the bus that we were supposed to ride on, four or five back seats. Now, if that bus has space up in front, you could not use it [and] when that bus got the four back seats filled, they left and left you. So you had to be careful getting back to the base and being on time because that was the only transportation you had, those buses coming in and out of Montford Point. But I tell you, at the time I was not bitter. I just took it in stride, because we were used to it. I mean, that's the kind of life we knew then. It was no animosity against the white or whatever. We took our position with pride. I didn't feel any lesser than those guys. But I knew what I could get away with and what I couldn't.

There were other things [that] happened to me down there. I went on liberty one night. They asked us, if we go on liberty, try to go [out with] more than one, because the town wasn't very friendly to us, and other marines didn't want you there. So, I go by myself. I get all the way down the street and I saw these young [white] marines coming toward me. They were laughing and talking. They acted like I wasn't even there, so I am thinking I am going right on past them. But when I get up abreast of them, they literally knocked me off that street and said, "This is my street," so and so, you know what they called me, and went on about their business. Now, here come the MPs. They didn't bother those guys, they got me. And what they got me for, my cap had been knocked off and got dirty. And I had to go back to the base because my cap was knocked off by these two young men. So, that kind of upset me.

They sent some of the guys to Guam and some went up to Perth Amboy, New Jersey. It was . . . '49, I am not sure of the month. . . . Up in New Jersey, what we did, we would protect the ships coming in and out of that pier area. It was a navy base but the marines took care of all the security. Still, there, [our unit] was all Black, [the] only person we had was a warrant officer [who] was white. Everybody else [was] Black.

One other thing that happened there, there was an explosion. A navy barge blew Perth Amboy completely off the map almost. So, the governor, [Alfred] Driscoll at the time, sent out word to the marines at our base to go down to Perth Amboy and secure the town. We get there, [and] the white[s] really didn't want us there. They called us all kinds of names. But we had to go in and [do] combat with them because they were just taking over. We secured the town for two days. The marines took care of that town till some National Guard came and relieved us and sent us back to base. About two, three weeks later, the governor came on the base and called all the marines out that were involved with that.

And one by one he came down the line and called our names and hand[ed] us a certificate [of] appreciation for what we did with that Perth Amboy explosion.

I am vague on the month, but [in] the latter part of '49, maybe around August, we started our troop train out [of] New Jersey and we picked up marines all along the way, . . . Chicago, Milwaukee, Saint Louis, and on down to California. So when we get down to California, our troop train is long, we have all these marines picked up along the way. We get into Camp Pendleton [and] we start to get out of the train, [but] the marines down there are standing out waiting on us. And the first thing I heard out of their mouth [was,] "Here come the nigger marines." Like I said before, the word, that word, didn't bother me at all because I heard it so many times. And [we] just knew that that's part of their makeup to say that.

Thomas E. Cork Sr.
Corporal, unit unknown
US Marine Corps
Interviewed July 23, 2004, Louisville, KY
Montford Point Marines Project
Copyright © 2006 Randall Library, University of North Carolina at Wilmington

Direct Impact of Executive Order 9981

For those who had enlisted before Truman issued Executive Order 9981, the order to desegregate the military represented an opportunity for great change. Often, however, there was little to no change right away, certainly in the army and Marine Corps. Lt. Gen. Julius Becton Jr., who had served in World War II, found that his base commander openly refused reform. The only unusual aspect of Becton's story is that the commander announced his response to the order so publicly. Many, many other commanders followed suit, although they may not have gathered the troops first to announce it. As Congressman Charles Rangel recounts, not only was the executive order not followed; it was not even discussed.

Elsewhere, as Charles Berry experienced, the camp commander interpreted the decision quite literally, desegregating the camp and integrating barracks bunk by bunk. However, the sting of segregation was never far away. Before his group was integrated by bunk, Berry also experienced the persecution of not just local police officers but bigoted MPs while on training maneuvers in South Carolina. And also, as Berry explains, just being integrated, even by bunk, doesn't mean that people are going to magically understand each other's backgrounds. Desegregation and integration, even when applied with the best of intentions, could often be a painful learning process for all involved.

I was at Aberdeen Proving Ground [in Maryland] for reserve training between semesters in college—this was July 1948—when [Truman's] order was signed. The post commander assembled all officers in the theater, read the Executive Order 9981, and made a statement I'll never forget: "As long as I'm the commander at this post, there will be no change." And what he was saying was that we would continue to have officer club number one and officer club number two, noncommissioned officer club number one and noncommissioned officer club number two, swimming pool number one and two. And so forth. No change. Which was the attitude of the military. The senior officers did not want the president to sign the order. They felt they had [a] just reason for their position.

[When I was a] young lieutenant at Fort Lewis, [Washington,] I was pretty good at close-order drill, and as a result I was selected to be the drill team commander for the battalion drill team. Doesn't sound like much, but we got to be pretty good at it. We could drill between eighteen to twenty minutes without any commands, just by counting and silent drill. Also very fancy with rifles. The platoon could do that; I was just the commander of the platoon. We got so good that the regiment commander said, "We want you to be the regimental drill team." "Well sure, we can do that." Then I started getting applications from guys on the other battalions, white soldiers who wanted to join. And we needed more people, so I went to see the regimental executive officer, a lieutenant colonel, and I said, "Sir, we've got this situation. We need some people here, some volunteers, I would like to integrate." And the lieutenant colonel said, "The answer is no." "Sir, we are short [on] people." "Answer is no." "May I ask why?" "You'll break up the complexion." "The complexion of my unit? Have you seen the complexion of my team? Because we have people almost as white as you." "The answer is no." So I saluted and walked away. That was the attitude. Not to do anything about the proficiency of the unit but the appearance.

I dealt with that all my life and you find ways [to deal with it,] ways to get around it. It's not that critical. So what else is new? A lot of people ask, "Why would you or people who look like you put your life on the line for a country where you get secondhand treatment?" The answer is simple: "There's always the hope that things can get better."

Julius W. Becton Jr.
Lieutenant general, 542nd Heavy Construction Company; 369th
    Infantry Regiment, 93rd Infantry Division; K Company and
    L Company, 9th Infantry Regiment; 101st Airborne Division
US Army Air Forces/Corps
Interview by Kate Ellis and Stephen Smith, February 2003, Springfield, VA
American RadioWorks, Minnesota Public Radio

CHARLES DAVENPORT, WASHINGTON, PENNSYLVANIA

I was at Camp Lejeune in 1948 when President Truman integrated the services. And we started at 8:00 in the morning, and by 4:30 that afternoon, the Marine Corps at Camp Lejeune was completely integrated. With the people that I dealt with during the integration, we had no problems whatsoever. And it was a white sergeant, same rank as I was then, [who was] with the white troops that we were getting quartered [with]. He was from Mississippi and I was from Pennsylvania. We discussed the problem, and he said, "You outrank me by date of rank. That makes you in charge." And I told him, "No, you know the white marines, I know the Black marines, and collectively we have to make this situation work. So we can confer on what we're doing and so forth, so that we have the least problems to deal with." I said, "Because any problem that occurs, we have to settle it. So if we can settle it between the two of us, then [it] filters down to the troops, so we won't have too much of a problem," which we didn't.

Charles Davenport
Gunnery sergeant/acting master sergeant, 7th Marines, 1st Division
US Marine Corps
Interviewed June 29, 2005, Washington, PA
Montford Point Marines Project
Copyright © 2004 Randall Library, University of North Carolina at Wilmington

CHARLES BERRY, CHATTANOOGA, TENNESSEE

[Fort Lee, Virginia,] was nice, that's where I took my basic training. And that's where we learned to get up at 4 o'clock in the morning, 5 o'clock in the morning. And that [first] Friday, the sergeant told us that we were going to have a "GI Party," so to me, hey, [I thought] we were going to have us some beer and some music and some gals and some dancing, you know. So, he said, "After supper, we'll assemble for the party." So I said to myself, why eat supper, if you're going to a party? It didn't make sense. But I found out what the "party" was. [Drilling.] And so when I complained about it, he said, "I got a special job for you. Go get your toothbrush." So I went and got my toothbrush, and he said, "Now I want you to get a bucket of this GI soap and I want you to scrub this floor." And that's what I used. And after the bristles were gone I used the side of it, the point of it. So I learned to keep my mouth shut.

But the training was good. It's to take the civilian out of you and put the military in you. We trained separate [from whites]. We had all-Black units, and I tell you we had real esprit de corps. Especially when we'd parade — we had that rhythm, man. And we could march, too. And I used to carry a guidon [a military flag]. And we were good. It was fierce competitions between the whites and the Negroes [for who could drill best].

One time we had a guy from Cuba who was sent to a white unit, then they sent him to us because he was very dark, but he was Cuban. And he didn't like us and we sure didn't like him. [When] he had to stay over there [with the white unit,] they put him in a separate room until he learned what he had to go through.

Also while I was [there] we went on maneuvers in Greenville, South Carolina, and that was one of the worst maneuvers we'd ever been on. As far as the maneuver [itself] was concerned it was okay. We left Fort Knox and went down to Greenville, South Carolina, to the air base there. And as we were going through the towns, I was driving the jeep with the commander, and man, we'd go through them towns, them guys would be up on them fifty cal[iber]s with the ammunition everywhere, and we'd stop in them towns and the women would be calling up to us and kissing on us and stuff.

So we got to Greenville, to the air base there, and . . . we went into town. We asked this lady at the bar, she had a restaurant with a little bar in it, too, that served beer, we asked her, how much would it cost if we rent this place and fix dinner for all of us? And she told us, so that payday we pooled our money and she had already cooked. And the gals came up there, and man, we were having a good time. And one of our guys was asleep out there on a chair out in front of the restaurant. We was all in there drinking beer and soda pop and eating, and all the girls were there. And all of a sudden we hear McClure holler: "Owww!" And we heard these voices, we knew they were cops. So we went out there. They had hit him on his feet. And he was taking treatments for his feet! And they tell him, "Stand up!" and call him all kinds of n-words, you know, an assortment of n-words. And when we came out they drew their guns on us, and they took me and ten more to jail.

And in the jail we were treated just like murderers. They took our shoestrings out, they took our shoes off us, they took our belts, and they had handcuffed some of us. The white MPs were calling us all kinda names and the cops were no better. I told this MP, I said, "When I get back to base I'm gonna deal with you. You're out here now [in] your glory, but when I get you on that base I'm gonna show you something." And I got hit a couple of times, too. And this lady [from the restaurant,] one of the guys had told her to call our company and ask to speak to the 1st sergeant and tell him what happened. So the company commander—we had a white company commander, but he was a good man and he was a southerner—and he came and when they got us out of jail, and they called him an n-lover, and he said, "We are American soldiers, and these men will be treated as such." So this white MP said, "They ain't nothin' but a bunch of cowardly Ns." So when we got back to the post, charges was brought on that MP and he was discharged out of the service.

[We shipped out for Hawaii.] At that time, the Negro, we didn't have all the luxuries like the Caucasians did. My bunk was located on top of a shipping crate and we slept on the deck and stuff. The whites had bunk beds and all that stuff. And of course, I might say, there were quite a few fights. And it was very normal. I think I was called that n-word more times between the time I left Chattanooga to the time I hit Hawaii. And then when we got into Hawaii, we were on a little island called Sand Island, and the first time that we went into Honolulu, we experienced [racism like] I thought I was back in Chattanooga or Mississippi. The white soldiers was just everywhere, and they said, "You can't go in there." I couldn't believe it.

We went down to the Royal Hawaiian Hotel and they wouldn't let us in there. And so what we did is we formed a line asleep on each side of that door, left a passway through, and slept there on newspaper on the concrete. And then the cops came and they said, "Well, they ain't bothering nothing." And we said, "We ain't doing anything, all we wanted was a room." So I think that was probably the first sleep-in! But it did happen. [And] there were quite a few fights. We used to have a bar out there in Pearl City, which is right outside Honolulu, called Pearl City Tavern. They got monkeys in there running around in the back of the bar, and you see them guys getting high and talkin' to them monkeys! But we went in there one night, and the Caucasians [were] on this side [and] the Negroes on this [other] side, and the bar is here and the monkeys behind. At that time they was drinkin' what they call Red Fox Beer and the Caucasians had made a big pyramid [of beer cans] up there. I had about six beers and I kept looking at that pyramid and my buddy [and I,] well, we stood up and threw cans and just tore that pyramid up and a fight ensued after that. Years later, I took my wife to Hawaii [and] we visit[ed] that same bar and soon as I walked in the woman [at the bar said,] "No fightin' this time! No fight!" She hadn't forgotten me. That was a lot of fun.

And then we got orders to ship out. Now in Hawaii, most of the duties that we performed were stevedores, guard duty, truck driving, and engineering. We knew that we had Black pilots and stuff, but I had never even seen a Black officer in all this time. We integrated [after] we went to Korea. We had that meeting, they said that the military was going to be integrated. So about half the company was shipped out, down about six blocks to another company. And the sergeant picked me to be a squad leader. Then he had all the whites and Blacks, he said, "Okay, y'all go in there and pick your bunks, and then I'll be in there." Now when they went in the barracks, the whites got on this side and the Blacks got on this side. So this sergeant walked in and he said, "I said, we are integrated now!

Now fall back out!" So he said, "One Black, one white, one Black, one white," that's the way you got bunks. That's the way he integrated.

But I gotta tell you, a lot of whites, they don't take baths. I'll tell you. I'm gonna be frank with you, we had a problem with that. And then a lot of the food that we eat they didn't like. And then a lot of the religious beliefs were different. Well now, each person has to respect another's religion, even though you may not like it.

But it got better, it really did. [But at first the friction was] so thick you could cut it with a knife. It was just like you was out in a desert. And you could hear 'em get together and say, "Man, them niggers," and this, you know. And so I had the squad and I called them all together. And I said, "The first one of you use that word, gonna fight me. And I'm not going to fight you with my fists. I'm going to call you and stand you at attention and I'ma hit you with that rifle butt." I said, "The man says we gotta live together, then let's live together. We take care of each other. We cook for each other." And I said, "And a lot of you whites have been raised by Black women, yet we're not good enough to socialize [with] and sleep [next to]? Well, you're gonna learn!"

Charles Earnest Berry
Master sergeant, 25th Infantry Division, 24th Infantry Regiment
US Army
Interviewed by Michael Willie, February 13, 2003, Chattanooga, TN
Charles Earnest Berry Collection (AFC/2001/001/05950), Veterans
  History Project, American Folklife Center, Library of Congress

CHARLES BERNARD RANGEL, NEW YORK

I'm Charles Rangel, born June 11, 1930, born and raised in the village of Harlem in the borough of Manhattan in the city and state of New York, and I served in the United States Army, 2nd Infantry Division.

I was eleven years old when the war [World War II] broke out, but my elder, beloved brother who I lost some years ago enlisted in the army long before the war broke out. He enlisted probably in the summer of 1941, so when we went to war he was already in the service. And throughout the war, of course, I lived vicariously through him, being concerned about his safety, as did my mom. We had three kids, and . . . when we would receive his allotment check it meant all the difference in the world to the family and to a large extent that's why he joined the army. I never intended to join the army, but a group of guys I was raised with were concerned about the draft. President Truman had indicated sometime in 1948 that everybody was going to be drafted, but if you enlisted for one year and served for six years in the national reserve, then you wouldn't be drafted. So I went to accompany some of my guys that had dropped out of high school. I was working in a shoe store on 125th Street. But [enlisting] was interesting because it was adventurous — the whole idea that they would be leaving Harlem and New York and not knowing where they were going. And the recruiting noncommissioned officer was very, very, very good because he convinced me that this year would be the best thing for me. When he started talking about the ability to send the checks home, all I could think of was that smile on my mother's face when she got that check from my older brother. And before I knew it, I was shipped off to Fort Dix with hundreds, hundreds of eighteen-year-olds. And at that time the prefix to our serial number was US. And even today, you can distinguish between a regular army person, which is RA, and someone that was drafted. I confused them all because [as a] draftee [I] was US57, but I was only in the army four months before I decided that I was going to become regular army and enlist for three years. And so the US became RA, but the 57 stayed, and so people were utterly confused that I was part drafted and part regular, but I was discharged regular army.

Boy, oh boy, [training camp] was so confusing. This idea of one year had just started, and I was in Fort Dix waiting for southerners to come to organize [a Black unit]. As a matter of fact, I went home. People were asking me, "What are you doing here?" I had on my civilian clothes; I had changed, because it took almost a month. I would go back and take a look and ask who was in charge, and no one was in charge. Until finally the first sergeant came and I told him that I'd been around for two or three weeks and I knew that there were people there from New York and Philadelphia and New Jersey that were anxious to get started, but we couldn't. But gradually of course, the troops came in — they were all Black, and they were from all over, but the majority of them were from the South. And [with] those of us who were already there from Chicago and Philadelphia and New York, we formed that bloc, and we stayed through basic training. And sometime, in a couple of months, we all got on a troop train leaving New Jersey and riding to the state of Washington, hundreds of us on a train. We were going [to Fort Lewis]. And I'm telling you, that was some train ride. You get a bunch of kids, eighteen years old, with guitars and trumpets and energy, and a young 2nd lieutenant explaining to us why we can't do things. And then came Fort Lewis.

We all ended up in the 503rd Field Artillery unit. It was an all-African American unit in the 2nd Infantry Division. They had two Black units there — one was the 3rd Battalion of the 24th Infantry Regiment, and the other was the 503rd, which was the 3rd Artillery Battalion. We were the .115s, and then of course there were the .105s.

Forget about [integration]! We wished we could have laughed about it, because even raising it [wasn't possible]. People [in charge] ignored [the executive order]. And the history of the darn thing! Even when I left the army in

1952, there was segregation. I was discharged from Fort Sill, Oklahoma, and it was located in [Lawton, Oklahoma]. It had one Black police officer and he was dressed like a buffoon, with epaulets and brass, and he couldn't arrest white people. And we had a problem because they were about to allow him to arrest Black soldiers. We were at least able to overturn that and leave us to the military for anything that happened in town. But, no, a lot of people think that the executive order went into effect in 1948, and it may have [in some places,] but it sure didn't in the 2nd Infantry Division. Nobody even talked about it.

There was a massive joint service [training] operation called Operation MIKI that the 2nd Infantry participated in. We were "invading" Hawaii, and there were enemy troops — I forgot what we called them at that time — but they had all different ways of identifying who got wounded, who got killed, who won and who lost, who got captured. It was quite a thing. The invasion was very realistic because we had to deal with .155-millimeter howitzers and that, in Korea as well as Hawaii, was difficult. I might add that after we finished the operation, the racism and prejudice that we had in Fort Lewis had preceded us in Hawaii, in terms of the natives knowing that we were treated differently in the United States. They also restricted [Black GIs] from going into their places of entertainment. Having said that, most of the GIs in the 503rd outfit, as I pointed out, were in the army for one year. But at Operation MIKI, their time would have expired before we would have returned, so those of us who had reenlisted and the older soldiers from World War II that had reenlisted and stayed in the army, we went on Operation MIKI and left the others back. By the time the operation was over, these guys were discharged, all the guys that I went there [with who were in] for one year.

[Back at Fort Lewis,] I had made myself the information NCO. There was no such job in my outfit, but I just made it up. I stayed in a Class A uniform and had a clipboard, and I would inform the troops as to what was in the *New York Times* and the Seattle papers, and they thought it was a great service. And as a matter of fact, the commanding officer said, "Why don't you go to school for this?" "Go to school for what?" It was information and something, there was an MOS [military occupational specialty] for it on the battalion level, but I was in the battery. So, they sent me off to New Jersey to a school, and lo and behold, there was a Black guy from the 503rd, a 2nd lieutenant just of out of Howard University, his name was Smith, and he was with the officers, and of course I was with the enlisted men. And one day he came to me and says, "Rangel, you know, you're a bright guy, but you're trying to beat the system, and I don't know you well enough to instruct you. I'm not in your battery, but it would do you well to get your training and to learn to do something because it would help you in the army and it would help you when you get out." Well, at that point in my life, I didn't like people who had gone to college. And he was no different. And the closer he was to my age, the more I just resented him talking to me as though I was some kid from the ghetto and he was some kid from college. But after we came back to the outfit, he was transferred to headquarters, where I was. And of course, by that time, I was a big shot with no stripes. I was going all over to the five batteries, giving them information.

It was on a Sunday [that the Korean War started], and most of the fellows were on leave or on pass. I was stuck in the barracks, and I remember it so well being empty. We had to roll up the mattresses on Sunday and clean up on Saturday night. And someone came and said that the North Korean Communists had invaded South Korea and the 2nd Infantry was alerted to go over there as a police action to stop the takeover. We were so excited about leaving Fort Lewis, we said, "Wow, a police action," you know. And I guess different soldiers had different things in mind, but a police action just sounded like the democratic thing to do.

I had to find out what this Korean thing was all about, but I did a pretty good job [informing the troops]. I had no idea of the dangers that was involved, but I had studied up to know about the Russian-US compact and the 38th Parallel, and that the 24th Division and the 25th Division will be there. [I told them that] by the time we got there, this thing should be wrapped up.

And then came the time when Smith came to me, and he said to me, "And exactly what do you think you'll be doing in Korea?" And I was never more embarrassed, because it's hard for a know-it-all to admit that you know absolutely nothing. He says, "Well, since you're in Headquarters Battery, I'm going to train you on the boat to become a fire direction expert." Of course, that involved a lot of math, a lot of protractors, a lot of getting directions, getting orders of [the] location of the enemy that you can't see, plotting it on the map, getting the protractor, giving orders to the batteries, ordering how many rounds of ammunition to fire. And in thirteen days on that ship, from morning to night, he trained me in and out. And the poor guy got killed early, early on. But my life changed, in a sense, because there had been no need, I thought, for me to become responsible. No one knew me, they didn't know what I was doing. Everyone thought I worked in [the] downtown battalion. And the battalion thought I was working [elsewhere]. And so I didn't have to go out in the field. You don't send the guy in a Class A uniform and shiny brass out in the field, right? Right. And when we got to Korea, however, [I had to fight right away].

Charles Bernard Rangel
US representative, 13th District of New York
Staff sergeant, 503rd Field Artillery Battalion, 2nd Infantry Division
US Army
Interviewed by Col. Robert Patrick, director, Veterans History
Project, June 20, 2013, Washington, DC

EDDIE WRIGHT, WEST SPRINGFIELD, MASSACHUSETTS

My name is Eddie Wright. I currently reside in Feeding Hills, Massachusetts. I'm seventy-four years of age. I'm what they call a career veteran. I started in 1947 and retired in 1967. And I was in Korea in 1952. I was in the 4th Fighter Wing Headquarters as an administrative clerk. I am from Georgia originally. When I graduated from high school I had a scholarship to Morehouse. I would have been a classmate of Dr. King. But I'm the oldest of fourteen and I knew that if I took the scholarship that my next older sister and brother couldn't go to college. Sharecropper isn't "share"; you just go in the hole every year. We had no money, grew everything we ate. So that's the reason I decided [to go in the service]. Everything I did in the military was better than the fields of Georgia. I told my dad if it's ever as hard, I'll come back. It was easy compared to what I had done. We got seventy-five dollars a month! We had never seen seventy-five dollars in the time I was growing up. [I] sent sixty-five dollars home. When I got back, Dad had bought a piece of land in my name, but I didn't even know about it.

[In the South,] they didn't think anything of telling us, "Drink out of this water fountain in the basement, [not] that." I rode in the back of the bus from Georgia to liberate the South Koreans. I enlisted in June of 1947 at Fort Jackson, Columbia, South Carolina. I took basic training at Lackland Air Force Base in San Antonio, Texas, [and] from there [went] to Roswell Air Force Base in New Mexico. Was there for five months, [and] we shipped overseas to the island of Guam from 1948 to 1949. I returned in July of 1949 to be exact. I was there about fifteen months. From Guam I came back to Waco, Texas, Connally Air Force Base.

When I enlisted in 1947, the military was segregated — whites on one side of [the] base, Blacks on [the] other. It was that way even overseas. [We] traveled separately. It was like that when I went over in 1948. The Black troops went over in one part of the ship, white troops in another. Even when we reached our destination, the white troops occupied one side of [the] base and Blacks on another. [Then] in 1948 President Truman signed a decree that the military would be integrated. If you're in the military, you're in the military. You weren't Black or white. So we went over on segregated ships, but coming back in 1949, after the bill was signed in '48, we were in integrated units. Going over it was segregated, but yeah, coming back it was integrated. We just got on the ship, and you got a bunk wherever you found one. But it was a long time before [the military was] completely integrated. There were pockets of all-Black outfits for a period of time after the bill was signed.

In those days, there were very few jobs available to Black troops—cook, drive [a] truck or civil engineer, digging ditches for pipes, and things of this nature. That was one reason that I went to school. And I did that on my own. I didn't go to the air force tech schools that were available. They had a school at one of the army bases on Guam if you wanted to come in on the evenings after work, you could take typing or military correspondence, and that was one way to get out of driving a truck. To me, driving a truck was little better than cooking. I never really liked cooking in the first place [and] I didn't really want to drive a truck. I wanted the administrative part of it, which I was able to get by going to school at nights. Then when I came back from Guam, they were going to put me in the motor pool to drive a truck again, and I said, "I would like to know, if it's possible, I'd like to get into administration. I went to school, learned how to type, and a little about military correspondence." He called up the officer in charge of [the] motor pool, who says, "I've got a boy here who just came back from Guam and says he knows how to type," even though he is standing there with my records in his hand that said I completed the school. He said, "He says he knows how to type. Do you need a clerk down there?" There was a great lieutenant, Lieutenant Kimball from Philadelphia, Pennsylvania, and I had lost track of his guy, and if I could find him, I really would. Great guy, Robert W. Kimball. He said, "Yeah, send him over," and the guy at personnel said if I didn't work out as an administrative clerk, he would already be in the motor pool, you can put him on a truck. [The] essence was that I would go in as a clerk on a trial basis, and if I didn't work out, I'm already in a squadron that drives a truck. So they could just put me on a truck, but I knew that was my ticket home. Just so happens this Kimball was one of the finest officers I've ever met. So, we got there, and he knew what was going on. He said, "You don't need to worry about the truck." After a couple of days, he was very satisfied with the work that I had done administratively, and as a matter of fact, in a matter of two months, I was promoted to sergeant. This was in the earlier stages of my career. At the end of the enlistment, that was when I made sergeant just before the end of my first three years. I [transferred to] Savannah, Georgia, Hunter Air Base, [in 1949] still as a clerk, and after a few months there, I was promoted to next grade, staff sergeant. Then in November of the following year they started a new unit . . . called the 3rd Strategic Support Squadron.

I was at Hunter Air Force Base in Savannah, Georgia, [when I] received orders—I didn't know I was going [to Korea] at the time. On the bus that I rode to [get the train] from Savannah, Georgia, to San Francisco, California, to get the ship, I rode in the back of the bus going to liberate the South Koreans. If you stop to think about that, I was restricted to where I could ride, where I can sit, whether or not I can drink out of this water fountain or that. That's the way we traveled back then, what we call the "old days."

I ended up at Kimpo Air Base in Korea. I was there about a year. Went to Korea in 1952. I was just a clerk there, just trying to get over and back. I was very fortunate. My experience was [in] an integrated unit [with the] 4th Fighter Wing Headquarters. I didn't experience [racism]—I guess I was in the right place. I'm sure it was there, but fortunately for me, I didn't experience it.

Eddie Wright
Senior master sergeant, 451st Fighter Wing
US Air Force
Interviewed by David P. Cline, October 14, 2002, West Springfield, MA
American RadioWorks, Minnesota Public Radio

MELVIN BOYKIN, MEMPHIS, TENNESSEE

My name is Melvin Boykin. Presently I live in Fayetteville, Georgia, [and] prior to that lived in Connecticut for forty years. [I served] with the 187th [in the] 7th Division. [The] 187 was a regimental combat team that absorbed [the] 2nd Rangers, which were [the] first Black paratroopers. The 187 was from [the] 11th Airborne, Campbell, Kentucky, but I came from Fort Bragg. I enlisted in the army . . . to get away from my home, my family. Got out of high school early and didn't want to go to college. My father said, "You go to college." My father weighed 240 pounds, so I went to college! [But] halfway through my freshman year, I put my age up and went in the army. When they heard from me next, I was in Fort Dix, New Jersey, for basic training.

My father and mother came to get me out of the service with my birth certificate to show I wasn't old enough to be there. I told them, "If you do this, I'll run away from home and [you'll] never see me anymore." My mother thought about it. My old man was a hell of a person, [a] big guy that wasn't afraid of anything, except my mother. She said, "Leave him alone." Gave me a key to the front door and five hundred dollars and said, "You can always get home, and this will get you in the house." And they left. So I finished basic, was sent to [Fort] Bragg, [and] from there to jump school in Fort Benning.

[I volunteered for jump school because] their uniforms looked better than everybody else's and they paid [an] extra fifty dollars per month for jumping out of the airplane! That was the reason. My old man used to ask me, "Melvin, why would you jump out of a perfectly good airplane?" I said, "Because they pay fifty dollars per month." He said, "That's not enough, you're risking your neck." I told him, "No. You got this parachute, blah, blah, blah." It was youthful exuberance, I guess — I was seventeen years old, what the hell did I know?

I was in Fort Bragg, North Carolina, [when Truman signed the executive order]. We laughed, it was funny. The president took five months to do something that Gen. [James M. Gavin] did in one day. That's why I laughed. [Truman] signed in April '48, but we had been integrated into [the] 88th Airborne since December '47. That year we played football — I was what you called a jock, played football, ran track, and boxed, so I didn't have to do much soldiering. We played [the] Cherry Point Marines in North Carolina [and] they refused to play us because we were an integrated team. That was 1948. After [the] Second [World] War, [the] Triple Nickles [555] were trained for combat but were used for fire jumpers in Oregon and California. [General] Gavin's thing was that as effective as they were, they should not be ignored. When they had the big parade down Fifth Avenue in New York, he insisted that the Triple Nickles be part of it. So they marched in that parade. I don't know that he was so set on integrating, except that he was a very fair person. He liked people. Everybody loved him — Black, white, you name it. He was a general that led by example. Whatever he was asking you to do, he would do. If the whole division was doing it, he was doing it too because he was division commander. He was that type of person. Slim Jim was his nickname. I recall once there was a situation where some guys were placed on company punishment for little infractions — for getting VD, believe it [or not]. Gavin came to [the] 3rd Battalion of [the] 505 — which is what we were after we had been integrated — he said, "These guys look better than everybody else, are sharper than everybody else, soldier better than everybody else, and they probably [screw] better than anybody else, and I don't want any more company punishment for it." He stopped it. That was crazy! It was a funny kind of thing, but he did that. He was that kind of person.

When I say they integrated the 82nd, you have to realize, it was integration of sorts. You've got three battalions that make up a regiment — 1st, 2nd, and 3rd — and the heavy weapons. We [were] the 3rd Battalion, the 05, which was all Black. The other two battalions were all white, but we were part of the same umbrella group, the 82nd. We were not integrated [totally] — nobody in the same barracks or whatever. In fact, when the Korean War started, they reactivated the 101st Airborne Division as a basic training unit, and they were all Black also. They had some white units for the 101st, but they were someplace else. The Black units were in basic training at Fort Bragg.

I guess I really didn't think about [being in a segregated unit] really. It might sound crazy to you, [but] I didn't think about it. There were certain advantages to it, I guess, and there were naturally disadvantages. I never really thought about it, that I'm in an all-Black unit. I was born in Atlanta but lived in Connecticut for a long time. I'm familiar with this. It was something I never really considered. [But] I was always in trouble because of it. Used to raise hell and do all kinds of shit. There was a store in Atlanta called John Jarrell's. They've closed now. It was a specialty store, a men's store. A nice store [or] nice-*looking* store I should say, because when you say "nice store" you're including everybody associated with it. If you were Black and went in there, tried on a pair of shoes, slacks, jacket, whatever, even if it didn't fit, it was yours. [You had to buy it.] That's the kind of thing you ran into. I used to go in there, try on a lot of shit, and say, "I ain't got any money." That was my only way of getting even.

I knew I was going to be going [to Korea] because I volunteered to go, wanted to get out of [the] outfit I was in. I was sent down to Fort Stewart as part of cadre to train National Guardsmen that had just come into the army. After two months I wanted out, but I couldn't, so I volunteered for Korea and they couldn't stop that. [But] a whole lot of things happened [because around that time I was playing football and] we were playing a team at Fort Myer, Virginia. [The] Cleveland Browns were in town to play [the] Washington Redskins, and Paul Brown came to see our game, sent somebody to the locker room after our game to ask me what I planned to do after the army. I said, "I don't know." He said, "Come and see me." The Browns needed a larger running back. I weighed 220, could do a pretty good hundred [yard dash], 9.7, 9.8 [seconds]. [They] offered me a free agent contract. They sent me a check for five hundred dollars and a round-trip plane ticket to come to Hiram, Ohio, for their training camp. I had twenty-seven days left in the army [when the war started]. Harry Truman said, "You can't go nowhere." They froze all discharges and extended everybody—that's how I ended up in Korea. I was gonna get out and play ball.

Melvin S. Boykin
Specialist 1st class, 187th Regiment, 7th Division
US Army
Interviewed by Kate Ellis and Stephen Smith, September 5, 2002, Memphis, TN
American Radio Works, Minnesota Public Radio

Segregated Camps after 1948

Before Truman's order, most training facilities in the South observed local Jim Crow customs, but so did many bases outside the South, importing the US Army's own brand of racial segregation into otherwise integrated parts of the United States. Even after the executive order, many training facilities enforced segregation. For example, Joe Tamayo recounts below that in 1951, Fort Benning, Georgia, was still starkly segregated, the Black soldiers relegated to inferior accommodations in a rural part of the base called Sand Hill. In some camps, there was a mixture of policies—all-Black units would be housed and fed separately, but the larger base itself would be integrated. Many times, even without total integration and especially in towns in the Deep South, the base could end up feeling like a relatively safe and progressive place in comparison to the surrounding community.

And so segregation in military camps in the United States persisted even as desegregation was becoming commonplace on the battlefields in Korea. In fact, segregation persisted at stateside bases long after the disbandment of the army's 24th Infantry Regiment, typically heralded by historians as marking total integration of the armed forces. In some cases, Black soldiers from integrated units, wounded on the front lines in Korea, were segregated during their stateside recovery, then reintegrated when they rejoined their units.[3] War may be chaotic and often nonsensical, but the military's slowly unraveling racial policies, and the insistence by some individuals to cling to the tatters of an old order, took the experiment in illogic to an extreme.

Fort Benning in Georgia, where wounded members of the 24th Infantry Regiment were reassigned to the segregated 30th Infantry, remained a steadfast holdout to integration, even when its own brass demanded change. In the summer of 1951, Maj. Gen. John H. Church returned from Korea to become commander of the infantry school at Fort Benning. Church, considered to have served heroically in both world wars, most recently had commanded the 24th Infantry Division in Korea after the capture of its original commander, William F. Dean. Leading his troops through fierce fighting despite frailty and arthritis, Church was awarded the Distinguished Service Medal before being assigned to lead the approximately fifty thousand soldiers stationed at Fort Benning. Church found the post still segregated, and local Georgia politicians were determined to keep it so despite his efforts to integrate the facilities.

According to reports in African American newspapers, Church had no true leadership of the base because "it is actually being run by the Southern politicians who run the nearby town of Columbus."[4] Despite the major general's protestations that his soldiers were not "colored and white" but "just American soldiers," base facilities such as swimming pools, barracks, and even the toilets in the post's engineers' building remained segregated, and no Black officers served either as company commanders or in the fort's headquarters. Further, no Black officers or their families were housed on the main post or in recently built homes adjacent to the main gate but instead lived in a segregated area ten miles from the base called Deveauxville, named for a regimental chaplain in the all-Black 24th Infantry Regiment.[5] Base schools for children, waiting rooms at the post bus station, even guard duty in the guardhouse—all were strictly segregated by race, and even the celebrated Black paratroopers, the 7th Infantry Division's all-Black 2nd Ranger Infantry Company (Airborne), were trained and housed separately.[6]

Fort Benning wasn't the only facility that segregated the education of the children on base. In 1952, the NAACP approached the secretary of defense to complain that Black children also attended inferior segregated schools at Fort Bliss and Fort Sam Houston in Texas, at Fort Sill in Oklahoma, and at Virginia's Fort Belvoir.[7] Only about fifteen miles from the White House, Fort Belvoir remained segregated at least through early 1952, with US Highway Route 1 actually running through the middle of the camp, dividing it into an African American area, known as Young's Village, and the all-white and more modern Gray Village across the road. The only exception was a few single, white student officers who were housed in the bachelors' quarters on the Black side of the base, but no Blacks lived on the white side. Segregation was so complete and well known that local nicknames emerged for the two sides of the base, with the Black Young's Village area known colloquially as the Union army and the white headquarters area on the other side of Route 1 as the Confederate army.[8] The situation was so bad that one Black journalist described Fort Belvoir as run "according to the dictates of the white South [and] the Confederacy, and the State of Virginia assumes the same attitude toward colored soldiers that it did toward colored men who supported the Union cause during the Civil War."[9]

White soldiers could apparently cross the color line, most notably to dance with the Black hostesses at the service club on the Black side of the base, but Black soldiers could not do the same at the all-white service clubs. The Black service club was also the site of a fatal shooting in 1949, when white MPs responding to a report of a fight, shot an unarmed and innocent Black soldier in the back.[10] And while the service clubs on both sides offered guest housing for visiting families of servicemen, the facilities on the white side of the base were said to be excellent while those on the Black side lacked even running water.[11]

As of the winter of 1952, despite the availability of federal funds for a new integrated school building, Fort Belvoir's Black children were taught in the segregated Young's Village schoolhouse, a two-story shack, half of which had been condemned by the post's fire department and which the Afro-American newspaper described as "a disgrace to the US government." Post officials allegedly claimed that they were forced to segregate schooling to comply with the laws of the Commonwealth of Virginia, even though state laws do not apply to federal property.[12]

In contrast, the school at the marine base at Quantico, Virginia, only a few miles down the road, was fully integrated.[13] Camp Pickett, near Blackstone, Virginia, likewise won praise from African American reporters for its early and strong commitment to basewide integration, including among civilian employees. But even at Camp Pickett, some segregation remained, since National Guard and reserve units assigned there for training remained racially segregated during their brief stays.[14] At another Virginia camp, however, Fort Eustis in the Tidewater region, Brig. Gen. Harold R. Duffie successfully desegregated the entire base within a few short months in the summer of 1951, earning praise from Black soldiers and journalists alike. As one Black soldier, a World War II veteran, put it, "This is it. General Duffie is convinced integration is the best thing and Hell and high water is not going to stop him from putting his idea in effect. It's a far cry from what [we] experienced over there [during World War II]."[15]

Even though military bases fell under federal rule, differences in integration policy often varied by locality. And not always in the ways one might assume. Fort Knox, Kentucky, remained segregated in August 1951—"The Army brass, especially at Fort Knox, don't give a hoot about the President and his no-jim-crow orders . . . no matter how many Negroes die in Korea shooting up the Asiatics to maintain American democracy," read an article in the Cleveland Call and Post. But so, too, did bases in Honolulu, Hawaii, where "along with other things that are imported from America, a good sized cargo of Jim Crow" was also brought along.[16] In early 1952, Fort Meade in Maryland, which was integrated in other ways, still segregated all newly arrived inductees, thus introducing recruits to the army with a cold blast of Jim Crow. The policy toward inductees was created at the whim of the director of the base's reception center and without the knowledge of the camp commander; nevertheless, it persisted.[17] Veterans frequently mention how they would run into a policy of segregation in one place only to have it replaced by integration and vice versa, as a consistent standard remained elusive.

At times, multiple policies competed with one another even on the same base as camps moved painfully toward adopting a new policy. At the US Army's Fort Hood in Texas in mid-summer 1951, post commanders had ordered total integration, including several commands in which Black officers led white soldiers, and all had gone without incident. However, Fort Hood was also the temporary home of the 1st and 2nd Armored Divisions, higher commands each directed by generals who outranked the post commander and both of which maintained a number of Jim Crow units, although the 2nd Division did integrate its MPs.[18]

At other camps, individual unit commanders could be resistant, even if they didn't hold higher rank. Alabama's Camp Rucker, for example, was completely desegregated in 1951, even its service unit, except for the holdout 406th Engineer Brigade, whose commander maintained segregation because he claimed not only that he lacked the authority to end it but also that "his troops preferred being segregated in a jim crow unit."[19]

Segregation could affect all parts of life, and military families were subjected to the indignities of local segregation laws off base. In Mississippi, soldiers who returned from the war in Asia attempted to settle near bases with their Japanese or Korean spouses only to be told that state law prohibited marriages between white persons and "Negroes or Mongolians." Military policies trumped local concerns on the bases themselves—an air force sergeant lived without incident with his Asian wife on Keesler Air Force Base in Biloxi, Mississippi, in 1952, for example. In some cases, these examples did bleed over into life off base as well; an interracial military couple in Greenville, Mississippi, was apparently tolerated by local officials who "'see but don't see.'"[20]

However, the military's integrationist policies sometimes did run into friction with local policies at joint military-civilian operations, such as South Carolina's Charleston Naval Shipyard. Even after segregation at all naval and Marine Corps shore stations had been banned, complete compliance was slow in coming. The result was partial integration of the Charleston Shipyard; by September 1953, signs over drinking fountains had been removed, but restrooms and cafeterias remained segregated "until further notice."[21] Occasionally, local mores contrasted with military policy in the opposite way. In March 1951, for example, a delegation of Minnesota politicians, including Sen. Hubert Humphrey, accompanied by NAACP director Walter White, visited the Department of the Army in Washington, DC, to complain about segregated basic training at army induction centers in their state.[22] The army was also accused of importing southern-style Jim Crow to Massachusetts' Camp Edwards, which in the summer of 1951 featured a number of segregated units as well as segregated recreation and training, all in a community described as previously having "a minimum amount of race prejudice."[23]

The US Air Force, too, experienced difficulties at some bases, even up through the war period itself. Some experiences went well; ten weeks after the air force ordered the end of segregation, the commander of Lackland Air Force Base in Texas reported that "the integration of the base was accomplished with complete harmony," and in Washington, DC, Howard University president Mordecai Johnson praised the integration of Tidewater Virginia's Langley Air Force Base.[24] At Robins Air Force Base in Georgia, as of June 1951, a Black reporter found that under the "courageous" command of Brig. Gen. R. V. Ignico, "there is absolutely no segregation or discrimination of colored airmen at this strategic materiel base located in the heart of Georgia. . . . There is nothing to remind one that he is in Georgia. Every single facility on the base from training to recreation, from flying to swimming is open to all on an equal basis."[25]

However, only an hour's drive away, at Shaw Air Force Base in South Carolina, Jim Crow was still firmly rooted, while at the air force's Maxwell Field in Montgomery, Alabama, as of July 1949, African Americans rode on segregated local buses to and from the field and Montgomery's USO facility remained whites only with no comparable facility available for Black servicemen.[26] The base, whose commanders had followed Truman's orders and had opened its facilities to all, seemed to be spoiling for a fight with local political and business leaders who remained committed to racial segregation. By 1951, however, it seemed that the locals had won and their segregationist traditions had, at least for the time being, held fast and had even started to erode some of the progress on base. Reporter Collins George, who was traveling the country reporting on the racial practices at military installations, claimed in mid-April that "there is no getting around the fact that segregation exists at Maxwell" and that "the vicious effects of Montgomery (Ala.) prejudices have crept in and are influencing practices on the base."[27] George described what he called the "split personality" of Maxwell Field, in which whites and Blacks toiled side by side together in most units during daylight hours and then at night settled into segregated housing facilities on opposite sides of the tracks and at which one unit, the 3817 Base Service Squadron, remained all Black. The base commander at Maxwell maintained that African American airmen had voluntarily self-segregated to the area known as Shantytown—George claimed that white airmen had plenty of other "unprintable" nicknames for it—and in fact had insisted on keeping the service unit from integrating.

But, George wrote, "I have lived in the South long enough to recognize Southern practices and I knew that Maxwell Field, across the tracks, held all the Southern resentments that Southern ghettoes breed." A Black sergeant confided in him: "I'd rather spend nine years in Korea than three more months at Maxwell." George ended his article with a direct plea to James Evans, the civilian aide to Gen. George C. Marshall, who he invited to come to the base with an eye toward eliminating the segregated service unit. "Jim," he wrote, "the boys across the tracks at Maxwell Field isn't happy at all."[28]

Among the services, the Marine Corps was the most resistant and intransigent when it came to heeding Truman's order to desegregate, and although a few advances were made before the Korean War, it was really the manpower demands of combat that forced full integration. The increasing number of Black marines was certainly a major factor in the corps' eventual transformation; in May 1949, just 1,523 African Americans served in the marines, 600 of them as stewards, but by October 1953, out of the 17,000 Black marines in service, there were only 500 segregated stewards, constituting 5 percent of total marine enlistment.[29] The last all-Black unit designation was canceled in 1951, though segregation persisted long after that. There was also often dissonance between what the camp brass claimed as policy and what the troops experienced, especially as Marine Corps brass claimed to be outpacing the US Army in providing equal, integrated facilities. In January 1951, the personnel director of North Carolina's Marine Corps Base Camp Lejeune claimed that "there is no damn friction here and we don't aim to have any." However, the Black marines themselves complained that their housing remained segregated, that they were not assigned to *jobs for which they were trained, and that they lacked enough warm clothing. Yet change did eventually come, and by March 1952, marines at the base were singing a different tune. Contrasting Camp Lejeune to the army's Fort Belvoir, an African American correspondent claimed that "life in the Marines is a happy one, for both they and their families."[30] He noted, however, that there was still only one Black officer at Lejeune.*

The stories of those who experienced these training camps give much-needed testimony and detail to the ways in which desegregation was really—often painfully—achieved. Much of it was shocking then and remains so now: the fact that Black military personnel, on their way to offer their lives for their country, were often hidden behind curtains on trains and buses, so that their mere presence wouldn't offend white customers, is hard to imagine but is an image that recurs repeatedly. And when white and Black troops did mingle during transport, again the curtains were drawn to preserve local mores. The irony and brutality of this situation was certainly not lost on the fighting men and women, even if it may have been to their superiors or to the governments of the states through which they traveled.

JOE TAMAYO, MOUNT HOLLY, NEW JERSEY

My name is Joe Tamayo. I was born September 26, 1928, and I'm seventy-four years old. I live in Mount Holly, New Jersey. [I served with the] 7th Division. [I grew up in] Meridian, Mississippi, [and] I was drafted in the army in New York. Believe it or not, I tried to enlist when I come out of high school in '48, [because] I wanted to further my education, but it was so segregated they told me I couldn't enlist in Mississippi. But soon as I came to New York in 1951, they drafted me! I was in New York, working in the days and going to school at night. I was wasting a lot of my time, because I couldn't put time into my studies like I wanted. So when the army drafted me, I figured it was the best thing that could've happened to me, because I wanted to go anyway.

When I left New York, I went to Fort Devens, Massachusetts, [to be sent on for basic training]. There weren't but two places for a man to go [for basic] who was any race other than Caucasian. It was Fort Benning, Georgia, and they had [one] other camp.

Because I was drafted, I had to take what they would give me, therefore the infantry. So by me joining the airborne, they sent me to Fort Benning, Georgia. At that time it was segregated. I didn't think it would be segregated. I figured it would be good training and would help better my education. Most of the people from New York were sent south, and most of the people from the South were sent north. That was to mix them up. I think it was a good idea, so they could see how people live in the other place. But me, already being from the South, I knew. Some people needed to see how much better off they were than people in the South. That's the only thing good about that.

They segregated us when we got on the train. They pulled all the shades down, so we asked the white sergeant why was that. He said it was a secret, so that people couldn't see what troops was moving, but I found out when I got to Fort Benning, they didn't want to see us mixed up with the white soldiers. At the train station[s], they got all the white guys to the front of the place to eat, and they took all the Black soldiers and anybody else that was Black to the rear of the station [to a] "greasy spoon" to eat. And when we went down to Fort Benning from Fort Devens, it was so segregated we didn't know what was going on. 'Cause up in Devens, it wasn't segregated, it was mixed in. When we got to Fort Benning, we weren't allowed to go up on the main post. They sent all the Black soldiers and troops who weren't white to Sand Hill, that was in the rural section of the base, and that's where we took our training. It was a disgrace. We couldn't go to the main post or to the main theater on the post. They had a club for the soldiers we couldn't go to 'cause it was for whites only. We had a little, small place that served beer and sandwiches and stuff for the Black troops. I played football on the segregated team. And the only time it started mixing up . . . at Fort Benning [was] when they put us all together, Black and white, to play football. And that's when I started figuring out what was [going on,] 'cause I started playing football with the whites. It was a disgrace. This is 1951.

Why should you put up with a segregated post? Like when you go downtown on the bus line, they had a sign: Black and White. This was just on base. If they didn't have enough room, you didn't go. When we went on the bus, you didn't go through the front door, you went through the second door. This was on base! The [leadership] didn't have much to say. Our officers were white. The only Black officer we had was a chaplain, and he couldn't say too much. I didn't have to put up with that junk down there of no rights.

Couldn't even go up on the main post. They kept us up in the woods all the time. By being in that segregated unit, whites got better food than we got. We got leftovers. We got the same coffee grounds for three meals—they just kept it in the pot and added water. The white troops got the best. When we started mixing up it was the best thing that happened because we got the same food they got. We got the same supplies, the same weapons and stuff like that. But . . . we didn't get the clean blankets the white guys got each time we got new troops in. We kept the same blankets, so you can imagine what was on some of them blankets. [And] we had to wash our own clothes. The whites sent them to the quartermaster laundry on base to wash their clothes. We didn't have that till they started integrating, then the Blacks got the same rights as the whites.

Joe Tamayo
1st sergeant, 187th Infantry Regiment, 7th Infantry Division
US Army
Interviewed by Ellen Guettler, November 23, 2002, Mount Holly, NJ
American RadioWorks, Minnesota Public Radio

CLENTELL JACKSON, APPLE VALLEY, MINNESOTA

Fort Knox, Kentucky, is where I had my basic training. That was segregated. [I] didn't [see] integrat[ion] until I got ready to go overseas, and then we were on the water, in the ship, when they changed our orders. [From Fort Knox,] I went to Virginia, Camp Lee, Virginia, for the NCO training, that's noncommissioned officer training, that's the one with the stripes. My company commander, he was picking certain guys to go, and he picked me because I could read and write. There were a lot of Blacks who couldn't read and write in the service. [Then] I went to a leadership school in South Carolina. I guess they thought I had the smarts to do it. They sent me there from Fort Benning, my base camp. I went to leadership school for two and a half or three months, and then I went back to Fort Benning. I went to three different schools while I was in the service. They weren't integrated.

[The instructors were] white and Black. I know in South Carolina there were two Black ones, and all the rest were white. And at these schools, your company commander and all your instructors, except these two, [were white]. I guess their jobs were pretty important. I don't know if they were there just for show, it could be because most of the students there were Black. There was no desegregation then, [but m]orale [among Black soldiers] was good. We knew what the circumstances was. We knew that trying to fight the circumstances, we'd end up in trouble, so why start trouble when you don't have to?

We signed up for Korea. And that was two weeks after it started. I wanted to get away from Fort Benning, because even the Black enlisted officers were on anybody Black from the North, like me and another kid from New York. They called us smart alecks because we, I don't know if we knew more than they did, or weren't segregated against in our home town or whatever, but it was a jealousy and they made it real hard for us. I had this sergeant and I hauled off and hit him, hit him right in his mouth. He made me so mad. He gave me the worst jobs, everything. Anytime they needed someone to clean the latrine, he'd say, "Get Jackson, he'll do it." He could've got me in trouble. He was a sergeant, but he was smaller than me and I laid him out and then I swore up and down that I didn't touch him. It was my word against his. I said, "No, I slipped and accidentally, as I was going down, threw my arm back like this so I wouldn't fall too hard on the ground." I said, "I'm sorry, I was falling and I, instead of hitting my head on the ground, I brought my arm back like that and caught myself." I'm lying like crazy.

There were a whole lot of guys that signed up [for Korea], a lot of them didn't go, but my orders came down and in a couple of weeks I was gone because this one sergeant said, "He's nothing but a troublemaker, he'll keep everything disturbed." Same with the kid from New York, same thing happened to him.

Clentell Jackson
Technical sergeant, 25th Regiment, 24th Infantry Division
US Army
Interviewed by Tina Tennessen, September 10, 2002, Apple Valley, MN
American RadioWorks, Minnesota Public Radio

GERALD L. BAILEY JR., BLOOMINGTON, MINNESOTA

[I'm Gerald Bailey. I was born] in Minneapolis, 1930. My mother was born in Saint Paul, and my father was from Colorado. Our neighborhood naturally was primarily Black. The people I ran around with, the kids I played with, were Black. [But] I went to . . . Catholic schools and [they were] predominantly white. [There were] maybe half a dozen Blacks at Incarnation, and for one year I was the only one at DeLaSalle, and then two more came in. By the time I graduated, there were three of us.

But other than that, Minneapolis was a fairly liberalized city, primarily due to Humphrey. But we still at times noticed some biases, other than housing, which was strictly biased. There were a couple eating places that didn't want to serve us; they did eventually, but they didn't want to. We didn't pay too much attention to it. It was brought up occasionally at the city level.

I enlisted [in the army] in June 19[48,] about a month after graduating from high school. I think it was more of a whim than anything else. I just saw a sign one day and it says, "Uncle Sam Wants You," and that was it! I never really thought about the other branches of the service. If I would've stopped and thought, I probably would've gone into another one. It was really a whim; I don't know why I did it. I knew a person who was in the army and he was stationed in Fort Lewis, so I suppose that influenced me somewhat. I enlisted and told them I wanted to go to Fort Lewis, Washington, and that's where I ended up after basic training at Fort Knox, Kentucky. We had eight weeks there, and then I went to Fort Lewis.

[Basic training in Kentucky] was my first experience with real segregation when I got down there. I'd never seen it before, where you weren't allowed to eat wherever you wanted, go wherever you wanted. I had no idea what it was like. It was all new to me. That was in the city. Being on the base, in basic training, you weren't allowed to go anywhere anyway, so it didn't really matter! We were in an all-Black outfit [in] the 3rd Army Division, I don't remember what regiment it was or battalion.

[In basic] we did calisthenics, rifle range, combat training, some class-type work, but you learned an awful lot about a rifle or a carbine and how to tear it down and clean it and how to shoot it. I even had a swimming class one time. But mostly it was marching drills, bivouac, walking out to the camping areas, camping out for two or three days, going through military exercises, coming back.

I was the only one from our outfit that went to Fort Lewis. We went out on a troop train, and parts of it went different places, I ended up going from Ogden, Utah, to Tacoma, so I didn't know anybody when I got there. I didn't know I was going to 3rd Battalion, 9th Infantry. All I knew was that I was going to Fort Lewis, Washington. I was assigned to L Company, 3rd Battalion, 9th Infantry Regiment, 2nd Infantry Division. The 3rd Battalion was an all-Black battalion within a white regiment. In fact, it was the only Black unit in the 9th Infantry at that time. I know there was one other field artillery battalion that [a] friend I knew was assigned to, and that was all Black, [but] we saw very little of them because of our location on the fort and the different kind of training.

[We] basically [did] not [interact with the white battalions]. Most of our training was done in the battalion. We went on maneuvers a couple of times where the whole regiment was involved, but ordinarily it wasn't. I did go to a leadership school that was integrated, that was not too long before we went overseas, sometime in the spring of 1950. I have no idea [why that was integrated but the battalions were segregated].

What [opinions on integration were] like at the commanding levels, I don't know. I'm sure individually everybody had their own opinion of what they would have wanted or would have liked. But basically I don't think it was a real issue, at least with the people that I associated with. I'm sure most of the individual soldiers, and many, many of them were from the southern states, but quite a few also from California and the Midwest, had an entirely different outlook from some of those from the other states. So it was, I suppose everybody had their own thoughts. I never gave it a thought one way or the other. I never remember wishing I was in the 1st or 2nd Battalion. Sometimes I was wishing I was out of it altogether, but that was about it.

I always thought the morale was pretty good, the esprit de corps was very good, they were proud of their organization, as most soldiers were at that time. We did an awful lot of parading in town—I don't know, that may or may not have been because of who we were, but it seems like we were always going on parades somewhere, and if we didn't go into town we were parading on base. Many of those parades, especially on base, the entire division was parading.

Sometimes we would go to Tacoma or Seattle and parade. Many times it was the entire regiment. So that was a big one. [Our commanding officers] were African American. Our battalion commander was a professor from either Grambling [University] or Prairie View [A&M University]. He didn't end up going overseas with us, but he was our stateside commander. There was another company commander who had been a teacher or a professor or something.

There were no rules of segregation that I knew of; the only thing was that we were a Black battalion within a white regiment. The regiment was all in the same living area. We didn't live in the same barracks as them because you never do in a battalion, a company is by itself. I think, when they were up to count, there were 205 people in a company, that's how many beds we had. A battalion is made up of four companies. Each company had three platoons living in the permanent barracks and one platoon living in a regular army barrack, a wood barrack. The permanent barracks were brick two-story building[s, and] the typical army barrack is a two-story wooden building.

Each battalion had their own quarters. We were in permanent barracks. One battalion butted up against another battalion in these barracks, so when you talk about segregated living quarters, it isn't so much that. To say that there was a line drawn between the 3rd Battalion and the 2nd Battalion, that's just not true, there wasn't. They were there and we were here and we were right next to each other. Each company has their own mess hall, and you didn't eat with anyone else, and a company is a lot smaller than a battalion. But we weren't on one side of the fort and the whites on the other side of the fort; we were all in the same group of buildings, including the other battalions such as the tank battalions and those kinds of people.

There were no segregation laws on the post, like you couldn't go here or you couldn't go there, there was nothing like that. If there were, I never knew about them. And as I said, I went to leadership school that was integrated. It was the first class of its kind — the leadership school — it was the first class of its kind. It was just indoctrinating noncoms in how to lead, a lot of clichés they use, the same things being used now in business. The one I remember the most is, "Familiarity breeds contempt." In other words, keep your distance from those you're trying to supervise. That's the only one I remember, and I've heard it since then in business.

I was in a machine gun squad. I think I was the gunner. I wasn't the squad leader. Then after that I transferred to Headquarters Company of the 3rd Battalion and went into the reconnaissance and intelligence section, and there wasn't a squad leader there. We had a sergeant, and the rest of us were all corporals. I just ended up there and I left my buddies, and in some ways it might have worked out pretty good for me . . . because a lot them in the old group didn't make it back, not as many, percentagewise, as our group did.

Gerald L. Bailey Jr.
Corporal, 3rd Battalion, 9th Infantry Regiment, 2nd Infantry Division
US Army
Interviewed by Tina Tennessen, August 3, 2002, Bloomington, MN
American RadioWorks, Minnesota Public Radio

HAROLD WOODMAN, MEMPHIS, TENNESSEE

My name is Harold Woodman. I'm from Louisville, Kentucky. I initially served with the 555 at Fort Bragg in [the] late '40s, early '50s. During the Korean War, I served with the 25th Infantry Division and the 187th Airborne Regimental Combat Team commanded by Colonel Westmoreland. I went over [to Korea] in 1952.

Initially, when I first entered the service, it was totally segregated. [The army] posts were like segregated towns [with] separate sections. The colored section of Fort Bragg was called Spring Lake. My basic training unit was all Black. We had white officers, Black noncommissioned officers. All of the trainees were Black. [I] Went to Fort Bragg after basic training [and the] 555 paratrooper infantry battalion was all Black, all of the officers were Black. This continued up until late '49 [or the] early '50s when we started getting field-grade white officers from the 82nd Airborne Division.

We thought those officers that they sent over were somewhat inferior and it might have been punishment for the white officers. However, we did get one outstanding battalion commander, a former ranger, Colonel Garrett. He was a fine solder. He came in and whipped the battalion into fine shape, and gained the respect of the men right off the bat. At the same time, we had a wonderful division commander of the 82nd Airborne, Gen. [James M.] Gavin. His previous service after OCS, I believe he served with Black troops in the 9th or 10th Cavalry. He had experience [with] Black soldiers. We had his respect right away. He was the one who fought so hard for integration of the military. The 555 Parachute Infantry Battalion was the first of any Black unit to be integrated into an all-white unit.

Now, integration at that time was not integration as we know it today. The military bases were just like any other segregated town. We had a section of the post where we trained, we ate, [went to] theaters [and] service clubs, and we caught the bus to go into town. This little area of Fort Bragg was called Spring Lake. However, when the division went to the field, when the division had training, they sent vehicles over to pick us up and we would go and parade in our portion of the formation. Then you would be returned to your area. We still trained separately, but on occasions we wore the division patch. We were considered one battalion of the division. Separate but equal—that's the only time I can really say that that term applied. And that's the way it was. [The] training was equal, the equipment was equal, and I thought that the billets were equal because General Gavin saw to that, and he was over quite often to see that everything was up to par and that we received [the] same treatment as the other two battalions.

In 1948, the biggest operation the 82nd Airborne Division had after World War II was [a] mass jump at Camp Campbell, Kentucky. We went in with part of the division, and we made the drop just like the other soldiers. We did the training. However, at the conclusion of the exercise they have a briefing and graders. And we were being graded by the Kentucky National Guard. This was somewhat of a surprise to the people in Kentucky when we showed up as part of the division. During the critique, the two sister battalions, all white, received favorable comments from the critiques. Of course, when the chief grader got up to speak about our battalion, which was the 3rd Battalion 505, he said, "Now, let's talk about that other battalion," and the tone that he set with his initial remarks just left everybody cold. He was very disparaging. As a matter of fact, Colonel Garrett stopped him right in the process of his denigrating our battalion, called us to attention, moved us back to our bivouac site, and said, "Before the sun sets today, this man [will] apologize to my battalion." And he [did].

I'm not saying many of the officers [in the army] wanted [integration] to happen, but I was in an outfit where the division commander wanted it to happen, and he was up at the Pentagon asking for it long before it happened. He was a pioneer. [He] had this experience with Black cavalry soldiers. He respected Black soldiers. [He was a] famous general, [a] wartime commander with a lot of clout with the 82nd. He had pull. He wanted to use this for some good. He fought like the devil to get the 555 integrated into the 82nd. He [was] just that kind of man. He had problems with junior officers and many officers [who] felt integration wouldn't work. I think Eisenhower was one of them—he made some disparaging comments about [how] white soldiers just wouldn't want to be with Black soldiers [and] that they couldn't live together, couldn't bathe together, and they couldn't train together because it would cause some friction. But the thing that really accelerated it, we ended up doing a paper exercise on integration . . . that made it look good. Everything that went into the Pentagon looked good on integration. Not that anybody in the Pentagon tried to rush it along. They had been hammered with this thing from Truman. And the military, you know, when you give them orders, they've got to stand up and march, [but] nobody wanted to make it really take off and go the way that it eventually did.

In 1950, I was one of 150 troops that left Fort Bragg and went to Fort Campbell, where they had the 11th Airborne Division, and the 11th was all-white, white attitude and everything, if you know what I mean. They had just returned from Japan. We went up there, [and] they put us in [the] same situation as at Bragg.

We were all together, but we were on this side of the firebreak [and whites were on the other]. We had all white officers. That was something that we had to get adjusted to, [but] again I ran into a wonderful situation—we had a fine CO from Paducah, Kentucky, my favorite state, and he and I have been friends a long time. He passed a couple years ago, and he never came to Louisville but he didn't look me up.

But war changes everything. Wars will change people's minds. At first in Korea [there] were all segregated units. Then they disbanded them, [and] started spreading them out. When we got into the Korean War, we went in with understrength units. We were just overwhelmed by the size of the Chinese forces that they threw at us. It took its toll on our few infantry divisions that we had over there. And as the war progressed and attrition took place with the troops, they just kept throwing in Black soldiers . . . they shipped us right into these units. When I went to Korea, I went directly into an all-white unit. I guess there must have been about five [other] Blacks [too]. I commanded a platoon of forty whites and had two Black soldiers in that whole platoon. We had a very fine, efficient[ly] operating machine. It went well.

And of course when they came back from Korea into the United States, [they came] into these never-segregated units because it was just over—segregation in the army was over, it was totally over. And I don't know if it accelerated be-cause of the war, people forgot the prejudices they [held because] they had a more important mission, or just the attitude of men in general. Some of my dearest friends [there] were white and from the Deep South. My foxhole buddy was from right there in Clarksdale, Mississippi. Once you got into integration, soldiers didn't fight it. Not everybody liked it, but we had a higher calling. It just moved right along with very little friction. We was soldiers, [we] didn't think about race.

Integration came easy for me and I didn't have the problems that some of my fellow soldiers had. You have to accept some things, you can't let all these things tear you down, get inside your head and drive you crazy. If a person got a problem, it's his problem, and you moved on from it. You just have to have the right attitude about it. My opinions might be different from some of my com-rades who've had a harder time with integration. I loved the army too much— I was born, raised, [and] will die a soldier.

Integration in the army . . . was one well-oiled operation. First of all, men in the service see you as a soldier. You spend so much time together. You live to-gether, train together, especially after integration took place. And the camara-derie between you [because you're both] just soldiers, and this is why you gel so well on the battlefield—they're just soldiers [too]. And these other prob-lems, they seem to just disappear. The biggest problem was going to town. This is where you encountered segregation again. But life on the military post was wide open.

Even during the riots [in much of the country in the 1960s] we lived in [a] separate society, military society. My wife was amazed how things moved along in [the] army. She said, "You're not living in the real world." I understand what she was talking about.

She said, "You just don't live in the real world. This is a phony world you're living in. When you leave the army, you're going to find life is a little different on the outside." Of course when I retired and entered into civilian life, I kind of ran into some of that stuff again. But it was in Kentucky, a border state.

Harold Woodman
Major, 25th Infantry Division and 187th Regimental Combat Team
US Army
Interviewed by Kate Ellis and Stephen Smith, September 6, 2002, Memphis, TN
American RadioWorks, Minnesota Public Radio

WALTER LEE DOWDY JR., CHATTANOOGA, TENNESSEE

I am Walter Lee Dowdy Jr. I served in the Korean War. I was in the army. I was with the 25th Division, 24th Infantry Regiment. My highest rank was corporal. I was born in Osceola, Arkansas, in 1930. It's a little, small town. My parents moved from Osceola, Arkansas, to Michigan. [They were] sharecropping [in Arkansas, and it was] bad in those days. Came there in 1932. There would be nine of us kids after we got to Benton Harbor, Michigan. And we was raised in Benton Harbor, went to grade school there and junior high and high school.

Me and two other buddies, we were going to be doctors. But during this time, if you can remember historically, Eisenhower was talking about universal military training. So we said we don't want to go and get into medical school [or] get into college and drop out a couple years to go in the military, so we said we'd enlist. My two friends enlisted before I did. I was a holdout, but I finally enlisted, and I told my parents, and my father and mom, oh, it broke their heart. They was crying and crying and crying, but I went in. I mean, we had already fought the war to end all wars, right? There wasn't going to be anymore wars. And November 1948, I enlisted. And they shipped me off to Fort Riley, Kansas, Camp Funston. The reason I remember it so well, my father was in World War I. He went into the military from Mississippi, [and] he took his basic training, guess where? Camp Funston, Fort Riley, Kansas. And he had a picture of him in his britches with his campaign hat on, you know. And so we went there, and I finished basic training. At Fort Riley I was in an all-Black outfit.

But now, when I got in and started reading about the army, I wanted to be an officer. I wanted to spend at least six years in the military. They didn't ship me out. They kept me back for cadre for the next people because I had passed the army [officer] test. I was going to Officer Candidate School.

Cadre are the ones who train the recruits who come in. We help the sergeants and the other higher-ups to train the new recruits. So we [trained] two groups [that] came in, [but] I still hadn't gotten my orders for OCS, Officer Candidate School. Then they shipped me out to Fort Leavenworth, Kansas, to Command and General Staff College. So I was there, [and] I started cooking now. I cooked for the officers at the Command and General Staff College. Officers from all over the world came to be trained there. I'm waiting for officer orders, [but] my orders still hadn't come. So the next thing, they shipped me out, and I got orders to go to FECOM, Far East Command.

I wanted to be an officer badly. If I would be an officer, I would make it a career. But then all my time from 1948 to February 1950, I'm just bopping around, bopping around doing nothing. Here a little, here a little. No orders. [Finally I was assigned to] duty station [in] Japan. We left February 14th, 1950, going to Japan, fourteen days on a merchant marine ship. [This was] before the Korean War. When I finally got to Japan, February 28th, I got settled in Camp Gifu. And, man, I've never been in a foreign country before. The smells, the noises. We get off the ship, went to the train station, and I saw a guy, Japanese, urinating right there in the street. And I says, "My Lord!" And I was a scared little boy, man. It sure is different.

Got to our duty station, and they got me cooking again now at this Camp Gifu in Naka in Japan. So my orders finally came. My orders — this is February, March, April — my orders came for Officer Candidate School. I had to take another physical. I was under orders to leave Japan in September 1950, come back to the United States, go to Fort Benning for OCS. I was going to be a ninety-day wonder! And so I took my physical and passed my physical and everything, and I was on orders for September 1950. You know when the war started? June 25, 1950. And they called me up in Japan.

And, man, we were on alert, and I've never been on alert before. And we had blackouts, and I had to stand duty in the mess hall because I was one of the cooks. And when we finally got on alert to go over to Korea, they issued us live ammunition and combat gear. We had to sleep in our clothes ready with our packs in front of our beds and ready for combat any time. Be ready to go any time. The first sergeant, he said, "Well, Dowdy," he said, "you [were supposed to be] in Officer Candidate School. We don't need cooks in Korea, we need soldiers, so we [are] going to give you a choice of a machine gun or a radio." And in basic training I had learned that machine guns don't last long in combat, [so] I took a radio. Forward observer, you know, with a radio on your back. So I took that [and] I learned that quickly. But you know what now, some strange things happened. When I was in Camp Gifu before we went on to Korea, we had white officers. When we got on alert to go to Korea, they changed to all Black officers. I went in combat with an all-Black outfit. Black officers, everything Black. But in Japan we had white officers. We had a white captain, white warrant officers, and everything. My first sergeant was a Black man, Sergeant Laday. He got killed in Korea. But I thought about that because I thought the army wasn't segregated. I thought Truman had fixed that up.

Walter Lee Dowdy Jr.
Corporal, 24th Infantry Regiment, 25th Division
US Army
Interviewed by Michael Willie, February 18, 2004, Chattanooga, TN
Walter Dowdy, Jr. Collection (AFC/2001/001/20008), Veterans History
    Project, American Folklife Center, Library of Congress

JEANNE L. BEASLEY, NATIONAL HARBOR, MARYLAND

I enlisted in the army, Women's Army Corps, 1949. I [had] just graduated from high school. I was living at home in Cleveland, Ohio. [I joined up] just for the job opportunity. [It was a] very poor year for job opportunities that year, and a recruiter came to our high school and said they needed clerical people. And so since I had taken clerical courses, I had filing, sales, and typing, so I enlisted. And it was my first job at a desk, and I was typing and I had a good [words-per-minute] time.

I went in in September of '49. They didn't tell me [training camp would be segregated]. When I got down there, Fort Lee, Virginia, the white girls went to a different company, but we would see them all day long. So they were segregated in a separate company. At that time we had sixteen weeks of training. I was at Fort Lee, Virginia, and so I completed my training there. Mostly marching and drill, close-order drill. We had what they call weapons familiarization, not the program now where the women fire. We only fired that one time. But now they have a regular program for them. And then after that I had two months of leadership course, and then I was assigned permanent party cadre. Then we were squad leaders.

I just felt like I had a little advantage over some of the others. We were all just coming out of high school. But they joined for different reasons. Most of them wanted to go in the medical field. Everybody avoided food service. Nobody wanted to go in to be a cook. But I knew right away from my first day of going to school I typed fifty-four words a minute.

They said, "You're not going to school; you're going to [do] on-the-job training." [I] was just happy to be out and get a job because there was no jobs available. [Later, I served] during the Korean War [with the] 2nd Team Major Support in Yokohama, Japan, [as] logistical support personnel.

I went in [the army in] September '49 and then in June, after the Korean War started, they integrated the army so everybody went to different places, and I stayed there at Fort Lee. And they sent me down to the officers training detachment, and I was the only person in that company. I was like a typist. They sent me more to get coffee. The little cook over there, said, "Come on in the door. You ain't going to get no coffee standing at the door." Every night she would bring me the cookies and I think, she likes me. She gave me a blouse for my birthday. But I never really had [any racial] trouble. I know other people said they had trouble with different things, but I never really had trouble. I came from such a poor family. I was so glad to get three meals a day and a place to sleep. I didn't know what to do. I didn't care. I just wanted to be happy. It was the first job I had.

Jeanne L. Beasley
1st sergeant, unit unknown
Women's Army Corps
Interviewed by William L. Browne, August 7, 2009, National Harbor, MD
Jeanne L. Beasley Collection (AFC/2001/001/73466), Veterans History
*   Project, American Folklife Center, Library of Congress*

REAMER C. BELL SR., CINCINNATI, OHIO

I am Reamer C. Bell Sr., of Cincinnati, Ohio. I was with the 999 Armored Field Artillery and joined them in spring of '51 in Korea. And stayed until spring of '52. I was a driver of the M41, the vehicles that carry the .455-millimeter howitzer, and I drove that for that year. So that's basically what I was doing there.

We were used to being an all-Black unit. Okay, my basic [training] was Black, okay; the unit I was in was Black. We didn't expect whites to be there, you know. We were on the Black side of the post in Fort Bragg, North Carolina, where I went after my first basic out of Fort Dix. Everybody in our unit in Fort Bragg was Black, even the commanders. They were World War II carryovers. We were on the Black side of the post when the whites had the headquarters, where the golf courses are, you know. So anyway we were just accustomed to it, and if you think back, that's what we've always been accustomed to, you know, the back-of-the-bus type of thing. We were just accustomed to it, and when they began to integrate, I took it with a grain of salt because I don't meet strangers and that worked out really well. [When we got to] the point where 999 had to have a white battalion commander, okay, we were all Black except the leading officers. And that, we always grumbled about. What could we do about it? It was a way of life, you know.

But when they did integrate, that was good. I thought it was very good. 'Cause this is what it is supposed to be like. You fight in the war for the same country. You come and you live, you know, and you just do what you got to do, and it should always be that way, and it should never have been any other way because we, we did our share, you know.

And I don't have bitterness because of it because that was history. That's past. Like I said, I had friends, even in high school, I went to a like 1 percent Black [school]. I had white friends there. Pete Rose, you have heard of him, I was there with his brother at Central High School. We had good buddies and we had fun.

You know what, I didn't even think about segregation. I really didn't. I didn't think about it. And I have seen the signs, colored water fountains, going around the country, I remember that. My parents moved from Georgia and I just happened to be born in Ohio. But that was the way of life, and I had been on a bus from Fort Bragg and I saw the water fountains there in Virginia, colored, you know, white, you know, what the heck? But I couldn't do anything about it and accepted it, which we all did basically.

Reamer C. Bell Sr.
Corporal, 999th Armored Field Artillery Battalion, X Corps
US Army
Interviewed by Stephen Smith and Kate Ellis, August 23, 2002, Little Rock, AR
American RadioWorks, Minnesota Public Radio

Integrated Camps

The integration of training camps mainly followed the pattern of desegregation elsewhere in the armed forces. And as we've seen, the individual character and choices of the commanding officer usually governed the way race relations were conducted.

Whereas many Blacks experienced discomforts in crossing racial and cultural boundaries, some experienced outright hostility and violence, as Mark Hannah attests to below. And as Larry Hogan points out, although a training camp might be integrated, some commanders found ways to isolate and persecute Black soldiers. Still others, many others, attest to the trope that once people get to know each other their fear of the unknown other often disappears, especially if confined in the same barracks or foxhole.

What [Truman's] order was [really] was for each branch of the military to submit a plan, a proposal for desegregation of the military in their own delivery speed. And the air force was the first to submit it, and the air force had been approved while I was a senior in high school. They hadn't started, but they had approved it, and in order to go into the desegregated air force, you had to go north, because you could not enlist in the desegregated air force from the South. You could still only go to the segregated air force, okay. So I went to Detroit and volunteered and went to Sampson Air Force Base, New York, in [the] Geneva area. They had established a boot camp for Blacks and whites to go to boot camp together. I was in the first group.

[This was my first intimate interaction with white people], oh yes, because, you see, not only Mississippi, but Florida was as segregated as Mississippi. My only other experience was when I was fifteen years old, my daddy drove us to Detroit, Michigan, and he came back and left us there two weeks, and we rode the train from there, and that's the first time I knew that I was supposed to be inferior to anybody. When we got on the train in Detroit, it was integrated. When we got to Memphis, Tennessee, the conductor came back through and told me and my brother that "you boys have got to go to the colored car," and a white couple sitting across the hall said, "No, you all don't have to move. You paid the same thing we did." So we sat. The conductor came back through and said, "I told you niggers to go to the other car." I believe the white couple was still saying we shouldn't go, but we got up and went, and that was really the first time it really come clear to me who I was supposed to be.

[And], quite frankly, I cried every inch of the way from Memphis to Durant, Mississippi, where we got off the train, and I don't know if I've ever stopped crying, because that was a real experience for me. I was a prima donna. I always thought that whatever I was, was as good as it could get, and then to find out that everybody didn't think that! I mean, even the white couple sitting over there thought they was better than me. So that was a real, real eye-opener.

I finished boot camp, and I went to New Mexico Western College. This was the first time that the Black and white [recruits] had gone to technical training school together in the air force. This turned out to be a blessing—technical school was where I learned how to type. That's been the most valuable tool of my existence. We graduated from New Mexico Western College, and this was the first time they'd ever seen any [Black] GIs here.

James Meredith
Staff sergeant, unit unknown
US Air Force

Interviewed by Renee Poussaint, June 27, 2006, Jackson, MS
National Visionary Leadership Project, Library of Congress

JOHN B. JACKSON, HOUSTON, TEXAS

I'm John B. Jackson. I live in Houston, Texas; I'm seventy-one years old. I was drafted into the US Army, inducted in 1952. I served in Korea over fifteen months through 1954 with the 2nd Division, 32nd Regiment, and 4.2 Mortar Company. And I was a sergeant, up to platoon sergeant.

I was out of high school two years, and then I was drafted into the US Army [when] I was twenty-one. I did not even know about Korea when I was drafted in October 1952. I just had heard that name Korea through the news, I never paid any attention to it. I knew about Asia, but I did not know about Korea and . . . during basic training that's when it really struck me that I could be going to Korea because they were going different directions [from] Camp Roberts, California.

When I arrived [there] in October 1952 they had just integrated the bases then and it was new, so I was brought into an integrated army in basic training. I did not encounter much [racist] activity because our first sergeant, the day we landed at Camp Roberts, he made an order, a strict order, which I think scared us more than anything, that we had left the South, we had left all of the old beliefs that we had grown up with. He told us to leave them. He never wanted to hear about anything like that in the barracks while we were there. So I cannot recall whether [there] was an incident, I'm sure [there] was, but it was very rare in my company. I just didn't come across it. Everybody accepted everybody. Guys from Mississippi, Louisiana, Alabama, Illinois, Iowa, California, Indiana, North Carolina, South Carolina, Tennessee, Arkansas. We were of all races. I cannot recall ever going on restriction for something on the racial thing. All my restrictions were probably for not cleaning a weapon or something. We never went on detail because we did get along. I was in shock, though, because I came out of a segregated community in Texas.

When I say I'm in shock [it's] because I had worked with the different races in Freeport, Texas, at Dial Chemical Plant. I was working in Dial Chemical Plant for this construction company, and in 1952 Dial was segregated and Dial would not have African Americans in a [permanent] position on his payroll. We were only on contract with some other company. They could hire whoever they wanted and put on the job. But Dial did not. So I came out of segregated schools and community and I went into working in Freeport, Texas, in a segregated job, but we had integrated [tasks] because we had all races working together, either in the ditches we were digging, or helping the carpenter. [But,] see, that was just on the job. When I went into the army, we had to sleep with the different races and it was just, I was in shock that we were sleeping bunk to bunk, bunk on top of bunk. So it was just a shock to me to see it actually happen.

My brother-in-law and my brothers, they were in World War II, but that was a segregated system and they did not encounter what I encountered. And when they went to town they went as two races or three races or whatever. But when we went to town we went as buddy-buddy whoever your buddy was. It could be all Black, Black-white, Spanish, it didn't make any difference.

It changed my worldview. At twenty-one, getting ready to go into twenty-two, and I'm in a new world now. That's the way it was. And going overseas I didn't encounter any racial problems in Korea, [no] racial [problems]. I did encounter jealousy of rank: "Why'd you get your rank?" And stuff like that. [But] I did not encounter a racial fight or word. I did not encounter that. All of the guys with me in my company were very, I wanna say, cautious. Big Gordon from Alabama, he was just like a brother to you. Nick Lewis from New York. I wanna say that if we set aside two [fellows] of the same race, . . . the white from Georgia, they did not like the white from New York. It wasn't a fight thing. It was just they'd sit on opposite sides. We mingled both ways, and did not feel any different, they did not make us feel any different. We could join the conversation, eat at each other's plate [at the] canteen, whatever. It was just one of those things.

John B. Jackson
Platoon sergeant, 23rd Regiment, 2nd Division
US Army
Interviewed by David P. Cline, January 10, 2003, Houston, TX
American RadioWorks, Minnesota Public Radio

MARK B. HANNAH JR., HOUSTON, TEXAS

My name is Dr. Mark B. Hannah, Jr. I'm a retired educator, and I live in Houston, Texas. I was born September 3, 1933, and I went in the service [early] by [changing] my birthday, [which] was coming up that September, and I went in that April, 10th of April, of '51. I had a good, good friend. He signed my father's name, and a general signed my mother's name — that's another thing, I forged my mother's name to go in [the army]. I first was inducted in Kansas City, Missouri, and from there we went to Fort Custer, Michigan, and from Fort Custer we went to San Fran. We received shots overnight, and we were loaded up on the ship *General Black*. I'd never seen a ship in reality. It held over five-thousand-some soldiers. So immediately I was segregated [from other Blacks and] surrounded by Eurocentric young men. So after the fifth day they say, "Now hear this, hear this, *General Black* will be going to Hawaii to take basic training at

Schofield Barracks." So there I found myself the only—we were Negro and colored then in 1951—I was the only Negro in my company and I was frightened and immediately they went to work on me.

[In training camp in Hawaii] they would pull pranks on all the fellas, but they were pretty heavy with me. I was up on the third [floor of the] barracks— there were three levels, the main, second, third. They put snakes and a tarantula spider that had spiders on top of it about the size of a quarter in my bed and I found all types of insects. And—so I'm going to go ahead and say this—I once woke up with something going around my mouth and it was semen. So shortly after that, the next thing was, I didn't put a razor blade in my razor because I didn't have any fuzz or anything, and so I left my razor and went into the shower, and the next thing I knew the sergeant, I can't think of his name, someone told him I didn't have a razor blade, and so he began to make me shave in the morning and at night with a razor [blade], and I didn't know how to shave with a razor, and so it [permanently scarred and] blackened my face.

We had sixteen weeks of basic training and ten of those weeks I slept on the commode rather than get into bed. And one of those weeks I got permission one evening after cleaning my equipment to go down to the day room and write letters home. So this sergeant 1st class, this field sergeant, he saw me in the day room and he just came and knocked all my papers and just pulled me up and pushed me up the steps, and I scarred myself all up, and he just gave me a whippin' and beat me. They didn't take me to the hospital, but I was pretty battered and they decided to let me stay in the barracks. The other guys, they didn't want this to get out, but I refused [to stay inside]. I went out on my mission like everybody else, all beat up. So they told me that they demoted him and sent him on to Korea, I don't know.

I had this other sergeant, Sergeant Samuto, American Japanese sergeant, and he kept encouraging me. And I'd been taught by my grandparents and other folks that we as Negroes had to work two, three, four times harder than the white man. So I just put that to work. I did not let my mind get physical though I was called nigger, and I just lived above it and I did very good on my stuff and I was appointed battalion soldier of the month, and that was very encouraging to me because I was able to spend a weekend with the base commander and his family one weekend for that honor. And that's the first time I ever saw a municipal pool and I was able to swim in that. But I didn't go into Hawaii that much because we could not go anyplace downtown in Honolulu. There was no place that Blacks could go into, no place. This was '51.

Somehow, by the grace of God, instead of me going directly to Korea, as that unit did, I was sent back to leadership school in Fort Riley, Kansas, about eighty miles northeast of Wichita, Kansas, where I was born and raised. And that was very challenging because it was OCS, so we had to put pasteboards in our sleeves and shine our shoes and I was the only African American in that company, but it wasn't quite as tough. It didn't have the racial prodding that I had in Hawaii.

Mark Brady Hannah Jr.
Platoon sergeant, 224th Regiment, 40th Infantry Division
US Army
Interviewed by David P. Cline, January 10, 2003, Houston, TX
American RadioWorks, Minnesota Public Radio

LAURENCE "LARRY" HOGAN, BOSTON, MASSACHUSETTS

When I went to Korea [from] Fort Dix—even though it was an integrated army, and we trained together— ... [when] the camp split up, ... all the Black guys went one way and all the white guys went another way. I wouldn't say they were prejudiced, but the way the army was then, you [don't really] know. And I had a big discussion with the colonel. And the colonel said, what can I say, you know. Looking at it now in hindsight, some of that was prejudiced and somebody said send these guys here, but a lot of it wasn't. Maybe the next cycle, maybe the white guys went, I don't know, because it was all politics, too. Guys would go to Alaska. When I got to Korea, I would see ... a guy from basic and say, "Where the heck have you been?" "I was in Greenland. I was in Iceland. I was in Trieste." Guys had duty in certain places that it was so bad that they would volunteer to go to Korea. I would say, "I don't believe this! You volunteered to come here?" [Maybe] there was a method to the madness.

Laurence "Larry" Hogan
Sergeant 1st class, 31st Infantry Regiment, 7th Infantry Division
US Army
Interviewed by David P. Cline, October 25, 2002, Boston, MA
American RadioWorks, Minnesota Public Radio

Officer Training and Black Officers

In the segregated army, Officer Candidate School was always integrated for the simple reason that the army felt it was not cost effective to build separate facilities for training Black officers. So even during the heyday of the Jim Crow military, a counterexample of a multiracial military was readily available, although it certainly had its limits. William Cooke, who served in World War II, was an officer with the federalized 272nd Massachusetts National Guard during Korea. While attending OCS at Fort Benning, Georgia, he still encountered the trap-

pings of segregation. "Here we are getting trained," he recalled, "[and I] had to go to a Black barbershop, still couldn't use the base facilities. [And in] December 1951, on the train coming back to Boston, before we got to the Mason Dixon, they asked [us] to move."

During the fall of 1951, Collins George, a reporter for the Pittsburgh Courier, wrote a series of articles about two federalized African American National Guard battalions serving at Camp McCoy, Wisconsin: the 645th Combat Engineers from Pittsburgh and William Cooke's 272nd Field Artillery Battalion from Boston. As we have seen, the Black press was deeply invested in covering African American participation in the war. Journalists not only reported on how troops were fairing overseas but throughout the war monitored the conditions African American forces faced on the home front. And in at least this one case, George's press coverage of unequal treatment at a military base appeared to affect the outcome of a series of judicial hearings.

George detailed how the 272nd had been formed in 1947 with a group of officers out of the 372nd Infantry Regiment, which had a legacy dating to the Meuse-Argonne offensive in World War I and had later trained men for World War II and served in Hawaii after the war. Although many of the officers had previously held different specialties, they were formed as an artillery battalion and sent to Camp McCoy in September 1950. Once brought to active service, the 272nd was placed under the command of veteran infantryman Karl B. Russell, who along with other officers was sent for artillery training. When Russell failed to complete this training, he was replaced by a white West Point graduate named Cornelius A. Murphy in favor of the acting Black commander, Maj. George Bingham, a World War II veteran much beloved by the men and officers alike, according to George. Bingham was immediately reassigned to an infantry unit without explanation, and his brother 1st Lt. William Bingham was court-martialed for a list of minor offenses and reassigned to a radar outfit. Murphy then accused eleven other officers of the 272nd of incompetency because, alleged Collins George and the officers, he hoped to replace them with white officers. While awaiting trial the eleven men were required, on a day's notice, to undergo a ten-hour artillery examination. And before their trials were even held, Murphy had secured their replacements, all white.[31]

Though cleared by the review boards, four of the eleven accused Black officers were nevertheless transferred, two requested release from duty, two were put on inactive duty, and the remaining four were recommended for dismissal from the army. By October 6, 1951, George was reporting that morale in the unit had plummeted and AWOL incidents were soaring because "the top command and top officers of the outfit no longer now are Negro and the 272nd, like the miserable world war two outfits, has Negro enlisted men, Negro junior officers, and white top officers."[32]

The Courier's reporting revealed some of the fallacies and inconsistencies of army integration. According to William Cooke, one of the Black officers Murphy challenged, the 272nd was integrated after it was federalized. However, George reported that the unit was integrated only at the top level of command and that it was approximately 75 percent over strength with untrained enlisted men "because the Army as yet does not have integration outside of its training camps and schools and Negro enlistees can only be sent to Negro outfits." While all of this was going on with the 272nd, the white commander of the 645th Engineer Battalion, the other formerly all-Black National Guard outfit at Camp McCoy, also ordered competency hearings of a number of his Black officers. George reported that this commander had been "struck by the success" of the "Murphy maneuver" and was seeking white replacements of his own.[33]

At around the same time or just after the competency hearings, the unit was alerted and received orders to ship out for Germany rather than Korea. Cooke contends that the shift in location was due in part to the press attention the unit had already received, causing the army to want to put it out of sight on a "mountaintop over there in Germany." Largely because, apparently, of the Courier's coverage, the army launched an inquiry into the competency hearings but upheld them, causing the Courier to call the inquiry "entirely inadequate [and] . . . missing the main point entirely.[34] Governor Paul Dever and Senator John F. Kennedy of Massachusetts agreed and called for additional scrutiny of the "reorganization of the 272nd," stopping the unit from leaving port. With the unit at the time were three of the four surviving Black officers; one had transferred to an artillery unit in Louisiana, and the other three, including Captain Cooke, joined the unit as "excess officers" because their white replacements were already serving.[35]

Eventually the unit shipped out, and by mid-December 1951, five of the original Black officers were serving with the 272nd in Germany, three had been cleared of all charges but assigned to duty elsewhere, and four were still awaiting final decisions. Less than four months later, those officers in Germany had all requested transfer to other outfits, leaving "the entire top command of the outfit white with a bare handful of the junior colored officers remaining.[36] Colonel Murphy himself was relieved of his command of the 272nd in Germany. Although no official reason was given for Murphy's sudden removal in the first week of April 1952, the chief of staff of the 7th Army told Collins George, "We just had to get rid of [him]."[37] George added that a number of officers stated that Murphy had "conspicuously failed to win the respect and cooperation of his officers and men."[38]

Even without Murphy, conditions remained difficult for the 272nd in the supposedly disbanded army. In Germany they were quartered—along with another traditionally Black unit now with white command—about a twenty-minute *walk from the main part of camp that housed the only recreation facilities and at which were quartered two units from Texas that the Courier called "all-Dixie." Collins George was prompted to write: "One wonder[s] when the Army will ever learn that separate racial groups inevitably lead to explosive group antagonism, whereas, even in the South, integration bring[s] about, at worst, only conflict between individuals which can be easily controlled."³⁹ The Courier, however, also cautioned against integration that followed the "Murphy Maneuver" and belied the spirit of Truman's original order: "So long as true racial integration is not the picture in the Army, all-Negro outfits should not be reshuffled (regardless of how apparently 'legal' the manner of reshuffling may be) into a re-creation of the old world war type of outfit in which the enlisted men and junior officers are Negro, but the top command consists of whites using the outfit as a stepping stone to further their material careers."⁴⁰ These words were written on the same day that the army's once famous and now infamous 24th Infantry Regiment was integrated in Korea. On that very day, the 272nd, with its white officers and Black enlisted men, was stuck in port before embarking for Germany and its segregated camp.*

JOHN CONYERS, WASHINGTON, DC

The first night we got there [to Fort Lewis, Washington], there was a dance at the enlisted men's and we got in a fight that first night. Some guy said we were from the big "D"—Detroit was there—and words were exchanged and there was a big fight. They had to bring in the military police, and the word went out all over Fort Louis that these lunkheads from Detroit are here and this is going to be rough.

I was put in battalion headquarters at Fort Lewis and I started looking at this Officer Candidate School business. I said, "Boy, I could qualify [for] that and become an officer. Get the heck out of this unit." And so I went to the base commander and they said, "Yeah," and they started helping me fill out the papers. You had to first go to several months of leadership school in Fort Ord, California, and then you go to the engineering school in Fort Belvoir, Virginia. Here's fate working again. Papers [went] back and forth, school records, this and that. Finally they said orders came down cutting John Conyers Jr. from the 1279th, putting him in the casual detachment of Fort Lewis to await orders to go to Fort Ord, California, for the leadership training.

And while I was there by the way, in Fort Lewis, we had these musicians, jazz musicians. And I had gotten a letter in music in school, in high school, and I was a jazz aficionado even then. [I played] trumpet, but I was studying piano and chord formations. [My National Guard buddies] said, "John, they want us to play. We can teach you bass and they'll let you stay here and you can play bass."

They were playing, making extra money and having great fun, and I said, "No, fellas, I'm going to go to Officer Candidate School." They said, "John! What are you talking about, man?"

So I'd go by and visit my friends again, and these [guys], you know, [were going] from there to Korea. You would wake up in the morning at Fort Lewis and the whole battalion would be gone. I mean, they lifted up the tents, the pegs. It was just like nothing had ever been there. They moved the battalion out. That's the way they did it in those days. They went that night and that was it, they were gone. And you didn't have to wonder where they were going. And [the] 1279th was on the list, and that's what they needed in Korea. You're supposed to be able to fight and construct at the same time, shoveling and firing. I said, "Boy, oh boy. Too bad, you guys." My buddy said, "Boy, that Conyers, he's so lucky."

I went to California for months and months and then to OCS [in Virginia] for six months, which is where I started going eighteen miles down US [Route] 1 to Washington, DC, where I stayed at the Kappa Alpha Psi [house]. My fraternity let me stay there over the weekend, and whenever I could I'd go watch the sessions in Congress. And I'd come and sit in the gallery . . . 'cause it interested me. I was drawn to it. And I'd look down at the members of Congress, and they seemed to be sitting around talking to each other. And I said, "I could do that. What's the big deal?" And then when I went to Korea and served a tour of duty there, I said, "If I ever get back here alive, I'm going to find out why I got sent here in the first place to kill people that may be trying to kill me with no more of a clear understanding of why they were fighting us." And sure enough, boy, as soon as I came back I finished up my prelaw.

[When I] finished OCS, [I] was sent straight to Korea. Straight to Korea! And guess what happened? I'll never forget. Colonel McDavid of the 1279th and this wonderful couple of captains, they started petitioning the Pentagon and said, "You cannot send these kids to Korea. You can't. They're not ready. They're not trained. They're just scraped up off the streets." And do you know, the 1279th got taken off the list to go to Korea? They sent them to Camp Kilmer, New Jersey, and then sent them to Europe. And these guys were saying, "Oh, John, it's so great in England and the duty is so wonderful. It's just so marvelous and we really miss [you!]" Quite a few of them stayed and never came back.

John Conyers
US representative, 13th District of Michigan
Michigan National Guard, 2nd Lieutenant, 1279th Combat Engineers
US Army Corps of Engineers
Interviewed by Renee Poussaint, August 20, 2007, Washington, DC
National Visionary Leadership Project
Interviewed by Louis Jones, September 19, 2003, Detroit, MI
Detroit Oral History Project

My name is William Cooke. I live in Boston, and I'm eighty-four years old. During the Korean service, I was a member of the 272nd Field Artillery Battalion, Massachusetts National Guard. I [had] changed my branch from infantry to artillery, and I commanded a battery in the 272 Field Artillery Battalion. We were inducted into federal service and went to Camp McCoy, Wisconsin.

It was a Black outfit and it was integrated when we were federalized. Our colonel, who was a Black colonel, was [re]moved from office and replaced with a white West Pointer. His name was Colonel Murphy. And he more or less took over the battalion. Eventually we had problems with him because he would try to remove the senior Black officers and replace them with his own type—what we called the "Murphy Maneuver." Whereas I was one of the senior officers in the outfit [and] I was the senior captain—I was a unit commander, a line officer, not a field officer—he saw fit to try to remove me. Even though I had . . . [gone] to Fort Sill, Oklahoma, and completed the basic [officer training], went to Fort Sill, Oklahoma, and I completed the advanced.

I was the senior commander. I had the base battery that all other batteries fired on my data. So that's why he went after me, because I didn't shake hands with him and say, "Yes, Colonel Murphy, I'm your boy." But I guess he figured I had too much know-how in the battalion. So I was one of those [he tried to replace,] along with [a man] considered one of the better officers, one of the best officers in our outfit, Major Bingham, eventually Colonel Bingham. He tried to remove him also.

So in order to prove that we were inept, he gave a test. It was mainly for me because I completed the advance officer course in Fort Sill, Oklahoma— a course that some colonels in my class didn't even pass. This test started right after first call and lasted until almost recall in the evening. He gave a lot of simple problems right at the start, and then he gave all the tough problems to go along [with] firing a battery. You had to know a lot of trigonometry—you had to find an unknown by knowing two knowns. So he gave that test, it lasted all that time. In fact it got so bad you got writer's cramp. 'Course, you know, I was the only one who passed it. They were trying to say I wasn't qualified because he wanted to remove me. At the hearing, I had a right to look at the test. Now, he had passed me, but there was about four or five problems that were very tough problems, where I was laying a battery, that he had marked wrong. So I had went to the hearing and I challenged him. I got my old 6-40 [field guide]—that's the bible of the field artillery—and I went to each problem and I asked him how to do it. First I asked him how to calibrate the aiming circle! He told me, you take two readings and then you subtract grid North from magnetic North. I said, "Colonel, magnetic North varies, grid North is fixed! You subtract the magnetic from the grid!" "Oh," [he said]. So the funny thing about it, it was all these big colonels up there, they was head of the board, they asked to see. I had marked off the 6-40 just where the answers was. 'Course they had to give me more credit for this test. And [a] few other [problems] that he had marked wrong they had to give me credit for, and so my score went drastically up. So anyhow, he got so frustrated that he [said,] "Well, I can admit that Captain Cooke is a qualified officer, but there's just something about the man I don't understand." I know what he "didn't understand," 'cause I didn't take no crap from him and I let him know that I didn't appreciate what he was doing.

So my DC, that's the defense counsel, got up and said, "Oh, so you want this man separated from the service because there's something about his character you don't understand?" So anyhow, the head of the board had to tell him, "We won't have no arguments back and forth now, so let it go." Anyhow, to make a long story short, he had to admit I was qualified but he didn't "understand" my personality. Because I didn't Uncle Tom to him, that's why. So anyhow the board had to admit that I was qualified.

He was wanting to get rid of the top echelon so he could bring his people in; the white officers were there to replace the top echelon of the Blacks. Colonel Bingham, everyone respected him, and he could have taken that battalion and made a whole lot of history with them, but he was one of the men that [Murphy] tried to get rid of, trying to say that he was incompetent. We just realized that he'd have to prove we were incompetent and ask for a hearing. At my hearing, he had to admit that I was qualified but he said that [there] was something in my personality that he didn't like — it was that I didn't want to kiss his backside.

So they asked me [after the hearing,] did I want to stay with the 272, and I said I wouldn't stay with any outfit that this man commanded. I asked for a transfer out and I was transferred, but by the time I went to get my orders, they had alerted the outfit to go overseas. Then they realized they couldn't transfer me out because they had been alerted. So I went over with them, but I didn't have an assignment. But I got over there and I [had to] come out. I had an attack, a seizure, while I was over in Germany waiting for an assignment to another outfit. So I was flown home to the States, and I went to Valley Forge and they found out I had a nervous condition and started having seizures. So I had to come out of the service on account of that. But that's some of the issues as far as what happened in the 272nd.

And of course, they did move a lot of the Blacks out and put the whites in their position. But the reason I had trouble with Murphy was because I complained about some of the officers of my color were kowtowing to him to keep in his good graces. Because they had asked him, was he going to give all them officers a test? Well, see, the only persons he gave that test was those he wanted to get rid of. And of course some of them wouldn't take it because they knew they couldn't pass it. So it was just mainly to get me, but then he lost out on that because I passed it and I passed it easily. And I asked him questions that he couldn't even answer and he gave the test!

William Cooke
Captain, 272nd Field Artillery, Massachusetts National Guard
US Army
Interviewed by David P. Cline, October 23, 2002, Dorchester, MA
American RadioWorks, Minnesota Public Radio

Private 1st Class Edward Wilson of the 24th Infantry
Regiment, 25th Division, awaits evacuation after a
battle near the front lines, Korea, February 16, 1951.
Photograph by Private 1st Class Charles Fabiszak,
US Army. NARA *File no. 111-SC-358355,*
Department of Defense HD-SN-99-03053.

President Harry S. Truman, at his desk at the White House, signs a proclamation declaring a national emergency on December 16, 1950. *Photograph by Acme, US Information Agency. NARA File no. 306-PS-50-16807.*

Members of the 24th Infantry Regiment, 25th Division,
advance toward the front on July 18, 1950, Korea.
Photograph by Breeding, US Army. NARA File no. 111-SC-343967.

Private 1st Class Clarence Whitmore, a radio operator with the 24th Infantry Regiment, 25th Division, catches up on the news and grabs some chow during a lull in the fighting near Sangju, Korea, on August 9, 1950. *Photograph by Private 1st Class Charles Fabiszak, US Information Agency.* NARA File no. 306-PS-50-10721.

Julius W. Becton Jr. (back row, second from left) as a member
of the Lower Merion High School Track Team, 1940–41.
Courtesy of Lower Merion High School / Lower Merion Historical Society.

Julius W. Becton Jr. as a newly
minted 2nd lieutenant around 1945.
*Courtesy of Lower Merion High School /
Lower Merion Historical Society.*

Charles E. Berry in his US Army
uniform at the age of nineteen.
Courtesy of Charles E. Berry.

OPPOSITE
Corpsmen tend to a wounded
soldier from the 116th Engineers,
121st Evacuation Hospital,
Yongdong, Korea, August 17, 1951.
*Photograph by G. Dimitri Boria, US
Army.* NARA *File no. 111-C-6620.*

United Nations forces withdraw south across the 38th Parallel from Pyongyang, 1950.
NARA File no. 306-FS-259-21.

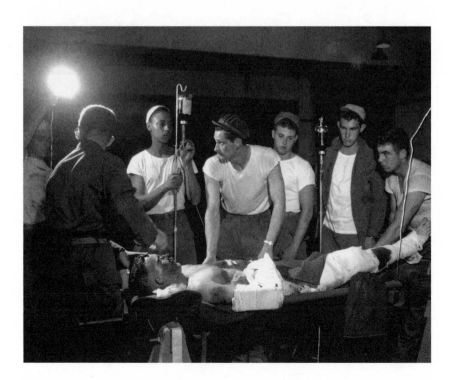

General Douglas MacArthur reviews troops of the 24th Infantry,
25th Division, at Kimpo Airfield, Korea, on February 21, 1951.
Photograph by US Information Agency. NARA *File no. 306-PS-51-10432.*

Sergeant 1st Class Major Cleveland of the 2nd Infantry Division directs
the fire of his machine gun crew, November 20, 1950, Korea.
Photograph by Private 1st Class James Cox, US Army. NARA File no. 111-SC-353469.

Personnel of the 822nd Mobile Army Surgical Hospital pose in Korea on October 14, 1951. Note the division by race and specialty, with the African American ambulance drivers some distance from their white colleagues. *Photograph by Cpl. Charles Abrahamson, US Army. NARA File no. 111-SC-382662.*

A mixed-race group of men from the 378th Engineer Combat Battalion hoist into place an underwater bridge support on the Pukhan River, Korea, November 19, 1951. *Courtesy US Army Center of Military History.*

Former POW 1st Lt. Alvin Anderson, 2nd Division, US Army, is embraced by
family members upon arrival at Fort Mason, California, September 14, 1953.
Photograph by Herb Weiss, US Army. NARA File no. 111-SC-431161.

Into Korea

3

No Bigots in a Foxhole
War Brings Desegregation

The Korean War integrated the US military. President Truman's Executive Order 9981, calling for the desegregation of the armed forces, was certainly important to him, and it was of utmost importance to African Americans, whose century-long commitment to using military service as a lever for final freedom and equality they hoped was finally paying off. But the order had less impact in a large swath of the military itself; cooperation with Truman's order was sporadic at best during the several years after it was issued. And for most white Americans, the desegregation of the military was for the most part a back-burner story in the postwar United States. Most white Americans in 1948 and 1949 were far more concerned with what they hoped was the peace and prosperity that had finally come to stay. White suburbanites flourished in newly built homes filled with washing machines and televisions and shiny-faced children. The reality for most African Americans, however, was far different and for them far from Perry Como's musical version of an America where "You can let your worries flutter by and do the things you please / In the land where dollar bills are falling off the trees."[1] There was no "Dreamer's Holiday" for a majority of African Americans in late 1949, when Como's version of the song hit number three on the charts, and for white Americans, the warm days following World War II were about to give way to the freeze of the Cold War. As the decade wound toward a close, carefree dreams would be replaced by what many feared would be nuclear nightmares. They were already gathering form. The Soviet Union detonated an atomic bomb in August 1949; on October 1, Mao Zedong announced the establishment of the People's Republic of China; in January 1950, the trial of accused Soviet spy Alger Hiss drew to a close; and in February, Senator Joseph McCarthy announced that he had a list of Communist Party members and evidence of a massive spy ring within the State Department. With the specter of Nazi Germany still lurking, leaders feared that the Soviet Bear posed the next big threat to both world peace and American democracy.

But no one, especially the United States, which had greatly downsized its armed forces following the war, expected war again so soon, and especially not in faraway Asia at 6:00 a.m. on June 25, 1950, when massive numbers of North Korean forces suddenly crossed the 38th Parallel, the line that divided North from South Korea. Truman gathered his advisers in Washington, DC, and furiously communicated by teletype with Gen. Douglas MacArthur in Tokyo. Believing that the Soviet Union was behind the attack and no less than the fate of the free world was at stake, the United States called on the United Nations to meet in emergency session. With the Soviet Union conveniently absent—they were boycotting the United Nations over its refusal to recognize the People's Republic of China—the UN Security Council voted to come to South Korea's aid with a multinational force under the command of the United States and led by MacArthur. It put the United States in charge and named MacArthur commander of the allied force. Twenty-two nations offered troops and other help, and an additional thirty-one nations registered official support. Although the conflict would be termed a United Nations "police action," it was in reality a war, and one led by the United States, which provided 88 percent of the 341,000 international soldiers sent to aid South Korean forces. And it was a war that the United States, and its ragtag band of allies, was little prepared to fight. In the first few weeks, the United Nations threw in troops as it could muster them and had them repeatedly overrun. In the first month, more than 2,800 Americans were killed. Overall, American casualties numbered over 36,000, with another 8,000 missing in action. Korean casualties, on both sides, numbered around 900,000 soldiers and some 2 million civilians.

American forces comprising what was called Task Force Smith arrived in early July, but initial victories along a northward drive back to the 38th Parallel were deceiving, and the international forces were quickly pushed back again to a small area around Pusan in the South, an area that became known as the Pusan Perimeter. The tide appeared to turn again with General MacArthur's daring surprise landing of US Marines at Inchon in the North, allowing a rapid UN counteroffensive from the South that drove the North Koreans past the 38th Parallel again, almost to the Yalu River.

Victory seemed certain—indeed, US forces were celebrating the thought of being home for Christmas—when suddenly the People's Republic of China entered the war, with thousands upon thousands of well-trained troops marching from Manchuria across North Korea's northern border. Chinese intervention forced the southern-allied forces to retreat behind the 38th Parallel again. Although the USSR did not directly commit forces to the conflict, the Soviets provided material aid to both the North Korean and Chinese armies. Several truce agreements petered out before the fighting finally ended on July 27, 1953, with the signing of an armistice agreement. This agreement restored the border between North and South Korea near the 38th Parallel and created the Korean

Demilitarized Zone (DMZ), a two-and-a-half-mile-wide buffer zone between the two Korean nations and patrolled by international peacekeepers.

Korea and the situation there, especially in North Korea under the current leadership of Kim Jong-un, continues to make the news, but most Americans still know little about this area or the war and its devastation. And fewer still know the roles played by African Americans in the war or the role that the war itself played in the history of the African American freedom struggle and a democracy that did not always practice what it preached. When US troops were sent to Korea as part of the UN-sponsored police action on June 25, 1950, segregated African American soldiers were some of the first to land and fight. But what indeed were they fighting for? Where was this place, Korea, a reclusive East Asian peninsula the size of Utah?

To understand how North and South Korea came to war in 1950, and how the United States got involved in a Cold War struggle half a world away, we must look first to Korea's long history of subjugation by a foreign nation. Long before the war that bears its name, Korea was a battleground for global politics. Japan, emboldened by victories over China in 1894 and Russia in 1905, made Korea a protectorate in 1905. From 1910 to 1945, with the blessings of the United States and Great Britain, Japan ruled Korea as a colony.

At the onset of Japanese colonization, Korean culture was quite uniform across the span of the country: its people shared a common ethnicity, culture, and language, and it had maintained consistent national boundaries since the tenth century.[2] Traditionally, Koreans had close ties to the Chinese and, like them, viewed the Japanese as culturally inferior. It was therefore a bitter pill that those whom they considered below them were now their rulers. Furthermore, the Japanese proved harsh masters. Japan chose to destabilize Korea's relatively strong cultural and political infrastructure through wholesale replacement with Japanese systems. They eradicated much of Korean culture with often-brutal army and police enforcement and replaced the Korean language and the Confucian classics with Japanese language and literature. Korea's traditional rulers, a scholarly and aristocratic group of officials, were either co-opted or replaced outright by a new class of imported Japanese elites.

Korean society before colonization was not, however, uniformly beneficial for all of its citizens. Under Korea's final dynasty, which lasted around five hundred years, a small aristocracy ruled over, and in some cases owned, a far larger population of peasant farmers, without any middle or merchant classes to speak of. The aristocracy, known as yangban, managed a civil service with a ruling class of scholar-officials and fostered artwork and education for members of this class. The new Japanese colonial rulers exploited this unequal class structure, often operating their colonial rule through these local landed aristocrats. The yangban even prospered briefly under colonial rule during the 1920s, when a relatively lenient period of imperial rule allowed their offspring to succeed in a series of professions, building what could have been the basis of a new ruling class for an independent Korea.[3] However, the 1930s brought global depression, war, and ever-harsher Japanese colonial measures. Korean elites, rather than being allowed to blossom into a new ruling class, were often turned into Japanese collaborators. Those yangban who refused to buckle under to the Japanese sometimes became underground nationalists who now found a common patriotic bond across class lines with their peasant compatriots. The climate was ripe, therefore, for the growth of Korean nationalism by the time World War II ended in 1945.[4]

The movement for Korean independence gained international support at the highest levels. At the international Cairo Conference, held in November 1943 as World War II raged on in Europe and racial violence peaked in the United States, China, which feared potential Soviet designs on Korea, joined forces with the United States and Great Britain on the Korea issue. They created a joint statement claiming themselves "mindful of the enslavement of the people of Korea [and] determined that in due course Korea shall become free and independent."[5] Two later international conferences, at Potsdam and Yalta, reaffirmed support for an independent Korean nation. However, the phrasing of the Cairo Conference statement hedged its demands with the phrase "in due course," revealing President Franklin Roosevelt's belief that it would be years before Korea was ready for truly independent status. In the meantime, the Cairo Conference statement mandated that Korea should be overseen by an international "trusteeship" consisting of the United States, Great Britain, the Soviet Union, and China.[6]

Multinational support for a trusteeship faded once the Soviet Union entered the war in the Pacific on August 8, 1945, occupying the northern portion of Korea as far south as Pyongyang. With Soviet troops on the ground in northern Korea and no American troops in the vicinity yet, the United States, without consulting Korean leaders, rushed to establish an occupation zone south of the 38th Parallel. This put the Korean capital of Seoul within its jurisdiction. The Soviets voiced no objections to the division of Korea, and it was made public on August 15, 1945, as Japan surrendered and Korea was declared liberated.[7]

American occupying forces arrived on September 8, 1945, under the command of Lt. Gen. John R. Hodge, a veteran of the Okinawa campaign. Hodge, however, was insensitive to Koreans' longing for independence as well as to their resentment of the Japanese who had formerly ruled them. Ignoring Korean wishes, his occupation government worked directly with Japanese former officials as well as with Korean collaborators, maintaining much of the repressive systems established by Japan. Thus, though supposedly liberated, Korea was once again occupied, and in such a way as to leave much of the oppression intact.[8]

The Soviet occupation of northern Korea had a very different feel, at least initially, than the American occupation of southern Korea. In contrast to the

US military leaders who were ignorant of or indifferent to local political realities and nationalist feelings, the Soviets styled themselves as liberators, routers of the Japanese overlords, and facilitators of a democratic revolution. Initially enthusiastic, Korean support in the North faded over the ensuing months as it became apparent that the Soviet Union's style of indirect control elevated only those North Koreans who shared Soviet political views. A truly independent Korea was not yet in the offing north or south. And envisioned plans for a country-wide Korean election in 1945, supported by both the Americans and the Soviets, were never realized. Instead, when the Americans and Soviets announced that Korea would be governed for the next five years under a Soviet-American trusteeship, Koreans responded with demonstrations and work stoppages. Although the Korean reaction was nationwide, it was also clear that different visions of an independent Korea were developing in the North and in the South, each with its own potential leader, Syngman Rhee in the South and Kim Il-sung in the North.[9] Meanwhile, as the Cold War emerged and then intensified, the Soviets and Americans took increasingly opposing approaches to each other, positions that played out in their Korean policies.

Like many other independence leaders of colonized nations, Syngman Rhee developed much of his philosophy, training, and planning while in exile. Born in 1875, he was involved in Korean independence activities as a youth, earning him imprisonment and torture under the Japanese. After participating in a failed revolution in 1919, Rhee immigrated to the United States, where he married, earned a doctorate from Princeton University, and began an academic career. He also formed a Korean government-in-exile with himself at the head.[10] The American occupation forces in South Korea turned to Rhee to help calm potentially explosive civil unrest that had resulted from the American suppression of political leftists in the South who had embraced Communism and established people's committees to undertake local governance. In order to pacify the civilian demands and calm the situation, the Americans brought in Rhee, who was both anti-Japanese and anti-Communist, to create a new base of power. Arriving in Korea on General MacArthur's personal plane in mid-October 1945, Rhee founded the right-leaning Korean Democratic Party and quickly established himself as the South's new political leader. His demands for an immediate reunification of Korea under an independent Korean national government, however, put the Americans in an uncomfortable position. Since Rhee embraced conservative landowners and did not champion the peasant majority, in order to counter Communism in all of Korea during the Cold War, the Americans had to also be willing to embrace an antidemocratic independent Korean government.[11]

Unlike the exiled intellectual Rhee, Kim Il-sung's rise within nationalist leadership had its roots in military resistance and Communist loyalty. Although many of the facts of his early life remain unknown, it is believed that in his youth he became a guerrilla resistance fighter against the Japanese, joined the Communist Party sometime in the 1930s, and continued to fight the Japanese along the Manchurian border with Korea. He then joined the Soviet army in 1939 or 1940, eventually earning the rank of captain, where he led a Korean battalion and trained soldiers for the fledgling Korean People's Army (KPA). Specifically groomed for leadership by the Soviets, Kim and sixty-six fellow Korean officers established the North Korean high command, with Kim as chairman of the Interim People's Committee, charged with establishing a civil government in North Korea.[12] An opportunist, Kim sought close ties with Joseph Stalin while eliminating local resistance to his establishment of a Communist government. At the same time, he continued to present North Korea on the international stage as a model independent nation.

With prospects seemingly dashed for a successful trusteeship relationship with the whole of Korea, the United States called for an UN-sponsored general election. Refused entrance to the North by the Soviets, the United States focused its efforts on the South, and the UN election thus became an election only for an independent South Korean government. Rhee's allies brutally suppressed attempts by the Communists and others on the left to influence the election, and Rhee was elected as the first president of the Republic of Korea (ROK), officially announced on August 15, 1948.[13] Despite South Korea's new independence, the United States kept a strong hand in South Korean affairs, especially in its developing military. A group of five hundred American officers and men, organized as the Korean Military Advisory Group, served as advisers but also held operational control over the ROK Army, giving the American military a great deal of power in the fledgling democracy.

At the time of the formation of the ROK, the possibility of a united Korea still existed. One hundred seats were even set aside for the North in the new National Assembly, although this remained a symbolic gesture after Kim Il-sung refused to participate in the elections or the new government. Instead, Kim Il-sung established the Democratic People's Republic of Korea (DPRK) in Pyongyang, north of the 38th Parallel, on September 9, 1948. The DPRK was soon revealed as a repressive totalitarian state whose constitution contained no protections of individual rights and that was enforced by a tight control on the media through a brutal police force. Kim also quickly built North Korea's army, formed around a core of thousands of battle-hardened soldiers recently returned from fighting for Mao Zedong in the Chinese Civil War.[14]

The North Korean government also supported a diverse coalition of rebels operating in the South. Composed of Communist Party members, other leftists, and even common thugs, the guerrillas operated out of the woods and hills of South Korea, attacking installations such as police stations and raiding small towns when they needed supplies. The guerrillas hectored South Korea for two

years, from 1948 to 1950, before Rhee managed to suppress them, although enmity remained on both sides. Conditions for a potential clash between North
and South Korea ramped up when both the Americans and the Soviets withdrew
their armed forces.[15] As part of a consistent policy of downsizing its military in
the years following World War II, the United States pulled out the majority of
its troops in June 1949. The Soviets had removed their own forces the previous
year and seemed to have other, more strategically important positions in mind
for them in Eastern Europe and elsewhere in Asia.

With most Soviet and American troops now gone, the two Koreas began
spoiling for a fight, harassing each other with border incursions instigated by
the armies of both North and South Korea and brief skirmishes occurring with
increasing regularity. The United States threatened to remove its five-hundred-
strong force of military advisers from South Korea if Rhee's men continued the
attacks. In addition, the Americans refused Rhee's requests for tanks and heavy
artillery for his ROK Army, which by now had expanded to a hundred thousand
troops, roughly equal in size to the North Korean forces.[16] When North Korea
escalated from border raids to a full-scale invasion early in the morning of June
25, 1950, instigated by Kim but with the permission and support of the Soviet
Union, the South Koreans were unprepared—and their army underequipped—
to respond properly.

Recent scholarship has revealed that Kim Il-sung himself was the main pro-
ponent of the attack and convinced the unenthusiastic Soviets to support him,
although at the time President Truman and his advisers were convinced it was
the Soviets' call. Alexander Haig, the four-star general who would serve as President Ronald Reagan's secretary of state, was a twenty-five-year-old aide in Mac-
Arthur's Tokyo headquarters when North Korea invaded the South. Years later
he recalled, "I think both MacArthur and the President concluded that this was
an action that could not be tolerated because it was clearly instigated by the
Soviet Union."[17] Although this turned out to not be exactly the case, Stalin did
support the attack. Stalin, who first consulted with China's Mao, did not desire
a war with the United States, but he was convinced by Kim that his forces
would win a quick victory in the South and that the Americans, whose forces
had already been withdrawn from the region, would not have cause to become
involved.[18] Still, Stalin insisted on protecting his own interests should Kim fail to
win the South quickly or provoke US involvement. Stalin required Kim to seek
Chinese support and refused his own nation's military involvement. During a
secret meeting in Moscow before the attack, Stalin reportedly demanded that
Kim get Mao's support, saying, "If you get kicked in the teeth, I shall not lift a
finger. You have to ask Mao for all the help."[19] Nevertheless, he gave his blessing, and in the weeks immediately before the attack, the Soviets shipped large
quantities of armaments to North Korea.[20]

While the troop strength of the northern and southern troops may have been roughly even, the North Korean Army was far more experienced from its time fighting in China and better equipped, with 150 Soviet tanks and sixty-two light bombers bolstering its arrsenal.[21] To this day, it is unclear whether North or South Korea invaded first; each side claimed that the other first crossed the 38th Parallel at the remote Ongjin Peninsula, northwest of Seoul. Whatever actually happened, the North used it as a chance to launch a full-scale invasion. Within hours, forces clashed at another site along the parallel, just south of Chorwon, where KPA forces crashed through ROK Army defenders and began moving toward Seoul. They met little resistance, as poorly trained South Korean units, fearful of the North's superior firepower and with little faith in the Rhee government, turned on their own commanders or fled before the advancing northerners. The Rhee government and the remainder of the southern troops retreated south of Seoul, which fell to a northern force that numbered only about thirty-seven thousand troops. When the fighting stopped several days later, half of the southern troops were dead or missing, and the survivors retained only about 30 percent of the equipment and weapons with which they had begun.[22]

Most Americans at the time, including President Truman and his military and political advisers, were not aware of Kim's secret meetings with Mao and Stalin or of Stalin's hesitancy and demands. Instead, they assumed that the Soviet Union and China had designed the attacks themselves as a Communist incursion of a democratic country. Secretary of State Dean Acheson pressed for US intervention, believing that the North Koreans had attacked American prestige by invading a country crucial to the United States' efforts to rebuild Japan. His arguments were endorsed by the president and subsequently brought before the Congress and the United Nations for approval. Despite the extreme reluctance of the Joint Chiefs of Staff, who believed that US armed forces were not numerically prepared for a war against the North Korean army, let alone the huge numbers of reserve forces in the Chinese People's Liberation Army, US ground forces were committed to battle in Korea on June 30, 1950.[23]

The Joint Chiefs of Staff were right to be concerned. American armed forces, which had peaked in size at 12 million during World War II, had been drastically reduced following the end of the war. By 1950, only 1.6 million remained in the armed services, and the US Army, which suffered the most severe cuts, was down to 593,167 personnel.[24] The army had four divisions stationed in Japan— the 7th, 24th, and 25th Infantry and the 1st Cavalry—but numerically they were short an entire battalion. As one former lieutenant colonel recalled, "All of the divisions were filled with new replacements and were in a poor state of combat readiness. With only one exception, all of the regiments had only two of their three infantry battalions, and the artillery battalions also were short one of their firing batteries."[25] Despite the legitimate concerns of the Joint Chiefs, Douglas

MacArthur approached the war with characteristic bluster. On the first day of the war, he claimed, "I can handle it with one arm tied behind my back," and initially requested a regimental combat team only. His request, however, soon increased to two divisions and, within a week, to four divisions and then eight.[26]

In addition to being understaffed, the divisions were inadequately equipped and not battle trained. Life in Occupied Japan was relatively laid back with plenty of leisure of time for the troops. Lieutenant Col. Charles M. Bussey, a former Tuskegee airman who was then serving with the 25th Infantry Division on Honshu, Japan, recalled, "Good living was the order of the day. Occupation meant occupying the best of Japanese facilities, holding a glass in one hand and a Japanese girlfriend in the other, and seeing how much food and drink one could indulge in and how much hell one could raise."[27]

America's first ground troops, Task Force Smith, composed of the 1st Battalion, 21st Infantry Regiment, 24th Infantry Division, was drawn from these ill-prepared forces and sent to Korea on June 30, 1950. The rest of the 24th arrived on July 1, 1950, followed nine days later by the 25th Infantry Division and the 1st Cavalry Division. Among the first into battle were some of the army's remaining all-Black regiments. The poorly trained and poorly equipped troops, Black and white alike, suffered great losses at the hands of the better-prepared and armed North Koreans. The United Nations added more troops as soon as they were mustered, but saw them repeatedly overrun.

Within the first two weeks of the war thousands of African American troops were among the five-division force now on the ground. Variously described by stateside newspapers as Negro, Colored, or Tan, African American troops arrived with the 2nd Infantry, the 3rd Infantry, and the 82nd Airborne. But the best known was the 25th Division's 24th Infantry Regiment: the Deuce Four. This regiment included the 10th Cavalry—the famous Buffalo Soldiers—as well as the 369th Infantry, which fought in World Wars I and II and became known as the Harlem Hellfighters, and the 555th Parachute Infantry Battalion, the Triple Nickles. The three battalions in the 24th Infantry Regiment were three thousand strong and made up one-sixth of their division; still, when they arrived in Korea two weeks after the start of hostilities, African Americans (and Puerto Ricans) made up less than 10 percent of the total force.[28]

As the most famous historically Black regiment, the 24th was closely followed from home, aided by a phalanx of veteran Black reporters who frequently accompanied them into battle or interviewed them afterward. Just days after arriving in Korea, "Tan GIs Go into Action," trumpeted the Chicago Defender, describing the men of the 24th Infantry as "the first United States footsoldiers rushed into the fury of the Korean Conflict."[29] This was a slight exaggeration, but fervor could be forgiven. Even more of a stretch was their description of the 24th as coming from "strenuous maneuvers in the Tokyo area." But those easy days on occupation duty would be quickly forgotten as African American soldiers, sailors, and pilots found themselves thrown into a series of bloody battles, some of which they turned into heroic victories, much to the enthusiasm of the Black community rooting them on from the home front.

"Eyewitness Tells How Negro GIs Won First U.S. Victory: 24th Takes City," ran the headline of the Pittsburgh Courier on July 29, 1950, after the 24th helped capture the city of Yechon, and marked the first UN triumph of the newly minted police action. Black newspaper reporters could not temper their excitement. "Sputtering machine guns coughed out their staccato rattle, the sharp zing of bullets whizzed overhead—now and then thudding into the dirt—and keen-eyed tan infantrymen wormed their way forward foot by foot as they drew nearer the North Korean lines . . . [before] all hell broke loose!" Describing the sixteen hours of fighting, the paper painted a stirring racialized portrait: "Brown-skinned doughboys became spattered with blood. Some of it was their own. But most of it was that of slant-eyed North Korean Reds who found themselves in hand-to-hand combat facing America's oldest and most battle-tested and proved Negro infantry outfit."[30] Black soldiers were, said one paper, "clothed . . . in glory," their effort on the battlefield "an eloquent plea for full integration in American life."[31] The victory, after two weeks of hellish fighting and loss of territory, was most welcome, especially, as the Chicago Defender wrote, "to Negro America." The victory at Yechon was "'the big lift' in the morale of a group whose war against segregation had also been marked with the torment of defeat."[32] Between the lines, the paper seemed to suggest that the bigger victory over Jim Crow must soon follow.

That battle, however, would continue long after the conflict in Korea reached a stalemate, even after nearly all vestiges of segregation had been eradicated in the ground troops during the war itself. But in those early days, much seemed possible, even historically determined; as one newspaper noted, "negro heroes" had fought in America's wars since Crispus Attucks, and asked, "Who will be our heroes in the Korea campaign?" To African Americans, that answer was certainly the men of the 24th Infantry, at least at first, as well as those from a handful of other units. Folks at home had reason to be proud and to believe that their men would indeed be thought heroes. President Truman joined this chorus, noting on September 11, 1950, that in a war he described as "a great struggle for the minds, hearts, and loyalties of millions . . . America's Negroes are destined to play an ever more historic role. All of America is proud of our Negro fighters in Korea."[33]

The 24th Infantry continued to be closely followed by the Black press and mainstream media alike, turning into a bit of a litmus test on Black soldiers and, by extension, Black equality. Through August, Black newspapers were reporting that "our boys are demonstrating again and again that skill and courage know no color line," and even noting that "tributes to their remarkable stand have come from the entire nation's press and that all Americans are proud of their achievements."[34] This would prove to be an overstatement as the early victories of mid-July were followed by lost ground and many lost lives and, with them, eventually, the reputation of the 24th Infantry.

By mid-August 1950, the 24th Infantry had been in continuous fighting for a month straight. On August 14, the troops held the line in heavy fighting near Haman, but they were reported to be wearing tattered uniforms, lacking equipment, and taking heavy losses. The "crack regiment," a Black newspaper reported, "is continually being sent into the line without vital equipment necessary for combat and at a time when the casualties in the regiment approach a staggering total which is steadily mounting." It was also reported that some of the equipment brought with the 24th from Japan had been in such poor condition that some of the men had hired civilians to fix it when the army refused.[35] At no time, however, did the army or the mainstream media suggest that Black troops were at best getting the short end of the stick and at worst being intentionally assigned to the most difficult duty with the greatest possibility of fatalities and, ultimately, defeat.

As the late summer of 1950 ground on, UN forces continued to encounter heavy fighting and to retreat, finally being driven back all the way to Pusan, where they were able to hang on long enough to establish a defensive perimeter. The men of the 24th and other units suffered heavy casualties—as much as 50 percent—while trying, without success, to hold the line.[36] It was a tense time, with the very real possibility that the UN troops would be pushed right off the Korean peninsula. And newspapers and magazines at home made much of the retreating units, especially those who were overrun and forced to abandon positions and equipment. Much of this ire was directed at the men of the 24th Infantry, who were of course only one small component of the larger force.

The Black community was well aware that its soldiers had been unfairly singled out. As one Black reporter wrote in mid-August, "Every single regiment here has at one time or another run off and left vital equipment on the field. A better yardstick might be to compare the number of dead and wounded in the 24th with the number of the other regiments." He also pointed out that resupply drops favored white units and that the men of the 24th were supposed to fight and hold the line with broken equipment and even, at times, barefoot, since their summer clothing and boots had long since worn out.[37] They were also being led by often-unprepared white officers, such as Lt. Col. John T. Corley, who in late August was charged with threatening to shoot a Black 1st lieutenant.[38]

At last, more American troops began to arrive, along with much-needed tanks and artillery, but the tide really turned in the United Nations' favor on September 15, 1950, when General MacArthur audaciously landed a surprise attack of two amphibious divisions of US Marines at Inchon, a port on Korea's west coast, about one hundred miles south of the 38th Parallel and twenty-five miles from Seoul. Criticized as taking excessive risk, MacArthur insisted on the landing, and caught the North Koreans completely unawares, then drove his marines inland, liberating Seoul—captured by North Korea at the start of the war—within a month. Buoyed by the new forces, the 8th Army, which had hunkered down at the Pusan Perimeter, now pushed northward, breaking through the retreating North Korean force.[39]

This sudden turn of events presented the UN and US forces with a new challenge. The UN resolution supported defending South Korea against the northern invasion, not invading North Korea itself, although that is what both Syngman Rhee and MacArthur both urged. Still not believing that China or the Soviet Union would risk war in Korea, Washington backed the plan to attack north on September 27, 1950, and a UN resolution concurred a little more than a week later. United Nations forces crossed the 38th Parallel en route to the Yalu River on October 9, 1950. As in the first days of the war, segregated Black troops were again at the forefront of the offensive. In fact, the men of the 24th turned the drive toward Inchon into a competition against the other two regiments, both white, in their 25th Division, to see who would arrive first. The 24th Infantry, with the help of the all-Black 77th Combat Engineer Company cutting roads and erecting bridges, won the race.[40]

Exemplary service from Black troops did not necessitate equal treatment, however, and from the home front came increasing calls for desegregation, spurred in part by the army's recent decision to embed South Korean troops with white units on the ground. "Now is the time" to desegregate ran an editorial in the Courier newspaper. Since Koreans had been integrated into white units, it read, "for any officer to contend now that likewise integrating American Negroes into 'white' units 'would not work' becomes not only ridiculous but criminally stupid if not downright disloyal." Playing into the Red Scare and Cold War fear, the editorial argued that desegregation must be fostered immediately in order to stop the scourge of Communism: "Certainly the only way to answer effectively Soviet propaganda against American Jim Crowism is to demonstrate on the field of battle that this propaganda is false."[41] This was an argument that would gain strength throughout the building Cold War, as America tried to counter accusations of "Communist propaganda that has made the most of racial discrimination in American society as proof of our hypocraisy [sic]."[42]

The NAACP seized on the news of white-Korean integration and anti-Communism and threw its weight behind this argument immediately, announcing in September 1950 that America could not win the battle over Communism "by guns alone" but, in order to gain the allegiance of nonwhite peoples around the world, "will have to demonstrate that democracy is a living reality which knows no limitation of race, color, or nationality."[43] According to historian Mary Dudziak, "The lesson of this story was always that American democracy was a form of government that made the achievement of social justice possible and that democratic change, however slow and gradual, was superior to dictatorial imposition. The story of race in America, used to compare democracy and communism, became an important Cold War narrative."[44] In the hands of the Black press, it was used to put greater pressure on the government—if African Americans could fight and live as equals, if "Jim Crow at least doesn't wear an American uniform," went the argument, surely the superiority of the American system would be without question.[45]

With the North Korean forces largely destroyed or in hiding, the UN troops moved quickly, occupying Pyongyang, the North Korean capital, on October 19. United Nations forces moved through Pyongyang and began to set up near the Yalu River, and expectations of a quick victory seemed on the verge of realization. Eisenhower was promising turkey for Thanksgiving and victory by Christmas, and the troops were already imagining the taste of their dinners. But the Chinese don't celebrate Thanksgiving, and leaders in Washington failed to predict that China, with its massive forces of battle-hardened, trumpet-blowing, supposedly drugged and enraged soldiers, was about to enter the war on the North Korean side.

Chinese troops, in fact, had begun crossing the Yalu into North Korea in October, and by the time Americans were imagining turkey and cranberry sauce, several hundred thousand had amassed. Staying hidden in the hills, the Chinese waited until US and UN troops had passed north on the narrow mountain passes, then poured out, advancing from the front and neighboring hills while cutting off the rear. Soldiers grimly joked that the Chinese troops were formed not into platoons or battalions but into infinite hordes. "It was the most depressing, extravagant use of human resources I've ever seen," recalled Haig, "The Chinese would attack against a steel wall of heavy fire over and over and [their] bodies would be stacked up like cord wood."[46]

As the war slogged into winter, the North Koreans drove UN forces south some two hundred miles, back below the 38th Parallel again. MacArthur's stubborn advance toward the Yalu had cost dearly, with thirteen thousand UN troops dead, wounded, missing in action, or taken prisoner and thousands losing body parts to severe frostbite. As the UN troops retreated all the way back to Pusan, Black soldiers continued to be featured in some of the scant victories still to be had. Lieutenant Harry E. Sutton of the 15th Infantry Regiment of the 3rd Division was awarded a Silver Star and lent his name to Sutton's Ridge after his men held off a North Korean assault for around eighteen hours in fierce fighting outside Hungnam.[47] The ten-year army veteran, who had fought with the Triple Nickles during World War II, was not to survive the war, however, dying in another battle two months later. He would join the large number of Black soldiers lost in the first six months of the war.

African Americans had answered the call of their country, but was their country watching? Some certainly were, although their reactions must have been violently mixed. Back in Meridian, Mississippi, for example, both Blacks and whites read news in late September that the "Town's First War Dead Are Negro."[48] Fourteen years later, Meridian would be in the news for a different reason, the infamous 1964 abduction and murder of civil rights workers James Chaney, Andrew Goodman, and Mickey Schwerner. Was the sacrifice of Meridian's Black soldiers in vain?

Strangely, alleged poor performance of segregated Black soldiers and reports of superior, heroic fighting by the very same men both were forecast as speeding necessary desegregation in the army. In late August, Senator Herbert Lehman of New York had an article on the bravery of Black troops read into the record, including a line that quoted a white officer as saying, "The quicker the entire Army adopts the policy of non-segregation, the better." Lehman added that "if those troops are accorded true equality of treatment, which means non-segregation, they will fight with a greater will and a greater determination for victory in Korea in the battle against communism throughout the world."[49]

When the army announced on October 1, 1951, that the 24th Infantry Regiment would be disbanded and its men reassigned to other mixed units, with the remaining vestiges of segregation supposedly soon to be jettisoned also, the loss of a proud tradition was noted, but the majority of readers of the Black press celebrated and felt that their people deserved credit for fighting both against Communism and for desegregation. Writing in his column Civil Rights Watchdog in early August 1951, Charles Lucas said, "All Americans should be proud of the action in Korea toward integrating Negro troops with other divisions fighting under our flag" and credited Thurgood Marshall and the NAACP's exposure of "excessive and outrageous courtsmartial . . . which led to the recommendation by commanding officers in Korea to abolish the segregated pattern."[50] Lucas went on to wonder aloud why the praise that had greeted the 24th's early battle victories had turned to condemnation, "as if in a concerted effort to discredit the record of the Negro fighting men." Only in integrated units, he concluded, would they now find the respect they deserved. And the integration of the men of the 24th Infantry was just the first step, he wrote, inviting readers to keep the pressure on until all aspects of the military followed suit. "Don't relax brother, our battle is just begun. This development is only the first step. We have this segregated jinx to face here at home in scores of training camps both north and south. No, the NAACP is not satisfied to rest on the initial victory of integration covering the 24th Infantry and other Negro troops in Korea. We insist on COMPLETE CONVERSION. The army must catch up with the air force and the navy. Separate National Guard units (such as we have in Ohio) must be liquidated. Our homegrown brand of racial inequality in the armed services must be genuinely cleaned up. Stick with us a little longer and help finish the job. Let's take the other necessary steps so that we can stop apologizing to other countries for our segregated practices with our precious warriors."[51]

The deactivation of the 24th and the desegregation of the army that followed was not solely the result of the alleged poor performance by Black troops or the pressure continually applied by the Black press and groups like the NAACP. In some ways it was the eventual — if slow — result of Truman's executive order, army studies, and the work of the Fahy Committee. Although the army was still segregated by the start of the Korean War in 1950, thanks to the steps taken since 1948, chiefly the Fahy Committee's abolishment of racial quotas, integration was now a viable option. Another side effect of the army's abolishment of quotas in March 1950 was that in the first four months directly following that action, the number of African American recruits went up from 8.2 percent to 25 percent of all enlistments.[52] The hungry maw of the battlefield and its need for replacement troops regardless of color rapidly increased the timetable of army desegregation but also gave conservative army brass an out; racial integration could be attributed not to social engineering or moral certitude but to military efficiency. "Everybody knows you've got to be able to use all available manpower, and we have some 13 million Negroes," said one commander interviewed for a sociological study. "That's a vast pool."[53]

Plenty of examples were also to be found of integrated units working well. One newspaper article in early September 1950 profiled the 89th Medium Tank Battalion, which after a scant three weeks of fighting had racked up a strong record based on interracial cooperation: "Tan Yanks are integrated in almost every level of the tank crews. They include commanders, drivers and gun loaders. Prime requirement of the five-man crews is that the men be able to work together in harmony . . . [since] close contact in the small chamber of a rolling hulk of armored steel requires good comradeship, and unity of purpose." Particularly striking was that most of the white soldiers were from the South, had knowingly volunteered for the mixed unit, "and many state that they would not have it any other way." The white commanding officer of Able Company, Capt. James Harvey of Los Angeles, summed it up: "All of our colored personnel are darn good. We would not trade them for whites. That's a true picture of what we think of the fellows."[54]

Desegregation, coming as it did after the abolishment of racial quotas, also coincided with an overall growth in African American troops as Black enlistment and reenlistment rates increased and the proportion of Africans Americans in the army, for example, rose from 10.2 percent in April 1950 to 11.7 percent in January 1951. And just as had happened with desegregation of military bases stateside, the proclivities of certain commanders also hastened integration, especially within the hard-hit 9th Regiment. Those commanders of the 9th who embraced desegregation saw their battalions perform especially well, which did not go unnoticed by military analysts, who also noted that by May 1951, 61 percent of combat infantry companies in Korea were now racially integrated to some extent.[55] This fact is interesting for both how quickly desegregation moved once it started and how bold-faced the lie was that desegregation was widespread by the beginning of the war.

Encouraging reports from newly desegregated units on the front lines also indicated the psychological impact that desegregation could have on the weary troops. Warrant Officer Raymond Burden, for example, returned stateside in October 1951 after thirteen months with the 573rd Engineers Pontoon Bridge Company, reporting that "the mixing of the fighting units has done more to boost morale than anything else could possibly have done. They've gone all the way too. Even the 1st Cavalry is integrated and the men are getting along together, understanding each other, fighting together like real teammates." This was notable, the reporter added, because the 1st Cavalry, while on occupation duty in Tokyo following World War II, had earned a reputation as "Negro haters."[56] If the racists of the 1st Cav could embrace Blacks in their unit, it seemed to say, then this segregation thing would not be nearly as hard to topple as predicted.

Still, as willing as the troops on the ground may have been to embrace their new colleagues, segregationist attitudes remained deeply entrenched among some at the top of military leadership, especially in the US Army. General MacArthur had favored retaining segregation, and his second in command, Lt. Gen. Mark Almond, was known as one of the fiercest segregationists, and most personally prejudiced leaders, in the military. Learning of the quick progress toward desegregating the 9th Regiment, Almond tried to stop it, ordering further study and instructing his new 2nd Division commander, Maj. Gen. Clark L. Ruffner, to cease placing Blacks in "white" combat troops and to use new replacements to restore the previous segregation of the units. Ruffner was a believer in desegregation, however, and subverted the order by assigning Blacks to white noncombat units until a further change in command could replace Almond.[57] And when Truman relieved MacArthur of command in April 1951, at a time that MacArthur's Tokyo staff was still grinding through a study of Black troops, hope was raised that his segregationist ways would be on the way out, that "now that General MacArthur has been fired, why not fire General Jim Crow too? He must be fired for the sake of democracy."[58]

MacArthur's replacement, Gen. Matthew B. Ridgway, favored action over surveys. Even as the independent Operations Research Office at Johns Hopkins University began a major study of the social implications of military integration, to become known as Project Clear, which would become one of the defining products of the Korean War era, Ridgway was moving forward. He considered segregation to be demeaning, to inhibit growth and leadership, and to be "both un-American and un-Christian." Ridgway believed that integration would both encourage fighting spirit and make best use of the personnel at his command. Project Clear revealed that a slight majority of troops in Korea were actually hesitant about desegregating, but in May 1951, their commander abolished racial segregation in the 8th Army and throughout the Far East Command. Although Project Clear recommended that African Americans make up no more than 20 percent of the army, even in integrated units, by 1951, Blacks would account for 30 percent of all combat replacements. Mark Almond was reassigned from commanding X Corps to become president of the Army War College, and he left Korea in July. The 24th would be decommissioned on October 1, and smaller units would be gradually desegregated through color-blind troop assignments and guided by an informal maximum of 12 percent African Americans in any one unit.[59] By the end of the month, 75 percent of the 8th Army had been desegregated, with completion within the Far East Command supposedly achieved by May 1952.

Sometimes the version of events that becomes accepted as historical fact differs to greater or smaller degrees than that experienced on the ground. Ralph Hockley, a white Jewish artillery officer with the 2nd Infantry Division in Korea, remembers a very distinctive version of how desegregation was instituted in October 1951:

> I know what Ridgway says, but the actual thing that happened to change it from one day to the next was that in 1951 General MacArthur's assistant secretary of defense was a little lady about five foot tall by the name of Anna Rosenberg, who was an advertising executive in New York. And I don't know how General MacArthur knew her, but he took her and made her assistant secretary of defense [in November 1950]. And Anna Rosenberg came to Korea in 1951, and she got rid of the [racist] generals. She talked to the troops, and somewhere she became aware of the fact that the army in Korea was not integrated. And after she researched that and asked enough questions, at the end of her stay she got ahold of the top generals, and she gave them two weeks to integrate the army in Korea. From my personal experience that's what happened.
>
> At the end of October or beginning of November I got called in. By this time I'd been in Korea for over a year, and I was the only guy I know who got seven combat stars, but the last two months, after being in the 37th Battalion, in the middle of October I was transferred into the 87th Anti-Aircraft Battalion as a platoon commander. And while I had this

platoon, I was called in and they said, "Okay, tomorrow morning you're going to receive ten Black soldiers. Use them as you see fit." They were all from the 9th Infantry. They busted up the 3rd Battalion of the 9th Infantry, the Black battalion. In so doing everybody got some of their soldiers. There wasn't a document that was handed to me that said what the army wants you to do.

So I decided that I would take one of these soldiers and assign them to each squad. So I would have one at each squad plus two at HQ. There was one sergeant, there were two corporals, and the rest were privates according to class, and I assigned the sergeant as an assistant squad leader, and I assigned them to different vehicles, and that was my integration. When I assigned them, . . . I told [the sergeants,] "As far as I'm concerned, they're American soldiers [and] they're going to be treated no better or worse than any soldiers that you've had."

Four weeks later, all the sergeants asked to talk to me. And they said, "Lieutenant, we have heard that the army or the division is being cut back by 10 percent"—which I knew nothing about, probably a rumor in the first place—"but we just wanted to ask you, if you have to make a decision on releasing 10 percent of the platoon, that you keep the Black soldiers." And they said that they wanted me to know that since the Black soldiers had been assigned to the platoon, morale problems had absolutely disappeared.

There is some kind of moral to this story. A soldier whether Black or white is a soldier. He can be a good soldier or a bad soldier, but whether he's Black or white doesn't mean he's good or bad. My experiences have been that it's the individual who counts, not his background of any type.[60]

By the beginning of January 1953, the Black press at home was declaring desegregation a success. "The U.S. Army has effected a major social revolution in Korea by abolishing racial segregation and the troops today are fighting better because of the change," read an article in the Chicago Defender, adding that the process seemed to have gone smoothly. "A frontline [white] private commented: 'When the commies start moving in, you don't care whether a guy is Black or has two heads. . . . All you care about is can he fight? These boys are fighting." Acknowledging that "social significance is more or less secondary since the Army is mainly interested in increasing combat efficiency" did not diminish the achievement.[61] And observing it gave those who championed civil rights hope that it would serve as an example for more widespread change. By May 1953, one reporter in Korea claimed that "the word 'race' seems to have been abolished and a man's color or kind roams about unnoticed. Out of the blood and stench and dust and mud of this battleground someone has found a solution to the race problem."[62]

Pockets of segregation persisted, however, often in National Guard units and in some stateside training camps that maintained Jim Crow at the whim of their commanders. Even where it gave way, some army leaders refused to change their long-held opinions; Gen. Mark Clark, former UN commander in the Far East, never ceased his support of a segregated Jim Crow military and in 1956, three years after the war had ended, still insisted on the inadequacies of Black soldiers and that desegregation was therefore the wrong move from "a military standpoint."[63] Some southern senators objected as well, but their voices were soon drowned out, at least when it came to racial policies in the military, and in 1954 the army's official report on desegregation was published, titled "Breakthrough on the Color Front." On October 30, 1954, the secretary of defense announced that no segregated units still survived in the United States Armed Forces.[64]

The armed forces, of course, were far bigger than just the US Army, and each branch had its own unique path toward ultimate desegregation. The Marine Corps' story of segregation and its eventual dismantling followed a path similar to that of the army, but perhaps even more so. Whereas the army went to war in Korea with some segregated and some mixed units, Marine Corps leaders utterly ignored Truman's desegregation order and entered the Korean War strictly segregated. Black marines served only in noncombat positions, half of them as stewards. As early as the first few months of the war, however, the Marine Corps began to experience troop shortages that prompted the shifting of Black service units into combat augmenting the 1st Marine Division. On the ground, given the choice of maintaining segregation or sending raw service personnel into deadly combat unaccompanied, many field commanders chose to break up the Black units and distribute the men among experienced combat troops.[65] Some Black marines found themselves single-handedly integrating a white company, as Private 1st Class Richard B. Dinkins of Columbia, South Carolina, did with a company in the 5th Marine Regiment. In general, those experiences went relatively smoothly; in Dinkins's case an awkward moment of silence at this arrival was quickly dispelled when a tall, white Texan invited him to share his shelter. Over the next few months, Dinkins went on to become the best marksman in the company, with an estimated eighty-five kills by the start of December 1950. Echoing the "no color in a foxhole" sentiment that would become gospel in years to come, his company commander noted that on the front lines, "we don't worry about color much up here. They're all Marines to me."[66]

Interestingly, the fighting esprit of still segregated Black soldiers in the army may have also done something to convince the marines that African Americans could fight. In early October, the commander of the 1st Marine Division sent an official letter of thanks to the all-Black 96th Field Artillery Battalion "for giving brilliant and effective support and saving the lives of many leathernecks."[67] And as in the army, once in the Marine Corps, African Americans like Dinkins proved themselves on the line, and in August the first, experimental racially integrated replacement units landed, arriving from Camp Lejeune and Camp Pendleton.[68] When the Marine Corps conducted an official review of its racial policies in the fall of 1951, it resulted in a December decree that from then on men would be assigned regardless of race. Throughout 1952, this policy rendered the remaining segregated units officially desegregated, and Black marine enlistment skyrocketed, rising from 1.6 percent of all marines at the start of the war to 6 percent by the time of the truce in July 1953.

The postwar Marine Corps still did feel some repercussions of its previous policies, however. Although now mandated to be open, the Steward Branch had no success placing whites and such a strong decline from Blacks that major personnel shortfalls and poor morale resulted. Worse still, was a stipulation in Marine Corps regulations that Black NCOs could be barred from certain positions if such was "in the overriding interest to the Marine Corps."[69] Thus certain commanders excluded Black NCOs in certain southern towns where the locals objected, and some special services also refused them entry, especially to positions in honor guards or other units with public standing. Thus, even though officially eradicated, racist segregation persisted in small pockets of the Marine Corps for years.

Of all the branches of the military, the US Air Force had acted most quickly on Truman's order, and by the time his Fahy Committee held its first meeting on January 12, 1949, an air force desegregation plan was sitting on the table. Beyond abandoning segregated units, it called for abolishing racial quotas and standardizing and integrating all training. Some reported general wariness about integrating barracks or banning African Americans entirely from air force service soon gave way to acceptance of an organized and systematic implementation of the new policies, with the general overseeing Lackland Air Force Base in San Antonio, for example, reporting that "the integration of the base was accomplished with complete harmony" among the twenty-six thousand troops stationed there.[70] But despite the air force's commitment to ending segregation in both operations and training, some neighbors of its southern bases had other ideas, and a few Dixiecrat senators vowed to ban Black airmen from "white bases." The air force simply ignored the senators, although the branch was not immune from local laws and the same bus incidents that plagued the army visited themselves upon the air force. Black airmen from Maxwell Field were forced to sit in the rear of Montgomery, Alabama, public buses taking them to and from the field, and the white woman managing the segregated USOS refused to combine them despite a national order.[71] The air force, however, was putting pressure on southern mores, and it was indeed a sign of things to come, especially concerning the segregated bus system of Montgomery, where Martin Luther King Jr. would rise to prominence as the leader of a bus boycott just a few years later.

After the bases came desegregating the forces themselves, which proceeded apace. When the 332nd Fighter Wing, which had an unfortunate reputation for lacking battle readiness, was disbanded, its men were fairly reviewed on their own merits and 95 percent of them retained in the service and reassigned. With the successful reassignment complete, the air force quickly moved toward attempting full integration. On July 15, 1950, two weeks into the Korean War, the Pittsburgh Courier reported that "tan flyers are well integrated . . . and are taking part in all phases of the operations over Korea . . . [and] are turning in commendable performances." Indeed, the paper said, the "great results" the Air Corps had achieved in integrating its men were "one of the main reasons why embattered US forces are still able to cling to even a foothold in the rugged South Korean fighting." In the nineteen Air Corps units under the 5th Air Force Command in Korea, eighteen were integrated and the last was about to be. "Integration over here is spelled A-I-R C-O-R-P-S and the Air Corps likes it that way."[72] Although it hadn't reached this goal by the beginning of the Korean War, by the end of 1950 the air force was 95 percent desegregated, with the final vestiges eradicated by 1952.[73]

The air force also gave the US forces one of its first Black military heroes of the war, fighter pilot Capt. Daniel "Chappie" James, who commanded a squadron of white flyers, flew sixty-four combat missions over Korea, and survived two crash landings. His exploits were followed closely by African Americans during and after the war, when, as leader of the 437th Interceptor Squadron, he commanded four hundred white airmen.[74] The other Black hero to emerge during the Korean War period was Benjamin Oliver Davis Jr., son of famed US Army brigadier general Benjamin O. Davis, and in 1954 himself made a general, in charge of the operations and training for the Far East Air Forces. Although he "avoided becoming involved in nebulous racial conflicts," his achievements were held up as an "inspiration to Negro air crews" and proof of the legitimacy of equality of treatment and opportunity in the air force.[75]

Another Black pilot hero emerged from the US Navy, which moved toward desegregation with even fewer difficulties than the air force. The navy's post–World War II racial policies were already mostly in line with what was called for by Truman's executive order and then elaborated on by the Fahy Committee. Unlike during World War II, when most African Americans in the navy served as messmen and cooks in the Steward Branch, afterward they were widely dispersed among the specialties and were fully integrated in training and living arrangements. Their numbers remained low, however, and there was a paucity of Black officers, who had arrived in the navy only in 1947, with just five on active duty when the Fahy Committee first met in early 1949.[76] The committee concluded that despite the racial changes it had instituted, the navy had done little to publicize them and to alert African Americans that they could now do more in the navy than wash dishes. In May 1949, the Fahy Committee declared that the navy would have to better publicize its racially equal opportunities, standardize promotional opportunities within the Steward Branch, and reform its entrance standards to along the lines of those of the army for the purposes of allowing greater Black participation.

Some of these now challenged practices had taken on the form of cherished naval traditions, and letting them go proved difficult, although the navy did accede to all changes but lowering its entrance standards. And although it showed good faith in implementing these changes over the next several years, results came slowly. Whereas in 1949, 65.1 percent of all Black sailors were in the Steward Branch, that figure fell by 1953 to 51.7 percent, even though the Steward Branch itself still hired few whites. Despite its efforts to integrate, the navy's overall percentage of Black sailors fell during the Korean War years. The experience of naval desegregation was a stark lesson that traditions and public perception would be almost as difficult to overcome as de jure segregation and could often amount to de facto.[77]

A great deal of visibility, however, was accorded a few Black naval flyers, most notably Ensign Jesse L. Brown, called "one of the best pilots in the air group" by his carrier commander. Brown, who in 1948 had become the first Black naval aviator to earn his wings, on October 13, 1950, also became the first to fly a combat mission, taking out a series of railway targets near Chonji, Korea.[78] He set another unfortunate record in December, however, when he became the first Black naval officer to lose his life at war, succumbing to injuries sustained in a fiery crash. A fellow white flyer from his unit, Lt. Thomas J. Hudner, attempted a daring rescue for which he would later be awarded the Medal of Honor, landing his own plane next to Brown's well beyond enemy lines and attempting to extinguish the engine fire with clumps of snow.[79] This act of selflessness for a Black colleague was in itself an important statement about equality and overcoming racism.

Beyond the naval flyers, other Black seaman played crucial rolls in the war from its first days. Artillery bombardment from ships at sea helped "soften up" the lines for army ground troops, and one admiral described "splendid coordination as an integrated crew under wartime conditions."[80] A review by a reporter for the Black newspaper the Chicago Defender found in September 1950, however, that the crew of the aircraft carrier Philippine Sea had less than 10 percent African Americans among its crew and that most of these were in the Steward

Branch. Still, the navy, with its limited successes, was heading toward desegregation and equality of opportunity.[81]

Changes were also slowly coming for those few African American women who served in Korea during the war; in fact, at the beginning of the conflict, only even thousand nurses of all races were in the armed forces, and only a few hundred served in-country despite a continuous call for more. The draft never applied to women, and so all females were volunteers. The first army nurses to arrive did so almost immediately after North Korea's invasion, establishing a hospital in Pusan in July 1950 that by August had nearly a hundred nurses on staff. By the spring of 1951, the army had more than three hundred nurses working throughout Korea, and a small number of air force and navy nurses staffed air evacuation teams and hospital ships. And although most women in the war effort were restricted to positions as nurses, they often not only did unsupervised medical procedures that would normally done by doctors stateside but were the ranking officers on hospital trains and evacuation flights. Indeed, the workload and responsibilities afforded many women a chance for relatively quick advancement in rank. As was the case for men, desegregation in the armed services for Black women mostly came about during the war itself, often out of necessity. The army was the only branch that had enlisted and commissioned significant numbers of African American women in World War II; now the air force and navy saw more Black women enlist and become officers, and women were among the first African Americans to serve in the Marine Corps.[82]

At the start of the war, women's official status in the armed forces was still relatively new, having been won only a few years earlier by the passage of the Army-Navy Nurse Act in 1947, followed by 1948's Women's Armed Services Integration Act. While these acts created opportunities, they also limited them, for example setting the maximum for the Women's Army Corps at 7,500, with 500 officers and the maximum number of female officers throughout the services at no more than 2 percent of the total. It also continued to apply a 10 percent quota for African American WACs and to segregate Black servicewomen through at least the mid-1950s. All Black WACs entering training were assigned to the same segregated company, and despite Truman's executive order and the dismantling of segregation among men in Korea during the war, women's training and facilities remained segregated, with the only exceptions being women's Officer Candidate School and certain army specialist schools.[83]

Mary (Smith) Teague's experience was typical. When she enlisted in November 1948, she ended up in the Women's Army Corps after the US Navy told her it was not enlisting African American women at all and the air force reported that it had filled its quota. She proceeded to segregated basic training, followed by integrated OCS and leadership schools, and then, following her commission as a 2nd lieutenant, was assigned back to segregated units. When she complained

up the chain of command that white women from other units were being promoted faster than women in her segregated unit, she found herself transferred
to Japan while nothing was done about the discrepancies in promotions. "I will
always believe they reassigned me to get rid of a troublemaker," she later recalled.[84] And Lt. Col. Lucy Bond, although she enlisted after army integration
was supposedly official, found herself segregated from white troops she was es-
corting on a stateside train. "It was frustrating," she said, "but there was nothing I could do about it."[85]

The Marine Corps added its first two Black women in 1949 and a third in
1950. The air force, as we have seen, was relatively quick to respond to Truman's
order, with the last segregated classes going through at the end of 1948. The first
air force women into the Asian theater was a squadron of forty-eight assigned to
Tokyo in September 1950. African American army women came in even more
slowly, with the first six Black nurses arriving in early 1951, such a novelty that
it made national news stateside, while less than a handful actually served in-
country.[86] One to do so was Sgt. Eleanor Yorke, a six-year army veteran from
Orange, New Jersey, who worked twenty-eight months in Japan and then eight
months near the Korean front lines before being rotated stateside in October
1951. Serving with a mobile surgical unit, she said she treated the wounded "20
to 45 minutes after they were hit." She described an endless parade of helicopters
and ambulances bring in the wounded and being "rocked to sleep in my Army
cot" by the sound of artillery fire. "It was a terrible eight months but I was too
busy to be scared."[87] Black newspapers reported that at the same time that that
army was publicizing a great need for nurses, nursing training programs were refusing to admit Black women.[88] Yokohama, Japan, emerged as having the greatest number of African American women at the time, including about a hundred
WACS and about fifty Red Cross volunteers. Sylvia Rock recalled that as a Black
Red Cross worker in Tokyo in the fall of 1950, she was such an anomaly that
"when I walked down the street, I would be surrounded by crowds of people who
would gingerly touch me to feel my skin, my hair, and my clothes. People turned
around while driving to watch me on the street. I have never felt so conspicuous
in all my life." Visiting a nightclub in Yokohama, she found it as segregated as if
"I were back in Harlem."[89] Jim Crow may have been starting to slip in the military, but there was still a long way to go before it would fall in the United States
or in those foreign countries that hosted its military forces. Those changes that
had come about so far, and would be steps on the path from segregation to desegregation to integration, did so because of the war itself.

4

African Americans and the US Army in Battle

Segregated Units

African Americans in both integrated and segregated units were among the first troops into Korea. While much has been made of the 24th Infantry of the 25th Division, African American soldiers served in a number of segregated units from the front lines to the rear. Their stories reveal that the Black experience of Korea in those first bloody months was far from universal. The 9th Infantry of the 2nd Infantry Division, for example, was understrength when it was ordered up and consequently found itself training truck drivers for combat through shooting practice off the back of the transport ship. As we will see below, there was some difference of opinion between the officers and the enlisted men on exactly how prepared they were for battle. When the men landed in Korea early in the war, a seemingly racist decision sent the all-Black outfit away from the rest of their division and off to guard an airfield. But when they were sent into combat, still segregated, they were more than up for the fight.

JULIUS W. BECTON JR., SPRINGFIELD, VIRGINIA

[I am] Julius W. Becton Jr., retired lieutenant general. [I] was in the 2nd Infantry Division, 3rd Battalion, 9th Infantry. Started in Saint Louis, and we were the first major unit to go to Korea.

I had just gotten married in January of '48. We were expecting a child due in December and I was a premed student in Muhlenberg College, the first Black to attend. We were having trouble making ends meet. We had just bought a home with the money I saved from World War II, and I realized that as a premed student that I really didn't want to be a medical doctor. I had liked what I had done when I was in the military. So, I came back on active duty, requested recall, and received it. That was in '48.

When I was recalled to active duty, I applied for a regular army appointment. It was important to me that if I was going to be a career soldier, I do so as a regular officer, not as a reservist. That was because I thought I would have a fair chance with the integrated army, which I thought could happen right away. [It] did not, I might add. I had competed both in OCS and as an officer before. Look, I had been around long enough to understand that a lot of things might be said at the top, [but] what happens at the bottom is going to take a long time to make a difference. [Integration] was a good example of that. Senior leadership was opposed.

It goes back to prerevolutionary days, when Blacks were used only when they had to be used. Blacks were considered to be slovenly, lazy, untrainable, and certainly could not lead anybody. [African Americans were mistreated] in every case from the Brownsville incident, which took place in 1906, where Blacks were blamed for something that never happened, to World War I where the 15th Regiment, which became the 369 Infantry Regiment, was assigned to the French because Pershing and the American military leadership did not want Blacks fighting as such. They went to the front and did a very fine job, [a] commendable job. [In] World War II [there was] complete segregation until the Battle of the Bulge took place, where they went looking for volunteers and they got volunteers to come into units to integrate it and they also took in platoons — Blacks being led by whites — and they found out that they [could] make it. But as soon as that was over, they reverted back because [they] did not want to have . . . Blacks leading whites.

[But] when we went to Korea, we had a Black commander. He was a Black lieutenant colonel, a PhD from Leland Stanford [Junior University], which you don't find too many of. [He was a] hard taskmaster, but he was going to make sure that [as] the only Black battalion in that division, we were the best battalion in the division. He had orders in April of 1950 reassigning him to an ROTC assignment, but he was not supposed to leave till summer. So, when the 25th of June took place, he was still there, and a lot of us felt that the army would change his reassignment orders and leave him there. Wrong, they did not. They brought back Lt. Colonel Chase, who was white, the commander who had the battalion before. Again [an] example of "We cannot afford the appearance of Blacks being in charge." Of course, [I] didn't know all those things back in 1948, but I felt there was a better chance [for advancement] than there had been.

I was recalled as a lieutenant, in fact 2nd lieutenant, because I received a terminal-leave promotion at the end of World War II. So, when I [was] recalled as 2nd lieutenant, I didn't talk to generals, but I can tell you what was published. There was a complete rejection of having people in combat when there may [be] a question of their character and capability. I was not in the inner circles, but when the 2nd Division arrived in Korea — we were the 1st Regiment, the 9th Infantry — we arrived [in] Pusan, they took our battalion and sent us off on a separate mission, not with the division, not with the regiment. And we were sent to P'ohong-dong to provide security for an airfield. No one told the soldiers, or a young lieutenant, why they did this. I later found out, when I went back to the archives and looked, there was a great discussion back in MacArthur's headquarters: What about this Black battalion? 'Cause the 24th had already been there and they had their own problems. I didn't know that at the time. I had no way of knowing it. The whole army was in pretty bad shape in Korea. And they said, "Well, we have to break them [in] easily." This is recorded history. [They] weren't too sure of this 3rd Battalion, so they sent us off by ourselves. And we rejoined the regiment about a month later, after we had, quote, "proven" ourselves.

That too is an example of the thinking [at that time]. Ned Almond, lieutenant general, commander of the 2nd Division, is considered by a lot of folks to be a racist. He had the 92nd [during World War II], therefore he was considered to be an expert about the Black military. He was now the corps commander under MacArthur, [and] apparently he was listened to. As a result, we went off our separate ways.

Providing security for an airfield is not all that difficult, [but] from a personal standpoint, this is one of those examples [of being put in harm's way]. Right before the battalion moved out to P'ohong-dong, I got pulled out of my company—I was a platoon leader—and I was told to report to Taegu [now Daegu], regimental headquarters. I had no idea why. I had a squad of soldiers. Once we arrived, we were given transport and were told to escort a radio rig, [a] truck, [from] Taegu to P'ohong-dong. I later found out that was to be the radio link with army headquarters. The battalion became part of a task force that went off on this mission, but we were the major elements of the task force. And it was our job, the radio rig's job, to maintain communications with [the] division, MacArthur's headquarters, and everyone else.

[For] the road that we took, I was given a map and a sketch. I asked a question, "Is there any reported enemy activity?" "Nope, clear." So, we tool down this road and arrived in P'ohong-dong, and an hour later, when the battalion started down this road, they got ambushed. Didn't do a lot of damage, killed a couple soldiers. Point being, they were there when I went down this road and they let us go through, the North Koreans. They could have done far more damage if they had knocked us out because we had an important piece of equipment. So, was there danger? No matter where you are in combat, there's always danger.

[Now,] go back before the war and look at what the units were doing in Japan. The 25th Division was there with its three regiments, and they were having more good time[s] than they were training. They were excelling in athletics, marching, and drill. They were excelling in VD, drug use, all those negative things that impact the unit. Not just the 24th [Regiment], that was typical of the [whole] division, Black and white. As a result, you have the leadership above the 24th — when you have a segregated unit, you don't have a lot of hard-charging officers wanting to get there. If they're white, it's a no-win situation. With the Blacks, there were not that many senior officers. You have a major or a lieutenant colonel that are either a medic or a chaplain, but not that many field-grade officers who are combat arms. So, you don't have the best of leadership, [and] you certainly don't have the best of equipment [or] training opportunity.

But the 24th Regiment trained in Gifu. For all practical purposes, it was a Black island, they had everything. When you have a segregated unit, you always have in your mind, "How it is on the other side?" Grass is greener on the other side. You never know. [But] I don't think the 24th was treated any different in terms of pre-Korea. Once they got to Korea and had some of the challenges that [they] were faced with, what everyone was faced with, it became a much bigger visibility when what happened to the 24th did happen. [They were the] only unit that got disbanded later.

Not everyone went over with the proper equipment. . . . We had summer clothing. I've been cold in my life and probably been colder [than in Korea], but I don't remember when. There you didn't really appreciate how cold it was, you had nothing else to do. You were there. What you had on was what you had, no need to complain. Everyone looked like you. And those idiots who built fires to keep warm — we found out when the Chinese came in — they became an aiming point for artillery and mortars. So yes, we were ill-equipped. And [was] that true for everybody? I suspect so. But when you have the perception of a segregated unit, a unit that is not being equal, that is happening to *you*. So that is one of the problems . . . you *believe* that there are people getting the proper equipment because . . . we know that the whites always get things better than we do. It doesn't do you any good to bitch and moan and groan about what you don't have. But I later found out that it wasn't just the Black units; everybody was suffering the same thing. We didn't have the proper equipment.

[The army units] were not in great condition [overall]. Take my unit, the 2nd Division that came in from Fort Lewis. We did a lot of training, but the day the war started we had 120 some people in our company [and] we should have had 186. When we arrived in country, we had 186. Now who were those people that we got as replacements? Were they well-trained infantrymen right out of basic training? Hell, no. We got all the rag-tags from the West Coast. They emptied out the stockades. Drivers and port people who knew nothing about infantry. We gave them orientation on the fantail of the ship as they fired their weapon for the first time, shooting off into the water. No way to train in terms of tactics. That's what we went with. And we weren't by ourselves; most of the army got [untrained personnel and] was understaffed. We were still following the falloff from World War II. People with the army in those days, in many cases, were not the serious veterans. They were folks who wanted some adventure, couldn't do anything else. In those days, they still had the draft, and sometimes in certain places, you got the choice [of] either jail or the army. You had some students who couldn't make it in school. It was not a pretty sight. I'm talking 1949, 1950.

We had had several small attacks in P'ohang as we provided security for the airfield. We had some patrol action against the North Koreans, [so] we felt pretty good about ourselves when we were put back with the regiment. The regiment was happy to see us because they knew how good we could be. We had trained together back in Fort Lewis. Same officers. They were getting in a posture to break out of the Pusan Perimeter and cross the Naktong and start back up north. Five or seven days [later], as we were breaking out of the Pusan Perimeter, I had my first combat wound. For the next six weeks. I was resting, recuperating in Japan. But the regiment did break the perimeter, cross the Naktong, and start back out to Seoul. Not much later they had the landing at Inchon and attack[ed] up into North Korea. By that time the regiment was integrated. We had not a large number of white soldiers, but we had Black commanders, company commanders in the 1st and 2nd Battalion[s]. [We were] well on the way to doing the right thing.

When the Chinese crossed the border up in North Korea, I got my second wound, and that probably saved my life. If you read *River and the Gauntlet*, it described the 2nd Division and the problems that it had. That was right down [from] our regiment, just south of Kunu-ri. The 3rd Battalion, 9th Infantry, was on the left flank of the division, the 2nd Battalion, 24th, was on the right flank. I [wasn't thinking about the 24th much because] right before the Chinese came in full bore, you were only concerned about the real estate you're standing on and the folks to your right, left, you don't pay attention to that unit. Nice to know there's another Black unit over there, but so what? As long as they're qualified and can protect your flank.

I got wounded because of [an] interesting discussion: the 2nd Battalion commander from the 24th was talking to my battalion commander, and I had come off a hill adjacent to where they were. We had sustained fire, and I came back to report to the operations officer what I had found. The major from the 24th said, "I don't believe that, there's no enemy here. We haven't had any contact, I don't think you've had any contact either." My battalion commander took offense to it, but he complied. "Becton, get back up there." I go tooling back up the hill with my platoon, and within two hours, I get shot and I come back down and they're still there. "And are you satisfied now with the comment I made?"

From our battalion we had five officers escape with a handful of enlisted soldiers. And one of the people to escape was a chaplain. I had gotten wounded two days before all this happened and I was evacuated back and flown by aircraft to Japan. The officers in my company who survived all that, one was captured and one escaped. Wasn't [a] very pleasant time. But I point out that I've been very fortunate. This time the round that I took was almost a spent round. It went into my left ankle at the Achilles heel and it went between the bone and the tendon. It didn't touch either. Not much space down there. If [it] had varied, I would have been crippled [for the] rest of my life. All I have is a mark and that's it. I did have a chance to make a snide remark to this major from the 24th, who was white by the way. I was rather outspoken in those days to be a lieutenant and survive. [But] my battalion commander wouldn't have let [any repercussions] happen. I'm his boy, let's face it.

The rumors [about the 24th] had been there from the very beginning. The "bugout blues," stuff like that. But that happened to other units. It just happened that this was a Black unit. Was I concerned about them leaving us? No. I probably knew the lieutenants over there, because the army is not that big in those days and you get to know each other, and you put a lot of faith in each other.

I did not [witness any "bugging out"]. The closest thing we had to that was a battle that we had south of Naktong when we rejoined the regiment. I was leading a patrol up a hill, and back in training, we would have many bull sessions and I made a statement that, "If any of you ran away from the enemy in my unit, I would probably kill you." They looked at me, "You wouldn't do that." Reason why I said that is if you run away, I will have less people to do the job and you're not doing us any good. Some of that was just being boisterous and some I really felt. I can recall days of veterans of World War II telling how they would get soldiers to get out of trenches to move forward. Fear on the field — you deal with that by overcoming that [fear], and if you have a soldier that will not get out of the trenches, you have to put [him in] greater fear. Best way is to drop a grenade. They have a choice, stay and get blown away, or get out and go with you. [So] I said to my guys, "You run and I'll shoot you."

In August we were going up this hill, near the top of it, close-air support of the US Air Force were being called in to help us, and they hit the wrong hill, they hit the hill we were on. When they came in the first time, we hugged the ground very tight, 'cause you want to get as small as you can, and they didn't hurt anybody. As they came around again, some of my guys went running back down the hill and I took one look and without even thinking about it I unloaded my carbine in front of them. They knew I was shooting in front of them and some of them remembered what I had said. Same time as the plane was coming around, my messenger jumped up and took our panels and waved it in front of the pilot. The pilot then recognized that they were in front of the wrong hill. They dipped their wings and went over to the next hill. My guys got back up the hill, and I put the messenger in for [a medal,] he got a Silver Star for that. After we got off the hill, a couple of the guys said, "Hey, would you really do that?" I said, "What you think?" And the answer is that I probably would because the one thing we did not need to do was to show the enemy or those fighter pilots that they got the right target 'cause we're running from them. We were able to reestablish the lines. So "bugout," if you call that a bugout, then it happened, [the] quote, "perception of bugging out." But the perception [of the army brass] was, "We told you." The army leadership [felt] the "bugging out" reinforced what they had said. It [gave] substance to the argument that Blacks are not to be trusted. [They said] nothing about the 27th Regiment or the other regiments that [also] did do that. [And] the white regiments had the same problems. I don't have feelings or views on whether it was a conscious decision to have this approach [to retreating problems] or this was a coincidence. America has had such a sordid history in terms of race relations, you become almost immune and you assume that this is the way it should be. In a Black unit, I had to convince the soldiers under my control that we're just as good as anyone. And given an opportunity, we'll prove it.

We heard radio propaganda [directed to Black soldiers], not a great deal but some of it. "Hey, give up. Why are you fighting for a country that treats you like that?" Same as they used elsewhere — they used it in Europe, and you can find the same thing. Bet you I can find places in Afghanistan and Iraq where we're dropping leaflets. It's part of warfare. Remember I was a lieutenant and we are not supposed to know anything [about politics,] just get out there and lead. Now if you said later on, when I had a chance to become a battalion commander or division commander or corps commander, we did a lot of talking.

But [I will] also tell you that, I'm told in the Kunu-ri area, as the units were moving south without any discipline and control, the historians have pretty accurately described what took place. A mob action, not pleasant. [But] we felt pretty good about [our] unit. Even though we had people coming in who were brand-new, it didn't take them long to find out the way we did business. We were a pretty good unit. [And there's] no question about the way we were treated compared to the 24th. [Blacks were disproportionately court-martialed in Korea,] yes, that's a no-brainer. Take a look at today's prison population. I don't think the crime wave is that much greater, Black versus white. But clearly in capital punishment, when you look at those on death row, it doesn't make any sense. So I think this is a cultural thing.

Again, we didn't have the problems that they had in Gifu, no port duty, no VD, didn't have absence of family and [too much] booze. Our families were with us in Fort Lewis, we were able to live together and train together. Also we were part of a regiment, part of a family, [although] a couple of things happened that might make you say, that's not quite accurate.

The Black officers I knew were good at what they did. Very good. [There were] a lot of good white officers who knew that. Our regimental commander knew how good we were. And he reinforced what we did. Of course we had idiots like that lieutenant colonel, but you have that around. I dealt with that all my life and you find ways to get around it. It's not that critical. So what else is new? A lot of people ask, why would you or people who look like you put your life on the line for a country where you get secondhand treatment? Answer is simple—there's always the hope that things can get better.

Julius W. Becton Jr.
Lieutenant general, 542nd Heavy Construction Company; 369th
    Infantry Regiment, 93rd Infantry Division; K Company and
    L Company, 9th Infantry Regiment; 101st Airborne Division
US Army Air Forces/Corps; US Army
Interview by Kate Ellis and Stephen Smith, February 2003, Springfield, VA
American RadioWorks, Minnesota Public Radio

GERALD BAILEY JR., BLOOMINGTON, MINNESOTA

We were prepared for combat because of the constant maneuvers we did. And when word came that a war was starting over there, at least the invasion of the South, it wasn't unexpected that we would go, even though none of us really wanted to. Why were we going? I guess because an ally of ours was being invaded. War was never declared against Korea, so President Truman was using his powers and calling it a police action so that he didn't have to declare war and didn't have to have the approval of Congress to do it. So that was the difference. But nobody really appreciated that, calling it a police action. Why was it different from any other war? Bullets are just as bad, and so forth. And one of the sayings was, we didn't have enough policemen and the beat was too big.

The 3rd Battalion left I think the 26th or 27th of July [and] we got into Korea the 1st or 2nd of August [1950]. We did a lot of training on our way over there, especially rifle shooting off the back of the boat. I guess we thought we were ready. We read our propaganda that we were the best-trained outfit in the army—that's why we were going, they said. There was a lot of apprehension—I don't think anybody was anxious to go—but we all went.

We were shipped out and went to an airstrip on the east coast called P'ohongdong. We stayed there from the first part of August until the mid-part of September. The first combat was up there. The first engagement we had was shelling, mostly. They had not put out a full-scale attack on the air base, so it was a defensive position we took up. There was shelling on both sides, in fact the navy was shelling from offshore, that kept it pretty quiet, [but] we did have some run-ins, the line companies did. Our group did have to take prisoners back to headquarters, did some interrogations, find out who was there and why, all that stuff.

[Integrating the battalions] started maybe a month or two after we got over there, primarily because of necessity. As you ran out of people, you had to replace them. In my opinion, race didn't play a part of where you went, it was who needed the people. That's the way I saw it being integrated. If your unit didn't need a replacement, then you didn't get one and you stayed the way you were, but that was only a few organizations, and we were fortunate enough that ours didn't at that time. So ours stayed Black, but we were no longer in an all-Black company or an all-Black battalion.

As I recall there was some [propaganda aimed at Blacks,] I don't remember what it said, but I know there was some. There was all kinds of propaganda to throw down our arms and surrender and see your friends in the North, and so forth, but then we were sending out pamphlets, too, the other way around, getting them to surrender. In the first few months of the war, it was pretty, I don't want to say disorganized, but it wasn't the way that you would normally . . . expect. It was pretty [much] in an uproar, because we were getting pushed back, we'd been pushed back so far that it was bad. And that's when the Chinese or the North Koreans used their propaganda to try and get people to surrender. And the same way, when we started pushing north and were overrunning them, that's when we were using our propaganda to get them to lay down their arms and come back and we'll treat them fine. So that's taking advantage of a situation. So they were trying to take advantage of the situation at the beginning of the war, and some of it I understand was aimed at the Black soldiers.

The 1st and 2nd Battalions went to the west side of the Pusan Perimeter, on the river, [and] in September we joined them. They were preparing for the move out from the Pusan Perimeter, so that's when we rejoined [them,] staging up for the attack across the river, to break out of the perimeter there. I don't remember [our] exact assignment [but] I remember the 2nd Division was the first one to break across the river. It wasn't the 9th, it was the 38th that did. We were assigned just like any other outfit along those lines.

When the Chinese intervened in North Korea, we were cut off . . . in the [Kunu-ri] Pass. That was where the [Bronze Star] medal came out of. That was the Battle of Kunu-ri. The entire division was cut off. What happened is the enemy got behind us and [had] taken out a lot of our rear echelon, people and equipment. We had one road to go on, and it was being blocked by a bunch of cars and trucks that were being disabled. And the only way to get out was to go through that roadblock that they had set up. They had people on both sides of the road, it was a mountain pass, and all the high ground, they had it. We were in the bottom, and we were caught in crossfire. So in running that roadblock, I was driving one of the [trucks,] just attempting to move the unit out. Truck driver wasn't my job, but there was a truck there and I was driving. But it got knocked out and I had to get out. I saw a soldier who was hurt and couldn't walk, and what I did was pick him up and carry him out. In fact, he was our section noncom, our section leader, I think he was from Pennsylvania. Supposedly saved his life, I guess. Anyway, that was it, it doesn't sound like much, it isn't much. Except to him, I'm sure it meant a lot to him. [The] Bronze Star was awarded [to me] over there by my commanding officer.

The 9th Infantry lost all but three or four hundred people. We had air and artillery support—but there were just too many of them, and the position was not good. So we came through there, and that was probably one of the toughest battles the 9th Infantry had. In fact, it was one of the toughest battles the division had, because after that the division had to go back and regroup and get additional supplies and people at that time. The 3rd Battalion took a very good beating that day. . . . If look at casualties, you'll see an awful lot of people who were injured or killed on November 30, which was the day we came through there. In fact the last week of November was a bad week, but it wasn't just the 2nd, it was almost all the divisions over there. The marines had a very rough time [too].

So we were back maybe a month or two. The bad part of that was that we thought everybody would be home for Christmas, because we thought everything was going well in our favor. Morale was a little low then, but there were so many new people, they didn't know what happened. So it didn't hurt too bad I guess, as far as the division goes. [But] you go back [to the rear] and hope you have replacements coming, which we did, hope they're trained well enough, because at that time you had battle veterans and brand-new entrants who hadn't seen combat. Fortunately, the little unit I was in, the intelligence and reconnaissance, had only lost one person so our replacement wasn't that big of a deal. How we got through there like that, I don't know. But we did. We were fortunate.

Gerald L. Bailey
Corporal, 3rd Battalion, 9th Infantry Regiment, 2nd Infantry Division
US Army
Interviewed by Tina Tennessen, August 3, 2002, Bloomington, MN
American RadioWorks, Minnesota Public Radio

Of course, the 24th Infantry became synonymous with the Black soldier in Korea, but the men's experiences were far from singular from other Black troops, nor were they wholly like. The 24th had a unique and proud heritage to uphold and, despite heroic fighting in the first horrible months of the year, found not just its flanks under attack but its reputation, too. The men of the 24th fought the North Koreans and the Chinese on the field of battle, but they fought for recognition and fair treatment from both the US Army and the folks at home. The many years that have elapsed since the end of the Korean War have somewhat recti-fied their shameful image and reduced the sting that came with it, but so much more about them is revealed when one goes beyond the superficial stories of a Black unit struggling to maintain discipline under heavy fire to hear about every-day life, in combat and out.

WALTER LEE DOWDY JR., CHATTANOOGA, TENNESSEE

I'm loaded—I got combat everything. I got ammunition, I got a radio, and I'm ready to go. They told me I'm ready to go, I got to go. I'm scared. Oh, man, you talking about scared. Anybody going into combat say they're not scared, they're crazy. You hear bullets, you hear bombs falling, you hear airplanes flying over-head, you hear everything, you hear groaning, you see your friends get—it's a mess out there.

So my first duty [was] in a jeep and we were going forward, and we got under attack, and we started moving back, and I says, "Captain, why aren't we going to stay and fight?" Because I want to shoot. I want to shoot, you know. He looked at me and said, "Man, the American army never retreats. This is strategic with-drawal," he told me, so I kept quiet. We came back in the staging area, the com-pany command post, [and] we got a [incoming] mortar barrage, and everybody was digging their holes, and I'm trying to string wire for my company position down to the mortar position. We got to throw them back at them.

I came down near a guy named McGruder. I came down the hill, I looked around: Bam. Everything was Black. I felt something running down my face. I said, "McGruder, McGruder." "Hey, Dowdy." I said, "Man, I'm hit, I'm hit." And I didn't see nothing, and I passed out. I didn't know nothing. I didn't know nothing. When I came to, I was on the airplane going to the hospital in Japan. MacArthur came. I shook his hand there.

I got hurt July 26th, 1950. The war started July 25th. The 25th Regiment was first in, under General [William F.] Dean. [The] 24th, we were second, the sec-ond outfit there. And we were on the 38th Parallel. We were fighting the North Koreans, not the Chinese. They're later, way later. And so I got hurt July 26th, 1950.

Walter Lee Dowdy Jr.
Corporal, 24th Infantry Regiment, 25th Division
US Army
Interviewed by Michael Willie, February 18, 2004, Chattanooga, TN
Walter Dowdy Jr. Collection (AFC/2001/001/20008), Veterans History
   Project, American Folklife Center, Library of Congress

[I'm] Jessie Brown. I was in the 25th Infantry Division, 24th Regiment, 2nd Battalion. We left the States [and] we crossed the International Date Line on December 23rd, 1948. I forget the dates that we arrived into Yokohama, but we get into Japan and [I] believe it was January. It was an experience. We stayed at place called Camp Zama in Yokohama. We stayed two or three weeks processing before we left to Camp Gifu and we were assigned there. I enjoyed the army so much; I knew I was going to do a total career there.

I remember when Truman [called for integration]. But my unit stayed segregated while I was there. When I left [it after combat in Korea] it was still that way. I was back in Japan as a cadre [when] I heard about the 14th Regiment. [The 24th] had integrated into the 14th. I thought to myself, "I wonder why?" It didn't bother me no more after that. About integrating the army, I don't know how to explain how I feel about integrating the army.

Gifu was not [a soft assignment] for us as infantrymen 'cause we trained hard. We would go into bivouac up into Mount Fuji, and we would stay up there forty-five days out of a year. We trained very hard. Back in camp, life was good but when on duty, we were on duty and we trained hard. I say we were good soldiers. Some of the best in the world. The war started June the 27th of '50. And they got us ready, processing. We left out of Japan 'round the 11th of July . . . and then we landed in Pusan about July the 12th.

I read about [the 24th's reputation for bugging out] after I left there . . . [but] it didn't [sound like the unit I knew and] it hurt. I was hurt [by that]. I remember in August of '50, when the United States was being pushed back to the Japan Sea, they called on our regiment. I was there, to hold that perimeter. We held that perimeter and we did not fall back. They did not push us into the Japan Sea. It was my regiment, the 24th Regiment, that held that perimeter and did not fall back.

[The] first big memory [I have] was we went up into [the] mountains with a lieutenant, myself and one of the squad leaders. Just the three of us — went up into [the] mountains as far as we could go. He wanted to observe, see what was going on, had his binoculars. On the way there we discovered where the Koreans had been. They had been eating. There was rice there and there were scraps on the ground. We observed a while and looked around and he said, "Let's go down now." And we started back down the mountain. The rest of the company had circled round the base of the mountain. We came down the mountain and just as we got to the base, the [North Koreans] opened fire on us with bird guns and everything they had. The company at the base of the hill, the platoon, they were pinned down. From there, way up into the morning, we were pinned down in that valley. I always called it Death Valley.

Recently, I met one of the guys that was with us that morning. After fifty some years [we] got back in touch. He says the name of the place was Sangju, Korea. But as far as I'm concerned, I don't care about the name. I was just there. I asked him if he remembered that morning and he say, "Sure I do." That very lieutenant got hit that morning — he got hit with mortars or whatever it was. He got hit real bad. He had went up a little ways, back toward the [hill.] Some of the guys went up in the hills where he was and pull[ed] him out — he was just bloody — put him on the front end of the jeep and turned around, under fire.

We were laying there, we were pinned down and they were firing at us with everything they had. Mortars and antitank weapons, whatever they were shooting out there. [It was the] first time I heard men hollering and crying and first time I had smelled as much blood as I smelled laying there on the ground. Guys that I knew hollering out. We couldn't see one another, we were just calling out, "Who's hit?" They were saying who was hit, calling names. And they were hollering, "Medic, medic, medic." Some of the guys from that morning I never saw again.

I got hit from a piece of shrapnel. I laid there and I like to have died from the pain. [The] only way we got out of there [was] they called for the 1st Battalion to come in, to draw fire off of us. I found this out later. I didn't know that's why we got out of there that morning, but we were able to get to our feet and they brought a jeep in close as they could. I was one they said couldn't get on 'cause they said that I wasn't as bad as some of the guys. I had taken a piece of shrapnel and some of them were shot. They loaded us on the jeep, and I begged for a place and I got a place right on the corner on the back end of that jeep.

We started out of there and they began to shoot airbursts after us, shooting mortars in the air and the shell would explode over your head. And then they tried to cut the road in half with artillery so we wouldn't get out with our jeeps, our weapons. But our jeeps ... had front-wheel drive [and] they couldn't stop the American vehicles. I passed out from the pain. We moved forward till they got us to [the] aid station. We unloaded there and they brought us in on the stretchers and I remember laying there and there was a colonel. He asked me how I was feeling, and I was trying to tell him to do something for my pain, something quick. He broke something, [I] think morphine, did something ... that kept me from dying 'cause I was hurt so bad.

I went to sleep right after that. We hadn't had no sleep. That morning they moved us from the table to another room in that building. I remember that, I talked to my wife a lot of times. I was laying on that floor on the stretcher thing and sun was shining through the window and we began to hear some rumblings. And it was them, moving toward the hospital, the aid station where the wounded were. So I heard somebody holler, "We got to move, we got to get them out of here." And that morning, they got us up and got out [those] who couldn't walk. Got us in the hospital carrier, with a red cross on the side. They started driving up a road with us. I closed my eyes and said, "I don't ever want to see this place again."

They got us to the hospital ship and loaded us all on. On that ship that morning, I saw my captain. He was wounded [too]. He was on there, [along with a] couple guys I knew, guys from the 1st Battalion. They shipped us to Japan to [a] hospital and that hospital is where I took my treatment. They come along and took our pictures for the paper. My dad said he saw me in the paper in my hometown. I stayed out of Korea I forget how long. But I was wounded, still had on my bandages, [when] they put me on a ship [and] sent me back to Korea again. I went back again and join[ed] my unit. There wasn't many of them then, wasn't but a few guys.

On my way back [I] stopped at HQ . . . and stayed till [the] next day to get transportation back to [the] front lines. [An officer] came along and asked me, "Soldier, what are you doing in the hallway?" I said, "Sir, I'm on my way back to the front lines." "From where?" "From the hospital." "Well, you can't sleep in here tonight." Now these guys are cruel to me. I'm on my way to the front lines and they tell me I can't sleep in officers' headquarters. And naturally I couldn't. He said, "Find somewheres to sleep."

I got up and started walking. Across the way was [a] little building thirty feet long. And I thought, maybe I can bunk down in here. It began to rain. I went in that building, pitch dark in there, and said, "Hey, fellows, any extra bunks in here?" It's a memory I won't forget.

It was so dark. In the army they told us when it's dark, get down and you can see better. So I got down on my hands and knees and began to crawl into the building, touching the guys as I went. These guys were lined up just as pretty. I said, "Any extra bunks? Hey, hey, any extra bunks?" I began to feel the toes and legs of these guys. These guys were cold. These were troops from the front line in body bags. And they were storing them back there in that building. None of those guys were able talk to me so I turned around and crawled back down to a hallway where the officer couldn't see me. And I went to sleep, stayed there against the wall all night till daybreak.

Next morning, [a] jeep came by with a captain in it and one of the officers hollered out, asked the captain where he was going. "Is this guy's unit anywhere near there? Take this guy back to near his unit." So I rode on the back of [that] jeep and began to see burned-up American trucks that had been hit, burned up, just charred. I began to see dead North Korean soldiers or South Korean soldiers along the road, swollen up. Rode all the way on back there and he let me off, "Your unit is in here somewhere." I found this one boy, his name was Donald Brown. I walked over to him and I said, "Where is everybody?"

He . . . was sitting on the porch [of a Korean house]. He was just going with a motion, . . . rocking [back and forth], and he looked at me and he says, "Where have you been?" "At the hospital. Where is everybody else?" "Brown, they all gone." And we was full of strength when we went in there. [A] regular company should be about 160 men with everybody attached. He says, "[There's] about nine men left in the company." So I went up and joined where I was supposed to go, [but] there is a blank [memory] there: I don't remember sleeping, I don't remember eating. It's just not there. But I remember seeing him sitting up on that porch.

That night I remember laying there and it was raining, monsoon rain. And I met this new guy . . . from Fort Lewis, Washington. He came in as a replacement. Told him where I had been and what happened and everything. He says, "I just got here, I'm replacing. I don't know how to shoot this M1 rife." I said, "Why not?" He said, "'Cause I'm a signal corpsman." I don't know his name, but we talked a while. We spent the night there together on the ground wherever we were.

Next [thing] I remember, we were taking this hill. We went up this valley, went up this hill. Sun was going down, it was raining. We were taking this mountain. [They] told us not to fall. "Don't fall, don't fall, they'll pin you down. Don't fall, don't fall." We had to cross this river. We made it to the top of the mountain. We were shelled all night by our own artillery. All night they shelled us, shelled us. We like went out of our minds. Somehow, they couldn't get the radio to make contact with them. We laid down [on] top of the ground 'cause the mountain was rock, we couldn't dig in. There was a corporal with me. [I said,] "I don't know why my insides are shaking." His name was Corporal Peeples. He was new, said he was in World War II. He begged me to be calm all night long. He said, "We're going to make it, we're going to make it, Brown. We're going to make it." They were shelling us with white phosphorous shells and the smell was just awful, like sulfur. We lay on that hill until daybreak and finally they stopped shelling and we came down that morning. The guys were wanting to fight one another; we were touchy. I remember [a] guy . . . drew his carbine on another soldier 'cause he tripped and slipped against him coming down the mountain.

My being is quivering when I get to talking about [that battle]. Don't know why. I talk about it I have to stop. I don't talk about it too much. I tell my wife about it [but] none of [my] children. I never really sit down and talk to my sons—one of them is in the marines—but I never talk to them about it. [They're from] a new generation. I've got a daughter, she's forty-four. She knows more about it. She hears me talking. [But] I get the feeling—and I just quit. I'm just quivering.

[I] went through that [combat] and came on back to Japan as a cadre [in] Yokohama, Camp Drake. I stayed there as a cadre processing guys to go to Korea. I was [the] only Black guy in [a] white company, [the] only one till I left there. They were nice. I experienced a lot of things I didn't experience in my all-Black company 'cause I got a lot of breaks, donuts and things, [at] certain times of day. We didn't do that in the infantry. In that cadre company, I enjoyed and experienced a lot of things. Made a lot of friends They were nice to me, just GIs, regular soldiers.

At that time, guys were marrying the girls and bringing them home. I had a . . . Japanese girlfriend. I had known this girl before we went to [Korea from] Japan and she joined me where I was stationed when I came back and we stayed together until it was time to leave. We decided we wanted to get married. Her mother told me she had been married before and she doesn't have a divorce. "If you're not going to marry her, don't have her clear that divorce up. But if you're going to marry her, she'll do that and we'll get the papers all straightened and get her clear for you." I said, "Okay," [but] I was hesitant. I said, "I like the girl but why bring someone from that far away, of another race, all the way back to America? What's going to happen when she wants to go back and see her people? I'm not financially able [to] start a family." It's just a feeling you have when you're away and you see a woman. And that's natural; we're all just soldiers.

But I was glad I didn't [marry her] after this happened to me: I went up to the sergeant major. He was a white guy from Atlanta, Georgia. He was sitting behind a desk and he said, "What you want to do?" I said, "I want to come in to get the necessary forms and papers to get married." He said, "You do?" and I said, "Yeah." He says, "What company you in?" I told him and everything. He says, "Uh, huh." He listened to everything I said. He went and got my records. He pulled them out and looked at them. He said to me, "You're on your way home. If you don't catch that plane you're going to pay six hundred dollars for the seat." Couple of days [later], I was on orders [to go home] — it didn't take but a day or two to leave. So I left. [I] said good-bye to her, said, "I'll be back, I'll be back. I'll reenlist. Come on to the States, I done my time." On the way from there, I was glad the sergeant did that for me 'cause I got back and grew up. Wouldn't have wanted to bring her from over there to here, don't think I would have.

It's all behind us now. War is war. There's many more who have tasted the same thing. We walk around, not zombies, but we have memories. World War II, guys go back to D-Day and they'll cry, they'll cry. First time I've seen grown men lie on their bellies and cry. I'll never forget Death Valley, though.

Jessie Brown
Private 1st class, Company 2, 2nd Battalion, 24th Regiment, 25th Division
US Army
Interviewed by Stephen Smith, January 7, 2003, Chicago, IL
American RadioWorks, Minnesota Public Radio

[I served] with the 24th Infantry Regiment, 25th Division, 8th Army, Korea. We were all Black. I was from Chicago, and so I went to school with white kids, white kids were my friends, they lived next door to me. I didn't come up in a segregated place, so that was new to me. The first time [I faced segregation] was when I joined the army. We used to have white outfits and Black outfits, and the sergeants used to say, "Y'all better look good now, the eyes are all on you." After we got assigned to the 24th Regiment, we knew what was going on. It was obvious. We just wanted to get it done and go back home.

I was there from January 2, 1951, and I stayed there until I was rotated back home in November of the same year. A lot [soldiers] didn't have the proper type of clothing for that weather [earlier in the war]. A lot got frostbitten. It was cold over there, very cold, down to thirty-five or forty below zero in the valley and mountains, too. Especially when you got to sleep outside, it was rough.

I got there just after the Chinese had came into the war, and my unit was being pulled back when I joined them, back beyond the 38th Parallel. We were being pushed back. We had to hightail it. I remember one incident, we were being run down the mountains by the Chinese and the US Army vehicles were heading south. I asked the chaplain, "Can you help me get outta here?" He said, "I'm lost, too, soldier." I saw a lot of bodies lying on the side of the road.

I never did see [the 24th bug out]. We were over there, so we were wondering where they got the stories from. We saw we were up on the front lines more than anybody else. [It didn't bother me], because I knew what was going on. We were always in the thick of the fight. We stayed up on the line longer than anybody else. Some of the outfits that were out there were mostly white, some were integrated. Ours was never integrated, but we had white officers. I didn't see no problems with [the white officers]. We respected them and they respected us. Some of the outfits were National Guard units, and they would always be pulled back, and we were always up on the line. As soon as we pulled back, they would tell us to get up in the front again. I believe it was both [because we were Black and we were good fighters]. [But] they were doing strategical withdrawal, so everyone was pulling back.

We jumped across first [but the good reputation mostly] went to the [27th Infantry, the] Wolfhounds. Probably because they were mostly white. But we did what we had to do. We stood our ground, though. We captured some Chinese soldiers, and they told us, "If you pull out the 24th Regiment and the 27th Wolfhound, we'll run the rest of these soldiers out into the sea."

One time . . . I was down in a foxhole with a steel helmet on and it was night. That's when the Chinese would attack. I heard a Zing! And I looked a little deeper, took my helmet off, and there was a bullet hole right through it. I'd been shot at. It doesn't get closer than that. [Although] I remember one incident up in the mountains. My sergeant told me never zip your sleeping bag all the way up. The Chinese attacked that night, and some of the guys who had zipped their bags all the way couldn't get out and were killed.

They just couldn't get out. I remember a friend of mine, we were attacked, and he was sitting behind a boulder. He must've been in the wrong place. A mortar round hit him, and his whole head came off. It was Black and smoky and burnt, and his head was off. And I thought to myself, "What am I doing over here?"

On my nineteenth birthday, March the 15th, we crossed the Han River. It was cold, cold. We ran into a lot of resistance. I said, "Ah, man. I'm nineteen years old and I'm trying to cross this river." We were trying to [gain] position, but the Chinese were fighting like mad. They didn't give up easy. It took us maybe four or five days to take that hill. I remember they had in the paper, the *Stars and Stripes*, talking about Truman called it a police action and I thought, these the baddest crooks I've ever seen over here.

There is so much that probably hasn't been told [about the Korean War]. Maybe they should tell more. It's like [the war] didn't happen. The 38th Parallel is still there, it's still the same thing. And they about look like they want to go to war again. Politics, that's all it's about. We didn't get the recognition we should have. It's all [because of] Vietnam. We lost more soldiers in Korea than in World War II or the Vietnam War. We lost a lot of people. Now they got the Vietnam Wall in Washington, DC. We fought over there and didn't get that kind of recognition. I don't have no hard feelings. It's just one of those things. [You'll] wake up with headaches all the time if you worry about that.

Isham McClenney
Corporal, E Company, 2nd Battalion, 24th Infantry Regiment, 25th Division
US Army
Interviewed by Stephen Smith, January 7, 2003, Chicago, IL
American RadioWorks, Minnesota Public Radio

ISAAC GARDNER JR., CHICAGO, ILLINOIS

[I'm] Ike Gardner, from Lynch, Kentucky, Harlan County proper, [the] coal mine section of the state. I enlisted in the army in 1950 because I didn't want to go into the coal mines. I was in the 25th Infantry Division, 24th [Infantry] Regiment, Company L, 3rd Battalion. I was a rifleman. My weapons were an M1, a couple grenades, and bandoliers. We were riflemen.

I wasn't surprised to be in a segregated Black unit. Number one, I was a young guy, and number two, I'd been in the South all my life. It was a way of life; life was structured that way. Some of the guys from Illinois, Pennsylvania, [or] Upstate New York would complain [but] my main concern was getting back home. I was born and raised in the South, so I had accepted racism, that it was everywhere. When I went in the army, I just expected it. You don't have time [for it]; I don't care what color this guy is as long as he's fighting. Once you get back and you have time to think, those kind of things come up in conversation, [about how] we were second-class citizens, we were gonna get second best in every doggone thing, but that was just an accepted fact. I think Mr. Truman started integrating on me. When men were getting killed so bad and wounded, they started integrating, but it was still 95 percent Black. The commissioned officers were mostly white, but the body of my battalion and my company was exclusively Black. I had some nice white officers — Captain Spencer from Atlanta always said, "Let's go" [and led the way].

I've seen decent white folk everywhere. Racism does exist, no doubt, but you just have to deal with it. We ran into it. Even some of the guys in the hospital [later], some of the white guys, tried to get smart. But we just played it off, you know. But on the post, if we went to the theater or something, yes, we've had scrimmages, but there were always officers who would break it up. And you have to ask yourself, if we had control, would we be any different? It's just human nature to look out for your own first. Because most of them are from the lower echelon. Blacks, poor whites, Mexicans, and inner-city kids fought that war. In Korea, the average guy on that line had about a tenth-grade education. And I don't care how you talk about race — there has never been a race war. Wars are fought because of economics.

I did my training at Fort Knox, Kentucky. About two weeks before I finished basic training the Korean War broke out. I came out of basic training, and I went home for ten days, and after that they need replacement[s] so bad, and I didn't know where I was going until I got there. We stopped in Hawaii and [they] took us to one of the nicest restaurants I'd ever been to in all my life. When I got to Japan, they gave us a refresher course and a pep talk. They said, "Some of you are not going home." And that's when I knew I was in a blizzard in my BVDS. That's when it really hit home what things were about.

After about two days at Camp Drake, we took a train from Tokyo. It was pretty. About a day after we got to Sasebo, they put us on a ship to Pusan. Then we took a train to Taegu. That was the Korean perimeter. I was lucky because the day after I got there, the marines came into Inchon. I got up on the line at 9:00 p.m., and I could hear small arms fire. They put me in a foxhole with a [South] Korean. He didn't speak English; I didn't speak Korean. We heard gunfire. They were prodding, trying to find out our position. They didn't hit us, but that next morning they hit us real hard. My first night on the line, I didn't know what to do. I didn't do much fighting. The next morning, they went down the hill to collect the dead. It was the first time I'd seen a dead man. Looked about fifteen years old.

[I heard about the 24th's bad reputation] when I got up on the line. When you're fighting, you do what you're supposed to do. What you're thinking or saying doesn't matter; I just care what my fellow soldiers think of me. We had some guys who didn't put out, but the real warriors didn't want anything to do with them, didn't eat with them. [But] Black soldiers gave a good account of themselves. Now, . . . I will say this about any outfit — only three out of five men on the line fight. Some [are] crouching, some cursing, some praying. Because with the firepower that the average American infantryman has at his disposal, if all of them fight, wars will be much different. They had the numbers, but we had the firepower. [But] the pen is mightier than the sword [and] as long [Blacks] as were doing something wrong, [whites] like to read about that. But I've seen some brave soldiers, Black and white.

The [North] Koreans started withdrawing. We were on the offensive. We got a little stiffer resistance as we pushed up to Cheonan. We whipped North Korea [through] just about the first of October. The rumors started then that we'd be home for Christmas . . . and it was going to be a cakewalk. We'd go down the river and put the flag up and be in Japan for Christmas.

I was close enough to smell the [enemy's] breath at times. But it didn't get serious till a couple days after Thanksgiving. As we got further up, the stiffer the opposition got. We were up on a little ridge near the capital of North Korea, and a guy from Oklahoma, he was mixed race, Black and Indian, and he told us, "A man said there's some horse dung down here." He picked it up and broke it open to find it moist. We knew then that the Chinese were coming down, because the Koreans didn't have horses. As we got further up, we had a pretty stiff fight. They hit us — tatt-a-tatatatat — and they moved back down the hill. Then they'd come back. The Korean's battle cry was "Banzai." One guy [in our unit] had a nervous breakdown; he just lost it. The next morning, we moved up farther. And we were supposed to put an identification plaque out. We'd dig us a foxhole and just then we'd get the order to saddle up and get ready to take another position. Now, I don't know exactly where I was because the only way an infantryman can find out anything was to get the military papers. I didn't know what part of the country we were in. Most of the time you find that out after you've established a beachhead, but we were moving. We'd just dig a foxhole for the night. We thought we were gonna be home.

[The] sergeant, the squad leader, took an eight-man squad out. We went down into this village and he put me on point. We got some opposition. There was a farmer pulling potatoes or something like that . . . [and] the farmer came at me with a machine gun. A bullet came right by my face. I don't think the guy wanted to kill me; he just wanted to get my sleeping bag.

As the rest of the squad come up, we just wanted to make contact and find out where they were. Anytime [the enemy] got the high ground and a thirty-caliber and you just have eight rounds — you'll have to reload — you're at his mercy. Unless your buddy can put down enough fire to give you time to reload. We see six of them. We're on their turf. A young guy from Texas got killed. I took his sleeping roll, so I was good for the night. A guy from Louisiana named Bernard Foster said, "You got something to write home and tell mama about now." He said, "You're a real soldier now." We started moving. We were eating C-rations. Sergeant Gise said, "Hey, Kentucky" — he called me Kentucky Slim — "You can come on over here and eat with us." That meant I was accepted, I was one of the boys.

Now the Chinese, they had buglers. He could blow the worst rendition of "Stormy Weather" I've ever heard in my life. They try to work psych on you, you see. They get bold sometimes. They come down to the bottom of the hill and make their fire and eat and get high off their opium. And when they get done, they'll holler, "Yeeeeee," and it just sent cold chills. Because you know he's coming, and you know he's enforced. Sometimes they were everywhere, and they got those snow-white suits on, and you got to be steady. Young recruits need to be with a seasoned veteran. A scared man runs but he stops. A coward runs for his life. They just had us outnumbered. One night patrol, they mauled the devil out of a twelve-man patrol.

Any man that was in combat, whether he's white or Black, he'll tell you that in December 1950 we didn't have a prayer. There were just too many Chinese. Too doggone many. It was overcast all the time and our fighter planes couldn't come in and help us. Those Chinese soldiers had just whipped Chiang Kai-shek and they were seasoned. And Mao Zedong sent those veterans down. Now I'm on the line, and most of the men were like me, four or five months out of basic training.

Like I said before, I was fighting to get home. The Chinese would capture some of the soldiers. They would take their shoes, take their ammunition, hit them upside the head, and turn them loose. But they were trying to use psychology. We captured a [Chinese] soldier and he told me, "A milky soldier — a white soldier — is number one, *hak gwai* — that's Black in Chinese — number two." I knew he was telling the truth — what could I say? Another experience — we went down into a home, and a fair-skinned guy from Detroit and I went down at the same time, and a little North Korean kid pointed at the other guy and said, "American." Then he pointed at me and said, "African." He got his textbook and showed us a picture of Africa and a picture of a white kid that said, "American."

We woke up one morning out of chow. For two days we didn't eat anything. The plane that dropped us ammunition and food missed the DZ [drop zone], and I guess the Chinese were as hungry as we were. We had a pretty good fight, lost six, seven guys, just trying to get that food. Some ate so much they regurgitated. We had to give the food back so the sergeants could ration it. We got a little further and we were encircled. As we were moving a tall lieutenant from Dayton, Ohio, got shot. We didn't see any blood. We tried to pick him up, and he said, "I'm too heavy, you guys go ahead." Lieutenant Baroni was an Italian lieutenant from Upstate New York. We were getting out of there; the Chinese were all around us. "Halt, Joe, you're my prisoner," so I turn around. Boom! Whether I killed him, hurt him, I don't know. I don't know if I ever killed anyone. But I've popped some. I took him out. When you're on the line, it's just like a football game.

We've gone down the hill, and here's some young [North Korean or Chinese] boy who's gut shot, just laying there, looking. A guy named Rick from Little Rock, Arkansas, said, "Shoot the frickin' so and so." But I just didn't have the nerve. So he walked up and shot him about four or five times, and that was the end of that. His words were, "He's been tried, convicted, and sentenced." It was a cold, brutal thing. I didn't feel good, [but] I didn't feel bad, because I was in a war. It was them or us. I wasn't fighting for mom's apple pie; I was trying to get home. You start to stiffen, too, especially after some of your buddies get hit. A friend of mine named Bill Morrison, he and I took basic together and he got so sick they had to take him to the aid station. He had TB. He came back with a tag around his neck. He stuttered and said, "I got that million-dollar wound now. I'm going home." He gave me his carbine and a banana clip.

Some of the smarter heads said it was one of the coldest winters they'd had for fifty years. It got so doggone cold the ground would sometimes be frozen six to eight inches. December 8th, I think it was, and the people said it was forty below, but I don't know. There ain't a dime's worth of difference between zero and forty below. We were just about freezing. We commandeered some farmers' homes. I don't know if we did it in the proper manner or what. We would stay in the foxhole for a while and so many of us would go down to the homes. The way they heat their homes [is] with clay floors and straw mats on top, with something like a furnace under that. We were able to sleep on the floor for a while. But we began to throw up from frostbite. We went back out and they kept saying exercise that trigger finger. But the body has a system of its own. Quite a few people, fingers just swelled up and burst on them. It was terrible.

One morning, we were going through some of those ponds, and you don't have time to change. I stepped in the water up to here, and I was like a human icicle. It got so bad out there, we lost the use of our hands. Now for a soldier to go out and take a constitutional, he can't button his pants, so his foxhole buddy had to warm his hands for a while just so he could [help him] button his pants.

When we went down to the Yalu River, they just had superior numbers, that's all it was. Someone said, we're not retreating, we're just attacking to the rear. But we were trying to get out of there, because of that doggone cold, you see. We didn't have the proper supplies and they were everywhere, they were just all around us. But the 24th did get a bad knock. We had inferior [white] officers, we were ill-supplied, and we didn't get the support, in my opinion, that the other regiments got. I've seen some brave guys in the 24th, and some cowards, and some marginal.

They were pushing us back so fast, now we were trying to fight the rear guard. We had to try to keep the bridges and the roads open. My feet were so doggone bad, I could hardly walk. At the aid station, they took my shoes off and my toes were blue and swollen. After that, they put us in the ambulance. The roads were nothing but ruts. We were like sitting ducks. One guy got hit in the shoulder while in the ambulance. We get out of the shooting part and we get down to Seoul, I think it is. They put us in a tent hospital. They gave us a real good hot meal and deloused us. Then they flew us to Itazuke [Air Base,] Japan. And from there, they flew us to [the] 8th Army hospital in Osaka, Japan. I stayed there for three weeks and then I went to the hospital in Fort Campbell, Kentucky, [in] my home state.

I can't stand too much cold weather even now. Every morning I feel like [my toes] are swollen and my feet, too. If I take a hot shower and some aspirin before I go to bed, it helps. I think about the war more when it snows than any other time. It really gets to me.

Isaac Gardner
Rank unknown, Company L, 3rd Battalion, 24th Infantry
    Regiment, 25th Infantry Division
US Army
Interviewed by Kate Ellis, September 2002, Chicago, IL
American RadioWorks, Minnesota Public Radio

The men of the 24th Infantry carried an interesting burden as both one of the oldest and proudest regiments in the army and as the symbol of military segregation. It was therefore a somewhat mixed response to the news at the start of October 1951 that the 24th Infantry Regiment would be disbanded. Adding to the sting felt by some was that the 24th was dissolved, not to put an end to unequal treatment of Black forces, but as the result of the army's concern that the all-Black troops had failed in battle.

The nail in the coffin was a devastating article in the Saturday Evening Post on the alleged cowardice and poor fighting of Black soldiers in the segregated 24th Infantry Regiment. Ironically, by the time the article came out on June 16,

1951, the 24th had been integrated for about nine months; in mid-September 1950, US Army integration unofficially began with the assignment of twenty-three white replacements to the 24th and eleven Black replacements sent to two previously all-white units. Brigadier Gen. Vennard Wilson, assistant commander of the 25th Division, noted at the time that "[in] my personal opinion, I think it is a good step forward. We might as well face the facts. Integration is working in the Navy and in the Air Force. I am interested in presenting a strong solid force front against the enemy, regardless of race."[1] Needing warm bodies on the front line, no matter their color, sped up the army's timetable for integration, although it would remain unofficial until autumn 1951. It was certainly hastened along by Saturday Evening Post writer Harold Martin in his article "How Do Our Negro Troops Measure Up?" in which he tried to make a case for how integration improved the service of Black troops, but along the way it promoted harmful stereotypes, including that Black troops were afraid of the dark, often fell asleep on duty, were quick to run away in the face of danger, and did their duty well only when alongside white soldiers. As one southerner wrote to the magazine, "The whites alongside of him make him fight, just like we make them work down here."[2] Martin claimed that the men sang a song about deserting their positions called "The Bug Out Boogie" or "The Bug Out Blues," which went in part: "When them Chinese mortars begin to thud, the old Deuce-four begins to bug."[3] Sung to the tune of Hank Snow's "Moving On . . . ," the song was not in fact the anthem of the 24th, as Martin described it, but was created by white troops about their own rivals; it was sung throughout Korean War as a way for one unit to make gentle fun of another, such as a version in which the 2nd Infantry Division made fun of the 1st Cavalry.[4] All units ran at times in those first terrifying, underequipped months of the war, but only for 24th and its fellow Black troops was the reason given as a moral failing of their race.

The double-edged message that integration was good, but only because Black soldiers were so bad, presented a conundrum for African Americans promoting the integration of the armed services. Walter White, director of the NAACP, for example, promoted Martin's article as mandatory reading for military brass, and in the end, it contributed strongly to the eventual breakup of the 24th Infantry Regiment and to wide-scale army integration. But the 24th, that historic and proud Black regiment, paid with its reputation, which would not be restored — or at least partially so — until the army officially revisited its case in 2005. More than fifty years after the war's end, military historians would argue that while the 24th did indeed underperform in battle, there were causes and reasons for this rooted in the demoralizing effects of racism combined with poor training and leadership and grossly inadequate equipment and supplies.[5]

Adding weight to this argument was the work by Thurgood Marshall in early 1951 on behalf of the NAACP to investigate the disproportionate number of courts-martial and conviction among Black soldiers. Marshall focused on the 25th Division and comparison of statistics from its white regiments and the 24th Infantry to demonstrate that African Americans made up the majority of court-martial cases, that their punishment was far more severe than that of like cases among white soldiers, and that courts-martial proceeded at such speed as to deny defendants an adequate defense. Of the 118 complaints he examined from the 25th Division, he found that twice as many Black soldiers as white servicemen were charged with cowardice and disobeying orders, although white soldiers outnumbered Black troops four to one. Thirty-two Black servicemen were charged, and thirty of them received ten or more years' imprisonment; one junior officer, Lt. Leon Gilbert, who had refused a white commander's order to march his ill-equipped men into certain death, was given a death sentence. Only two white soldiers were convicted in the same period, each receiving less than five years' imprisonment.[6] Marshall concluded his report by finding that the root cause was racism within the military and institutionalized racial discrimination, primarily through segregation.[7] Marshall himself took on Gilbert's appeal and got the death sentence commuted to twenty years' in prison; he was released after five.[8]

The 24th was deactivated by the US Army on October 1, 1951, just three months after the appearance of the Saturday Evening Post article, garnering a range of responses from African Americans. Most applauded, including activist and civil rights leader Mary McLeod Bethune, who cheered the unit's closure as finally making "one Army under our great government."[9] But the soldiers of the 24th, who had picked up on army rumors of their eventual disbanding for poor performance a full year earlier, were resentful and credited the "bugging out" reports to white jealousy over their superior fighting and their ability to persevere despite the longest frontline service of any unit. (Indeed, at the same time that the unit was being decommissioned, three officers and thirteen soldiers of the 24th were awarded Bronze Stars for valor, and three were awarded the Distinguished Service Cross, the nation's second highest military honor after the Medal of Honor.)[10] Others believed that the army, embarrassed by its overall performance and inability to hold the line, had made the 24th its convenient scapegoat, "the whipping boys of the campaign."[11] Still others pointed out that although integration was "a step forward," the experienced Black officers of the 24th, in being reassigned, were being routinely passed over in favor of less experienced white officers.[12]

But all of this was still to come when the 24th was rushed into the front lines in July 1950 with broken World War II rifles and thin summer uniforms. Joining the 24th Infantry as the other all-Black unit to see immediate action was the 503rd Field Artillery of the 2nd Division. Arriving after the North Koreans had successfully pushed their way all the way down to Pusan, they quickly pushed their way up from the south as MacArthur's daring marine landing at

Inchon came down. The American forces began a premature celebration and MacArthur promised they'd be home by Christmas. But the Chinese army, sitting just on the other side of the border with Manchuria, had other ideas. As they came streaming across with drums thumping and trumpets blaring, the segregated 503rd got stuck in the Kunu-ri Pass, the same pass where General Becton had been pinned down with the 9th Infantry, and took a savage beating. One of the lucky ones to survive that battle was a young high school dropout named Charles Rangel. His experiences in Kunu-ri would send him on a path that eventually took him to the US House of Representatives.

CHARLES BERNARD RANGEL, NEW YORK

When we got to Korea . . . we had to stay out in that water for a long time because Pusan was then considered unsafe. The 24th and the 25th Infantry Divisions had been almost wiped out — they'd been driven from the 38th Parallel to the Pusan Perimeter. And actually we had to fight our way from the perimeter back north. And the thing that I remember the most is that we were not shocked at seeing dead bodies on the way to the front, and they had exploded with gas and they smelled terrible, and we would see peasants out there with their white dress, apparently they were farmers, and as we were rapidly traveling north in these six-by-six big trucks, a couple of trucks were coming from the opposite direction. And they had what we called topfolios, which [were] canvas covers of the cargo. And the cover blew off and we saw Black soldiers from the 24th or 25th stacked up dead in that truck and piled on one another like wood, going to graves registration. And even though we thought we had absorbed all of the terror of war, aw, we cried, we threw up, we were just a wasted group of young men. And they said that we wouldn't get live ammunition till we got to the front, but you can bet your life we stopped that convoy and everybody got loaded [up] in a way that just didn't make any sense from a military point of view but emotionally we just [got] prepared. And it didn't help that when we stopped these guys and they were talking to us and we all dismounted to hear what the hell was going on, they told us that even the people out in the rice fields was the enemy, that they had changed clothes. And all during the nights that we were going up you could hear machine guns going. Sometimes it was just cows or the wind or whatever, but we were truly scared to death.

Well, after we passed some of the great battles of the Naktong River and whatnot and we were moving north, it was then that we heard of the Inchon landing. And that's when Douglas MacArthur, with the navy and the marines and others, were landing far north of where we were. And when they landed, it meant that all of the North Koreans that got caught in that net, there weren't a whole lot of heroes there. It was just a question of surrendering. And we swiftly moved past the 38th Parallel.

There were battles on the way—[some] people didn't know the war was over—but being in Headquarters Battery and seeing the maps and seeing where the intelligence had shown where we were it was just a question of just staying alive long enough to get back home. You can see light at the end, you believe that you can get home, where when you lose a friend, immediately and vicariously, you figure that's you. And when he has on your uniform and you know the guy and you were training with him, that's you. And when you see other people [who] look like you [go down], it's scary. And when you don't know really [know] what the hell it's about and what is victory—we didn't have the Star Spangled [Banner] and this kind of thing going for us. They were just Asians and Koreans and we didn't know North Koreans from South Koreans and they were changing clothes, and it was a mess. But when you hear the news that [the] enemy is surrounded, then your job then is to make certain that you're not one of the people who's going to get killed when victory is in sight. We thought. We thought. We thought. . . .

And it was September when we got up there, the temperature was dropping. We were singing songs about going home. And pretty soon we started thinking about Thanksgiving and the holidays and New Year's and singing. But it was so cold, so very cold, and we didn't have any winter clothes. So they told us that there was a supply depot miles south of us that was supposed to bring the clothes up. And we went to the supply depot [instead]—it was like being in Macy's warehouse: "Size nine is over here! Well, extra-large is here! Whatta you got down there?" And everybody went back to the outfit overdressed. We may not have been ready for the Chinese but we were damn sure ready for the winter, you know? [We were] still thinking we were going home. And then I remember so well that someone had said, "Sergeant Rangel, some of our people on patrol got captured, and they released them. And it was Chinese that captured them."

Now we had lost a lot of men on the way to North Korea and I had told the new people—I don't know where I got it, probably I made it up—but in order to get them not to fall into the feeling that the war was over, I told them that the Communist Chinese were going to parachute in. And then when I heard that story, I wondered it was an extension of the lie that I had told to scare the hell out of the recruits! Or whether Chinese really had parachuted in! Well, they didn't parachute in but they damn sure were there. And for three days they, at nighttime, would come out and it was just a nightmare. They would blow the trumpets, they would talk to us in broken English, they would drop pamphlets on us. And they would remind us that this was a civil war, and Blacks have no business being there. And, "You can't go to the resorts or the swimming pool back home." Then they would name some of us. And then they would allow some of the people that we knew that were captured to talk and they would tell us, you know, that this is not our war, the Chinese didn't want to hurt us, and we should surrender and go to Lieutenant Dunn and Captain Smith and just tell them that you don't want to fight this war against people that you don't know. None of it was effective. But very few of us got any sleep at night. And the air force would just bomb the mountains where they were located, but we couldn't see them. And later we found out that they had buried themselves deeply into the ground, but they would come up at night and shoot the flares. There were no mortars or any artillery, but it was a psychological feeling that they knew they had us and there was no place for us to go and they would explain how we were completely surrounded. And then another thing that you hear stories about, how white superior officers above the rank of majors was actually heli-coptered out of the Kunu-ri Pass. Because we were on a mountain pass and we were cut off on one end, cut off on the back end, mountains on one side and just falling off the mountain on the other. And the river that they came across sepa-rated Korea—because we were north of Pyongyang—from Manchuria, where they'd come from.

So the [commanders] had heard all of this stuff [too], and I went to the cap-tain, and [said], "What the hell [do we do?]," and he said all he could do was tell us to pray. I mean, it was really so painful and disorganized, it was beyond your worst nightmare. Beyond your worst nightmare. It was surreal.

Then finally after the third day, they started their mortars. And that's when we knew they were coming. And they told us when they were coming! And the horses and the screaming and the bugles and the mortars, and they just swamped us. And you could see the people falling and being captured and I was shot off of a truck that we had put the wounded on, thinking we could get the wounded out. And then I end up in a ditch and listening to all of this and saying if I'm gonna die, die fast. Or praying. And that's where the whole concept of my life began anew because I knew then that I was dead. And my heart was beating so fast and so loud that I thought everyone could hear it. And I thought if I just stay down halfway under this truck, just like the movies they'll come, and they'll take bayonets and they'll stick into everybody.

And I don't know, I just felt that if God was going to help me and I didn't think that he would, [but] that he couldn't help me if I was bleeding in a damn ditch. So the only thing on one side of this Kunu-ri Pass was this damn moun-tain. And you could see the tracer bullets going, just sweeping the damn moun-tains. But I saw a guy named John Rivers—he was a sergeant 1st class when we went overseas and he was a World War II veteran—and I saw Sergeant Rivers, there was a full moon, screaming and yelling that there were dogs after us. And it was clear to me that he had lost his damn mind. And then my choice was to try to follow this crazy man or to stay down there and just let the Chinese capture me like they were capturing so many others.

And on this mountain, there were so many mounds of dirt, which of course I hid behind. They were all over. And it turned out to be a Korean graveyard, in a sense, because they would just put a little hill there [over a grave]. And to me it was just a place to hide behind. And then other people came, and they thought I knew what I was doing, and they came with me and before you knew it, there was a whole gang of people with me. And I talked like I knew what the hell was going on, because I was "in charge." I had a map I couldn't read, I had a compass I couldn't read, I had all these things. And I'd given all these damn lectures, because that was all I could do, was talk.

And then the air force came and started strafing the whole damn mountainside. And we're on the hill looking down and we can't wave and say, "Hey, don't shoot us!" Because the Chinese are [right] there. And they're killing the Chinese and any damn Americans that are wounded, too. So it looked like it was going to be over one way or the other, till finally a glider came, and they saw us, and they dropped some C-rations to us. We were starving. And they would circle in a way that would indicate to try to follow them. And I think someone said during this time that the Chinese said that they were going to let us go through. I don't remember, because my mind wasn't my own, but I do know, I ended up in some damn hospital and some officer congratulating me for my heroism and I don't know where I am or what I'm doing or what the hell is he talking about? And it was hard for me to believe that I was alive, that this rotten nightmare had ended.

And quite honestly, from that day on, I became somebody. And I had a lot of time to think. How the hell did I live? And how many people that became my buddies were dead? And what the hell did I promise anyway? And how do I keep that promise? And I don't know, but I know one thing. It was easy to keep. And that's why I made up my mind that I would never, never, never, never, never complain about anything that happened to me because my life was spared. And there would be nothing, nothing that would happen to me in life that could be as frightening as what happened to me that day. And I've been tested. You know, a lot of things have happened, but if I could just grab myself and say, God damn, you're living, you're breathing. If you got a problem, dammit, deal with it, but don't moan, don't groan, and don't complain.

And so, when you look at it, I went in the army as a high school dropout and with all the medals I came out [with], I was still a damn high school dropout. And when I went to get a job and people asked me what could I do, well, I couldn't tell them, "run around with a clipboard." And Korea defied the rules of having an occupational specialty, you know, "firing .155-millimeter howitzers" [doesn't translate to civilian life]. And I had this idea that at least I'm alive. And so I was back to the [New York City] garment center. Getting in overalls, it was sign of poverty really, and I went to work for some people that were proud that I was a veteran. And they told me that I had to sweep the place and close the place up and carry these big, awkward boxes of lace. And I remember it was raining and I had this hand truck and it slipped out of my hand and these boxes went all over 6th Avenue. And a cop was cursing me out, saying that I was blocking the traffic. And I had been on such a high before I was discharged, you know? I had been one of the first to go to Korea, one of the first to come back. Some people thought I was crazy, and they left me alone, some people thought I was a hero, and they left me alone, but whatever it was I was okay, until I got discharged.

And then I just walked to the VA from 36th Street and 6th to 23rd Street. And I told them, "Hey, I'm in trouble. This ain't working and I don't know [what to do]." And the resistance I got! Because all of the people there were white and World War II veterans and most of them were disabled. And Korea didn't impress them worth a damn. And they gave me a hard time. But I stayed with those rascals, it took me almost a year, [before they said], "What the hell is it going to take to get you out of here?" And I said, "I gotta get into college, I gotta get into law school." And they said, "No way in hell for a dropout to get that much out of the GI Bill to do that." I said, "Well, do the best you can." And they worked out something. I went to high school, went to NYU, got out, and got a scholarship. And I haven't looked back since.

Charles Bernard Rangel
US representative, 13th District of New York
Staff sergeant, 503rd Field Artillery Battalion, 2nd Infantry Division
US Army
Interviewed by Col. Robert Patrick, director, Veterans History
    Project, June 20, 2013, Washington, DC
Charles Bernard Rangel Collection (AFC/2001/001/89089), Veterans
    History Project, American Folklife Center, Library of Congress

---

Edward L. Posey served with the airborne 2nd Ranger Infantry Company, the first and last all-Black Ranger company in the US Army. The company conducted the Rangers' first ever airborne assault, capturing Hill 151 near Munson-ni. The company was highly regarded and highly decorated, earning multiple Silver Stars, including one for Posey. But, as he points out, African American soldiers—even in the elite Rangers—had to perform at twice the level as whites for the same recognition. And even that would not be enough: the medals awarded the 2nd Rangers, he says, would have been much more and of higher levels had the men not been Black. Those who won Silver Stars would have won Distinguished Service Crosses, he says, but for the color of their skin.

EDWARD L. POSEY, FAYETTEVILLE, NORTH CAROLINA

[I'm] Edward L. Posey, [from the] 2nd Ranger Company in Korea. The army was segregated at the time, only Black units and white. Airborne was different because they didn't have a Black school for it. [In] Ranger school [we] trained as an all-Black unit, [but] segregation in Ranger training was not the same kind of segregation as in the rest of army—we trained with whites, in the same training areas, but as a unit. Accommodations were [separate but] exactly the same—not very good [but] all the same. The Rangers did treat us as a Black unit equally as they did the white unit. At that level, they considered themselves above and beyond segregation, but didn't have authorization to do anything about it.

I [do] think they wanted to see if we were capable of being Rangers. Like with airborne school—they wanted to see if we'd jump out of airplanes. Will Blacks jump and will they fight? After all this training, they wanted to see if we'd function in combat as Rangers. And Rangers have a different kind of mission from the rest of the army.

[A Ranger] fights behind the lines, disrupts enemy communication, can walk farther, fight harder—[he's] trained to be a super, airborne soldier. That kind of training we got. [And] demolition—we broke a lot of things and blowed up a lot of things. And we did this and done it better [than the whites]. We had to do twice as much as a white unit to get [the] reputation we needed. We understood that. We was gonna make it regardless. We only started off with 131 [men], and we took 126 to Korea with us. That's guys that dropped out, had to go on emergency leave, didn't finish training because of injuries, et cetera. Our loss ratio was very low.

The 2nd Rangers was the first all-Black paratrooper unit and it was the last Black Ranger unit. We were the first Black troopers to make a combat jump behind enemy lines. We fought harder, captured more ground—we had an outstanding combat record. Of all the Ranger companies, we had the highest rating . . . because they had to do everything twice as hard. We were motivated. We never expected to be part of the Rangers—it had been inconceivable. Rangers have always been the best [and] I was having the chance to be an airborne Ranger. All the restrictions to being Black took second place to what we wanted to be. The US was our country and we'd fight for it, prove it over and over. We didn't dwell on segregation [although we] lived it in our hometowns, grew up [with] it. [But] we'd do our part regardless, just like we always have.

We realized [our] special burden, [but we] also realized segregation wasn't going to last, would pass in our lifetime, it had to pass, it was outdated, didn't work. We just knew the country had to change, and we were going to be part of it. We done our part to make it change. [As] an all-Black unit, we had our own officers, chain of command. We was in a different army. They shielded us from any attitudes the whites might have. [My] second time in Korea, the army had started integration. I found no resistance there, in Korea. We didn't have time to figure out who was Black/white, et cetera. [We were] just doing our job to stay alive.

[I earned seven Purple Hearts] because when you're trying to do your job, people shoot you. The guys on the other side shoot just as good. Some was flesh wounds and you had a hospital stay of three or four days. Time was critical — you'd go back with bandages on. We had a small company, so everyone counted. The unit meant more than your own personal aches and pains, your own life. Guys didn't goof around. In our unit every man received probably about two to three Purple Hearts. When you're doing your work, you tend to get hurt. We lost a few people.

[There] was an attack on the .45 position. We went into the attack, people [were] getting killed. [There was a] machine gun nest [and] we were assigned to take it out. I got shot in the arm, so couldn't use my rifle. I got my pistol and called more troops and we charged and destroyed the nest and killed the people in it. Somebody thought that was deserving of a Silver Star. We had to get that nest — if we didn't, they'd get us for sure. I wasn't thinking about honors, just about getting over the fight. We had to take out this position — the situation dictates what you do. We were all stouthearted, but I was the one that got recognized. In our company we had people that probably should've got a Silver Star every day we fought. But that's not possible.

[But there was still discrimination.] If you see a Silver Star then you see a Distinguished Service Cross [DSC]. When I see a Black man with a Silver Star, especially during those times, that man would've earned a DSC if he'd been white. I had a company commander who got a Silver Star. If he'd been white, he'd have gotten the Congressional Medal of Honor [CMH]. In fact, we're in the process right now of trying to get ours upgraded. If I'd been white charging that nest that day it would have been a DSC or CMH. That was DSC work.

In combat, you can't [afford to be prejudiced] — you've got to be there for each other. You have to lay down your personal dislikes and do the job. There is time to go back to [prejudice] if that's what you want to go back to, [but] you'll also always have people believing the right thing. [The] army reflected what civilian life was. If you're going to keep people oppressed, you can't give them Congressional Medals of Honor. That's not good for that kind of society. It was the same fears — [you] didn't want Blacks to get status because you can't control them anymore. Then it was: "Know your place." Now we don't have a place, we're our own people now. As the army integrated, you still had the lingering effect of racism. But I think the army took a real look at themselves and have done an excellent job of integration. It mattered a lot less to soldiers than to civilians. The top brass had a mission, getting it done. The military's got a different agenda than civilians. If you fight the general's integration order, you've lost the battle already, because he can find somebody to do it no matter what. In civilian life, it's different. When they don't want to do something, they'll find a million ways not to do it. The army only has one way and that's to get it done.

[There] might've been [racial] problems in the States, but not in Korea. We had a chance to change parts of it—we knew if the military changed—one of largest and most powerful organizations in the US, civilians would go along. If they can do it, civilians will come around. [Still, change] didn't come fast enough.

[As Black soldiers, though,] we didn't have many political views, us as a people and especially as a soldier. We'd go anywhere and fight anybody, though we didn't have anything against anybody—we'd have went to Africa as well as we went to Korea. That didn't make any difference. We just didn't enjoy the privilege of being politically inclined—we didn't even know what a Communist was. Whatever the Communists were, couldn't have been no better than the situation we was under at the time. That's like apartheid in South Africa. Well apartheid and Communism, people don't have opportunities. Regardless of what you call it, it's the same thing. So we didn't have political views, didn't talk about them.

[But] I think [the Korean War] was worthwhile. That kind of war for those reasons might not be the thing we'd want to do now. We're a lot more sophisticated in our judgments of things, but that was a nonnegotiable war. We had to preserve the line. We had made pacts with countries to defend them. We need as a country to keep our word. Especially when dealing with other cultures and societies.

I think Korea was a just war. With the spread of Communism, when I found out what it was, [it] had to be challenged somewhere. Looking back, I think it was worthwhile. Yesterday's Communist people [are] today's friends—so you look at that and say, what was the war all about. At the time people thought it was a bad thing, now we can live with them. Shame we didn't know how then.

Edward L. Posey
Master sergeant, 2nd Ranger Infantry Company (Airborne)
Interviewed by Kate Ellis and Stephen Smith, August 5, 2002, Memphis, TN
American RadioWorks, Minnesota Public Radio

Another unit to see combat in the first six months of the Korean War had, like the 24th Infantry, a proud record of service in previous wars and was similarly segregated. The 999th Field Artillery had made its name in World War II, landing in France one month after D-Day and winning merit awards from both the French and American military. Launching 200-pound shells from huge howitzers they towed into position, their motto was "Never Die," and they fought with such valor that they were allowed to incorporate the arms of the French town of Colmar, where they were based, into their official insignia. In Korea, the designation of "armored" was added to the unit's name and they were transferred over to M41 Howitzer Motor Carriages equipped with 155-millimeter howitzers firing 95-pound shells. They supported the Puerto Rican 65th Infantry Regiment in October 1950 and the 1st ROK Division in the spring of 1951.

WILLIAM L. JACKSON, RESTON, VIRGINIA

When I got to Korea, it was November. I left the States in August [and] we spent two months in Japan, then went ashore at Wonsan, Korea, in November 1950. We were told at that time that there was a system whereby you could accrue points to be rotated out. It was called a rotation system and with thirty-six points you would be rotated out, and go back to the States, or go someplace else. You accrued points, first of all, by just being in Korea, secondly by being inland or in combat, and then you accrued points if you were wounded, et cetera. The minimum number of points to rotate out of Korea was thirty-six. We hit Korea in the evening, so the first day we started into combat, we were on the combat line, and we began accruing points. So at that rate we would have had enough points to rotate out in April 1951.

I think that [segregation] was a reality in 1948 when I went in the service, and [in] 1950, when I got commissioned, it was a reality that a Black officer was going to be assigned to a Black unit. There were only a few all-Black units and your career would be limited to the opportunities that would present itself in a Black unit. That was a reality and not a concern. I mean, you knew it. There were also some other things that I learned as I went along. Because while the 999 was a segregated unit as far as enlisted personnel was concerned, the 999 was integrated as far as the officers were concerned, particularly junior-grade officers. Top-grade, top officers were all white, your 1st and 2nd lieutenants were mixed. So that was a characteristic I think in quite a few of the units at the time, although in Germany officers were all Black. But [that] was a reality: if you were going to [be in] the army [in] Korea at that time as a Black officer, you would probably wind up in an all-Black unit or assigned to some other administrative position. As a combat officer, which was what I was, you would probably be in an all-Black unit in 1948, '49, and '50. It's only in 1951 that I saw [that] change.

When April of 1951 came, we were told that there was nobody to replace us. That's when we realized we might not come out at all. There were no replacements in the pipeline. As far as my world was concerned, my world was [the] 999 and we weren't being replaced, so we weren't going anywhere. And I am assuming that other units that were fighting in Korea had the same problem. They were not being rotated because there was no replacements.

I think there's no place on earth that can be as bad as North Korea was when I was there. Korea was the coldest place I've ever been in my life and it was the hottest place I've ever been. In my opinion, the US Army was committed to a combat situation ill-equipped and not supported by its own government. Many of the people who went into Korea when the war broke out in June of 1950, they went in summer clothing. They got caught in North Korea in forty-below weather in summer clothing. You cannot fight like that. Our own country, in my opinion, did not support [us]. They committed troops to a situation and then they did not support them. That's why I didn't get rotated in April because we were committed but not supported by troops in the pipeline to replace us. We fought with stuff that was left over from World War II, nothing new. A lot of the equipment was not in the best of condition. So based on the ingenuity of your mechanics, your motor personnel, they kept it running. You fought in subzero weather. That's not good on equipment.

The people I worked with, the people I fought with, the people who supported me, the enlisted personnel, I thought were the best in the world. Whenever as a forward observer, I was designated to go out on [an observation post,] I always had volunteers to go with me. An observation post is always gonna be on the front of the line. You're gonna be exposed to danger. A forward observer, which is what I was primarily when I was in Korea, goes out with a jeep driver and a radio operator, and while you're on OP, you three are out by yourself and I always had people volunteering to go with me to the OP. And in some cases the assignment of OP was certain death. You know, the enemy is trying to find the eyes and ears of their opponent [and the] forward observer is the eyes and ears. Now if you knock out your forward observer, then there's nobody to direct fire. So you try to figure out where the forward observer is. Nine times out of ten he's going to be on the highest point to see the most. You watch the highest point; you watch the movement, send out a patrol, find him, and kill him. Well, I never had any trouble getting a guy to go with me on OP, the troops were supportive. When I was not on OP I would be back on the battery and I would work on the fire direction center firing the guns. I could walk out and there was nothing that I could ask of the men that I could not get them to do, and they did not show resentment. And primarily it was because of my style. I walked among them.

When they were out working, cleaning the guns, I walked among them. I did not separate myself from my men. They knew who I was. If they were relaxing, I'd come out and chat with them to try to maintain a sort of closeness to them because I knew that . . . [an] officer is not anything without the men to support him. So you gotta have the support and you gotta be able to trust it. If you get in trouble, you gotta know that they'll support you and help you get out. If not, they're gonna take care of themselves and they're gonna leave you. So that's why I think I had some of the best men that existed.

I can say with [an] amount of certainty that the men were more comfortable with Black officers than they were with white officers. It probably is a carryover from the fact that white officers had preconceptions about the abilities of their African American enlisted personnel and may have exhibited some of that in their attitudes, whereas we did not have that problem. So I think that the men felt more comfortable with us. I know that there were a number of white officers who did not have that attitude, who respected the men for what they were able to do and would not have carried that kind of baggage in with them. I can't say that for everybody, but there were some.

I never had a white soldier under my command. The unit became integrated while I was in it, but at the time they started bringing in white enlisted personnel, my job was as a liaison officer with the Korean battalion—I was sort of being rewarded by not being exposed to the danger anymore. I had a safe job as a liaison officer and other people were going out and sitting on top of those hills. So when they started bringing in enlisted personnel and other officers both white and Black into the battalion, I was living the life of Riley. I had a choice job. I didn't get dirty anymore. So I had no white enlisted personnel under my command during any of my military career.

[There was] not a lot of discussion [about being second-class citizens, but] there was an acknowledgment of it. And there was a feeling among all the young [Black] officers, [although] it depended on where we came from. I think some of the young GIs, enlisted personnel, would have been a little bit more belligerent, a little bit quicker to take another person's life if they felt that person was stepping on their toes or somehow making them less than a man. There were some, maybe some of the officers, that had an attitude that they won't take anything from anybody: "If I'm going to be required to come here and die just like everybody else, then I'm not gonna go home and take any crap." There were probably some that said, "Okay, I'll go back, and I'll do my best to change." There were different, I think, attitudes to that issue. I don't think anybody would say, "I won't fight because I won't be treated as a full citizen when I get back." I don't think that attitude existed then. I never saw it. I think there are people who have said things like that, but I don't think anybody who ever said those things [was] ever in a combat situation. [My attitude] was similar to most of them, that it doesn't make any sense that you want me to come over here and get shot or killed to defend my country and my country won't defend me when I go back and try to get an education, try to move into a new neighborhood, et cetera, et cetera. No, I didn't like it worth a hoot . . . [but] I did not have any type of vision about coming back and saying I'm going to devote the rest of my life into correcting it. I think you know within yourself that you'll reach a point where if a thing bothers you like a segregated society that you will deal with it your way, when you have to. Sometimes it's best not to tell people how you're gonna deal with it. But you'll deal with it your way when you have to.

[Segregation in the army] cost them victories. It cost them lives. There is no rational way you can justify segregation. Every officer is taught certain things about tactics. A bullet can't see color, so you don't commit people into combat based on their color. If our military made decisions on whether or not to commit troops into combat because of the color of their skin, number one what that means is that all the white troops are going to be the only ones exposed to the danger of being shot when they got off board, when they come ashore on the landing craft. If they don't have the reserve troops to come in and relieve them because the troops have to be Black, then they stay online. You can only be affected for so long. You can only take that for a while. You've got to be pulled out in reserve, pull somebody else in, and give them a breather. If the military practiced segregation to the point that they would not commit an all-Black unit into combat because of their color, you're gonna waste some lives.

Almost in any phase of American society, . . . African Americans were kept down because of their color and then at some point they were allowed to compete on an equal basis. You'll find that they would excel or exceed if given that opportunity. That does not mean that everybody's gonna do it. But as a group you'll find that if given an equal opportunity there will be some who will excel or exceed their counterparts. That's true with the military, too. I think [segregation] was a grievous mistake. I think the good old boy network, which ruled the army up until the '50s, which was primarily controlled by West Pointers because they looked out for their own, did more damage to the military and to American society than they ever realized. President Truman was not a West Pointer and decided he needed all the help he could get, and President Truman decided this isn't right to begin with and ordered integration of the military. That's the only time they saw it and since that time people probably think, "Well, why didn't we do this before?"

I think there were other aspects of it, too. Maintain[ing] a segregated society has a lot of cost that people don't admit. You gotta maintain separate housing, separate facilities, separate training, separate everything. It's like separate but equal education—you gotta have two schools, two labs, you gotta have two of everything, and the segregated army was no different. To maintain the segregated society is costly. There are some people who are willing to accept the costs. I think today you'd have a hard time trying to sell that.

There are a number of African American generals that have come through since that time. I have two friends who retired as generals who came out of my high school. When I went into the army there was one African American general who later had a son who became a general. That was the only one, Benjamin Davis was the only one that I knew of. Now you can't name the number of African American generals. But I'm sure that all of the African American officers who stayed in the military can say that the integration of the armed forces was paramount to their advancement in the military, and I think enlisted personnel probably would say the same thing. I just was not in to see it.

William L. Jackson
2nd Lieutenant, Headquarters Battery, C Battery, 999th
   Armored Field Artillery Battalion, X Corps
US Army
Interviewed by Kate Ellis and Stephen Smith, August 23, 2002, Little Rock, AR
American RadioWorks, Minnesota Public Radio

REAMER C. BELL SR., CINCINNATI, OHIO

We had a racist battle commander that came to replace the one that was there when I arrived. He was from out of Tennessee originally, came in with his second-rank officer. They just treated us like dogs. He was a racist from the word "go." He came in very prejudiced. He had his kangaroo court set up. He even set up a [stockade], a chicken-wired fence over six foot high. That's where anybody who got out of line, he'd lock him up, and assign a guard around it. I mean it looked like a pigpen, when it would rain. And you can imagine what a rice paddy used to be, nothing but muck. He would put these guys in a tent, and that's where they stayed, fed them through the fence, like they were feeding a pig or something. I doubt very much [white soldiers would have been punished the same] 'cause [we] were already integrated; they were there in our unit. They were there, this was late '51. The only ones in that pen was Black, and this is what he did. I have had to walk around my own buddies. I wish I could have done something about that, 'cause that was criminal. He should have been [called] on the carpet. He should have been known about higher up in the military, and he should have been court-martialed. The man should have been court-martialed.

And they would sneak up on our posts, which took a lot of nerve. This little 2nd lieutenant he brought up with him, just as racist. Now, we were up on our post, and our guns [were] down in the valley, and we got bunkers dug up there [above them]. And he would come around all of a sudden; he'd try to catch you when you're asleep. That was his reason, to bust a Black guy. We would see this lieutenant . . . looking at the foxholes. That's scary; he could have been blown away. Guys thought about that, too, and it would have been justified. Hey, you don't sneak up on somebody sitting there with a BAR [Browning automatic rifle], and all those automatic weapons, and we looking down at the front line. I can go on and on about that. And that happened in '51. This was hateful, but that didn't bother me. But other than that it was good to be integrated because we should be. So I have no bitterness about it, I just wish it had always been integrated, you know.

I didn't get my sergeant's stripes until I was back in the country. And it came through headquarters. My company commander — and now this was another Black unit in 1954, we are still all Black, 100 percent — the company commander, when he came up, he says, "You got your sergeant stripes." And he says, "I couldn't have stopped them if I wanted to." 'Cause I was supposed to have gotten them in Korea. We are always behind. They caught up with me in 1953, and I should have had them over there in 1951.

You know about the [civil rights] marches and the demonstrations [later]. Look, we've fought for this country, [and] when we came back [from Korea, Black] lieutenants and up were not allowed in officers' clubs, can you imagine that? Now this is the army. They weren't allowed in the clubs. And that is talked about a lot, you know. It is still hurtful. We talk about it, you know, . . . 'cause [when] Blacks get together, there is a little bit of aggression, whether it be the dance floor, whether it be sports, and lo and behold, in combat. A lot of guys have not been given their [just] rewards, you know, that they deserved years ago back when it happened. But it is beginning to come in, and that hurts [too] because a lot of those guys are gone, they are dead . . . [and] a lot of them didn't get [it]. But other than, it is just that I did what I had to do, and I really would do it again.

Reamer C. Bell
Corporal, 999th Armored Field Artillery Battalion, X Corps
US Army
Interviewed by Stephen Smith and Kate Ellis August 23, 2002, Little Rock, AR
American RadioWorks, Minnesota Public Radio

ADEN R. DARITY JR., BOSTON, MASSACHUSETTS

I came out of the service [after World War II but] was very dissatisfied. I couldn't get myself together and I went back in. When I went back in, I stayed at Aberdeen [Proving Ground, Maryland] for a period of time. And had a chance to go to NCO school. They sent me to Fort Benning, Georgia. At that time they had a trucking outfit, medical, and I worked there. While there I had a chance to go the second-echelon school, I also had a chance to be a motor sergeant, and that's what I was doing just before Korea broke out. My enlistment ended and I reenlisted just a few days before Korea. When I reenlisted, I enlisted with a field artillery outfit called the Triple Nine. At this time it was supposed to be the latest equipment they had, with the 155 howitzers mounted on tanks. The enlisted men [were African American] . . . we had all-white officers.

They assigned us to the 3rd Division. We transferred out, stopped in Japan for a period of time to train. At this time it was the early part of the Korea conflict. The outfit I was with was the last one to leave out on the ship. And we landed in Inchon. My outfit fired cover for the marines at Chosin Reservoir, and it was in the very, very cold wintertime. I work[ed] as a service man, an automotive repairman. I was in the Headquarters Battery and my responsibility was to see that all the vehicles would operate there. I did have the chance to work with tanks. My duty was never in the category of combat. As a repairman, I stayed in the yard most of the time with the vehicles. As you know, support is important also. If we don't get the equipment there and the supplies that they need to do their duty, they can't do anything at all.

I've been assigned to a number of outfits, but I have always traveled alone — the only time I traveled with an organization was with the Triple Nine. The other times I traveled alone as a replacement. And I did have a chance to go back to Germany. And there were very few of us [African Americans,] but I did go in an outfit that was mixed. And I did well with them, I didn't have too much trouble. Because sometimes it depends on you, it depends on the person and their attitude. And how they can work with people and the situation as it comes and deal with the situation in such a way that after the situation is all over, we can walk away smiling. While I was in Germany, I did get married to a foreigner. I was the only one, in my section, that was colored. And they used to ask me every day, what are you going to do when you get to America? And I said I don't know what I'm going to do, but I know one thing: I'm gonna try to live, find me a place where I can make a decent living for my family. And they said, oh, and left me alone.

Aden R. Darity Jr.
Rank unknown, 999th Armored Field Artillery Battalion, X Corps
US Army
Interviewed by David P. Cline, October 25, 2002, Boston, MA
American RadioWorks, Minnesota Public Radio

One of the ways [the war] changed me [was] in terms of how I look at people. We were put together over there. Once in combat, no color. There were unpleasant situations, but . . . life is not for you alone, you share what you got. We shared a lot of things, gave each other small things, like longer breaks. By suffering you learn to care about others. Sometimes you'd take the place of somebody else if you felt you were stronger than they were. Sometimes guys volunteered and didn't come back. So the guy they'd helped would go visit the dead one's family—say I'm here today because of him. You don't think about it, just do.

Something else I didn't understand when I got there. I got assigned to all-Black outfit because that's primarily what was over there then. It was mostly Blacks over there, because whites weren't jumping up for military jobs. The enlisted were all Black, one or two Black officers, but [the] head of [our] company was white. And I'm supposed to be from a generation that wasn't ignorant anymore—a lot of guys with me had some college. We talked about that, about what we wanted to do when we got out, go back to school and change certain things—somebody gotta make a change. MLK started while we were over there; we read about him in *Stars and Stripes*.

The [enemy] dropped fliers while we were over there. We'd be sitting around, and we'd pick up the [fliers] from after they bomb[ed]. [The propaganda] was an embarrassment to us, for someone in a foreign country to know how we were treated. And we['re] over here fighting these people to make it better for somebody back home. Remember the guy that got executed in North Carolina named McGee? They had his picture on fliers dropped in our area. It did upset us—it [seemed] worthless, here's what we are risking our lives for and we still ain't counted. We talked about it, saying we're over here fighting a war and a man can't even get a fair trial because he's Black. And the chair malfunctioned, and they put him in it a second time and killed him. He died because of hearsay. A white lady said he winked or something. That's the part that really hurt when they dropped them fliers that said lay down your arms because you're not the perpetrator. They'd done their homework—they had facts that we didn't know anything about even.

[Integration] didn't make much difference to me. I had no problems with it. It wasn't a big deal. As long as people respected each other. [The] primary reason [to support integration] was [that there would be] more recognition and better [opportunities] for Blacks. When they brought white[s] in, it was a totally different feeling that we had—could have been because we were far from home—[but] we accepted them, told them things they needed to know. The army teaches the buddy system, so that's what we done. The first guy we got in—[I] think he was from New York—name was Lucas. We were off the line then, and we had these cots. You'd make it up like home. Lucas had a picture of his girlfriend up. The guys would go up and take her picture and say, "She's staying with me tonight." He didn't do anything maybe because he was the only white there. One guy, Batson, kept her for two days.

Samuel King
Staff sergeant, 999th Armored Field Artillery Battalion, X Corps
US Army
Interviewed by Kate Ellis with Stephen Smith, August 24, 2002, Little Rock, AR
American RadioWorks, Minnesota Public Radio

Integrated Units

As stated earlier, by 1951, African Americans in integrated units accounted for more than 30 percent of combat replacements in the US Army. Whereas Samuel King experienced the desegregation of his unit on the fly, some, like Larry Hogan from Boston, who went into battle with the 7th Division Bayonets, 34th Infantry, fought alongside men from many backgrounds from the start. Hogan's unit was one of the last still using fixed bayonets as they charged into battles, such as those at Pork Chop Hill, over and over. He served well over a year on the front lines, one of two in his unit to emerge unscathed. Long periods of unrelieved combat were common. Ernest Shaw spent seven and a half months on the line as an officer with the 31st Regiment, 7th Infantry Division, earning a Silver Star for leading a flame-thrower team into heavy fire to destroy an enemy bunker. "I felt highly gratified that I was perceived as a so-called hero and given that level of respect and recognition, especially as an African American," he would say some fifty years later.[13]

LAURENCE "LARRY" HOGAN, BOSTON, MASSACHUSETTS

I volunteered for the infantry. One of the things about the infantry: some people can be a doctor, some people can be a lawyer, nurse, policeman. Any of those jobs I wouldn't take on a bet—not my thing. But at the time I could do [the infantry]. I was psyched for that. I could do that. Knowing that you're going to go into the infantry and knowing what you're going to do made it a little easier for me psychologically. I'm just speaking for me as an individual. And the older I get I can look back on it and figure out some of the reasons why. One of the reasons was you got ten thousand dollars if you got killed—your family got that and ten thousand dollars back then was a lot of money. You got a pension— an allotment came home to my mother and sisters—that was good. I got paid about seventy-eight dollars a month, for my rank, the lowest rank, . . . and when I went into combat, I got another fifty dollars a month. I was sending it home, but my mother saved most of it. She saved a portion of it for me for when I got home. I was telling her keep it because you don't know if you're coming home. It was a couple a hundred dollars back then. So I was becoming a millionaire there in my own right.

That was my reason for going in the infantry, and I've never regretted it. I mean [there were] times when I wished I wasn't there, like anything else. But I've seen people who weren't in the infantry that suffered more psychologically, because if you were in the infantry you got four points a month for being on line—[in] nine months you got thirty-six points. And in theory you came home, if they weren't fighting. It could happen that at twenty-seven points they would rotate you out. So you could luck out. That's if you were on line. If you were a mile back you got three points a month, if you're halfway down the peninsula . . . you got two points, if you were in Japan you got one point. So you multiply that by the month.

[All] I knew [about Korea] was that's where the fighting was. I came from Harlem and like five guys had already been back. Really young guys. I went when I was seventeen. I think Arlington went when he was sixteen. Back and wounded. They were telling you what was happening. So I knew there was a war going on and everything like that. I went in right after I graduated high school. A buddy of mine, we went down in December, we were ready to go. I told my mom, and she said finish high school, get my diploma. So I finished. My buddy went in December. I went in that March.

[I got to Korea on] October 7, 1952—a muggy, misty, rainy, overhung day. Have you ever been up in New Hampshire in the mountains on a gray day? Gray all the time, gray. We went to Camp Drake, we took a boat over from Camp Drake to Pusan, and . . . halfway down the gangplank I looked up at the sky and you could just see the mountains just going up and then you don't see the tops of the mountains. And I was thinking, it was my mother's birthday. I said, Holy . . . . Well, that was October 7th. What's today? The 25th? I was fighting my ass off on the 25th.

On the 14th they ran a thing they called Triangle Hill, up in the Gimhwa Valley. [I was fighting within] five days. I always said they owed me something because they said, "You come in and go to the replacement depot and you'll get five days of training." I think we looked at three days. And they had started that Triangle Hill, and the next thing I knew we were on the back of a deuce-and-a-half goin' right up there. Right up there. That was the first big one I was in.

And I didn't find out this stuff till years later, but that was the part of the war where we had been pushed back and the talks were starting and everything like that, and Mark Clark was the commander at the time and he said, "We're going to make a push." So that's when we pushed all along the line. And that's when we pushed up to White Horse and Kumar Valley, and Heartbreak Ridge. You've heard of that from the other wars, but that was the Heartbreak Ridge they were talking about. Heartbreak Ridge, the 2nd Division was up there. They got slaughtered up there. White Horse and "Papasan," [Hill] 1062. They had the tunnels and the caves, and the things built into the mountain. They had hospitals and things built into there. I knew back then all about . . . what they used to talk about [later in] Vietnam. They send people down in the hole in the ground. Two years ago, I had the occasion to go back to Korea. [We visited a tunnel] they had built right under the valley. They were coming right across the valley, right under us. I think it caved in or something, so they found it. They kind of sealed it up and now it is a curiosity thing. You can come from both sides. You go all the way down the tunnel, you go down for maybe three quarters of a mile, and the bottom is a glass [window] there and we're on one side and the North Koreans were on the other side.

They had built the tunnel and they were already up there when we found it. That was one of many, but this was a huge one. They could run something like thirty-three thousand men up there — I can't remember the statistics now — in a certain amount of time. They had waystations where the tunnel went down. They had cooking stations, the kitchen, all down [in a tunnel]. See, we weren't used to living like that. It was hard to get us to build a little foxhole three feet deep until it hit the fan. You'll go crazy digging.

[Surviving] is dumb luck. It's belief in God — to me — and it's dumb luck. 'Cause anything could have happened. You don't get the four points a month if you don't do anything. You had to be there, you know. You had to be there. Four times we were on [Pork Chop] Hill . . . I had the occasion to be on that sucker four times. I didn't realize that until a while back. We were there in March, April, and July. Maybe June, but I know March, April, and July definitely. July was the last time we were there. April was the bad one. They were all bad, but April was the bad one. A lot of hills, different companies and different regiments and divisions, when they change over, they'll call the hill something different. . . . Like there was Old Charlie, and the 3rd Division called it Kelly or Jolly or whatever. But hills like Pork Chop and Old Baldy, everybody called those the same thing. Certain hills everybody knew. The Punch Bowl, Heartbreak, Pork Chop, and Baldy, T-Bone, they know those ones. It's just a trip, a trip.

[At Pork Chop,] we were fighting a war of attrition — we take it today, they take it the next day. Somebody comes up with a plan and says we're going to push up here and we do. We ran patrols at night, and you fight in the daytime. You jump off in the morning, maybe 4:30 in the morning, you jump off and you start up the hill. And we're going to take it today — we'll take it! — and you do a lot of fighting, and we take it. And maybe a day later they turn around and take it back. And you go back again, at some other time, you go back again. You get caught up into the battle. There were quite a few of them. A lot of time you get in just to relieve somebody. "Get a platoon, it's going up there to relieve Charlie company." Well, that would be the biggest battle you ever saw.

This is another thing that I think is very important, because like you're going to sleep and depending on people. It happens, I mean you got so fatigued you just fall asleep, you're not doing it on purpose, but that's [a] very important thing. That's when you come to depend on people, and in the dark, who knows who's what except that you and I are going home.

Now I couldn't speak the language, and the Koreans [we fought with], they had many a time [when they would call out in Korean] because they smelt that kimchi. They'd smell that stuff coming across the valley, you know, like you could get a whiff of anything. And when it's that strong, [they've got] a lot more people than we got. When you smell it out there, you got a lot of people coming. So that was the type of thing that we used to call "pulling your coat." Careful tonight — if they start overrunning us, we're out of here.

[I carried the] M1 rifle. M1, A1, model 19-18, M1, A1. Semiautomatic, clip fed, gas operated. It had a nineteen-inch bayonet. Do you know what the spirit of the bayonet is? It ain't for opening C-rations. The spirit of the bayonet is to kill. That's what it's for, that's all it's for. And I was in a regiment, that's what we were. Our division was the Bayonet Division — that tradition goes way back. The marine company might have fought the last one, but I think the 7th, we fought the last bayonet attacks in Korea.

When you go up a hill, you fix bayonets. At night, we'd have them on. And we didn't have the short — you see the little short bayonets — this bayonet is a nineteen-inch bayonet. This is like out of proportion — it's a big bayonet. You slash with that. There's a whole drill you do with that. Slash, thrash, hold. You see the bevels there? They're in there for a reason — you stick [a regular one] in, it comes out. [With this one a] body will grab on it, suck [it] right in there, ain't going nowhere. You want to leave the rifle there, but you don't want to do that — that's not a good idea. . . . You had to shoot it out. It ain't like the movies, see, 'cause if you hit somebody like that and you in that far, you're in there.

[One time,] we were on the line, they broke through on the left, I think, [with] the Triple Nickle[s], [the enemy] took their artillery pieces. They came through on the right. I don't know who the hell was on the right over there. We were up on our hills, and they came through and they got the Triple Nickle guns and they were firing the Triple Nickle guns at us! And Syngman Rhee let go a million prisoners on Koje-do Island. I said, "This is unbelievable!" And we just got this million-man Chinese army in front of us and they're on the bullhorns, saying, "Welcome men of the 7th Division, we know you're here." And see now you know you're in the war, 'cause now it's *you*. They're calling out people's names, people know who you are. It gets very personal. The whole United States Army gets down to the infantryman, even the pilot in the plane. Because if he crashes, he's mud. . . . That's the difference being in the infantry. It's really stupid and it's weird, but people do it every day and people sacrifice to do it, just like a doctor, lawyer, policeman, and fireman. And they will never get the credit for it, they will never get the credit for it, just to stand there. You're handling more just standing there because you're talking about a high-stress job when you know that—it's unbelievable—that someone wants to kill you. You're not even mad at them. Well, you'll eventually get mad!

The only two guys that I know [of from my initial unit] that didn't really get wounded were myself and a guy named Floyd C. Perry. His father was a reverend in Cleveland. He was like a sniper, had a sniper rifle. Perry and I, after the battles were over, we'd always just look up and look around for each other. And he'd look at me and I'd look at him. And we never used to say too much. 'Cause we're saying, man, oh man, because if you were hit, but not too bad, you're coming back. I've seen guys get hit five times. There were guys couldn't take that kind of stuff, guys shot theirselves, but if you weren't hit too bad, you're coming back [home].

Most of the guys I know [who] were in Korea . . . got wounded. And they might have got wounded in two weeks, they might have got wounded in three months, they might have got wounded in six months, and they might have saw a lot of fighting! The more I start thinking about this, I say, "Wait a minute— I didn't get wounded that bad!" I got concussions, shaken up, my knees—but nothing that you weren't gonna send me back in. Throw a band aid on me and tell me I'm going back. They say you gotta take R and R. Two weeks' R and R. I wouldn't take mine, because I'm staying on line. I'm four points away, I'm staying right here. I got away with it. I made seven months before I had to take R and R. They came and caught me!

We were on a hill one time, goin' up a hill, and we've got three-quarters of the way up the hill and we're getting the shit kicked out of us. And I carried a PR-22 radio, which is a big Black radio, nothing but batteries, I had that on. I had an M1 rifle, that's my regular rifle, and I had a couple of bandoliers. And somebody gave me the BAR and said, "You got to take the BAR up the hill, you guys got to take it up there." Because we didn't have that many guys, so if we got up there, that's more firepower. So the guy's going up with the rifles, and a couple of guys said, "Yeah, well I'm carrying an extra one, so when we get up there, we'll have one." Some guys said, "Put your M1 down," and I said, "Let me tell you something. I'll carry everything, and that's coming with me!" That's a very powerful weapon and you can depend on it. If it gets wet, if it gets cold, if it gets mud in it, if it gets sand in it, I know that I'll shoot that thing, and everything will come out. I'm comfortable with that, and a BAR you had a clip, and you get on the hill, and the artillery grinds the sand up so fine, it's like sand on a beach. You look at it, it's like a New Hampshire hill. You're no longer running up a hill, you're running with sand up to your knees.

We got up the hill, we got three-quarters of the way up the hill, and we got bogged down and everybody was eating the dirt. I was trying to figure out if I could just get these buttons off my shirt, that's how close I was. This captain or lieutenant stood up, and he got hit, got hit in the eye. . . . And he's bleeding and he's yelling: "Get up, get up, you yellow bastards!" And he's yelling everything at us just trying to motivate us. And nobody's moving. You're just going to get yourself shot to death anyway. Everybody's down and they're just firing like crazy. And he said, "Okay, hey, forget it, okay. You don't go up today, you go up tomorrow." Man! That guy said that to me! That resonated with me! And I'm three-quarters of the way up the hill! I got up and started boogying. We got up and took the hill. We took it. But it's amazing what motivates people any given time. That doesn't happen every day. Because I try to figure out what is a hero and what is a coward? It's just a matter of who's there at any particular time.

[My war ended] not with a whimper, with a bang. We were still fightin' up to the 25th. I left the line, they were still fighting, they were still fighting, right up to the last minute. The artillery was firing, they were doing some rumbling. I think they were still on Pork Chop and Hill 200 and all in there. They were still fighting.

But I left and I was going down the hill and I said, "Oh, shit." You ever get, you know, you ever get apprehension? You know, today you think the brick is going to fall off the roof and hit you? You ever have those days? All the time, all the time, and you know it's going to hit you right in the middle of the head, because you're saying you know what? This is too lucky. I'm not going to make it from here to that boat. It can't go like that. That's like when I said you get 27 points, you try to get rid of a guy, if you can. 'Cause after a while, the guy's no good. You got three points, two points, you don't even see the end. You don't even see it, don't even think about, don't even think about home. You don't even want to hear it. So your mind is, your churning on other stuff. Sometimes you don't even write home. That's why people don't write home. What am I going to write? I'm okay and I've got nine months to go? Are you nuts? I don't even want to write that, I don't even want to put that on paper, because if I put that on paper, then I'm out of here, you know? 'Cause this is real, you know, so you don't want to do it. Some guys, you know, they made it right up till the end, made it right up till the end. They say, "Where's so and so, he's rotating [out]." "No, man, that guy got hit."

A guy could be over there eighteen months in the rear and a little something something happens, and they need troops, he's goin' up to the front anyway. So now he's been there eighteen months worrying about going up to the front and it could be the last week [and he gets called up,] because if something happened, they pull guys from Japan, they pull guys from Alaska.

But it wasn't a Black-and-white thing that way. There were more white[s] in the divisions, but people were getting killed at a rapid rate—we lost just as many people in three years as they lost in ten years in Vietnam. Now in order to do that, you had to be doing some [fighting] every day. Continuously, day and night you know. We lost a lot of people. When that happens, it gets to be a very integrated thing very fast, very quickly, 'cause all you're looking for is a warm body, somebody to come up and fill this hole, replace this guy's, somebody you hope is well trained, or you can get along with, or whatever. So it gets to be cohesive in a quick amount of time.

[Now, there] was [racial] tension on the line, so I can honestly say I'm sure I had some [racial] thing, [but] you know it would just blow up for anything, it could be anybody. I mean if I try to think of incidents, it was another guy, just a guy, for any reason. You did see a lot of that [racial] stuff when you were going to the rear. Because these guys brought all their [attitudes] with them and they were terrified. [But I] didn't go back anyway to the rear that much, but say we had some down time, there'd usually be a fight over gambling—guys were playing cards. The rebels would get their guitars and we wanted to play our R&B and you know we just had arguments on that stuff. I saw individual guys get into where things happened but I never saw it where it was gonna be, "We're gonna get them," like they got up to in Vietnam. We didn't get into that, not in my unit. I come from New York and anyway the wind blows the breeze cools me, you know. I'm used to growin' up with all kinda people, you know. Nobody likes anybody period, but everybody loves everybody.

Laurence "Larry" Hogan
Sergeant 1st class, 34th Infantry Regiment, 7th Division
US Army
Interviewed by David P. Cline, October 25, 2002, Boston, MA
American RadioWorks, Minnesota Public Radio

CLENTELL JACKSON, APPLE VALLEY, MINNESOTA

I was born in Minneapolis, Minnesota, General Hospital, 1929. I was in the 25th Infantry Regiment and the 24th Division. I was in a heavy weapons company. There were four platoons to a company, and I was in the 4th platoon, the heavy weapons, the other three platoons were riflemen, and we were machine gunners, BARs. There were only twelve of us that integrated the service at the time, and they say that we were the first to integrate these white companies. I started out as last ammo bearer, I carried the ammo for the machine guns. And I worked all the way up to platoon sergeant. I think there were three or four Black guys in my platoon and the rest were white, maybe twenty-eight or twenty-nine men. In each platoon they had four squads and each squad had five to seven men.

They had one Black regiment [in Korea], the 25th Division, the 24th Regiment. That was the Black regiment, that's where they put me on orders to go there. That's where all the Blacks went, and we had orders to go over there. The Korean War had just broken out, it'd been going on for two weeks, and we were on the water, and they changed our orders right on the ship. [I was headed for] the 24th regiment in the 25th Division, then when they changed my orders, that put me in the 25th Regiment in the 24th Division. That's when they integrated. There was twelve of us originals that integrated [the 25th Regiment], and we integrated right on the ship, on the way over to Korea. We were [put] together, there was no segregation on the ship at all. They just changed our orders, that's all they did. They told us that we were going to the 24th Division, 25th Regiment. They let us know, so many to this company, and so many to that. There were twelve of us, I think in my company, and there were five of us, the four besides myself, that went to the machine gun platoon. The rest of them went to the 1st, 2nd, 3rd platoons, the rifle platoons, small arms.

Right after we got off the ship, they gave us an M1 rifle, with one clip of ammo, which was eight rounds, [and] put us on the train, heading to the front line. I met my officers and everything. We were on the train three or four days, up and back, up and down the line. We'd get close, you could hear the gunfire, the large guns, the large weapons that shoot maybe a half a mile or more. You could hear them booming. It's nerve-racking—you'd get nervous, but we joked about it and everything else, to keep everybody feeling good.

Of the twelve of us [Blacks] that joined the outfit, only three of them died. Nine of us came back alive. They died from the enemy's bullets, or you never know. Guys were paying other guys to shoot them over there. They were saying, shoot me in the leg or something at night. Two or three [men] died that way, they wanted to go home so bad. You really get scared, at night especially, because you don't know where the enemy is. We went out at dusk and were supposed to climb this mountain and set up a line of defense. We climbed all night and kept smelling this smell—we come up and there are Chinese, gooks, Koreans laying all over, dead ones. That was the smell. The next day we're kicking, and pushing them down the hill, trying to get away from the smell, but you can't. It's a hell of a smell. There's no fear, I used to walk around dead people and think nothing of it. Now you go to a funeral home, you feel kind of funny. At that time, it didn't faze me because there were so many, and all of us were going through the same thing. Some guys would really be fearful, but after being there so long, you just see one laying, and you'd push them out of the way, and you'd let it go at that.

Overseas I went right up in rank. I went from a PFC all the way to a tech sergeant, and that's all battlefield commissions, where you go up in rank. [They] told me to stay two more weeks and I'll make you master, but I told him, "No, send me home. I don't need that." They were killing so many guys, getting wounded, that's why it was easy to go up in rank. If you showed any promise at all and had an idea what was going on, they'd push you up. I had a fear of death. And I said to myself, I'm not going to get killed over here. And I really believed that. I said, "I'm going back home when this is over." And that took me all the way through, over there, during the war. [I served] three years, nine months, and eight days, I forgot the hours. I graduated from high school in May and I went in September of '48 [and served just] one [tour of duty]. I got the Bronze Star and two Purple Hearts in a cluster.

Let me tell you why I got the Purple Heart for frostbite, and also I got shot in this leg here and I didn't even know it until we were crossing this pond and the water got up over my knee and I felt a burning sensation and I ran around telling everyone. I was so happy because I was going to Japan, getting away from there! [The] other [wound came when] I got blown off a hill. They were throwing grenade rounds at us and this one hit about twenty feet from us and it just picked us up off the ground and kind of threw us and knocked the wind out of me. I didn't get hurt or anything. I had shrapnel in my back, but I didn't even know that because [with] all the excitement and everything you don't notice things. I went and sat down and my back was all red. I went to take off my shirt and I said, "Ooooh." The shrapnel was in my back, you know little pieces of steel. And it went through the shirt and it pushed the shirt into the holes, too, that's why it was hard to get off. Once I got it off they picked out the big ones, and I had one that came out about ten or twelve years ago, a piece of shrapnel, but it was so small you could hardly see it, but you could feel it. There were a whole lot of guys that that happened to.

My machine gunners, we were on the trail and we were going to set up a defensive line and we run into some Koreans and we didn't know they were there and they start firing right away. I had to set my machine guns up, like a dummy, I could've gotten killed and didn't even know it. They were shooting at me but they were so far away, the bullets so close, when you hear them pop, they're close, just inches from you. I told the machine gunner to get out on this ridge, it was a mountain, a point out here and another here, so we had to cross machine gunfire so no one could cross that hollow, that lane, because it dropped on both sides and then leveled off and we had to keep the machine guns going across both sides. I guess the sergeant gave me the Bronze Star for that. I was put in for the Silver Star but . . . the major, he was a captain and then he made major, I think he got wounded and never came back to finish the paperwork or something for the Silver Star.

I got along pretty good with the guys. There was never anything said about [race]. The whites knew new troops were coming in. We were in a war zone, so there wasn't too much rejection, the more the merrier. When they integrated the army, it was no big deal to us. To me it wasn't a big deal, because I had been around white people all the time, raised up, went to school together. But some of the guys, I guess it was a big deal to them. They were finally getting on the same level, and they figured this was a plus, but to me, it didn't make any difference — it went smooth with me because I'd experienced it already. I had problems with two or three guys, but I didn't worry about them, I'd get them. Some of the southerners did [have problems adjusting]. Maybe there were two or three that wouldn't associate with white guys at all and then others who'd do the opposite. You'd find bad on both sides . . . [but mostly], we'd crack at each other and just have a good time. "Minn-nin-apolis," they used to call it. We'd crack up, and we'd ask guys, "Where's Minnesota at?" And they didn't know nothing about it. We had more fun. They used to call me, not hillbilly, they'd call me, what was it, "Here's the Lake Man." 'Cause I had told them, "We got ten thousand lakes in our state."

I had a whole lot of good friends over in Korea, and the majority of them were white. This kid from Mississippi, he had me write his mother and his sister; he had blond hair and blue eyes, but he just really liked me. The reason I got to know him is he was on KP [kitchen police], and I was in the chow line, I was the last one in line and he came up to me and said, "Hey, boy, come help me tote this garbage can over there." I said, "What do you mean, tote? You better get out of my face." I told him he was just a private and I'm a private 1st class, I had more rank than he had. And we got in a little scuffle. He hit me and then I hit him. And I told him, "Boy, that's a pretty good blow you got there." And he said, "You got a damn good one, too," something like that. From then on, we shook hands and we were buddies, we were the best of friends. Guys would talk about me, he hauled off and hit a white kid who was saying something about me that he didn't like, hauled off and hit him. He said, "That's my buddy, you don't be calling him names," and he laid this guy out. I was real surprised. I said, "I got a real friend here." And I wrote his mother; his mother and sister, were really nice people. They knew I'm Black. The mother said, "You take care of [my son]," she'd write me letters, and "Don't let him do this, don't let him do that." I don't know what he told his mother about me, but he was a real friend. Then he wanted me to go home with him. I turned him down. I said, "No, no, not in Mississippi."

If they'd have been integrated years ago, years before they did, I think the whole country would be better. The people would think different of each other. We're living together, so I know almost as much about his ways as he knows about my ways, and my wants, and things I like to do. And I'd learn about things that he'd like to do and a lot of them get into your mind. I looked at certain guys over there and you can almost tell what they're thinking: is that hate in them, or do they envy you or are they friendly? You can tell by their expressions. They always taught us that "the man on your right, you look out for him, he's going to look out for you, and you'll end up alive and so will he." And that's the way the army taught you, in a sense.

[Now,] a lot of the Chinese [who were] captured . . . were educated in this country, [and knew a lot about our racial situation]. And they'd say, "Come here." And you'd walk over to see what they want, and they'd tell you all this stuff: "What are you doing?" I had a Chinese soldier say, "What are you doing over here? You should be on my side helping me. You're going to go back home and be segregated against and everything else." They'd be so convincing, it isn't even funny. They'd stop and make you think. I'd think about it a lot, there was a lot he was saying that was true. You can't hardly give him an answer to different things like that. You tell him, "Well, things will change," [but] you're probably saying to yourself, "They'll probably never change." This guy, he's [bringing me] down over there.

I didn't have an answer for him the first time. The rest of them, the rest of the Chinese just looked when he said that. I just stood up there and looked simple. I might as well have told him, "You're right." But I didn't. I did tell him to mind his own business, I told him, "Well, who are you to talk?" And let it go at that. It was kind of an insult to me. I felt funny about it, and I thought a whole lot about it. But I never let onto him that I was worried about it or thinking about it. I just told him where to go and what to do. I thought about it a long time and I talked to a sergeant over there, a Black sergeant. He said, "This is the way it is. It's been like this for years, it's something you'll have to deal with. Don't worry about it, try to throw it out of your mind, forget about it. Forget about the Chinaman, what he said." But it's kind of hard to forget because he was speaking truth the whole way.

And then I turned around and hit one of them . . . because he said, "All you are is a second-class citizen, and you're over here giving up your life for him, the white man, he's not going to do anything for you, he's not helping you one bit." And they had a whole lot of Blacks convinced of that. I should've never hit him, but you do get mad when someone says something that hurts, and you can feel it. The first thing I thought about doing was swinging, and it was the wrong thing to do. And there was a lot of hate over there. I didn't see a whole lot, but I seen some. I pulled different Black guys aside, and I'd tell them, "Hey, at least, you might be segregated against in the US, but it's not as bad as some of these other countries," and let them know that they'd have to educate themselves and they can get over different things.

Clentell Jackson
Technical sergeant, 25th Regiment, 24th Infantry Division
US Army
Interviewed by Tina Tennessen, September 10, 2002, Apple Valley, MN
American RadioWorks, Minnesota Public Radio

MARK BRADY HANNAH JR., HOUSTON, TEXAS

When I went overseas [to Korea] I was in [the] Honor Guard. I was a good soldier. I was really a good soldier, but the guys didn't want me there. They didn't tell me [they didn't want me,] they just shipped me out. They shipped me to H Company, Mortar Company 81mm. I [was] the only African American in that company. And so I got there and being a corporal, that would make me a squad leader. [But] the guys there in the 81mm company didn't want me to be in charge of their company and so they said, "Well, we'll just kill the nigger." [Now,] my father's a 32nd degree Mason and he was able to talk to the brethren at the lodge to let me go in as a juvenile at seventeen and I became a full Mason before going overseas. So the CO, he was a Mason and I was wearing my [Masonic] ring and he asked me to become his valet and his jeep driver. I refused. I told him my uncle told me that in World War II the only thing Negroes were able to do were drive jeeps or cook, and so I refused. And he sort of liked me and said, "I'm going to give you thirty days" to make up my mind to be the valet and I refused. [But] they didn't let me back on the mortars any kind of way, so I was just there because those guys said, "We'll kill him."

I wasn't quite used to that coming from Wichita, Kansas. After finishing grade school, you just automatically went to Horace Mann Junior High or North High or East High. My father finished high school and he was born in 1913. And we had our own park on the corner with a nine-holed golf course. We had tennis courts and a pool and field house, and they had two baseball diamonds and I thought everybody lived like that. [It] was Black, middle class. Dr. Forman and next to him, Dr. Scott, Dr. Jeeter. On my street it was Dr. Simms and Dr. Bell and Mrs. Flakes, and my grandfather lived right behind her. So this [kind of hatred] was all new to me. I knew we had problems but I didn't know anything that rough.

So they sent me up one night to [the] 224th, Charlie Company, and I'm the only Black there. And those guys were eating turkey and all that stuff and I said, "God, you guys eat well here," and they said, "Well, we frequently go up on Pork Chop Ridge," and I couldn't finish my dinner then. And they made me point man. [The Chinese] had this 348th [Regiment] and this tank deal and [there] was a battle that we lost and had heavy casualties. I was in a foxhole with four guys and a mortar came in and killed them and my right leg was burned. I'm getting together with some of my colleagues now that were a part of that company and division. And I went to a convention and I was still the only black there a couple of months ago in San Antonio. They've written letters that I should get a Purple Heart [for that burn].

Anyway, we moved after going off of Pork Chop Hill and then I was made platoon sergeant. And so one night the CO sent for me and told me that I would be going down to the foot of the hill [to] operate the tram that night. I was going home. And they needed me to take [the CO] up and show him around and stuff like that, and [then go back down the hill and] the jeep will pick [me] up tomorrow. I was on the tram . . . that night [and] my whole platoon got killed. I knew every one of those guys that were coming down that night. It was a whole platoon plus and there are forty some men in a platoon. Forty-eight men [got hit] if I can remember right, probably more than that. They said that it was a night that they couldn't believe.

So I just knew that they were going to send me back up there, but I went on [and rotated out], and so I go into Japan. [But] I only had eighteen points. You had to have thirty-nine to rotate out of Korea, I only had eighteen and [that CO,] he gave me wings. So the next thing I knew, I arrived in the States, in Camp Carson, Colorado. It took me a long time to deal with [having survived and gotten out]. As it did when those four guys got killed and I didn't, I just got burned. It was only, I would say, this last three or four years that a light came on. Every day I read the 27 Psalms plus other things and "The Lord is my light and salvation and . . . ." It goes on to say that "He protects us," and so I attributed it to that.

Anyway, I got back to Camp Carson, Colorado, in Colorado Springs. I didn't even think about going off base because I didn't know anybody in that part of the country. I was wearing my sergeant stripes on the base, and so I was arrested by two MPs on the base . . . about the sergeant stripes; they could not find any other records on me other than that I was shipped in there. And so the base commander said, "Well, this guy surely isn't AWOL because he's on the base. He was shipped in here but we have no records on him." And he said, "Where do you live, soldier?" and I said, "Wichita, Kansas." And he said, "How'd you like to go home for forty-five days?" and I said, "Yes, sir!" So he said, "Don't wear those stripes," [and] I said, "Yes, sir," but I wore them.

When I got back, they really didn't tell me anything, and the next thing I knew I was in a replacement company in Tacoma, Washington. They all were Black in the replacement company—it was supposed to be integrated and this was in 1952—but it was all Black in this replacement company. This was my first encounter with a lot of Blacks, and it was on the north [part] of Fort Lewis, Washington, and they frightened me too because I had never been around that many Blacks. And the guys, the way they carried on cursing and gambling, I just had not done those things. That's after coming from Korea.

But somehow by the grace of God they shipped me to the main fort [as a] replacement and I asked if I could change my MOS into a cook because I was raised up around hotels and waiting tables. And so I got this sergeant, Sergeant Greenberg—he was in the Philippines and had a good portion of his face cut out, he was one of those that went through real tough stuff—and he was very cordial to me and I went in as a cook. And I was a 1st cook and probably [after] three months I was assistant mess hall [because] I could do typing. In this particular company we fed probably from two thousand to three thousand per meal. Sergeant Whitaker was his name, he was the mess sergeant.

The officers wanted to have a party in the mess hall deal and I knew how to make hors d'oeuvres and how to cook the clams and they really liked that. I used to put on a show! Outside, they had four grills to make the pancakes and where they had four guys I did it all by myself, [making each batch and then] come back down and turn 'em over. And so they got rid of Sergeant Whitaker and I became the mess sergeant in the largest mess hall in the main fort. And that was a very pleasant deal for me, the best I had ever had in the service.

And I was wanting to be a disk jockey [when I got out] and I bought a lot of equipment. At night I would be over in the mess hall and I'd set up my turntables and a lot of guys used to come over there. In fact, I was the only Black in that company too. And they used to come over and watch me turn the tables and listen to the music and I liked jazz and Dave Brubeck. And so [word got] around and I started going to the radio station and doing that in Tacoma, Washington.

My time to get discharged [was] April 10, 1954. Well, two months before that they offered to make me a warrant officer if I'd stay, but I knew that I wanted to go into the ministry and I knew that I wanted to get married, so I got out.

Mark Brady Hannah Jr.
Platoon sergeant, 224th Regiment, 40th Infantry Division
US Army
Interviewed by David P. Cline, January 10, 2003, Houston, TX
American RadioWorks, Minnesota Public Radio

RUTHERFORD "JACK" BRICE, ATLANTA, GEORGIA

From Fort Knox I went to Korea. This would have been right before Saint Patrick's Day [of 1950]. An interesting anecdote: When I got to Korea, I was assigned to the 11th Airborne Division, 187[th Regiment,] and it was on Saint

Patrick's Day that I got to the reserve marshaling area. All the officers, every-body, was celebrating Saint Patrick's Day. However, if you looked around there was only one face like me. So I went to the officer's club where they were working. And an officer that I had known at Fort Campbell, Kentucky, said, "Well, Brice, I never expected to see you here! How you doin'?" you know, "Let me take you in." Real nice guy. And he says, "You know, this is an Irish party, so we got to do something about this." So he got a saber from the corner and he made me kneel down and he took the sword and tapped me on my shoulders, and then on the tip of my head. Said, "I christen thee O'Brice." I thought it was funny.

I was Special Forces as a jumper, and we had an advance drop 66 percent casualty [rate]. I was hit in my leg and sent to the Philippines, to Manila. It wasn't a serious kind of thing, it was more shrapnel than anything—just scraped up my bone a little bit. At any rate, I came out of that and I couldn't jump. So I was sent . . . to the 23rd Infantry Regiment, C Company, of the 2nd Division. I went to basically the same . . . marshaling area, [because] the reserve training area for the 2nd Infantry Division was just where the other one had left. That's when the 2nd was training to go into the attack for Heartbreak. And that was interesting because I was in an observation post the night before I was to join that company, C Company, looking at the preparation for and the jump-off for this attack. Actu-ally we called this thing 1069, the height of the hill. That was Heartbreak.

Heartbreak Ridge was one of the [fiercest] battles in that valley. Because Heartbreak Ridge—as I said, the height was 1069—was the predominant domi-nant landmass in that area. You could see all of the valley from there. And we had to have that land in order to see what was developing with the troops, you know, the enemy troops all over the place in that particular area. So that's why it was important to us. But it was really well fortified from an artillery standpoint. And nobody had really taken the hill and held it. I was in two situations like that where we were just back and forth. I mean they kicked our butts off, we'd kick their butts off. Same thing happened with Heartbreak. It was really a heartbreak. Climbing up that thing from the reverse slope was unbelievable, the paths there. They, the Koreans and the Chinese, had it all tunneled in, and they had artillery in the base, they'd been there for a long time. Finally we, along with the 24th, took care of that hill. They [were] routed and went off and we defense landed for I don't know how long because I went off to someplace else. There were a lot of people killed there, . . . at Heartbreak. It was one of the most [fierce] battles we had in Korea. Bloody Ridge, Heartbreak Ridge, Old Baldy, and Pork Chop. And I was in three of them. I was in Baldy and Pork Chop. Most of my combat action, from a commander's point of view, was at Old Baldy. I was company commander of the unit. I was platoon leader at Heartbreak. But I was a com-pany commander at both Bloody Ridge and at Pork Chop.

I think probably in my mind the most exciting and most responsible position as a company commander [I had] was during the siege of Old Baldy. I was the executive officer for the C Company of the 23rd Infantry Regiment, 2nd Division. And we prepared for this attack on Old Baldy. And I was in charge of the blocking position for Old Baldy. Old Baldy itself, the mountain, was I imagine about two and a half miles away from the blocking position. And the blocking position was to protect our troops in case they had to fall back. We used to say, "bug out." And I had the rocket launchers and machine guns, and two platoons of troops to aid in the blocking position. Let's just say — and I'm not really convinced I remember [exactly] — the attack went off right about 7:00 p.m. It was a night attack. It didn't really get dark until probably about an hour and a half or so after that. It's interesting, I guess about twenty minutes or so after the attack had started the company commander was hit. And he was evacuated. And the battalion commander called me and said, "Brice, get up there and take charge of the hill."

We had D Company and E Company on the sides, and my C Company was going up the middle. This thing had been going on for quite a while, so the hill was really pulverized with artillery. It was not a big top on this hill so it was very difficult to hit with artillery. So a lot of the rounds were coming off the back of the hill. So when I say pulverized — trying to get up that hill from the center, because that's where my troops were concentrated and that's where the observation post was — I had to go through this stuff, it was like climbing sugar. I mean, it was just very difficult. Patska was the company commander of D Company on the left flank, and a guy named Evansville was the company commander on the right flank, and my troops were in the center.

I remember two of my platoons were not there, they were still in the blocking position. But I took with me, as I went, the rocket launchers. I didn't take the machine guns, they were too heavy. Rocket launchers were easy to take [and] the ammo was easy because you could strap it across their shoulders. I laugh about this because I always tell about coming up this hill in the back and how it was like sugar or salt that you're trying to run up. As we were climbing up the back of this hill, I could hear this round. It was a mortar round. I could hear it coming. And, you know, when you don't hear it anymore it's about to drop. And I didn't hear it anymore. And crap went everywhere. It landed, but it didn't explode. It was a dud. And me and these two guys, it was like our butts took wings. I don't remember touching the ground at all till I got up to the top of that ridge! And I want you to know, that as much as I hate to tell you this, I peed all over myself! But it really didn't make any difference, and I was sweating anyway. So anyway, we got there, and we took care of organizing at that point.

Within seven days we had secured this hill and taken care of the enemy. We'd knocked out the machine guns, we got in good position. Air cover had gotten there and took care of their artillery, et cetera, and we thought we had secured it.

As a matter of fact we did. Remember that the 24th, the marines, a lot of people had been there before we were there trying to secure this thing. And I was on that hill seven days, [and] during that time what I remember is the only thing I ate was grapefruit out of a can during that whole seven days. I must have lost about twelve, fourteen pounds. I was recommended for the DSC [Distinguished Service Cross] and got the Silver Star, as a result of having, for all practical purposes, command of the battalion at that time. And that made me feel good. It was quite an experience. I did a lot of growing up during that seven days.

Rutherford Vincent "Jack" Brice
Captain, 1st Battalion, 23rd Infantry Regiment, 2nd Infantry Division
Interviewed by Frederick Wallace, April 22, 2003, Atlanta, GA
Rutherford Vincent Brice Collection (AFC/2001/001/05397), Veterans
    History Project, American Folklife Center, Library of Congress

JOHN B. JACKSON, HOUSTON, TEXAS

I arrived in Korea May of 1953, to Inchon, assigned to the 2nd Division, 32nd Regiment, 4.2 Mortar, which was a blessing to me because I was scared. I [had] realized sometime through training that we were fighting for democracy for a people I had never heard of. And I looked back and I said, "Jackson, wait a minute, you're going to Korea to fight for democracy and when you left Houston, Texas, you were segregated, you did not have the word democracy." And I was angered about this because President Truman is sending me over there but yet I knew that if I ever got back to Texas, I would still come back to that "undemocracy" system, that I would come back to the same one.

When I arrived in the 4.2 Mortar Company all the oldies were crowded around the truck because I was a replacement, and they welcomed replacements with open arms. And [there was] a "slack," and I was replacing him because he had the points to rotate out, and he just hugged and hugged me and all this, and he said [let's] go to my bunk and he got out a bottle of vodka, and I'd never had vodka before and he said, "Have a drink on me. Welcome to Korea." Here is a white guy doing this for me because he was ready to come back home. But he welcomed me as a soldier, as a man, and he just made me feel great. So I was very comfortable in Korea.

But you go in as a 4th ammo bearer, then you move up to 3rd ammo bearer. As 3rd ammo bearer, you drive the trucks and you haul the weapon around. So I had to drive several weeks and then I moved up — because of rotation you just move up: 2nd ammo bearer, 1st ammo bearer. Your steps move up and that's how my ranking came because I got there at the time I was able to get into the ranking of sergeant because of the rotation. And just because of good work, I guess. I was platoon sergeant. I was squad leader for a time and then I became platoon sergeant.

I was [on a] 4.2 mortar so I'm behind the infantry and I'm in front of artillery so we are stationary. The 4.2 has to be mounted and it's a stationary weapon, so I did not come in contact directly with any person on the other side. [But] we were hit . . . by our position [drawing] fire. I can only recall one casualty. An African American came in, recruit, brand new, and as they drove up and parked they were taking the equipment off of them and we were hollerin', "Get down, get down!" Because when you're under fire you learn how rounds sound and how close they would fall to you within your position. And we were telling him to get down and he did not get down and a fragment hit him while he was on the railing of the truck and that's what got him. So he never [even got off the truck]. I can see it when its infantrymen going out on the line of fire. But here's a person just getting in and it just happened to be an African American. I've thought about it — he didn't get to enjoy the democracy back in the US that would probably be in place for him where he could go back to his hometown, go to the front of the restaurant, don't have to ride in the back of the bus and give [his] seat up to another race. But he did not have that opportunity.

So those were the hurting parts and it was all races that died like that but with an African American it was just really hard for me to understand why did I have to go to Korea to fight for democracy when I knew that I did not have democracy in the US as it was [defined] by Webster.

I was there for the cease-fire. The night of the cease-fire was, I don't want to say dramatic, but very touching — that we delivered that much ammo and explosions into a community and they signed a treaty. The same people that you fired at last night, they're out waving at us and we're waving at them the next morning because they had signed a treaty to ceasefire. It was unreal. It was something to see. I did not think that much about it then but over the years, I thought about what it really did mean to be firing on people and then not firing.

We were rejoicing but we knew, we understood, that we'd still have to stay in Korea because when there was war you were going to be rotated by points, but then there was the cease-fire they eliminated the points. And you had to accumulate time and that's why I stayed there longer because they stopped the point system. So we just stayed there and worked the other tour of duty there. [But I] was just rejoicing because I didn't want to fight. I'm not a war person but I want people to have their rights and that's why I was willing to fight.

John B. Jackson
Platoon sergeant, 4.2 Mortar Company, 32nd Regiment, 2nd Division
US Army
Interviewed by David P. Cline, January 10, 2003, Houston, TX

We came from Fort Lawton by ship to Yokohama. We left the ship by train to Tokyo and had to process on the train on our way. Lawrence Wirdlow, he was my buddy and pal, we thought we would be stopped in Japan and we would have some garrison duty. We [thought we] didn't need to worry too much about combat as a 2nd grade lieutenant. So on this train, the captain came through and processed us. He said, "I'm going to give you three sheets of paper and two envelopes. Put your name, rank, and serial number. Put down if you don't have next of kin or someone, list who you would like to receive your money in case you don't come back." Then it hit me that things were moving kind of fast. I had gotten married in 1950 [and now] I didn't know if I would survive Korea, and I thought, well, whatever will be will be. So I had reconciled myself to deal with it. As I indicated, I had been in World War II but saw no combat. We had excellent training in Tuskegee [though,] and some of the officers were in combat in World War II. They integrated the concepts of war as being a necessary evil and if we were going to be good officers, we would have to adjust ourselves to the ways of war. It was a way of helping us acclimate.

We went by train from Tokyo to Sasebo, and that gave us opportunity to go through the two cities [where] we had used the bomb. I saw and thought it was midnight, but it was daytime. We went by truck to division rear and from division rear to the front lines. So it was moving fast. I didn't write any letters, I didn't whimper too much, [I] just put a little distance in my mind between what was going on and what I had expected to do.

When I did arrive in Chuncheon, which was division rear, the young man with me was so gung-ho, he went out with the chow truck to hurry up and get to the front lines. I told him good-bye because I wasn't going any faster than they required of me. He had already been assigned to a field unit and I didn't see him for a few months. I was given charge of Company A, 3rd Platoon, and my company commander was Dwight Haight. Captain Haight was a tremendous man, confirmed bachelor and very wealthy. He treated me genuinely. Didn't ask anything of me that he wouldn't ask his other officers. I was the first African American junior-grade officer to join that unit. The platoon I assumed leadership of was under the command of a sergeant, Sergeant Derflinger, [a] tremendous sergeant from Illinois. I was among fellow officers and they accepted me, and I gave it my best shot.

From my vantage [point as a Black officer in a mixed unit], it was fine. I had no misgivings about my role and responsibilities. Having gone through Tuskegee and being told, "Things won't be easy, but you'll be expected to do what you're expected to do," that's what I did. I felt confident because I had gone to Fort Benning for seventeen weeks of leadership training. And by then I had been exposed to Anglos, junior-grade officers and enlisted men. This was the first time I had been given to command mixed troops in a situation in the field, so that was new. Sergeant Derflinger, he had been in charge of that platoon before I came because the preceding lieutenant had been killed, so I indicated to him, "While I get orientated, you just keep on handling things as you did. If I have reason to countermand orders, I'll let you know." The battalion commander, the colonel, accepted me and made it clear that there might be folk that might not be too happy, but most folk aren't too happy with 2nd lieutenants. Not necessarily because of your race, but because you're new. [The commander said], "Any problems that transcend your authority, that's why I'm here." The first patrol I led over the lines, he was the last person who shook my hand. By then we had stopped moving, were running patrols every other day. Had several men who didn't return—of course, that didn't sit well with me or anyone else. But I managed the best I could and I'm proud I did.

It was a real opportunity to lead men in combat and lead men who were well trained and wanted to be led. I didn't give them any orders that I wouldn't take myself. When [I] was getting ready to leave seven and a half months [later], they indicated that, "Lieutenant, when you came we didn't know what to expect, but we would go anywhere with you now." I said, "Well, I'm going home." That's a true story.

[When we] moved into Korea, we were moving pretty fast. Most of my time was spent on the lines. It puts you in a state of alertness beyond normal range of what should be. That's part of training, you have to stay focused. I spent a winter there and it would get exceedingly cold. We had [better equipment] later, but the hardest part was our feet. Our boots—they later got a vacuum boot. Also [with] the cold, whatever we used for lubrication would move slowly. When you fired your weapon, you would have to help it along.

I followed the North Koreans and Chinese. But the big part of the fight while I was there was with the 2nd Division. They had taken high ground and we were their relief north of Yeongdeungpo. The name of the valley was Myungji Valley. That's where my unit was disposed with tanks, tanks dug down. We had a pretty bad night for New Year's Eve [1952]. We were on the front lines, dug into the main line of resistance. We had flares [and the] troops wanted to make like New Year's, and they wanted to shoot off a few flares. We lost a few men because instead of flares they were Bouncing Bettys, and Bouncing Bettys, they throw shrapnel in all directions. That was not good. I felt bad about that because I had given them permission to make like New Year's.

But I never asked a man to do anything that he failed to respond [to]. One of the troops I lost, named Nash, an Anglo from Arizona, volunteered to go with me on a patrol that he didn't have to go [on] because he wasn't in my platoon. But I didn't have a man in my patrol who had knowledge of using the flame-thrower and Corporal Nash said, "I'll go." And he didn't make it back. That disturbed me and still does. But I guess I'm talking about the fact these men were very loyal and courageous.

We put out listening posts, and we would have an outpost in front of the lines in order to alert the men of incoming enemy, and on occasion the enemy would infiltrate between listening posts and outposts and the main line of resistance. And we would lose those men. Not often. We were mostly running patrols while I was in combat. We ran patrols almost daily and nightly. We would go on prisoner capture missions and reinforce patrols, mostly platoon size or less. Invariably the goal was to get [prisoners] as quickly as possible, relieve them of any armaments, and pass them on to intelligence. In the military you have four segments in any group. In a battalion you have S1 personnel, S2 intelligence — and that's who we were to pass them on to, we were not to interrogate, just keep them alive — S3 training and operations, and S4 supply. And each subset would have its own people. As a junior-grade 2nd lieutenant, my job was to capture and pass them on back. Also keep them alive, and naturally when a man is angry, lost buddies, they are not placid as they would normally be. My job was to be sure to carry out the mission according to the order.

We also tied in with the Ethiopians, and they were good fighters. You could tell when they were your replacements or you were theirs 'cause the Chinese would not come too far into the lines 'cause [the Ethiopians] would throw their rifles down and use spears and bayonets. They were awesome fighters, too. As officers, we couldn't occupy the whole perimeter, but you had to make contact with the person on the right or left flank, and one of the requirements was that the officer accompany the squad to set up defense of that position on the right or left. I had already passed the point at which I should stop before I realized I was surrounded by Ethiopians, but the officers were English speaking, some had fought Italians in World War II. We would chat and exchange food. Some of the Hispanic fellows would get peppers sent to them and in a C-ration can you get corn[ed] beef hash, et cetera, and I would get some peppers to make it more palatable. My point is that it wasn't all bad and all traumatic. Not all fighting, some light moments. I had a chance to read mail. I remember one patrol, I had my wife's letter in a Bible, her name was Marie. But I wouldn't read the [letters] as soon as I received them because they would cause you to get overrelaxed. So I would wait to get back in reserve. A piece of shrapnel had lodged in it. When I opened my mail, there were little pieces of shrapnel that had penetrated the New Testament of the Bible. They didn't penetrate [me]; I had no visible wounds. I came back unscathed, according to the Department of the Army, but I did not. But I persevered.

[One time] we were over training [some] South Korean troops in [the] background in reserve. The colonel told us . . . "We didn't bring you to get killed in the background, so go where you have to go." While I was gone, the 2nd Division had taken the lion's share of Heartbreak [Ridge]. The 7th Division, of which I was a member, was given orders to give the 2nd Division night relief. I didn't go on recon, my sergeant went 'cause I was being brought back from this training mission by jeep. When we arrived, he came and he said, "Lieutenant, it's going to be awesome, it's going to be bad." At that point, I recognized that this might be it. I knew I had a job to do, but thoughts go through your mind.

I was sitting on my bunk cleaning my carbine and .45 and thinking about what might happen. We struck tents and went by truck and waited until night-fall [to give] relief. I don't know what platoon I relieved. It was night relief. [We were] instructed to leave our weapons at the bottom of hill and would relieve them on sight; that's how close we were to the enemy. I was disposed on a river-bed [in an area] called the Mundungnee Valley. I had almost a full complement [of men]. That night we fired all night. We had quad .50 machine guns firing up the valley and we did get hit, but we repulsed the enemy. The next day they moved the rest of my company into the valley. Heartbreak Ridge was quite an experience. We lost an innumerable number of men. As a junior-grade officer, you just do what you're told. But on that patrol, there was a company on the attack. We were on Hill 839 — Heartbreak Ridge is a media concept, [we didn't call it that at the time]. To my knowledge the 2nd Division took the brunt and we relieved them and what happened after I left, I can't know.

I was relieved of my assignment [after seven and half months] and left the front lines and became a motor officer for the battalion. I had been recalled in-voluntarily. [I now] think that was a blessing in terms of not having bit the dust. I was getting weary. I was brought off the hill by two Anglos, one arm around each shoulder of the men. I was injured twice, once by shrapnel and once by a grenade. I didn't yet receive my Purple Heart because it didn't show up in the record, but it did occur. I haven't given up hope on receiving it.

[I went] back to Japan, we just reversed the [path] and came back to Fort Lawton in Seattle, Washington, and on back to San Antonio, and came to Fort Sam [Houston]. My sergeant met me at the airport. We went out that night and several people said, "Shaw, where you been?" They hadn't missed me. Think that's why they call it the forgotten war 'cause they had forgotten I had gone somewhere.

Ernest Shaw
First lieutenant, 1st Battalion, 31st Regiment, 7th Division
US Army
Interviewed by David P. Cline, January 10, 2003, Houston, TX
American RadioWorks, Minnesota Public Radio

[My] second year [in high school] as a sophomore, a group of us got together and decided to volunteer for the army. We were being bussed from Johns Island to Burke High School in the city of Charleston because we couldn't go to the high school on Johns Island. It got to the point I couldn't even afford lunch, and was treated so bad, being from the country, and speak[ing] a language called Gullah, and folk always making fun. There was a feeling in our folk that if you spoke Gullah that you're stupid. You know I'm around people every day now from all over the world that got an accent, and everybody [says], "Oh, that's such a beautiful accent." But with mine, it makes me "stupid." I was sixteen at that time, but they really didn't care like they do today. They "let" my age be eighteen and I was able to go into the military. [The reason I joined the army was] poverty, just that simple. The military is a way up for a lot of poor kids.

[I served for] three years [in] the army. But you know . . . I've been the first in so many things. And I try to teach young people, especially young Blacks, you don't need to be the first. The first suffer more than any. If you can be second or third then you can do it, but being first is not a good place to be. I went in the army right after they integrated the army. What they did is that they couldn't send people that volunteered for the military out of the country for training, so I went to Hawaii. I took my basic training in Hawaii. And there were just four or five of us Blacks in each one of these companies. Again, I suffered more racism in the military than any place I've ever been in my life, especially on Johns Island. I mean racism was just so bad in the military. [As] I look back at it, I suffered more racism in the United States Army at Schofield Barracks in Hawaii than I've suffered any place in my life before or after.

And the bad part of it for me then is that we got our training in Hawaii and went straight to Korea. Everybody used to have vacations and come home, but we went straight to war, went straight to Korea, no vacation, no nothing, went straight to war. And they took us in on an LST [landing ship, tank], where they dropped the front of it in the water, where you run up on the beach with the guns and bayonets and stuff like that, and that was one of the scariest things [even though] we were about three miles away from fighting anybody.

The racism was real, real bad in Hawaii and Korea. And I realized, later on, it was 1951, right after they had just really integrated the army. There were four Blacks in our company, with one Hispanic, one Indian, and we were the really [the first among a group of whites]. I didn't realize until many years later that all of these people were poor white men who also had a lot of problems. And the only place that they could vent any of those problems was on people like me.

So, they had their own problems, reasons, and we had a lot of fights with that. I had physical fights.

And, you know, a guy would beat me, but I [would] end up being the one getting in trouble. I had such a bad temper, and I get real mad. I don't give up, so I don't stop when people say to stop. But they did so many things to the Blacks. We had one guy, one of my best friends, who died recently, they made him dig a six-by-six-by-six hole. And then the sergeant dropped a dime in it and then made him close it up. You know, those are the kinds of "stuff" that we went through. And a lot of it [is] coming back to me more and more now, [and I'm] just having a lot of flashbacks with that.

Even in Korea, in the war, [I had problems with racism]. I mean my 1st sergeant, who I didn't know, on the front line—we'd just fought for two days, and I was going up the hill, on top—and he said, "You Black son of a bitch, if you come up here, I'll blow your brains out," and he had a .45 on me. My rifle was in the [fox]hole, and I [thought I] could roll and get my gun, you know, like you saw in some of the movies. And then I decided after a point, that .45 will blow a hole straight through [me], because I had seen .45s shoot people, their whole back blown out. I went back to my hole and stayed there. When it was time for us to leave, he sent for me and made me lead the whole company out. Because, being in front, you get killed first, so he wanted to make sure that I was in front going out. So, there's a lot of stuff [like] that, that we can laugh about, because if you don't, you cry about it. But the racism was just really heavy.

And coming back, even into California when we got back as heroes, because I got wounded, and we were there in California, and they start calling out the white soldiers' names and then they called the Black soldiers. I never understood [why] until we got on [the train]. Black and white soldiers couldn't ride in the same train coach across America, you had to ride in separate coaches.

I stepped on a booby trap on, God, December 26, 1951. It'll never go away. And [it was one] one of th[ose] really odd things: the snow was almost two feet deep, and the rule was everybody walk in the same [track]. The squad leader walks there, and everybody, fourteen men, walk right in that same track. Because I was assistant squad leader, I was the last man in the [line,] and it went off on me. That's the kind of luck I've practiced most of my life! And, you know, it hit me, and I went up. It hit my M1 rifle and busted it in half. And then it was what you call a booby trap trip-flare that had went way up, about fifty feet in the air, and lit up. And that's how they used to shoot people, because they would show you where you are.

I knew I had not lost my leg, I felt it was there. Some of the soldiers said, "Well, we want to go get a stretcher for you and take you back," and I said, "No, I'll walk." So the medics said there wasn't nothing wrong with me, because I couldn't walk if something was wrong. And about four o'clock that morning we were attacked by the Koreans. We fought until about five or six-thirty that morning. And my foot is swollen up so big it's about to burst open. And the medic said, "Well, we'll send you down to let them check it." By the time I got to the aid station, the doctor said, "It's broken." And they put me in a jeep, then on a hospital airplane, and I went to Japan and spent four months in the hospital there.

I was in the hospital in Fort Jackson for four months for my wound. After my four months was over, [I] went *back* to Korea, on the front line! They changed the law [soon after] — all laws have always changed with me! Anytime you got a broken bone, you went home — except they changed the law right [after] that time. My luck was like that. I went back to Korea for another two months.

[When I got out of the army,] I got paid, got about five hundred dollars, which was a monumental amount of money back in those days. And we went into Columbia, South Carolina, and I ran into the Greyhound bus station. My buddy kept the bags, and I ran into the Greyhound bus station. And a cop came to me with his gun pushed down and said, "Boy, what's wrong with you? You know you don't belong in here!" And I never knew that I didn't belong in a Greyhound bus station, because I'd never been off of Johns Island to go through that kind of segregation. I said, "No, Officer, I didn't know I didn't belong here. Where do I belong?" And he showed me the back of the bus station where Blacks bought their tickets outside. And when the bus comes, whites loaded in the bus, and any seats that are left in the back, we had access to those seats.

My bitterness really began at that time, really hard. I just didn't understand it. At that point I began to call all white people racists, not because of what they do; because of what they didn't do. Here's this place full of soldiers that I fought with for a year, and all of them just dropped their damn head down. Nobody would say, "Well, Bill, stay in this line. Get the ticket," or, "I'll get the ticket for you," because I was trying to get the ticket for a friend of mine that was holding the bags. And what is that? Nothing. And I said to myself going home after the bus got all of the whites on and we got in the back of the bus, I said, "You got to be a damn fool. You're in Korea fighting for freedom for Koreans and you ain't free yourself." And I've been bitter ever since.[14] You know, the only place that I've ever *really* been an American was basically in . . . Korea and in Japan. I've never been an American in America. I've always been a second-class citizen in America.

[When I got back] I was about nineteen then, eighteen, nineteen, but I was still trying to be a man and I wanted to do some stuff to prove that I was. So, when I got [back] they sent me back to Fort Lewis, Washington, to Tacoma, and I went to administrative school. I took typing and all kinds of administrative stuff. I end[ed] up being company clerk and I was able to make [staff] sergeant before I got discharged. I was in charge of sending out people to get promoted, so I was in charge of who at least got to be eligible to be put in. So a lot of friends came back as sergeants! I end up making sergeant [myself] down in Fort Lewis.

William Saunders
Staff sergeant, unit unknown
US Army
Interviewed by Kieran Taylor, June 9, 2011, Charleston, SC
Civil Rights History Project
Interview completed by the Southern Oral History Program, under
    contract to the Smithsonian Institution's National Museum of African
    American History and Culture and the Library of Congress, 2011

It is important to remember that not all Korean War–era veterans served in-country in Korea, but for those African American sailors and soldiers stationed elsewhere in Asia, in Europe, or back in the United States, racial issues were never far away.

ALAN NELSON, MATTAPAN, MASSACHUSETTS

I am a Korean era veteran. I served three years in England, mostly in the London area, where I lived in Quonset huts . . . not too far from downtown London. I didn't want to get drafted [and] joined the air force to avoid combat. I was old enough to remember getting over World War II. That was a trauma in our life. Blackouts. Before I went in the service, some of the young fellas I used to play ball with got killed in Korea, so I decided to join the air force and have a little better say in what I did. [Still,] my mother cried like a baby when I went in. When you're a teenager it's a trauma. Most of [the air force guys] went to technical schools and from there they went to a final destination. You had to stay there until they shipped you off somewhere. Had they sent me to Korea, I would have went. [I had] firearms [and] gas training. But fortunately the shooting had stopped when I finished school and that's why I went to Europe [and spent] three years in England.

We were a novelty over there, [there were] not too many Black people over there [so the racial situation] seemed a little better. The women were very, let's say, *receptive*. There were Caucasian women just as fond of African Americans as they were of Caucasians. Little tension there. I had a good time over there. [There were] minor things among ourselves but in general nothing really to be worried or concerned about.

The section I was in was mainly Caucasian [but the] unit itself, Global Communications, had a lot of Blacks doing teletypes. [We did not have] too much trouble [with the white officers]. We answered to local sergeants and basically had no problem. At the same time, if their views were somewhat segregat[ionist], they believed they were right, quoted the Bible. Without my asking, they defended their segregat[ionist] beliefs: "It says in the Bible that we should separate." But never confrontations.

One time I was with a group of African Americans, and we had a little confrontation with "Teddy Boys," little English gangsters that didn't like Americans [and told us to], "Go home, Yank." So we had to run off. A white boy from Georgia was ready to stand toe-to-toe with me against these guys.

Alan Nelson
Rank and unit unknown
Interviewed by David P. Cline, October 20, 2002, Mattapan, MA
American RadioWorks, Minnesota Public Radio

5

African Americans and the Air Force, Marines, and Navy in Battle

The air force and navy were the first to respond to President Truman's order and instigate changes to race-based policies, and the marines were the most recalcitrant. At the start of the Korean War, African Americans made up 5.1 percent of the enlisted men in the air force but only 0.6 percent of the officer corps. The navy, which like the air force desegregated fairly quickly, had Black enlisted representation at 4.7 percent, but no Black officers. And, in fact, even the enlisted numbers are deceiving, since testimony before the Fahy Committee revealed that 80 percent of African Americans in the navy were cooks, stewards, or stewards mates, specialties that remained 98 percent Black.[1] Among those African Americans in the air force were veterans of the Tuskegee Airmen, the all-Black squad that had "integrated" the air force in World War II, but also African American women and men undertaking all manner of specialties on the ground. Among them was a young James Meredith, assigned as the first Black man on a B-29 bomber crew at Topeka Air Force Base and only a few years away from his historic desegregation of the University of Mississippi, a major turning point in the fight against Jim Crow and the advancement of civil rights.

Like the air force, the navy was quick to change following Truman's order, but African Americans still faced restrictions, with many sailors still stuck in the Steward Branch, while some found their way to responsible positions as hospital corpsmen and storekeepers. Black representation in the Marine Corps, which put up strong resistance to racial change, was even sparser, with no Black officers and only 1.6 percent Black enlisted men.[2] But every situation and every experience was different.

The day the Korean War started, there were just over 1,500 African American marines. Segregation was the order of the day, and about one-third of all Black marines were assigned as stewards, preparing and serving meals to white officers. By the time the cease-fire was signed in 1953, 14,731 Black marines were in service, and only 538 still served as stewards. As in the army, desegregation came about quickly once the marines found themselves in combat, with service units reassigned to combat. In the field, commanders often broke up the reassigned Black units, sending individual marines to whatever combat units needed a replacement. The performance of these Black marines in combat convinced the Marine Corps brass, which on December 13, 1951, made it official policy that Blacks could be assigned to any division regardless of race and, shortly thereafter, called a halt to segregating new units.[3] Throughout the war, the Marine Corps expanded rapidly while also desegregating all existing units, except the Steward Branch, which, despite an open policy, remained all Black. The officer corps, however, remained difficult to crack, and as the Korean War wound down, it remained to be seen if the Marine Corps had really changed its ways or just buckled to the pragmatic needs of battle.

Air Force

CHARLES WALTER DRYDEN, ATLANTA, GEORGIA

I flew with an outfit called the Mosquitoes. I tell you when I first learned I was going to be assigned to the Mosquitoes, I thought we were going to be flying the Mosquito, which is a heck of a[n] airplane from World War II, but that's not it. What we were, we were tactical air controllers, from the air, flying a T-6 trainer, two seats, one behind the other, no guns. And our job was to seek out potential targets, because the North Koreans were excellent at camouflage. And they would run a tank up in the side of one of their mud huts and cover it over with grass and you wouldn't even know it was there unless they had tank tracks leading up to it. And then not knowing that there was tanks and ammunition and so forth around, our troops, with extreme noise, would bypass it, and they would catch them from the rear. So our job as tactical air controllers was to find such targets and direct our fighters to knock 'em out. Like mosquitoes, we're supposed to harass the enemy. Well, I flew fifty missions of that and then returned to Japan and then returned to the States. So, I had thirty missions in World War II as a fighter pilot and fifty as a reconnaissance pilot in Korea. So, I survived both of the wars and that's why I say I'm blessed: to have survived two wars, two general court-martials, and two wives!

Charles Walter Dryden
Lieutenant colonel, 99th Fighter Squadron, 332nd Fighter Group, 12th Air Force
US Air Force
Interviewed by Myers Brown, February 28, 2002, Atlanta, GA
Charles Walter Dryden Collection (AFC/2001/001/43847), Veterans History Project, American Folklife Center, Library of Congress and Atlanta History Center

When the government of Mississippi tried to block the entrance of James Meredith to the University of Mississippi, federal government troops guarded and protected him. It was certainly not the first time Meredith had been surrounded by uniforms. He had been in the air force for nine years before his desegregation of Ole Miss. As he recounts below, it was a pivotal time in shaping his growing activism.

JAMES MEREDITH, JACKSON, MISSISSIPPI

My first assignment was [to] Topeka Air Force Base, Kansas, and that I'm sure had a great impact [on my future activism]. Because that was 1951, just at the beginning of the Brown [v. Board] decision. The Browns were from Topeka; I knew the Browns. You could not stay three years in Topeka and not know everybody, everybody Black! Blacks could only go to the skating rink once a week, on Tuesdays.

But I went to Topeka Air Force Base and I was assigned to a B-29 squadron, the first Black ever assigned to a B-29 squadron. The B-29 was the one that dropped the atomic bomb, it was *the* plane, it was *the* thing. So, when I went to my assignment, they were still living in the old two-story World War II barracks. And they assigned me to a room on the second floor, and when I got back from work the first day, everybody on the floor had moved, not just my roommate. But they left me the only person on a whole floor. Of course, that tickled me to death because I thought that's what I deserved! I'm telling you, this Black-white thing, this white supremacy thing, is serious business. It still is. It was then, but it still is.

Then I left there and went to Indiana, Peru, [to Bunker Hill] Air Force Base. This was 1956. This is five years after 1951, when they started [what] they called desegregation. That had gone so well, they decided to do a whole base and start from an integrated position. They still retained the old 10 percent rule, you see. The 10 percent rule was that not more than 10 percent of any unit could be Black, okay. Now, that's the only thing they kept, but everybody was coming [to] a new assignment, everybody coming to that base.

In addition to desegregating the military, they decided to bring in Black civil servants, so my wife was a senior at Roosevelt High School in Gary, which is known for both basketball and being a good school. She had been one of the choice students in the typing and administration [program,] so directly out of high school she was given a job as a civil servant on that base. I had been there five months, and I had established my control—couldn't nobody talk to a girl within a hundred miles of that base that didn't go through me, and that's a fact!

For whatever reason, I wouldn't let nobody else deal with her, so she ended up being my wife.

We got married and went to Japan together. That took some doing. Many people take their cars and their families eventually. I took my Cadillac and my wife to Japan on the same plane with me, and that took some maneuvering. [We were there] three years, the most important three years of my life [because,] number one, although I had this feeling of superiority, the reality made me wonder if I wasn't really inferior.

Because . . . the first time I came home to visit my mother in Mississippi, I not only had to get on the back of the bus, but the bus driver on the Greyhound went and pulled a Black curtain, and all the Blacks had to get behind that Black curtain to make sure you knew who you were. I had a real problem with being alive and taking all this crap, you understand. So I was really beginning to wonder if I wasn't really inferior like they said we all were.

[In] 1957, even though the desegregation thing had been going on now for six years, it had only been ordered in Japan, Tachikawa Air Force Base, Japan, six months before I got there, and that was very significant. Because before then, Blacks had to go out the back gate. Only whites could go out the front gate. As a matter of reality, all of the Blacks still went out the back gate, and all the whites still went out the front gate, although the rule had changed. The Japanese out the front gate, the Japanese out there would call you a nigger quicker than a redneck in Georgia, but the Japanese out the back gate loved Black[s]. Not only was Black beautiful, they loved Black. So, it came to me clear[ly] that all of this race thing, this white supremacy, was manmade.

The other thing that happened, my assignment to Japan was to supervise an all-Japanese administrative unit. For the first time, the United States hired Japanese to do some of their administrative work, typing and all that kind of thing. I was assigned to supervise that, and of course, there wasn't no supervising. All I did was play golf, but it was a very significant experience. Number one, it gave me an opportunity to travel, so I traveled Japan. [The] race [situation] was different. It was totally unlike white supremacy [but] I don't want to imply that the Japanese were all that good!

James Meredith
Staff sergeant, unit unknown
US Air Force
Interviewed by Renee Poussaint, June 27, 2006, Jackson, MS
National Visionary Leadership Project, Library of Congress

I'm Hansel C. Hall. [I served in the] US Air Force [in] Korea [with the] 5th Air Force headquartered in Tokyo, 502nd Tactical Control Group. I wasn't in Korea a year. I went [to Korea] in February '53, came back September '53. That was the last year of the war. I got a commission out of the ROTC at Indiana University in Bloomington. [I trained at the] ROTC encampment at Wright-Patterson in 1950. [It was integrated] but there weren't many minorities, maybe eight or nine African Americans out of four hundred or so, I guess. My brother went to Howard, [and my] adviser wanted me to go to a Black college [too, but] I went to IU because my parents paid taxes there [in Indiana]. Blacks couldn't get their hair cut on campus, had to sit upstairs at the theater. I decided I was going to work on that, and we formed a group and we did. [I joined the NAACP] when I got there, [but] they were all white, sociology majors. Step by step we made some inroads.

[Growing up], my dad was active with the NAACP. We were told we were better than other kids. My parents knew what I was going to face, so they tried to build me up. [My brother is] up in Saginaw, [Michigan,] we have a tennis rivalry. He went from kindergarten to PhD, and from private to brigadier general, and had fun all the way. While he was a colonel, he found the names of everybody on the House and Senate Armed Services Committees and wrote them letters [about how] he supported them, so when his name came up for brigadier general, they knew him! He got married to the first African American woman to teach in a white school in DC. Going to the wedding, we saw some kids picketing a restaurant and I said, "We've got time, so let's go and help them for a minute." She said, "I didn't spend all this money to get arrested!"

The air force [was] integrated and made a big point of that. That was one reason I chose [air force] ROTC, because [the] air force was integrated. [The] air force was better [than the army]. There were human beings there. Tuskegee had been tested, the story was known. They knew there were guys who had tasted what the war was all about. The army was so much older, [racism was] institutionalized [there], unconscious. The House and Senate committees [were] controlled by southerners. They had their sons sent to West Point. They say Benjamin O. Davis was never spoken to outside of the classroom [at West Point] for two years.

I didn't have any opposition [to the war] at all. I liked Truman, not all his policies, but the buck stopped there—the Marshall Plan, integration with women. They had a quota, women was supposed to be able to do anything but couldn't have more than 2 percent of them in service. In Korea you didn't treat them like regular GIs, made them comfortable. The nurses, [it is] interesting to hear them. The ones in the Korean War Association are white, but there were some Black women in [the] service. One is traumatized, too, [she] got raped by a guy over there.

[The] ROTC . . . paid you monthly and that's why I went. My folks had no money and I needed more to get into school. [The] ROTC paid, so I got in there. It was a good program. There are few colleges in [this] country that teach leadership. Most colleges you only get it in ROTC. I thought it would be boring but was intrigued by studying battles, et cetera. I was an honor student and [was] offered [a] regular commission, but didn't want to go that way.

As I look back, it was so intense at the time. You had to have your will finished, and that made you think you may not come back. [That] got your attention. I was in an [ROTC] encampment when the war broke out. All of a sudden, we started paying attention — someday these experiences are going to be valuable [in keeping us alive]. I was called in because the war had started and they needed officers. It was unusual for African Americans to even have commissions.

In [the] summer encampment, they had people from all over [and] southern schools were segregated . . . [and] the southerners wanted to get Blacks out of ROTC. Playing basketball, a guy from Georgia would push me into the wall. I didn't say anything, just made the basket. A guy asked me why I took that treatment, and I said, "I [don't] want to get washed out of the program." He said, "They do that again, I'm gonna deck him." He did! A fight happened. When the police got there, I was in the middle saying, "Gentlemen! Gentlemen!" And I got five points!

[Military integration was] positive, especially in the air force. [It] became less fashionable to discriminate. I went to East Saint Louis to get shots, [spent] three weeks there. One cycle [of shots] put me in bed for three days and made me reconsider. From there [I went] to Detroit, and stayed six weeks, which was unusual — didn't find out till later they were trying to figure out where to send me. Finally, Wilson, a Jewish lieutenant colonel commanding [an] Upstate New York outfit, a National Guard active duty outfit, said he would take me. I went up there as assistant personnel officer. [I was the] only African American on the base. [There were] no Orientals, no nothing, all Caucasians. [I was there] almost two years. I got along very well in New York, Niagara Falls. [I] became defense counsel in special court-martials — you didn't have to be a lawyer then — they just looked at my record and saw I had constitutional law. I enjoyed that because the government was always making mistakes, and I never lost a case. I even had to go to appeals sometimes because [the] commander would disregard court sometimes.

While I was there I wrote the commander and told him I needed to finish my degree. So they sent me back to IU, all expenses paid. During the war, the air force wanted all their officers to have degrees. While I was back at IU, they were reslotting people, and I said I'd like a shot at Paris. They slotted me for Korea [instead]. In Korea, I asked [the] legal counsel if they needed help, and they made me a prosecutor. That was the fun part—you had to put the thing together, call Tokyo to get a court clerk. They gave you a plane and a pilot. I'll never forget when I got ready to get on the plane, a two-seater, the pilot was drinking. I was a brand-new 2nd lieutenant and was uptight about that, so I ran back to [the] commander and told him. He said, "That guy flies better drunk than he does sober!" Matter of fact, he did.

I was in personnel and training, and I was trial counsel for special court-martials. Lieutenant colonel [was my highest rank]. As a personnel officer, we started testing guys for promoting and change in their career fields. So I was a testing officer and went up to the sites. The 502 had four squadrons with sites. You'd get a jeep and a driver, usually with a .30 caliber machine gun on the back. Officers had .45s, enlisted men had carbines, and you'd be riding along and a sniper would shoot [at you]. I had about three of those [situations]. [Sometimes an airplane would] throw out a bomb here, bomb there, and we had to run to our foxholes. Other than that, I wasn't in combat.

The [court-martial] case I got a commendation on involved an African American kid from Arkansas. They told him to go from one point to another point in combat [but] he went to see a prostitute on the way. Everybody did it. [But] he knew he [only] had a certain amount of time and was rushed, so he ran over a Korean kid [driving back], killed him. We all knew other guys had been doing the same thing and [he] just got caught [in the accident] rushing away. We had to call the Korean police. It had been six months when I came [on the case]. I told the kid I had to prosecute him—I'd be as fair as I could, would try to mitigate results. I'd been told to move the case [through] quick, so we had court on Sunday, but his defense said the kid had to go to church. I didn't know if the kid had ever been to church before!

It was [a] sensitive [case] because race was under the surface everywhere. They wanted to give him . . . a dishonorable discharge and prison. So I recommended a bad conduct discharge. He told me he had five siblings, was from a farm, [his] mother was getting an allotment [from the air force, and he said, "She] can't live without the allotment!" [But the] Korean kid case [was] complicated by race and rank. They weren't sure [whites] would be supportive [but] things were changing. I handled it with aplomb. They issued a press release on it.

The 24th Infantry had some bad experiences [with courts-martial], and wrote a letter to the head of NAACP, and they sent Thurgood Marshall over there. The petition . . . they sent to the NAACP said [African Americans are] getting more court-martials, while only 15 percent of the army was Black, and getting longer sentences for the same crimes. When I got to Korea, I contacted my fraternity, Omega Psi Phi, and we decided we'd take risks to show [African

American] heroism to overcome [the bad] publicity from the 24th. I met Thurgood afterward, and we talked about how ornery MacArthur was. Those were exciting times. Did you know [Marshall] memorized the Constitution? He said as a kid he memorized it for acting bad and it was a tremendous help. Constitutional law was not an easy course.

The outfit I was in was from South Carolina, so middle management was mostly from the South. I had an incident with my immediate boss, but I'd learned how to politick by then. He was one of the old southern boys. He'd tell jokes in the bar—jokes about every ethnicity—and I wouldn't laugh. I thought I had some responsibility to let him know subtly it wasn't okay. [He would] give us orders to do something illegal, [like] "Go pick up my Korean girl," but I wouldn't do it. That wasn't okay. They finally found he had done some wrong things—he'd gotten a typewriter for his girl—so I didn't get in trouble for not obeying him, [but he got] in trouble for cohabitating with her. My brother, David Hall, who became brigadier general [in the air force], dealt with illegal orders, too. He handled it by meeting [with] his boss's boss and asking [that] colonel what he would think if somebody did such and such. [The] colonel says, "Are you crazy? That's illegal." So, when my brother's boss ordered him again to do [that] illegal thing [again], he referred his boss to the colonel.

In any situation where I could make a change [toward racial equality] without violating the regulations, I tried to. I got some help from some Jewish guys in Korea. They understood, were sensitive. In Japan, the social life was segregated [for both] officers [and] enlisted [in the] Japanese places. We'd make reservations and they'd ask, "That brown lieutenant, with you? So sorry." I went to the guy in charge of the police district, who was Black, and he said the place we were going was illegal. I tried to figure out how to get a message across tactfully.

A guy didn't salute me at Scott Air Force Base [in Illinois] and I racked him back. Another captain came by and pulled me aside and said I could handle it differently because you can't be emotional as an officer. My brother went through ocs. Hotels in Texas were segregated, [and] for [his] air force graduation, they were going to have a party in a big hotel. My brother knew about segregation and volunteered to head the committee for the party! All these people are human beings—[they] learned this stuff and it can be unlearned. You catch more flies with syrup than vinegar.

There's no unanimity amongst minorities in how they look at the [racial] problem. Wherever there was a frat brother [in trouble], we took it as a challenge and tried to be strategic. You make up your mind when you get up whether it's going to be a great day. Some guys were very bitter. Some guys got shot because they were white or because they were Black. It got written up as combat statistics. Military press releases are never true, [they] always paint a nicer picture.

Some of the guys had a reunion and they had a lot of old propaganda [from the Korean War]. It would say, "What are you fighting for? Join us. It's the white world against the nonwhite world." They didn't have no dummies that were doing propaganda for Korea. Some of those guys went to Harvard. Some of our [soldiers] were caught up in that, went to the other side, [but I think they were] mixed up, unsure of themselves. I like to think I could've talked them out [of it]. Life's about overcoming hurdles—might as well do it in a place with more resources, like [in a] democracy.

I had support from guys, like the Jewish guys [I mentioned] earlier. We went on R and R together—Feinberg and Ruddleson—up into the mountains in Japan. We didn't have much chance to go around, so we sat around and talked about what we wanted to do with our lives. I was happy about it—we come from a damn good country. We had a conversation we couldn't have had in dictatorial countries. [My experience in Korea] sharpened my appreciation for the country, [gave me the] knowledge that life is short. When I came back to Chicago and hung out with guys who hadn't been to war and the way they talked, [it] made me see differences. They valued things I no longer did. I came back and had all this stuff in me and the guys I shot pool with didn't know, they thought I'd been on vacation or something. Occasionally you'd meet someone else who'd been there, and then you'd talk about it. But the Korean War Association didn't get started until years afterward. One guy is still uptight—everybody in his outfit got killed except him and he's still wearing that "Why did I live?," that whole thing. It's bad. In my unique case, [serving during the war] was a positive thing because I saw an opportunity to make change, to develop and mature.

Hansel C. Hall
Lieutenant colonel, 502nd Tactical Control Group, 5th Air Force
US Air Force
Interviewed by Stephen Smith and Tina Tennessen,
    July 22, 2002, Minneapolis, MN
American RadioWorks, Minnesota Public Radio

DOROTHY BOYD, DORCHESTER, MASSACHUSETTS

I'm Dorothy Boyd. I was in the air force during the Korean conflict. [The Korean War] was never declared a war. It was a police action. They call it the Forgotten War—as a female veteran, [I can say] that's true.

I worked in a communications center. [I worked with] emergency messages, I'd pull the tapes, and monitor the back of the vacuum system to monitor the messages as they came in. I like most base ops because I dealt with flight and weather and that was interesting. I worked five days a week and I could fly anywhere in the world I wanted to as long as I was back to work on Monday, no limitation on our passes until they separated the bases [by branch].

When I finished [a] course in teletype and they said you have the highest training but you might not get a job because they don't hire colored people in that field, I said, "Why does the government spend the money?" They said I was an astute student. I said, "I don't worry about it. I can work doing anything. I have a lot of training and once I've got it here in my head, they can't take it away from me."

I went overseas. In Newfoundland the bay freezes early, and if you don't get supplies and get out, you get frozen in. It was an interesting [time] . . . I learned a lot. Saw a lot. Dealt with a lot. [In Newfoundland there were] three branches of the military there. You have to go through that training in March or April, plenty of snow. Plenty, plenty, plenty. It's an experience. I came home because they wanted to send me to Kentucky and I said, "No, I'm not going back south, I'm going home."

They had a snowstorm [when I got back to Boston] and I had summer blues. I had to put on my winter uniform and just look around and see everything was so different, so changed. Everybody looks at you like, "You new in town?" I'd tell them who I am, but I know you. I said, "I knew you when you were that high." Kids that were this high when you left was this high when you came back. [There was a] whole new generation. I went back to school. I stress that to all the kids. Get your education.

[I've been active in this Veterans of Foreign Wars post] thirty years this year. I was past day commander. And I belong to the group called the 8 and 40 La Boutique [Nationale]. I did a year at that, [was] past district director. I covered quite a bit. The 40 and 8 is the French name for a group that does hospital work for children with asthma and AIDS. We work really hard. "Where do you get the time?" I find it. I can't sit still.

It took me eight years to become commander here [at the VFW post]. The guys said, "Oh, please. A woman. What can you tell me?" I said, "A lot of things, but I don't think you want to hear them." I ran every year. A man said, "If you didn't win what would you do?" I said, "I'd run again." He said, "You've got determination. You're going to get it." You can't let them knock you down, you got to keep pushing, but you have to keep learning. Can't sit in the corner and say, "Maybe one day they'll vote for me." A fellow said, "I notice something about you, you laugh." You gotta keep going. I laugh. You gotta keep pushing. And they'd say, "She's determined, she'll get there one day." After the eight years was up, [I got elected and] I'm here. But what I like about it is they work with me. Makes me feel proud and I let them know that. You have to let them know and let everyone else [see] you appreciate them. Let them stand up in a meeting and everybody see who they are. That means a lot. A lot of the guys say, "Nobody appreciated it." I tell them, "You guys are just like little kids. I don't have candy but I'll let you know I appreciate what you're doing." It's a great feeling. Getting everything moving. I'm having a ball. I give them citations, awards. Makes them feel wanted.

Dorothy M. (Phillips) Boyd
Airman basic, WAF
US Air Force
Interviewed by David P. Cline, October 20, 2002, Mattapan, MA
American RadioWorks, Minnesota Public Radio

Navy

LARRY "LEN" LOCKLEY, SPRINGFIELD, MASSACHUSETTS

I was on the soccer team on the ship [*Lake Champlain*], and we played different places, we played in Florida. And we were supposed to play Duke [University]. And all of a sudden the officer in charge of the soccer team came to me and said, "I want to talk to you, can you come talk to me in my wardroom?" And he said, "Len, there's a problem. Duke has a policy that they won't play against Black people." And I said, "Well, I know we got this game scheduled, and well, I won't play." And he said, "I don't want to do that, maybe the team . . . ." Well, one guy, I forgot his name, I think it was Galifianakis, he had gone to Duke before, he hadn't finished, but he was on the team and he came up and he said, "Len," he said, "I'm so embarrassed." 'Cause we had played in Haiti, all over. And he said, "We'll elect not to go." So the team didn't play Duke. It was supportive, it was really supportive. You didn't get too much [racism] on the ship. I mean really, I was really surprised. Well, I was the only Black corpsman, [and] the corpsman, that's your lifeline to a lot of things, I guess. But really, [I] had never experienced any real issues on the ship where guys were overtly racist or negative.

The billets were really kind of dispersed, racially dispersed. There were stewards and everything . . . [but] the guys I hung out with, the Black guys I hung out with, were a guy named Pemberton, [who] was a 1st class engineman or something—he had been in the Second World War—[and] another guy [who] worked in the boiler rooms. At that time the navy was really switching over and was trying to make an overt effort to get people integrated into different areas. Because on my billet, you know they test you for different things, and I think what I qualified for was a hospital corpsman, dental corpsman, or aviation gunner's mate. So, if you had the stones, they'd put you where they want[ed] to put you, that's all. But everybody knew me because I was the only Black corpsman on the ship.

[There were no Black officers onboard.] Oh, no, no, no. I think I saw one Black doctor in all the time I was there. The air force probably had Black pilots, and maybe there were some, but [I didn't see any], I don't remember any Black officers.

[As a hospital corpsman,] when you're on the line, usually there are four carriers on the line flying sorties into Korea, and we had people getting hurt and pilots coming back, resting, snapping, people getting hit by hung rockets, people walking into props, people getting hit by the bulkhead, getting their heads torn open and stuff, guys falling off the ship, all sorts of thing[s] happened. Guys getting their fingers missing. We had to just sew them up, do what you have to do, while there were rockets going off over the ship, bursts at different times.

I never saw any overt racism on the ship. And I never experienced any problems with guys treat[ing] me bad or anything like, never, as I can recall. The [racial] problems we had [were] when we got to Japan, when we had three R and Rs from Korea. I didn't like it when guys, my fellows, treated people overseas in a very bad way. They thought all the women and the people were stupid. I saw a guy damn near get killed in Yokosuka by a couple of Japanese guys because he was just being disrespectful. People don't take that, they really, really don't. And so, the whole thing about the Ugly American? It was. That whole [mind]-set kind of puts us as a country, I think, in a lot of embarrassing situations that we can't undo because we say some things that are really stupid.

One of the things that probably helped was I grew up in Springfield, [Massachusetts]. And in Springfield back then in my high school class there was probably five Black people in the entire class; Springfield was predominantly white; Massachusetts was predominantly white. People would let you go places 'cause you weren't going to "take over the neighborhood." You could go all around here, you could go to Boston. 'Cause people said, "Oh, they're just passin' through." So, the issues of overt racism really hadn't solidified in me. It was there, I'm sure, but it wasn't really noticeable to me because it really hadn't affected me before. And so, I just dealt with it. Sometimes there was a guy who was a pain in the neck and had a chip on his shoulder or something like this in a matter-of-fact way. I think my buddies took it more as a personal attack because I was oblivious to the whole thing at the time.

But it was just an experience, you know, that you went through. I'm sure other people had some other very different experiences that might have been regrettable. But I guess our group, what we were doing was needed, and when people are hurting they can rationalize and put some things aside. "Well, I need this, I don't care what color he is, I need this." So they kind of relinquish a whole lot of that stuff, and then it comes back, I think, when they're well. But when people are in need of help they don't care. They can rationalize. My group, I never saw them shy away or try to [or] be embarrassed because I was part of them. I never saw that, I never saw that. I hear stories from guys who had some real issues, and had some bad incidents there. We were just insulated, I was just insulated, I guess.

It happened at a time that Truman had made some decisions about how the service was going to be integrated, but I don't think anybody had any idea how to do that. Then I think the Korean War, because they needed people, it afforded the opportunity for that to happen. And then some of the naysayers probably figured, hey, if it can happen it can happen, just let it happen, political people said let it happen. And people in the service, like the guys I just talked about, I'm sure they went back to their little hovels or hometowns, and said well you know maybe I got a different feeling about this guy or that guy, you know. And I think that happened. People looked at a lot of guys in Korea and said, Black guys can do some things, you know, they have some abilities. I think the crucial moments like that when people are pushed to the wall about survival, they can cross the line. That can happen tomorrow, that can happen again, I guess.

I was talking with [my white buddy] Canazaro one time, I think the time he came up here with his wife. And I was trying to thank him, because for me it became more obvious that [my white friends] were more indignant about [how I was treated], because I was oblivious to it. And I was trying to thank him, and I said, "I really appreciate you taking me under your wing," because he was a 1st class and I was a corpsman, he was always over my unit. And I said, "You know looking back, I really want to thank you for kind of looking out for me." You know, we were from Massachusetts together and he'd always be hovering there, and he was kind of an assertive guy—he was a short guy, but he had a Napoleonic complex, so everybody was kind of worried about him, you know. He was Italian, that swagger. So, I said to myself, maybe that's the reason why I never got in trouble out there, you know, when you rerun the show. And he didn't know what the hell I was talking about! He was kind of, like me at the time, out of it, so he didn't see how he probably played some kind of major role in all of that—some kind of influence maybe, maybe not, I don't know. But I never experienced [difficulties] with any of the guys who came aboard, who joined our unit, any of the air groups, anything like that, never, never. And a lot of guys it's probably because God takes care of fools and idiots, you know, so you [go] into the Ku Klux Klan meeting singing, "We Shall Overcome," and guys are like, I don't know whether to shoot this guy or let him walk out of here, you know. I guess, that's what it is. So, because of my naïveté about all of it, it probably eased me through a lot of this stuff, where guys from the South saw it coming and recognized it right away. I don't know, I don't know.

I want to make clear [though], I'm sure it wasn't great. Like I said, I had a little piece. And part of it was, as a corpsman, you have a different type guy in there. You have doctors, you have nurses, you had guys that had some inkling about the realities of public health and the need for medicine and all that. So, the group itself, that I was tied in, was not a cut above, I'm not saying that, but a little more focused about the job they had to do, and they were more grounded. And so, they either suppressed some of these things or felt they would stand out if they made issues about these things. But I like to think that's what it was.

We were sent home and we pulled into Jacksonville, Florida—we had been around the war, to Suez and all that junk—we came in in December '53 after the Korean War. And I remember coming to get the train, I had to get a bus to the gate. And I'm waiting at the gate to get a taxi to the train station, I was waiting, and cabs kept [passing]. And one guy, an MP, shore patrol, said, "Hey, Doc, you're going to have to wait for a Black cab. No one's going to pick you up." And that kind of bothered me. Here we've been through Korea and we come back and have to go through all that. So there were incidents like that, little things. In Tokyo we had a problem at the club, they let all the rest of my buddies in and stopped me at the door, the Japanese did. And at another club, some guys were there from the army and we were all drinking and partying and stuff, and a guy said to me, "Hey, Doc, I got nothing against you personally, but when I'm home and I'm from the South, you can't be going out with the same girls I'm goin' with." So my group, they got all upset. And his sergeant came over and said, "Well, in a couple of days we'll all be back out there [in battle] and you wouldn't care what color he is then." But there were little incidents like that to let you know what we were in.

Larry "Len" Lockley, PhD
Hospital corpsman 2nd class, USS Lake Champlain
US Navy
Interviewed by David P. Cline, October 29, 2002, Springfield, MA
American RadioWorks, Minnesota Public Radio

ODELL GREGORY LOVE SR., SAN DIEGO, CALIFORNIA

My name is Odell Gregory Love Sr. I am a retired navy commander, Supply Corps, US Navy. I entered the service from Hot Springs, Arkansas, 1951. Right after high school I had the choice to go in the army or go in the navy. I chose the navy and that's where I made my career. I was barely eighteen at the time and I took my draft notice down, and the recruiter and I worked it out where I signed up, and that started a forty-three-year career in the United States Navy.

My mother saw me off at the bus station at Hot Springs and we went over to

Little Rock, Arkansas, where we were given our introduction to the service. Of course, 1951, that was kind of a tough year; things were happening, and in Little Rock at the time, of course, things were still segregated. So one of the comical things that happened there, that I always think about, was after we all got inside there and they told everybody, "Okay, it's time to come and eat," and everybody started out to eat and I started right out with the rest of everybody else. And I was the only Black person there. And all of a sudden, a hand went out in front of me. And: "No, no, you can't go out and eat with them. You gotta eat in the kitchen." Okay, no big deal. The cook was a Black lady. And she said, "Well, son, come on in. At least you're gonna get more chicken than they're gonna get!" So, I was introduced to the segregation part of the United States Navy.

Later on we took a train on out to San Diego, where I went through boot camp. And [I] still encountered a lot of the segregation because I was the only Black in the company of forty-six sailors. But I learned how to deal with that, and I had some good advice, of course, from my mother and my father back home who taught us a lot of respect for other individuals, and I gotta say that served me well in those early days in the military. And after boot camp, I went aboard ship and spent time on a repair ship, a heavy hull repair ship, ARH-1. It was a tender, city in itself. And that was quite an experience—I walked aboard and the first thing, one of the chiefs said, "Put him on mess cook." And the 1st class storekeeper says, "No, I need some people down in the main GSK store-room." And [the first guy said,] "I want Love to work for me." And the chief warrant officer settled the argument and said, "Okay, the 1st class can have him." And that began my career in the Supply Corps of the United States Navy. And I never did get to go mess cooking. And I was given a set of keys for the storeroom and I hung those keys on my side and I thought I was really something then. That was the first time that I had been given some kind of a responsibility—to be in charge of something, that felt good.

I had it made. At least I thought I did, until they told me who my section leader was, a big old segregationist, a 2nd class. And he didn't like me, so he kept me on my toes. He gave me a lot of mid watches even though I didn't have the duty. There were three watches in those days. So the 1st class [eventually] took care of that and he got the big guy off my tail and I went on to do my job.

You just didn't fight. Someone call you a name, the first thing you want to do is fight. [But my mother] told me fighting will only get you nowhere. You may win the fight, you may even hurt the individual, the individual may hurt you, then what do you got? But more than that, navy regulations say, "Do Not Fight." Even though it was kind of one-sided in the punishment in those days. I saw a lot of young Black sailors get put out with bad conduct discharges for fighting, fighting with people of different races. And of course, the other side of the coin, is the other guy just got slapped on the hand and was able to stay in the navy.

Odell Gregory Love Sr.
Commander, Supply Corps
US Navy
Interviewed by Edward Duling and Joy Leibbrandt, n.d.
Odell Gregory Love Sr. Collection (AFC/2001/001/17071), Veterans
  History Project, American Folklife Center, Library of Congress

CLARENCE JOHNSON, CINCINNATI, OHIO

I was born here in Cincinnati. I went to elementary school at Kirby School, Northside, Cumminsville. That's another little community, in fact I was the only Black in K-8. The story about that is that people had their stereotypes, but I had a dad who always kept me informed as to some of the things that I would have to be faced with, and he said, "Son, I don't care what you do, you keep your mind on the books. These things that come, I don't know how you're going to deal with them, some of them you're going to have to deal with them as they come."

When I dropped out [of high school] my junior year, I was kind of crazy at that time, I didn't hold a job and ended up getting drafted, got in December of '44. I didn't choose [the navy]. I didn't want to go to the navy for some reason. [But at enlistment], when you get up to the desk, the guy said, "What branch of service?" I said, "I'd like the army." Boom, "You're in the navy." So that's how I got in the navy.

[After World War II, I joined] the inactive [reserves, where] you don't have to do anything but [they] got you for four years. And that's where I made the biggest mistake of my life. Came home, got married, and within three months of that four months, Truman froze everybody and I ended up in the Korean conflict. Married, a son, I was depressed. All of us said we would never go back to the Pacific.

Well, you know, it's a new day now. Truman had desegregated [the navy] and I didn't know what to expect and I was shocked. I left Cincinnati, hit Long Beach, and I was assigned to the D. D. *Halsey Powell* 686, a destroyer. I went straight to the commander. I say, "Hey, I'm not shining any shoes, I'm not going to cook any meals . . . or there is going to be some trouble here?" And he says, "Hey, I thought you had heard, this is desegregated." I was assigned to the .20 millimeters, .40 quads, and those five-inch .38s. And that was the first time I got exposed to what sea duty was all about, what the real navy was all about on ships. We were with Task Force 58 when we went up to bombard those bridges around Wonsan in Korea. Japan is where we docked, we went into Sasebo, but we would go up there in the north sea by Wonsan and blast at those bridges. And they [said,] Russia was releasing mines into the convoy, and we would take those .20 millimeters and hit them, explode them. But they said they never could pinpoint Korea doing it, and word was Russia was helping them.

Another episode that I had on the destroyer: The [white] guys didn't like us. I can understand, you know, if you're not used to being around [Black] people and they've never been on your ship. And the boatswain mate would always send me down to the hull and I would have to take those readings on all the ammunition and see what kind of condition it was in. If it was damp or wet I had to record that in the journal. And I didn't know, I was going down there and doing my duty and I would always have to carry the book up to the executive officer. And after about the fourth week, I came in and [the officer] said, "What are you doing here?" "Well, I'm bringing you the book." And he said, "That's a two-week assignment. It rotates." I said, "I just follow orders."

So, [us Blacks,] we got to talking, and we got into it with one of the guys on the ship. This guy came down and he [grabbed me by shoulder and said,] "Hey, Smokey," and I almost hit him. And I said, "Look, I'll you what. Don't ever touch me again, because if you do, I'm decking you. If you give me some trouble, that's what's going to happen." And at the time the boatswain's mate walked up and he started telling me, "I'm going to put you on report." And the executive officer, I told him what happened, and I told him, "You know, you come over here to fight for your country and you got to take this kind of crap all the time." The next week, he sent for me. And he took me up on the quarter-master deck—there was a lead helmsman's thing there and there was a helm. And he told the leader up there, he says, "I want Johnson to learn both of these operations. I think he can do it. I don't expect any trouble." And the guys, they start showing me. I started operating: "Bring the ship on course, 245 . . . ," you know, I was doing it! And I look back and I could go: "Hey, this ship is doing what I [am] telling it to do. It was quite a [thrill]. And I really appreciated the officer. I see what he was trying to do. He [thought], "Well, this guy, he's sitting down there, working on the guns, he never gets exposed to this." I thought that was a nice gesture. And his response to whatever the boatswain told him.

All the time it was something. I guess my problem with that whole [segregation] thing [was] how do you rationalize, if you're fighting an enemy, you have a system [where you mistreat people?] At times, down in Virginia, I felt like I was fighting two wars. You go on liberty, marines, with their buckles, and we got our dirks, and I thought that was awful. I said, "Hey, we're from the same country here, man." But you went through a lot of that.

Clarence Johnson
Seaman 1st class, USS Halsey Powell
US Navy
Interviewed by Theodore Gardner, n.d., Cincinnati, OH

*Clarence Johnson Collection (AFC/2001/001/82722), Veterans History
Project, American Folklife Center, Library of Congress*

MAURICE GARTH, CHICAGO, ILLINOIS

[Born] Chicago, Illinois, 1931. Played semipro softball. I played softball until
I went into the service. I got a job as a mail boy for about a year, 1950–1951.
A. Phillip Randolph visited his school. [Then] they sent me a letter: "I want you,
[signed] Uncle Sam." I was ready because I had two friends and we had already
talked about going into the US Navy together. So one went in before I did, he
joined, and he went in and about a year later, I went in. But I was expecting them
to call me, which they did. One of my best friends had gone in the service and
he got killed the year before I went in. We graduated together. We had planned
to go into together, three of us, and each one went in separate. After they sent
me the letter, they were getting ready to draft me, and I went down to the navy
and told them I wanted to enlist. I was twenty [years old].

After about three months or so I was supposed to have gone in and they said
I had failed the eye test. So they sent me back home. I went back home and then
I went down again. They had given me another physical exam and the eye test
and I was straining! Because I had broken my glasses and I wasn't wearing them.
And they said, "Well, you passed." I was straining my best to get in there! At that
time [I wanted to go in], because I had told people I was going in and they had
taken up a collection for me on my job. But then I failed, and I went back, and
I felt kinda bad and I said, "Well, I have to give these people their money back."
And they said, "No, just don't worry about it."

I went in [the navy] because I didn't want to go to Korea. [Some others I
knew] were going in the marines and army, that's why I picked the navy, and my
buddies, they picked the navy the same way, because I felt that I'd be on a ship,
not on the battleground, that it'd be safer. Plus, I heard they had better food in
the navy!

I didn't know what to expect [in the navy]. I did know that they were kind of
prejudiced at that time, because it hadn't been too long . . . [since] Blacks started
going in the service [with whites], where they used to have to all be in the same
group, Black servicemen with each other. But when I went in it had integrated.
I was surprised that that was that way because I was thinking that maybe it was
gonna be Black with Black and white with white. So that surprised me.

I received fourteen weeks [of basic training] in Great Lakes, Illinois. We
went through marching, drills, then we had firefighting for one day because the
navy doesn't have a fire department, so if a ship gets hit by a bomb, you have
to put out the fire. So we spent one day on fighting fires. And that was something very interesting. Every day we would drill, we had classes, and we had

swimming. If you couldn't pass the swimming test, you couldn't get out of boot camp, and I didn't know how to swim. I didn't learn to swim until the fourteenth week that I was in there. We had eighty men in the company, and I was the seventy-ninth to pass the swimming test!

In the service, [life] was different. Discipline. That's the main thing I think about when I think about the service. You have to go to bed at ten o'clock and get up at six, every day you do the same thing. And then you had to work. I guess that was one thing that I wasn't expecting, that you'd be on the job [while] the war was going on. I didn't know where I was going so I didn't know what to expect, where I was going to work. And they would give you a test on four or five things to see where they were going to put you. [I was a] seaman recruit and [we eventually went] to Guantanamo Bay, Cuba. My first duty was I had to coxswain a boat. I called it driving a boat, they called it coxswain. I went down to Cuba and they assigned me to a boat. They had a 150-foot boat and a 90-foot boat, and they carried passengers.

But, this is a story: We went to the South after boot training. And while we were in Norfolk, Virginia, we were riding in a bus and the law was you had to ride in the back of the bus. And my best friend and I, we sat down in the middle of the bus. And nobody said anything because the bus wasn't crowded. But I guess some sailors saw us, they were watching us. And we went back on liberty again and we sat in the middle of the bus because it wasn't crowded. And the sailors were sitting in the back of the bus, the Black sailors. And the bus started filling up, and all of sudden people was standing all up over us. And we acted like we couldn't see them, put our heads down, but we could feel the hostility. We knew something was up, you could feel it.

So about a week later we got on the ship going to Cuba. On my ship there was 9 Blacks and the rest were white. But the other three ships that were traveling with us, our sister ships, most of them had about 30 or 35 Blacks and the rest white out of about 280. We were going over to Cuba, where we were going to spend two years. And some Black sailors came up to us, and they [said], "Well, we got a problem in Cuba. We have to have a dance every three months . . . and they bring in 300 Cuban girls, but they don't bring any for us to dance with." So we said, "What you want us to do? We just came in the navy and you guys have been in here ten or twelve years, why are you over here talking to us about it?" They had noticed us sitting in the middle of the bus, so they said, "We maybe thought that you could do something about it." So, we said, "Well, we'll see."

So, when we got out to Cuba, we talked to a chief petty officer and he said, "Now, if you guys are going to try to do anything you're going to have to go through the chain of command." So we went all through the chain of command. Every time we went to one officer, he said, "I can't make those girls dance with you!" So we'd go to the next one. Finally, we got to an admiral and we told him what was happening. I did all the speaking, my buddy didn't say a word. And he said, "Well, I can't make those girls dance with you." And I didn't know what to say [and he thought] that was the end of it. So out of my mouth came these words: "We gonna take this up with the NAACP!" And he looked me in the face and said, "Let me handle this." And I thought he was going to handle it alright, he's probably going to send us over to Guam or someplace like that, a fueling dump. And I said, "He's going to send us over there and say, 'Well, if you wanna dance, you dance with them birds over there!'"

Next time they had a dance, the guys went to the dance. And we didn't go, we went on liberty. And they told us, "They only gave us one, they sent only one Black Cuban girl over." So, we said, "We'll go back and talk to the admiral," so we went back and talked to the admiral and he said [again], "Well, let me handle this." So the next three months when they had the next dance, they brought twenty-five Black Cuban girls over." But we went that night! We went over to see what it was like and make sure everything was right. And everything worked out alright, but I always said that we thought that God had set it up for us. Because, you know, they could have sent us to a different spot where we didn't want to go. But the admiral knew us and from then on, every dance that they had, they had twenty-five Black girls. And the thing about Cuba they had about fourteen bases, naval air base, naval air station, marine station, Seabee station, and each one had their own gallery. So there was maybe about sixteen hundred Black sailors all over there and the rest would be maybe sixteen thousand white [sailors]. So, all the [Black] sailors knew us, but we didn't know them. Because we had our names on our shirts then, and we'd be walking down the street going to a movie, and they'd say, "How ya doin', Garth, how ya doing, Johnson?" Because they knew we were the guys who got these Cuban girls to come over, so they thought we were heroes! I felt that since we were all in the same navy and everything, I thought that there should be some changes made. But I didn't go in there to do that.

[As a coxswain] I put about nine boats out of commission so I learned they were going to transfer me and eventually I became a storekeeper. I knew if I went up on the ship, I'd be on the deck crew. I didn't want that job. And the navy, they were kind of prejudiced because I never could get the storekeeping job. I had to go through that — a lot of times they would freeze rates. And every time I would try to get to be a storekeeper they said the rate was frozen. I ended up being a steward after a few months of being on the deck. I didn't want to be on the deck, because they'd be scraping paint, and I didn't want that job. Plus, I would have more liberty by being in the supply department.

After one year, I became a storekeeper. I ordered the food for the cafeteria. Whatever they ate, I ordered. I also had a meat [freezer] and a refrigerator. And I was on that for a year. And I made out the menus for what they were gonna eat.

It was my duty to post the menus for three meals, what they would have each day. So I liked that, it was a lot of fun. [Then] I was assigned to a destroyer . . . for one year. They say all real sailors have to be on a destroyer: if you don't [serve] on a destroyer, you're not a real sailor.

Maurice Garth
Storekeeper I, USS Hale
US Navy
Interviewed by Courtney Thompson, n.d., Columbia, MO
Maurice Garth Collection (AFC/2001/001/66703), Veterans History
    Project, American Folklife Center, Library of Congress

JAMES A. "JACK" LUCAS JR., ATLANTA, GEORGIA

I'm James Lucas, called Jack, of course. I was born in Winston-Salem [North Carolina], January 16, 1933. My father was in World War I, and my oldest brother was in World War II. My daddy was an infantryman. My oldest brother was a medic. I'm the third of three of the males in the family to do this. I'm not really unique, I'm not the hero of the family.

And when I went in the military they had advertisements—it was right after World War II—and they had the signs up: "Join the Navy and See the World." There ain't no war, a girl in every port, and all that. I don't know what I'm gonna do with one in every port, I can't do with the one here at home. So I was lured! And I needed another adventure. I didn't know much other than Winston-Salem. I needed to get out and meet somebody else.

I was sixteen when I joined, but they were smart enough to not take me until the following year, when I was seventeen. That's how I got in. And then there was fellas in the neighborhood who had been in the military, other than my brother and daddy, [and] a few of the guys had been in the navy. The navy in my neighborhood was considered a kind of elite service, so to speak. You had to make certain grades to be in—they said if you flunked out of the navy, you could always make it in the army!

I had to go to Raleigh, North Carolina, to take the oath. That's where they shipped me to San Diego from. The only boot camp facilities available to the navy at the time was San Diego. They had closed up Great Lakes in Illinois. And I liked that, too, because I got the opportunity to take a bus ride all the way across the country. I got to see areas of the United States that I hadn't seen before.

I didn't think much about [race in the military] at the time. I ran into some Jim Crow situations, of course, going across country. Matter of fact, I ran across some at home. I had a very uncanny experience with my complexion, of course, not being light enough to be white and not being dark enough to be Black, so I had fallen somewhere between the cracks, I guess. One Black fella [said,] "Oh, you could almost pass for one of them!" Never did figure out what "one of them" was, but I got some idea! And he may have been right. I did at some time [get] offered positions that guys whose complexion were darker than mine hadn't been offered, and I did think that they done it only because of my complexion. And I thought that I lived up to that position that they were willing to go and get some even darker and move them on in. They had a name for guys like me, the first ones!

They had desegregated the military, so to speak, two years before I got in in 1948. Harry Truman, "Give 'Em Hell Harry," was president at the time. And many of the people who were in the military at the time didn't really adjust to it right off. You had those people who had always thought that with their complexion alone, it gave them some kind of authority over those who[se] complexion may have been a little darker, and this sort of thing. But now when you integrated, you find that some of those guys are moving on up to [an] upper echelon, [like] Colin Powell. And I like the idea that Colin Powell made a point of letting them know that he was standing on the shoulders of men who had gone before him who was willing to take the kind of punishment that we had to take. I liked that, because some people forget. But that man didn't forget.

Now my brother said, when he was in there, they had a general who was Black, his name was Benjamin O. Davis, but he said that he was not inspirational to the Black soldier. They said his conversation, when he came on their post, was [sending a message that] I'm your color but I ain't your kind. That's no way to talk to a man who's fitting to go out here and get killed for you. "I'm you're color but not your kind." What you mean? We're all the same kind! But that was the bad attitude that he had. Now that was the Senior, that Davis. Now, Benjamin O. Davis Jr., he had a better attitude.

After boot camp, they had amphibious training school there at Catalina Island. My first duty was [supposed] to be on the USS *Coral Sea*. That was too much ship for me! And somehow or another I didn't make it on that ship and I'm almost glad I didn't, it was too much for me. I didn't join the navy [for that], you go on a big ship like that you may as well not leave the land. But that was the first time I saw a Black commissioned marine officer, he was from Atlanta. Little short fella, but he was good at what he did! And he could fight, too. Because I saw him beat two guys out there who didn't want to do right, to do what they were told, because their complexion was different. He pulled his bars off and beat 'em. They'd been telling him, well, if he didn't have them bars what they would do. He said, "Don't let them stop you"—he took 'em off and beat both of them. And I didn't want that. When I graduated, he told me, he thought he was probably going to have to [fight me]. I told him, "I saw what you did to the last ones—I didn't want that!" So I went right on through that [training with a] yessir! And boy, you talk about a guy who knew how to wear a uniform. He was sharp, every day, creases in his pants. They couldn't have made a better lieutenant in the Marine Corps than that guy, when it comes to dress. I couldn't keep up.

Well, when I left there they put me on the USS *Dixie*, an auxiliary destroyer tender, as a passenger, not as a member of the crew, to go to Japan—my home port was [to be] Yokosuka, Japan—that was to get on board the USS *Pledge*, AM-277, [a minesweeper]. We were recommissioning that ship. That ship had been built in Alabama in 1943 but it had been decommissioned, so I went to work with the crew that they brought in to refurbish it and get it ready. And I'm seventeen years old, I'm the baby boy, everybody's teaching me because I know absolutely nothing. And that was my biggest asset—to know that I knew absolutely nothing. That meant that I could be a sponge and I could learn. I give those men credit, they took time and they taught about everything I need to know. Many of those men had been in sinkings before, they knew the dangers. It was called "The Suicide Navy," the mine squadron. We were a minesweeper. When they talk about policing, they're talking about go get a broom and go out there and clean up something. You're not going over there to arrest nobody, you're going over there to clean up! That's why you had your UDT [underwater demolition] teams and everything connected with them, they are your first responders. We cleaned up. If they spotted a mine in the middle of the Pacific, we got to go out there and try to get it, anywhere. Well, I was a mine demolition specialist at seventeen because of those men. And I went from fifty-two dollars a month to three hundred dollars a month because of those men. They taught me what I need to know. They need a ship's diver? Tell them you'll do that. And a little extra change looked good in my pocket.

I was a mine demolition specialist, part of the UTD, [just] a part of it. It's not a Hollywood thing. This is not Hollywood. My job was to run that minesweeping equipment, those cables and those cutters that we put out there on those paravanes, those dan buoys, that sort of thing. Then once we sweep, we gotta go back and we got put those buoys [out], make channels so the ships would know that they could come in, that it had already been swept. Well, my job was to make sure that it was done. I worked off the fantail until we'd go to general quarters, and then I go to my antiaircraft gun.

This ship, my first one, the *Pledge*, it sank at 12:36 in the afternoon of October the 12th, [1950], twenty-nine minutes after the USS *Pirate*, our flagship, [sank]. In fact, the flag on that ship, Lieutenant Commander Mullins, had been the chief boatswain mate on the ship that I'm on. He taught me. I used to cut his hair. And I wasn't no barber—he didn't care! But there weren't that many mine demolition experts after World War II, so they had to take Mullins [off the

Pledge] and put him in charge of the squadron. He was Comm 913. We were one of his ships. My ship and the *Endicott* and a few other smaller ships were part of his outfit. We were all part of Task Force 77 of the 7th Fleet.

I had been a Boy Scout all my life, and the motto of the Boy Scouts is be prepared. So, I had two lifejackets on, I had on a kapok and a Mae West. We also had two three-inch .50 guns, so I knew that those powder casings, they would float. And so I preserved me one of those. We were at general quarters [when we struck a mine], so when it hit, it lifted me out of my gun turret and it dropped me down on the fantail. My head was against the ladder there, that's what kept me from drowning, because my head wasn't in the water. The water was up on the deck. And I'm dazed. Many of the sailors on there are dazed, too—big explosion and this sort of thing. And then they're shooting at you from the beach. Well, I get up and start stirring and I hear, "This is your captain speaking, this is not a drill, all hands abandon ship." That ain't hard to figure out. It's easy. The man's telling you, if you ain't planning on going down, you'd better get off. I took him at his word. But instead of doing it then I walked up to the bridge. He'd lost an eye, the lieutenant commander. Like I said, I'm in a daze. I see him, one of his eyes is out. Our chief executive officer was holding him. Brave men. He's laying out under one of those three-inch .50s. I said, "Well, the man said abandon ship." I got off. We lost at least nine men, everybody that was in the engine room.

And when I got off the ship [I saw] the commercial officer, [a] lieutenant, somehow or another he knew me by name. And he said, "Jack, let me have that canister. I can't swim." And I gave it to him. And that evening, about six o'clock or seven, it was almost getting dark, I felt the kapok getting waterlogged. So I took it off. And I hit the button on the Mae West, and it filled it up with CO_2, and it kept me [afloat] till I got picked up the next morning. Right there around breakfast time was when they picked me up. And they made a joke of it, three guys up on the fo'c'sle, they said, "Boy, we had to pick up speed to get you. You was kicking up a wake eight foot high and your eyes were big as teacups!" Well, you can't beat that, I laughed with them. They had a boat hook that pulled me on up there, close enough to throw me a buoy, pull me on in.

They steamed me to the hospital ship to be assessed, evaluated, and this kind of thing. And I found out something there, this hospital ship was not just treating sailors, they were treating the army soldiers and everybody. And I saw another soul brother there. He had lost an eye and some stuff. And I said, "Well, I guess you're fitting to go home." He said, "No, I got to go back up! I ain't finished my duty." That was the army, gotta go back up to the front lines.

I was almost unemployable when I got out. I had to create my own business. And I was successful at doing it. Remember, my daddy was in World War I. And when he came back—my daddy's dark—they wouldn't let him eat in certain places. And my brother, some places he couldn't go eat [after World War II]. And it wasn't much better when I came back. And you had the white water fountain and the Black water fountain and this sort of thing. It was almost like I went out and defended some people who may have been a little bit [slow]. These people didn't mean to be mean, these people needed mental help.

[But] there are heroes all over the place. My mother was a hero. The domestic situation—[there were] those heroes who fought the domestic war for us: Dr. King, John Lewis, H. Rap Brown, Stokely [Carmichael], and above all, El-Hajj Malik El-Shabazz, Malcolm X. And one of the most intelligent men of our times, we must not forget him, a man who didn't really have a third-grade education, and that's Elijah Poole, the honorable Elijah Muhammad, a man who took so little and did so much. [My advice is:] Get to know each other, get to have confidence in each other. You're being exploited by people who want to divide you, tell you one thing and tell your friend another. But you and your buddy, your friend, are going to have to agree on something to get something done. Don't be afraid to see what's lacking and see what's causing it to be lacking, who is causing it to be lacking. And let them know: "I know that you are responsible for this condition and you ought to do something about it. If you're not [going to,] get outta the way so the rest of us can."

James A. "Jack" Lucas Jr.
Seaman, USS Pledge
US Navy
Interviewed by David Vassar Taylor and Rachanice Tate,
    November 3, 2017, Atlanta, GA
James A. Lucas Jr. Collection (AFC/2001/001/111026), Veterans History
    Project, American Folklife Center, Library of Congress

Marine Corps

FRED ASH, JACKSONVILLE, NORTH CAROLINA

I went to Korea from Earl, New Jersey. It was a segregated unit, 'cause all the NCOs, except for the officers, was Afro-Americans. The only whites we had was officers, all officers and navy personnel. And when I got transferred from there, I went to division in California, and then from there overseas. [In the division] we was at Tent Camp 2, and we all slept so many to a tent, and they was all integrated. And also when we would fall out for roll call or go to eat, we were integrated.

They organized us in different units. So, I left California in 3rd Platoon, George Company, 7th Marines, but I was in a platoon that they put on an ammunition ship, [the] ammunition supply ship for the whole division. Well, the

5th and 6th Marines is the ones that made the Inchon landing [and] . . . I was in the 7th Marines . . . [but] we had a, well, a gung-ho lieutenant that claimed he was gonna have us win him a Congressional Medal of Honor. We had to go ahead of my organization [the 7th, because] he volunteered us to go in on the landing at Inchon, at which I wasn't supposed to, and we went in on about the 26th or the 27th wave of the Inchon landing, and joined the 5th and 6th Marine Brigade.

You could still smell charcoal from burnt buildings and all kind of other odors. And everything was all ransacked and tore up. And there were snipers firing at us, but that didn't hinder us any. We kept walking. And of course, we couldn't fire back, 'cause we didn't see nobody to fire at, you know, they was hid. At this time they had already surrounded Seoul and we joined in, filled in on the lines that surrounded Seoul. And when they finally . . . went through Seoul, they claimed that they walked through it in thirty to forty-five minutes, but they didn't say anything about [how] they had been dug in around it, had it surrounded for about three to five weeks. Because they had [torn] all the buildings down and . . . the USS *Missouri* had bombed it twenty-four hours a day and burned everything down, and when they went through it the last time, they just walked through. I went through Seoul with the 5th Marine Brigade, 'cause they were the ones that made the original landing and capture. It wasn't nothing but ashes. We had to be particular to keep from stepping in a hole that had been bombed and was on fire.

I was [also] in the Chosin Reservoir [campaign] from the beginning to the end. . . . It started off around about the 15th of October, 1950. And we had Thanksgiving dinner. We had a hill we named Turkey Ridge that we had captured where we ate at, and it had already snowed. And what happened when the snow first fell in Korea, it doesn't never thaw out until that next spring. All the rest of the snow from that time on just piled right up on the first snow that fell around the 15th of October. And the temperature runs anywhere from fifteen to seventy-five below zero during the winter. And everything freezes up, even rivers, streams, freezes up hard. We ran tanks, amtracks [amphibious vehicle, tracked], and some trucks across rivers. Rivers would be so frozen. And then from there we went on up into an area headed toward the 38th Parallel. That's as far as we were supposed to go, and I went there twice up to the 38th Parallel. And before we got there, we was in an area we stayed for a couple of days, I guess they call it regrouping. That's where we met the Chinese, a great number of Chinese, . . . they would charge us and blow bugles before they would make their advances, and we knew they were coming. And when it began to break day, they would start out . . . toward us, [and] it looked like the whole hillside was moving, 'cause that's how many of them would be coming after us. And our instructors would just tell us to "Hold your fire, hold your fire until you see them and make sure you make every round count." We fought them off that night, [but] I can remember we lost a lot of guys that I knew there in that battle. And after that, we left Nightmare Alley and went on up, 'cause we thought we had destroyed all of them. We'd killed so many of them at that time, at that incident.

And we went from there on up to, I think it was maybe twenty or twenty-five miles farther up before we got to the Chosin Reservoir, and it was still cold. And got to Chosin Reservoir and they said that we had to move back fifteen miles below the Chosin Reservoir and dig in. But they ran us off. They got the firing going. They ran us off. They had planes and everything out there, the Chinese. In fact, I got run over there twice. And this is where General MacArthur got fired and we were all upset about it, because we thought he was doing a good job, but he was told not to go all the way up to the Chosin Reservoir. And I went up there, I know I went up there twice. I was there with him when he went up there the first time. Went up there the second time . . . [and] the unit was cut off. We stayed cut off for about four or five days. We couldn't get no supplies into us. And we were fighting the enemy from a semicircle all around, and we stayed awake from five to six days, twenty-four hours a day. And the only way we would get any supplies was from air drops, and if the wind wasn't right, the air drops would drop supplies into the enemy area, and then you had to try to destroy that to keep the enemy from getting ahold to it. But they'd drop tons and tons of artillery ammunition and also small arms ammunition right into the enemy area, and then they had the fighter planes that come in and try to destroy it as much as they could.

After we got supplied as good as we could — [and we] had trouble with frost-bite and pneumonia and all kind of sicknesses, gunshot wounds, and so forth — [but] after we got supplied we fought our way out and then . . . the people that was fighting rear guard for us [would] come through us and then we kept rotating and going on like that until we got back into the safe area. It [took] somewhere in the neighborhood of three, three to six weeks or better. We'd have [to] sleep sort of like in shifts, and it wasn't too much sleep then, 'cause you was fearful that whoever was on guard, watching for you during the time you were sleeping, they might fall asleep and end up we'd all get killed. So, we would sleep with one eye open and one closed.

I left Korea in the spring of '51. I came back to San Francisco, California. The main impact I think that being in the Marine Corps had on me as an American, it made things a lot better, a whole lot better. And I was glad that [integration] did happen after I went through it. That brought us to the point that where we were more or less looked upon as men and not second-class citizens. Not only that, it made things better all around, for us, our families, and even for the youngsters, our offspring that are growing up today, [it] made things better. And it got to the point where they were paying better wages, you get better promotions and then each, every organization, no matter what it is, you got a percentage of so many Afro-Americans and other nationalities in all organizations.

Fred Ash
Master sergeant, 7th Marine Division
US Marine Corps
Interviewed December 17, 2004, Jacksonville, NC
Montford Point Marines Project
Copyright © 2004 Randall Library, University of North Carolina at Wilmington

THOMAS E. CORK SR., LOUISVILLE, KENTUCKY

[During] my training there at Camp Pendleton, I picked up a couple friends: whites and one Black. We kind of went around to different places together. And some place[s] we [could] go in, some place[s] we couldn't. Some places the whites wouldn't allow us in, some places the Blacks wouldn't allow the whites in. [But] we stayed friends until we got on the ship to go to Korea.

We get into Kobe, Japan. There was a band playing, welcoming us to Japan. This young man, one of my good buddies, was standing behind me looking over at this band. And he said [in no] uncertain terms, "I didn't know they had a nigger band here in Japan." I stepped right down from him. That was the end of my conversation with him. I never spoke to him again. I heard later that he was killed. Over the years I kind of mellowed, but now I wished I had confronted him about it. But that really upset me [to] hear him saying it, of anybody. I took it in stride, but I never thought that would come out of his mouth. Because we had been such good friends. We ate each other's sandwiches, we read each other's mail. And just got to be close friends, as young men would do. But it came out. And it just hurt my feelings, it really did. Took me forever to get over that.

When we got into Kobe, Japan, they switched us off to get on the LSTs and we went in to Inchon. Now, by this time, I am the only Black in the outfit. The rest, they are white, and at first they didn't accept me. Wouldn't talk to me, wouldn't say anything to me. But as time went along they realized that I am part of their outfit and they are going to have to deal with me from then on. In California I [had been] trained on the light machine gun. That was my job when I got into Korea, that was my duty. [We] went on into Inchon [and] from there on, we would kind of move along. [By] those times the segregation part never crossed anybody's mind because we are in this thing together. Never heard another word, [no] calling me any kind of names. I became a marine like the rest of them. And that made me feel good. I felt welcome with them. Because here I am, a nineteen-year-old man being in combat the first time, don't know what to expect. And when you got people around you, they don't want you there, you got problems. But as it turned out they really accepted me. And they treated me like any other marine going into combat together. I'm a gunner and I had [an] assistant gunner, our [lives] depend on each other. He has to feed the ammunition to me, make sure I have the ammunition. Only thing I do is load it and cock, let it go. I found out later, I didn't know it at the time, the life of a machine gunner is very short. Because the enemy knows, they can see the fire coming from a machine gun, they know there is firepower. So, they concentrate on the automatic weapons, especially machine guns. So fortunately, I didn't know [that and] I made it through.

We went in [at Inchon] on about the 13th wave. The one before us, a lot of those guys were killed. And those bodies were just stacked up, you know. Young men going in combat. But strange thing about it, you really don't think about death. Your job now becomes survival. Once we get on land, we start moving north, and little by little we took town after town after town. We all went to Seoul. Went to Seoul twice [because] we lost Seoul and had to come back out and start all over again. There were some hills above [Seoul] familiar to a lot of people, Pork Chop Hill and, and those hills. We take them today and tomorrow we might come back down and had to retake them again.

[We] got on the hill one time [and] on the other side of that hill, there was another hill. We kept seeing these people going and coming out of this building. They['d] go in real fat and come out skinny. Go in real fat and come out skinny. So, we called back [to] the recon and told them what was the experience up there. And they said to sit tight. We try to find out what's going on down there. So, I guess by the third day, we see these people still going out, out of the building. Actually, we found out later they were enemy going in and out of that building. And a lot of them were dressed like civilians. That was one of the things, because they weren't in uniform like we thought they will be. They were military people but [hiding ammo under their] civilian clothes. It was an ammunition depot for them. So, the recon called up and said go for it. So, we started firing on it. Next thing you know, there was all kind of explosion. Because we had gotten this ammo.

The colonel came up. He calls us out and gave us commendations and talked to us about that. And then we moved on, and we began to move pretty fast. We went all the way into the Chosin Reservoir. Now, Chosin Reservoir is a story within itself. We were sent and went there. And we had thought the war was over. General MacArthur said, "You young men will be home for Christmas," okay. It didn't happen that way. Moved so close to China that we looked across the river and see Chinese on the other side just walking around. The marines were sitting in the middle, 8th Army on the right, and what they call the ROK Division, which is Republic of Korea, on the other side. Well, the Chinese came across on foot.

They had all their food on them, what little water they needed. Everything, rice, whatever they are going to carry in combat, they had on their body. They were literally walking past. Those Chinese came across in thousands and thousands, and thousands and thousands. Recon said they had found some Chinese back there behind us now. Then we began to tighten up and found out where these Chinese are coming from. But by that time they had us surrounded, completely cut off. It's about thirty-some below zero. The only clothes we have was those scout boots. And they were good boots, nothing wrong with that, but the problem was, your feet sweat in those boots and freeze. That's what happened to us there. We started coming back, and I think there was a general made a statement about "We are not retreating," we were attacking in a different direction. In fact, that's what we was doing. We had to turn around now and start back.

Now, one of the things that happened to us, we didn't have supplies. We only had, like, a one-day supply, so they had to drop our supplies to us. But when they dropped the supplies the Chinese was getting them before we'd get to them. So, the marines devised a decoy. They would drop dummy stuff down. And the Chinese would go for that. And then they'd drop ours down to us. And ammunition and food was [at] a premium. Water was a problem. If you all tried to make a cup of water out of snow, that's a project in itself. Because you got a cup of snow and you get about a teaspoon of water. That's what we had water from, from the snow. And when they finally got us out of there, the first person I saw was a British marine and a Turkish marine. [They] had a little [American] flag, like, waving it. Because I had no idea who these guys are—I never seen a British marine or a Turkish marine—I am thinking they are the enemy. And so they are making sure that we didn't shoot them, waving a little American flag. And they got us out of there. They were trying to take out the ones that they thought was in bad shape.

They kept asking me over and over again, "How do your feet feel?" As long as you had feeling in your feet, you are pretty well okay. But when your feeling disappeared, then that meant your [feet are] frozen. When the guys were taking me out, I said, "I am okay, I don't have feeling at all." They said, "You are the one we want. Because we know what's happened to you. Your feet are frozen."

[They] got me back to Tokyo [and] there was a hospital [that] used to be a hotel, and had these big mirrors around. They brought me on a stretcher. And I went past this mirror and I saw myself. And I am telling you, I was scroungy-looking. I hadn't shaved and bathed and whatever. And I asked, "Who was that?" And they just said, "That's you!" So, they started cleaning me up . . . but the problem with my wound [was] when they took my boot off, it was frozen. And the boot came off and part of my foot came out with it. So, that's why I lost all my toes.

I stayed in Tokyo I guess about a week. Then they sent me to Midway. Then they sent me to California, Travis [Air Force Base]. Then they flew me all the way across the United States to Westover, Massachusetts. And then, down to Saint Albans [Naval Hospital, Queens, New York]. One of the problems they was running into, they had never had that severe a frostbite. Not only myself, there were others. They never had that much frostbite, they didn't know how to handle it. At Saint Albans Hospital, they did have some navy doctors there that had dealt with frostbite before. And they tried and I am sure were successful with me. And what they was trying to do [was make sure] I don't get gangrene, which I did to a point but not [as] serious as they thought it would. Every hour on the hour, they was taking my blood to make sure that gangrene didn't go too far. They had to take the part of the foot that was all the way frostbitten. What they call the metatarsal in my foot, down from the instep down, they had to take that off. As a matter of fact, when I got there I thought my hand is going, too. Because my hand was frostbitten. Both feet and the tip of my nose was frostbitten. And my ear. They saved everything but my right foot.

They kept me in the hospital about, off and on, almost six months. Then they sent me down to Philadelphia, down at some place in Michigan, and then on to the veteran hospital down in Kentucky. And I stayed in that veteran hospital maybe about two months. I tell people this — they don't believe it — that in '51, it was still segregated there. I was on a ward that was an all-purpose ward, but I should've been on the surgical ward. But they put everybody [Black] down on that same ward. No matter what you had, if you were Black you were in the same ward. There were guys that had TB, there were guys that [had] literally everything wrong with him. Ward 31, that was the ward I was on. And as it turned out, this one friend I met in California, he lived in Canton, Ohio. Somehow he found out . . . what hospital I was in. He came to see me at the hospital. When he got there, they told him I wasn't in the hospital. And he says, "Well, I know that he is there. He is in this hospital somewhere." It turned out, I think it was a white nurse saw him and said, "Are you looking for a guy named Tom Cork?" He said, "Yes, I am." They wouldn't let him on the ward with me where I was. [I had to] get in a wheelchair and go out of the ward to visit with him . . . because he couldn't get in the ward I was on . . . because he is white. He was a white marine, you know, ex-marine. He was my friend — nobody would go that far to see somebody unless he cared about [him and] wanted to see him.

When I got out of the veteran hospital now the problem was trying to find me a shoe that I could wear. They start[ed] out with [what] I seen people [wear who] have one leg longer than the other, that kind of shoe. Well, that wasn't working because it was too heavy. My one foot was heavy, the other foot was light. My back was killing me. And the VA couldn't figure out what was wrong. They keeping X-raying my back. But a doctor came in and sent me to walk. And he said, the problem is, young man, you are walking wrong. That big old shoe you got, he said, that's causing you to, to walk different than you normally walk. It's pulling your back out. So, now he, they were trying to get me some shoes. So, they sent me to Saint Louis to get a specially made shoe for me. And what they had to do, they had to make those shoes the same weight. So, they had to add something to, to my right shoe to make it the same weight as the left shoe. Now, [the] veteran [hospital] is good to a point, but if you pardon the expression, [it] was hell to get anything done shoe-wise. I had to go all the way to the director at the VA hospital to get them to get me a decent pair of shoes. I was thinking that white marines might have these kind of shoes. I have one on my foot now. They was wearing them. I didn't have any. So, I saw [this] guy, I asked him, "Where you get those shoes?" He said the VA makes it for me. And I went back again. So, they got that corrected [and] now I got a decent pair of shoes, and that's all there.

With the VA, I had problems trying to get my disability. As it turned out, a guy from Houston, Texas, good friend of mine, he said, "What you need to do, go to a civilian doctor and just ask him to evaluate you, send all the information he has to the VA hospital." So, that's what I did. I went to a private doctor. He said, "I never seen anything like it in my life. I don't know why they are doing it to you. Because your foot's gone . . . and you have arthritis in your neck, hand, and every place else." He said, "I don't know why they don't want to give you your disability." It took them another three years to get my disability up to par. But the good news was, they back paid me. So, everything wasn't all bad. Then after that I went into the post office. I made my career [at the] post office. I worked there for thirty-one years.

Thomas E. Cork Sr.
Corporal, unit unknown
US Marine Corps
Interviewed July 23, 2004, Louisville, KY
Montford Point Marines Project

RUBEN LEMUEL HINES, CHARLOTTE, NORTH CAROLINA

This is the first time I've ever told too many people this, but [when] I got out of the Marine Corps [after World War II,] I found it very, very difficult to exist in civilian life. That was in [the] latter part of '45. And I was working at a furniture store in Birmingham, Alabama, and . . . the man who was in charge of the whole floor, name was Frank, . . . he slapped me. And I had a hooked big old knife in my hand. And I hooked him. And I don't know if you know what that term means. But I pulled it around way inside and cut his guts out. Then, that's when

I really panicked, being in the South, in Alabama at that time. I came back into the Marine Corps under an assumed name. And I went through boot camp at Parris Island [South Carolina].

That was in 1950, and they caught up with me about two years later. And I had made such a name for myself, I never will forget. The general who convened the board, name was Kaufman, . . . [held] a hearing to determine whether to let me remain. [The charge was] faulty enlistment, and they decided after the hearing that they would allow me to remain in the Marine Corps provided I promise them one thing. And that was to be one of the best marines that ever was. And I made that promise, made that vow. And I stayed in the Marine Corps from 1950 until 1969.

Now, the Marine Corps—I don't use the word integration no way, because it's no such thing [really]—[but] the Marine Corps desegregated quicker than any other branch of the service. They did [it], as a matter of fact, over the weekend. You're in an outfit, say, on Friday, and you were in a desegregated unit Monday morning. And that was it. It took the army and air force, took the air force, I think about five, six years. The Marine Corps did it on [a] weekend.

I went to Korea twice. I was in motor transport. And we were near the [Chosin] Reservoir when the Chinese crossed over. That's where the Chinese entered the war during that particular period. It was nothing easy and it was nothing wonderful—was cold all the time, freezing to death and all that. I never will forget one particular incident, if I may. When the Chinese broke through I had a buddy from Louisville, Kentucky. His name was Rudolph Hyde. And I was visiting him in the hospital. [He had gotten frostbite and] he had [his] feet in a basket. And the colonel broke through the tents and was telling us to run for it. Run for it, run for it. Run for what? He said, "The Chinks [are] coming, the Chinks are coming!" Well, I knew that's the nickname for Chinese. So, I started getting my gear and getting ready to head [out] like everybody else, and I remember Rudolph asking, "What about me? What about me?" The colonel told him, said, "Hell, go yourself!" Rudolph had forced me [to go on ahead, but] about ten, fifteen minutes later, who was running behind [me,] Rudolph with those frostbitten feet. He lost his feet later. But I never will forget. He forgot all about that pain and discomfort that he had, boy, and he was running with us, you know. It wasn't too good, but I remember him with a lot of fondness.

I was back in the States about two years before I went back [to Korea], still [doing] motor transport. I stayed in that same field twelve or thirteen years, [and] I did three full tours in Vietnam.

Ruben Lemuel Hines
Gunnery sergeant, unit unknown
US Marine Corps

Interviewed May 17, 2004, Charlotte, NC
Montford Point Marines Project
Copyright © 2004 Randall Library, University of North Carolina at Wilmington

JOHNNIE GIVIAN, JACKSONVILLE, NORTH CAROLINA

The Korean War was just getting heated up over there and beginning to fight. I got in our motor transport, and I volunteered to go to Korea. When I got there they had invaded Inchon about three to four months [earlier,] it wasn't long after. I moved up about thirty miles north of Inchon and that's where the DMZ was set up [and] I went up in there. They put me in a company called Item Company, 3rd Batch, 5th Battalion, a rifle company, a fighting unit. Up there where that line was where the North Koreans stopped and where the Americans stop[ped] at, that's where the line of resistance was. That's where I spent the rest of the time, which was about fourteen months. I fought there and Bunker Hill, I ended up on Bunker Hill.

When I first got there, we put in a defense force, we were at the line of resistance. And, what we did daily for three or four months, we would go out at night as a patrol, squads would go out. One would go in one direction, one would go in another. They were trying to keep the surprise of an attack from coming up on us. We went [out] just every night. We would go out and leave and go out and come back at the dawn of day tomorrow. And we would go check out what they call outposts in between our line of resistance and their lines of resistances. Sometimes it would be thirty feet and sometimes it would be three hundred yards. Sometimes it would be a half a mile, the distance between the two lines. And this [became] routine, this combat, people would die. They would get killed, and the next morning we'd find out their squad had two deaths because they ran into an ambush or something. Fear was there, yeah, but you got to brave yourself for that. And I must say I grew up during that time, I grew up to be a man. All that stuff at Montford Point was tough and bad and ugly, but I grew up because I had to face death and really did. We ran into gunfire, we got ambushed out there in the squad that I was in.

We had a man by the [nick]name of Freak, he was a student at Penn State College, and he was a sergeant. I was a corporal at that time, and he was a real strong man and he got killed and I took his place. Racism didn't show up then, nobody ever talked about it. It was almost forgotten. I was the only Black at one time there in our regiment of three-hundred-some people. The company commander made me squad leader when Freak got killed. So the racial problem wasn't over there then, you know. I knew I was Black, but that's all.... [You] become separated from everything else [but] just surviving.... I used to lay there when I got back off of patrol and meditate on how I was gonna get through that day or that night.

We ran into a lot of opposition. [These] hills that are like little small mountains [were] sitting in between us and the Chinese line, and we used to have to go out and stay on this outpost for seven days to make sure that we're not gonna be surprised with an attack or something. And then that outpost would get attacked. I was in a severe [fight] once. We was out there, it was a marine platoon and the support, which was two corpsmen, a radioman, and a chaplain; [we had] sixty-nine people out on that hill and we got attacked one night. And the next night I came up the hill and when I got back to our line, which was about a half a mile away, maybe a little further, I find out that it was seven of us walked off that hill. The rest of them didn't make it [out] on foot. So it was severe fighting over there.

The first time I was wounded, we was on the line where we got this trench dug, our line where in front of it is war [and] behind it you try to get peace. We was up in there one day and this captain, Hoke was his name, told somebody to fly some ice cream up there on the line. It was about 105 degrees. So he called up to me—I was the squad leader and the squad leader always wants to go get [the special treats,] but [when I went] out the door to go, I had this guy—I liked him but he was pretty rough—the guy reached and pulled me back, he gonna get [the ice cream] and he ran out. And a Chin[ese] mortar came in. There was half a can of gasoline [that] we used for our tanks [and] for these little Coleman stoves we had, and that mortar round hit that can and it went up in the air and this guy went down. He was 98 percent burned, burning like a torch and I was right behind him 'cause I was gonna pull him back again, but I didn't have time. And that's when the fragmentation from the thing saturated me [and I] lost my sight. They flew him out to Japan, me they flew me back down to Seoul. My eyes were blind, but then they figured out that it was just the blast, the heat from the blast. And I was just full of shrapnel.

Then, after so many days, I went back up to the unit. That was one time [I was wounded] and when the next time we was [on] X-ray, that was the name of the hill [where] we got attacked. That's the one where seven of us walked off of there, and when I came down I had been ripped open under my arm, by my ribs, like somebody took a knife and cut it, and I didn't know nothing about it till I got down there 'cause I wasn't even thinking about that. But that was the second Purple Heart I got. I left Korea fifteen and a half months after I got there, and I came back with the draft that I went over there with. It was 4,800 Marines that was in this draft, and [when we] went back it was 1,900 of us [left]. We landed there in California, and when we got off the ship, [we] went down and got processed, went through the medical things.

Johnnie Givian
Corporal, unit unknown
US Marine Corps
Interviewed August 17, 2005, Jacksonville, NC
Montford Point Marines Project
Copyright © 2006 Randall Library, University of North Carolina at Wilmington

ADNER BATTS, JACKSONVILLE, NORTH CAROLINA

After we left [training at] Montford Point, I came in as a steward, which a lot of the Blacks was going to [in the Marine Corps]. Most of them, by and large, [went to] depot companies [or became] stewards. Depot companies, of course, meaning moving equipment, ammunition, that kind of [thing]. And I was a steward cook, or I got them at least to let me show that I could cook a little bit. [I went to] the steward school . . . with three Black guys and about eighteen white guys, and we were at Hadnot Point [Camp Lejeune] with the Supply School Battalion. I was the tallest one out of the three of us, Archer, Stowalt, and myself, and I was [put] in charge on our way from the barracks to school. And it was another guy in charge of [the] eighteen whites. He would drill them, and I'd drill my two behind him. Can you imagine that? Huh? It's kind of comical, when I think about it today.

I was a private, but then we had a general's inspection, out on the parade ground, and the only Black people out there was Archer, Stowalt, and myself, on this front rank of Headquarters Company Supply Battalion at Camp Lejeune, [on the] parade ground. We had five hundred or six hundred people out there, or better, and we're on the front. This general came by, when he inspected us, he looked up and down, he said, "Why aren't these guys PFCs?" He said, "They look just as good as the fellows down at Parris Island." And I remember my colonel's name was Colonel Cloud. He said, "Sir, it was just an oversight." [The general] said, "Well, I think if a man has got enough to break boot camp, [he] should be at least a PFC." And so after we got back to the barracks and put down our gear, the battalion officer called, and we went down there, and they made us PFCs. It took a general to promote we three to PFC, kind of like a battlefield commission.

After that, I was assigned to one of the very places I worked as a civilian, with people that I didn't know at the time were stewards, as a cook, I was assigned as a cook. They were steward's attendants, and some of the same guys that I knew before was there, you know, telling me, you was crazy to come into the Steward Branch. [That was at the] Commission Officers' Mess, Camp Lejeune, North Carolina. Remember, I worked there, as a civilian, as a janitor, on the bar, in 1946, '47. And when I came into the Marine Corps, I went right back there.

And then, I was tired of the Steward Branch, I felt that I could do something that I would like more. During this time, the general commander and officer of the base wanted a cook. The officer in charge of the officers' club called me down and [told me] the general wanted a cook. Would I like to cook for him? Everybody here says, you [are] a good cook. And I said, "No, sir, I'd rather not." I remember the general's aide said, "Well, you'll cook for him if, if he wants you to." I said, "Yes, sir, I know that, it's no doubt about it. But I don't feel that I'm qualified to cook for a general. I don't cook that well." I didn't want to go cook.

I went over to Korea in '52. Came back '53. I was [in] an integrated unit. I was in Korea probably about sixteen months. I was over there when the war ended, as a matter of fact, but I was in the Steward Branch then, and that's something else, see? It's something that you wasn't trained for. I was a buck sergeant, E-4, then, but I had to set up [a] perimeter for grazing machine gunfire there because I was a sergeant, but I was actually a cook. I hadn't had no machine gun training. Well, you had to qualify with the M1, and other weapons you had was the .45, the carbine, and, the BAR, Browning automatic weapon. Other than that, that's all you had been training with. I was cooking, [but] like I said, when [the] time comes, I was manning . . . or setting up machine gun positions, setting up perimeter, pulling out, getting out the standing guard, and that kind of thing.

After Korea, I stayed in the Marine Corps twenty-eight years, ten months, and one day. I came back [from Korea] to Quantico. By then, my letter was in, and I stayed up there about a year or so, and I got a change of MOS. I'd heard about the Marine Corps Institute, and so I took an MCI course at the Marine Corps Institute, in engineers — international, diesel crawler, or tractor repair maintenance, and then I put in for the change of MOS, and I got it that way. My new MOS was engineer, 1345, Engineer Equipment Operator. And I came back to Camp Lejeune as an engineer man [and] I went up through the line.

Adner Batts
Master sergeant, unit unknown
US Marine Corps
Interviewed June 29, 2005
Montford Point Marines Project
Copyright © 2006 Randall Library, University of North Carolina at Wilmington

PAUL HAGAN, JACKSONVILLE, NORTH CAROLINA

[After training at] Montford Point [in 1946], we boarded a train on the railroad track at a place they called Dew Drop between Jacksonville and Camp Lejeune. We loaded on a troop train, all Black, and we went from there to California, all the way segregated, all the way through with all Black, and when we got to California, we [went to] a place called Treasure Island. . . . We board[ed] a ship[and] we went to Guam. Eight Ammo Depot in Guam [was the] first duty station for me. We handled ammunition. All we done was handle ammunition when we was on Guam, . . . [for] about eight or nine months. [Ammunition handling] is all we were trained [in]. We had no infantry training at all. Just a little hand-to-hand combat.

Then I was transferred to Hawaii . . . [and] I joined the stewards over there after I left the Eight Ammo Depot. We got to Hawaii, and . . . they had all the officers assigned there, [and they] assigned the Blacks to be stewards in the officers' clubs, had us working for them. And a navy captain and above, we worked for them also. That was our job there. No ammunition [handling] there but we done a lot of cooking and waiting on them, making up beds and stuff like that. [We had] a very little training [as stewards.] They just talked to us, that's all. I didn't stay there but about I think approximately six months.

I remember coming back from Hawaii to the United States, that was in '49, I think. Anyway, in, in '50 that's when we [were] over there training at Dew Drop [and] they go to [war in] Korea. While we was on the ship there—we was on the ship for sixty-two days—the president of the United States passed that integration bill, integrated all the branch[es] of service in 1950. That's when we was going in, getting ready to go into Inchon. On the ship I was on [was] ammunition handlers only, . . . [but] what they done, they integrate[d] everybody in the armed forces, and when we landed, so many [would go] to the infantry, so many to different outfits and like that, that broke [up our all-Black unit] up. And then they bring us all together [racially], and we had no experience of combat during that time. [We were assigned to] different [integrated] units, all of us.

[At] Inchon, after I landed there, I was assigned to come back to service school. [But] after we was in the south at Inchon getting ready to go to battle, no, [they needed me for combat]. We split up, and like I said, some of them, cooks and bakers and everything, was over there fighting during that time, too. I was in this unit that was doing all the fighting and everything. And that's where I received my award. My job then was handling ammunition and stuff like that. Carrying it to the front line, and stuff like that. But we were all working in the front line during that time, too. One thing I remember is that when we was on our way up to the Chosin Reservoir, it was thirty-five below zero and our men's feet was busting open in their shoes they were so frozen. And there was many men up there. We lost vehicles up on the mountain, we lost a lot of troops up there. And due to the fact, like I told you, that we was not trained, [had] no combat training, we just had to dig in and do the best we could. Because we did not take that training before we was sent overseas. The medal I received [was] when I was in there.

I met many [whites] 'cause we was integrated. We worked together, they were friends. I worked with so many different peoples. We were all were friends over there, we were friends to each other over there because we know we had a job to do and we all done that job together.

I went from Inchon to the Chosin Reservoir, all the way to the Chosin Reservoir, next to the Yalu River, where the two hundred thousand Chinese cross[ed] to come over to fight us. We [were] aboard ship [when] they cross[ed], and we [retreated] when they got there, we went back [out] to the ocean. We were moving away from those Chinese. This was called vacillation—we don't call it retreating in the Marine Corps—but it's still retreating. Then we come back to Japan. I did not have to go [back] to Korea after that.

I was awarded the Silver Star. [Actually,] I was awarded six Bronze Stars. Now, [a] Silver Star [is] in lieu of five Bronze Stars so it would add up to be six Bronze Stars, or use the Silver Star with one star. So I had six Bronze Stars. And that was what I rated over there. But there was a lot of confusion when I left there to go back to the States about the ribbons that I wore. We had a battalion inspection and I was in the ranks. I was a sergeant then, and the commanding Officer of the battalion came up to me and checked my ribbons over, and he called the sergeant major and had him take a number of every ribbon I had and what the meaning of those ribbons was. . . . They wanted to get me busted . . . because he felt that I did not rate those ribbons. . . . I was one of the most decorated men up there in the battalion. . . . I had more ribbons on my chest than the commanding officer had on his. I believe [they went after me] 'cause I'm African American. 'Cause he did not stop the other people, white [marines]. I believe in my heart, that's why they done it. And they took my name and sent into headquarters, Washington, DC, to see what ribbons I had in my record. And they sent the letter back . . . that I rated every ribbon and every star that I was wearing and also one that I rated that didn't have in my record. And that's when they dropped the case, but I rated all the stars and ribbons that I was wearing.

[When I got back,] I was in TMO, that's transportation, being in charge of the Marine Freight Traffic Management Office. I was stationed over in an industrial area, Building 1011, in [the] Traffic Management Office, Camp Lejeune—the Main Side, not Hadnot [where Montford Point was]. I stayed over there about three years because I was backwards and forwards all the time. I went overseas six times—Guam, Hawaii, Japan, Japan, Japan. I think overseas I was treated like any normal American over there, [a] marine.

We had good liberty overseas . . . [but] in Okinawa, they had the place over there they call B.C. Street, all white. We had a place they called Four Corners, all Black. In other words, we had a different area that we mostly went in and whites had a different area they went in. But the living was good and we was all treated right. [By] the [late] '50s, after everything was integrated, we worked together most times then. I mean, we caught the buses together, went on liberty together. And we come back together. And we slept side by side in the barracks and we ate in the mess hall. In other words, everything seemed to be a lot better than it was when I come through at the beginning.

Paul Hagen
Sergeant, 8th Ammunition Company
US Marine Corps
Interviewed May 25, 2004, Jacksonville, NC
Montford Point Marines Project
Copyright © 2006 Randall Library, University of North Carolina at Wilmington

6

African American Prisoners of War

The official number of American POWs in the Korean War is 7,140, of whom 2,701 died in captivity, a rate of 43 percent. Thousands more deaths may have gone unreported or occurred between capture and arriving at a POW camp, and in the first year, before management of the prison camps was turned over to the Chinese by the North Koreans, prisoners may have died at a rate as high as 75 percent. Somewhere around 3,000 men likely died between November 1950 and April 1951 alone. Many of those who did survive endured imprisonment for two years or more, and most survived death marches, abuse, severe malnutrition, inadequate clothing and hygiene, lack of medicine, torture and deprivation, and the freezing cold.[1]

Those captured in the first four months of the war, between July and October 1950, ended up in the hands of North Korea, which was not a party to the Geneva Convention. Captured soldiers were beaten, tortured, and killed, some of them dying in group massacres of up to sixty men. Survivors were often stripped of most of their clothing, including their boots, and forced to march into the frozen north of the country, a quick pace encouraged by a steady rain of blows from fists and rifle butts. Frostbite was endemic. Those who could not keep step were murdered by the side of the trail.[2]

Once the Chinese entered the war, little improved for POWs. Like those captured previously, they were often housed in improvised temporary camps, including caves, for up to several months, before being forced to move again, marching at night to avoid strafing by UN air forces. Many died along the way; the "lucky" survivors ended up in a series of permanent camps along the Yalu River.[3] There, still denied adequately warm housing or clothing, they endured a meager diet—most lost up to half their body weight—as well as rampant lice and dysentery and near-constant abuse from their captors. At long last, conditions improved slightly in October 1951 with the resumption of peace talks at Panmunjom. Prisoners received quilted Chinese winter uniforms, blankets, and shoes. And the scant diet of millet and sorghum was now occasionally supplemented with rice and flour, but most prisoners, still lacking enough nutrients, suffered night blindness and other ailments associated with malnutrition.[4]

The Chinese also brought another innovation into their handling of the POWs: so-called education classes. Typically, captives were subjected to prolonged interrogation, followed by a regimen in which they would be "broken"—kept cold, hungry, and often sleepless—while being forced to attend hours of lectures on the superiority of Communism and of the allegedly peace-loving Chinese to their American capitalist aggressors.[5]

African American POWs were subject to a particular brand of this indoctrination. Reports after the war stressed how the Chinese used race to divide prisoners of war, segregating Blacks from whites and teaching African Americans classes in US history with a strong focus on Black struggle and freedom denied. Black prisoners were continually asked why they were fighting against other people of color and why they would fight for a country that had historically and continuously denied them basic freedom and dignity. Corporal Donald Rogers States of Newton, North Carolina, told reporters after his release, "They would tell us that minority races were discriminated against and never had a chance under American democracy. Maybe a few of the guys listened. I didn't. I knew they were the enemy and I wasn't going to let any bastard outsider tell me anything against my country."[6] Other Black prisoners were more unsettled, some noting that it was the first time that they had ever learned their own history.

Prisoners of war were generally sorted by their captors into three categories: Progressives, those who went along with the Communist indoctrination, helped to promote Communism in various ways, and in some cases became informants; Reactionaries, who refused to comply or who actively resisted; and Middle-of-the-Roaders, who attended compulsory classes and even did some self-study but neither helped nor hindered their captors.[7] Fellow prisoners generally called the Progressives more colorful names, including "rats" and "stool pigeons."

Some African American prisoners were drawn to the so-called Progressive groups with promises of privileges, including jobs, better food and living quarters, and medicine, but also after being subjected to prolonged campaigns focusing on the unequal treatment of Blacks stateside. This sometimes did its job of finding a sore spot on those who rankled against segregation and indignities at home; it also exacerbated an already stressed situation within the camps by amplifying racial tensions, with some POWs later reporting the presence of Ku Klux Klan chapters among the prisoners. Indeed, one postwar study found that the KKK was considered one of the more active organizations in the camps when it came to resisting Chinese propagandizing and "encouraging" fellow prisoners—through intimidation and sometimes even violence—not to collaborate[8] Black newspapers back home reported how the Chinese exploited these potential racial divides and "attempted to instill vicious racial and class hatreds" by "play[ing] one group against the other to confuse and disorganize the Americans," and, according to some, "tell[ing] colored prisoners that the whites did not want them around, even as POWs, and the whites that they had something better," seeming to offer Black soldiers preferential treatment.[9]

The Chinese showed a sophistication in their propaganda techniques and a deep knowledge of US racial politics. Indeed, some of the officers had been educated in the United States. As one repatriated GI reported, "They told us how hard we should try to fight for rights of colored people, that we should join Paul Robeson and fight for peace, but ridiculed [NAACP director] Walter White." Robeson, an acknowledged Stalinist and Black activist leader, was repeatedly held up as an example, and his records, in both English and Russian, were played over camp public-address systems.[10] Eugene Fleming, a Black POW who had served with the 503rd Field Artillery, reported, on returning home to Philadelphia after thirty-two months as a prisoner, "those commies made it tough in order to set us off against one another. And they doggone nearly did just that."[11] Corporal Richard Barnes of Houston, Texas, said that the Chinese "made the most of racial problems" and that Black soldiers were sometimes shown leniency in order to stir up resentment among white POWs. "Nothing would happen to me for doing something. But if a white boy did it, he would get from six months to a year in jail." The Chinese also regularly reported to the prisoners any news of racial bias from back home, hoping to provoke new racial conflicts in the camp. The Chicago Defender reported in August 1953 that "Red Chinese 'indoctrination' was so severe in some cases in stressing class struggle that some of the prisoners became mentally unbalanced for prolonged periods of time."[12]

African Americans were perhaps more frequently among the Reactionaries and were often targeted for punishment for their refusal to comply with orders, as one survivor recounted: "At first most of us were made to attend lectures. Then some of us just refused to go and for that got the hardest work detail."[13] Eugene Fleming recalled one incident from early on when one of his captors caught him with a stolen blanket and stared at him and "looked bad, 'North Korean style,' and I just stared back and looked bad, 'South Philadelphia style.'"[14] Another Reactionary, Col. Page Thomas Baylor Jr. of Washington, DC, imprisoned for thirty-two months, was eventually moved from Camp 3 to Camp 5, which was set aside specifically for Reactionaries. There he was beaten with rifle butts and sent to "the hole," a dug-out space in the frozen ground "not big enough to lay down in" and covered with a log lid, for a total of forty-eight days.[15]

Acts of resistance could take other forms, including conducting and attending religious services and forming bands playing on homemade guitars, bass fiddles, and drums. Prestee Davis, whose story follows, crafted an enormous bass fiddle out of salvaged materials, earning himself the media-coined nickname "Stradivarius the Second."[16] Earl Dantzler, of the 503rd Field Artillery, was elected band leader of the group they called the Cats of Harmony. He recalled that "the Chinese took propaganda pictures of us and sent them around the world, calling us 'The Interracial Cats!'"[17] Some African American POWs reportedly used Black slang, or bop, to confuse their captors.[18] Others said just finding small ways to be happy, showing joy, and having camaraderie—laughing and joking around among themselves—during the attempts to break them down could be an enormous act of resistance that often befuddled their captors.

Black POWs were also conspicuous in their participation in the bizarre sporting event the Chinese put on in 1952 known as the Inter-Camp Olympics, a propaganda effort designed specifically for the Chinese to highlight to the world the supposedly robust condition of the United Nations prisoners. Belying the often horrific reality of the camps, the prisoner-athletes were divided into teams by camp number and even given team sweatshirts to wear for a host of track and field competitions, boxing, wrestling, softball, basketball, football, volleyball, soccer, and other sports. The "Olympics" were highly featured in Chinese propaganda declaring the prisoners healthy, well fed, and provided with recreation and other amenities, a far cry from the dominant reality.

It was clear to the prisoners from the start that the festivities were yet another form of highly staged Chinese propaganda, and some refused to participate. Those who took part did so for various reasons, very few of them actually supporting or believing the incredible hype of a souvenir program—supposedly published "at the request of the P.O.W.'s"—that claimed to be evidence of "the harmonious atmosphere that prevailed at all time among men of various nationalities, races, creeds, and colors." The program even bestowed praise on the "Korean People's Army and the Chinese People's Volunteers" without whose "efforts such a tremendous undertaking could not have been possible." The program "author," George R. Atkins, continued: "At all time the cooperation, generosity, enthusiasm, and selfless energy displayed by our captors was perfect and left absolutely nothing to be desired." Another writer, Clarence B. Covington, enthused, "I am certain that no one in his sane mind will ever say that prisoners of war over here are not the best cared for in the whole world today."[19] And interracial unity was much on display in the accompanying photos, including one with the caption, "Whatever the nation or race, everyone has a smiling face."[20] As one archivist would later write of this prose: "One can only wonder which of three voices is speaking: that of the brainwashed prisoner, psychologically conquered by his tormentors; the pragmatic collaborator, dutifully repeating what his captors want to hear; or the wise guy, laying it on thick and knowing that nobody back home would be fooled by such a charade."[21] Even purposely introducing typographical errors into the program could be a small act of sabotage or a subtle signal to those on the outside that the work was done under duress.

Prisoners of war had many ways of taking agency: what could appear to be co-operation on the surface could in fact be an act of profound resistance.

Most of those who did take part in the Inter-Camp Olympics did so in order to see their buddies from other camps, to highlight their unity and athletic skill, and simply to take a chance to recreate and enjoy themselves after months or years of deprivation. Rather than viewing the spectacle as an act of collabora-tion, many of the athletes felt that they were turning their captors' public rela-tions stunt against them, wresting individual meaning and pleasure from the games. Team A from Camp 5, an all–African American team, won the football championship with players that included Prestee Davis and Robert Fletcher, both of the 24th Infantry, and Claris Levert of the 2nd Infantry Division, 8th In-fantry Regiment, whose stories follow below. Clarence Adams, one of the twenty-one Americans who famously refused repatriation and who later stayed in China for twelve years, boxed as a lightweight. While Adams acknowledged that some refused to participate, he also recalled that Reactionaries as well as Progressives and Middle-of-the-Roaders welcomed the "diversion from the tedium of their daily lives . . . [that] made us forget where we were at least for a few days."[22] Another participant in the camp games was Earl Dantzler of the 503rd Field Artillery, who spent thirty-three months imprisoned. Dantzler recalled that by 1952, a truce was on the horizon and the food and recreation improved as the Chinese prepared for press coverage. He competed in the walking competition and in basketball for Camp 5, playing with bare feet since the Chinese could not find shoes sized 12D. Years later he exclaimed over a propaganda photograph of himself taking a jump shot. "I don't know how they did it, but the Chinese had painted shoes on my feet!"[23]

When the truce was finally agreed to in 1953, rather than follow the typical Geneva Convention protocol of a total prisoner exchange, it included a provision that prisoners could voluntarily forgo repatriation. The result was that about forty-seven thousand North Korean and Chinese former prisoners stayed behind in South Korea. Embarrassed by this mass desertion, the Chinese and North Koreans highly publicized that twenty-one American POWs also refused repatria-tion at the end of the war. At a press conference in the neutral zone on January 26, 1954, the former prisoners denounced conditions in the United States, re-quested to be accepted "as free men" by the Chinese, and said that they hoped to return to the United States "at some time in the future when we can fight for world peace without being persecuted."[24] Not surprisingly, most were already considered "progressives," and many of their fellow prisoners figured they would stay behind rather than face charges of collaborating with the enemy. Among the twenty-one were three African Americans, Cpl. William White of Plumer-ville, Arkansas, Sgt. Laurence Sullivan of Omaha, Nebraska, and Pvt. Clarence

Cecil Adams of Memphis, Tennessee. Adams had only eight years of formal schooling, was accused by fellow prisoners of voluntarily collaborating, urging the adoption of Communism, attending special voluntary classes, and informing on other POWs. Fellow prisoners noted that he had been rewarded with a "cozy camp job as librarian." Private White, who had twelve years of formal education and had been rewarded with a job as camp mailman, was said to have willingly accepted and preached Communist ideology and informed on other POWs. Sergeant Sullivan, a former cafeteria worker with eleven years of schooling, worked on his camp's newspaper, where he wrote pro-Communist articles and made propaganda recordings.[25]

The limited schooling of the three men was in keeping with that of the twenty-one POWs overall, who had an average of only two years of high school, with only six having graduated.[26] But the three Black POWs were more than capable of articulating exactly why they had decided not to return. Refusing to return to racial bigotry and "beatings by white policemen," they had chosen freedom, they said. "It is taken for granted [by the Communists] that we are free men," said White. "We have asked [them] to accept us as free men and they are doing it." Adams added that he would be willing to return home, but only "when living conditions improve—everyone knows what I'm talking about."[27] Sullivan elaborated, "The American people know how the Negro is treated in the United States. Definitely this is one of my reasons [for staying in Asia]. Of course, my desire to work for world peace is the main reason," he quickly added, remembering his talking points, "I can't speak out for peace in America without being persecuted."[28]

Home-front newspapers rushed to condemn the twenty-one men and to seek answers for their defections. Most suggested that they were the products of broken homes, limited education, and "weak" values. One POW who initially refused repatriation, then changed his mind, reported that the Communists had promised the twenty-one that they "would be masters of our country. The Communist Party of the United States would plan when the revolution would start and we would be shipped back [to lead] when the time came." In the meantime, he added, they were told that while in China "they could have plenty of women and a good home."[29] Some quoted fellow GIs suggesting that the "turncoats" were all Progressives of the worst kind who had collaborated with their captors and against their fellow prisoners, and so feared prosecution and the retribution of their fellows once home. As one officer commented, "Those punks aren't Red, they're just plain yellow."[30] Taking another tack altogether, Newsweek claimed, without evidence, that the "sorry bunch of losers and misfits" were "bound together more by homosexuality than Communism."[31]

The three Black former POWs posed a particular threat on the home front. Did their refusal to repatriate suggest that the Chinese indoctrination had found a welcome home among Blacks who, fed up with Jim Crow, would now embrace Communism? Both mainstream and Black newspapers rushed to reassure their readers that the numbers—three out of twenty-one defectors, three out of more than four thousand surviving POWs—were too low to be representative of larger Black belief.[32] The African American Cleveland Call and Post joined in to describe the defection of "only three" Black prisoners as a victory, stating that even though Black POWs were targeted with propaganda, "special treatment and inducements, [Communist] pleas fell on deaf ears" with the vast majority.[33] The paper contrasted the three Black defections with a report that "thirty-six men from the white company at Camp 5 were indoctrinated. Thirty of them reportedly were returning to the United States with the intent of organizing communist cells."[34]

Still, it could not be denied that much of the Communist propaganda aimed at Black POWs was rooted in the disgraceful truth of American history as it pertained to African Americans, or as a reporter who had interviewed some of the returned men put it: "At the heart of many of the men's confidential comments was the recurrent theme that a good bit of the wearisome propaganda in the camps was true when it came to the American race problem."[35] One Chinese technique was to reteach American history with a focus on African Americans, the first time that many prisoners learned anything about their history. Years later, while in China, Clarence Adams would remark to a visiting W. E. B. Du Bois, "Doctor, I never heard of you during my school days in Memphis. But in the P.O.W. camp, one February, some of the fellows staged a play about you. Imagine how I felt when I, a Negro, had to be told about a man who they said was the greatest living Negro."[36]

Interestingly, one of the two white POWs who initially refused repatriation but changed his mind within days and returned to the United States was later accused of writing pro-Communist propaganda in camp newsletters, including articles castigating US racial policies. Cpl. Edward Dickinson, of the interestingly named town of Cracker's Neck, Virginia, even asked that his "blonde, gum-chewing wife," Lottie, let reporters know that her husband "believed all people were the same [and] he wanted Negroes here to know this."[37]

In his court-martial trial, however, Dickinson claimed that the three African Americans who had stayed behind were key to a Communist plot to foment a revolution in the United States within five years and that they would return to reunite with a number of already repatriated POWs in a secret rendezvous to take place in Chicago. He said that Adams, White, and Sullivan were told they would receive specialized training in organizing "minorities" and that while in China they could have their choice of Chinese wives or elect to have one imported from Africa. They would later be secretly slipped back into the United States to reunite with the other Progressive repatriates who would by then have established a network of secret Communist cells.[38]

This was obviously not to be, and it is unclear whether there was any truth to the story. In any case, Sullivan returned to the United States in 1958 and White in 1965. That same year, American troops in Vietnam were surprised to hear a male American voice on North Vietnamese radio, broadcasting propaganda to them alongside Hanoi Hannah and in the tradition of World War II's Tokyo Rose. It was Clarence Adams, the last of the three Black POWs who stayed behind, and he focused his broadcasts primarily at Black soldiers. He recounted that he had been captured after his segregated unit, the 502nd Field Artillery, 2nd Army Division, was left behind during the retreat from the Pusan Perimeter, and that his training had prepared him to find the North Koreans and Chinese to be barbarians. "I am the living truth that the American bosses have lied about the Asians in the same way that they have lied about Africans and Latin Americans," he said in one broadcast. Speaking directly to his Black comrades, he asked, "Fellows, are you on the right side of this? You are in the wrong battle here. You are fighting the wrong war. Brothers, go home. The Negro people need you back there."[39]

Adams, too, yearned to return home, as he admitted to a visiting Shirley Graham Du Bois, the author and activist and wife of W. E. B. Du Bois, in 1959: "My greatest ambition is to return to the United States, trained, rounded, ready to serve, to walk with dignity, to be a credit to my race. I want you to tell my folks I am not running out on them. I'll be back and I'll be a much better man than I would have been had I not come to China."[40] Adams would eventually return to the United States after a dozen years in China. During the Cultural Revolution, he found himself on the outs with his hosts and under suspicion, and came home. He and his Chinese wife raised their two daughters in his native Memphis and ran a successful series of Chinese restaurants.[41]

Another African American POW, Rothwell B. Floyd, unflatteringly distinguished himself while in the camps and was the first POW to be tried and court-martialed after the war. He was initially welcomed back along with his comrades as a surviving hero and lauded in the pages of Jet magazine, and he testified to reporters that he'd seen Chinese soldiers throw a prisoner off a cliff during a march.[42] But his facade would soon crumble, and the twenty-eight-year-old newlywed from London, Kentucky, was arrested October 3, 1953, after accusations from fellow POWs revealed that it was he who had thrown the American POW from a cliff, among a slew of other heinous crimes. Floyd was later indicted for a second murder, with assaulting a superior officer, for mistreating fellow POWs, and for larceny.[43] Of the fourteen POWs who faced courts-martial after the war, Floyd was the only one not charged with collaboration and was one of two accused of murdering a fellow prisoner.

Known by the ironic nickname of "Tiny"—he stood over six foot two and weighed 250 pounds—Floyd preyed on the weak and dying in Bean Camp and later in Camp 1. Fellow prisoners testified that he routinely stole food from fellow prisoners and money and valuables from the sick and dying, hit one man in the head with a rock and regularly kicked and beat others, and sold food he'd acquired from Korean civilians at extortionist rates, amassing a fortune of fifteen thousand dollars. Fellow prisoners repeatedly mentioned that Floyd maintained his considerable bulk while those around him starved to death. In the first of two murder allegations, he was accused of drowning a fellow prisoner while crossing a stream—he had been tasked with carrying the sick prisoner—by knowingly let him drop into the water. He was also accused of throwing a dying comrade off a cliff, after robbing him, during the infamous death march from Bean Camp to Camp 1 in which half of the six hundred prisoners died over a twenty-one-day period.[44] Floyd, it seems, was an equal opportunity oppressor, victimizing Blacks and whites alike. In one incident, recalled during testimony by a fellow soldier, "Tiny" stole the special portion of "sick food" given to three other Black prisoners. When one of them dared to speak up, Floyd responded: "You son of a bitch, you don't need it. You are going to die anyway and I'm going to live."[45] While the more serious murder and assault charges were dropped due to lack of credible witness testimony, Floyd was eventually found guilty of striking an officer, Lt. Col. John Keith, of "wrongfully mistreating" fellow prisoners by assaulting them and stealing food meant for them, and of larceny for stealing wallets and jewelry from the dead. Floyd was sentenced to forty years at hard labor, later reduced to ten years by the US Army Board of Review.[46]

Aside from Tiny Floyd and the three who refused repatriation, African American POWs generally conducted themselves with honor in the camps, and their ability to stick together and help each other through the ordeal was especially strong. Some former POWs recounted a song they had sung, to the tune of "Sleepy Down South," in the early spring of 1953: "Cold wind blowing through the Chosin trees / POWs here about to freeze / Won't Uncle Sam come and hear my pleas? / Jack, its cold in North Korea!" A scant four months later, these same men filled the first two truckloads to arrive at Freedom Village for repatriation and a voyage home. Now one group of men started up a chant: "Be light / Be bright / It sure is good to be back / To this little piece of Uncle Sugar!"[47]

SAMUEL J. FARROW, TACOMA, WASHINGTON

[I'm] Sammy J. Farrow. I got captured . . . [when] we was going up [into] North Korea. We had passed the capital and there's a river north of Pyongyang. We knew the Chinese was up there because in October they put [up signs] in Chinese and English that if we crossed the Manchurian line they was coming across and this is what they did. And they broke through with one of their cavalry out-fits and that's the way they got behind the 2nd Division.

It started snowing right after Thanksgiving [1950]. Maybe about two days after Thanksgiving is when the stuff really hit the fan. The Chinese had broken through. It's the type of terrain that you can't turn the vehicles around. You have to be able to make a big circle and we was in something like a ravine and this one road is just [the only] way up. And they knocked the front vehicles out. So we are at a standstill. We couldn't go any farther.

I still had a hand grenade with me — my weapon, I'd got rid of it, say about a day before then, because I was out of ammunition. But I did have a grenade with me, because we had ran across a couple Black prisoners that they had tried to take the skin off, and I wasn't gonna be taken, captured alive. But it didn't turn out that way. When this group did catch us, I guess it was about six Chinese guys, we first thought [they] was Korean. We thought we's in pretty good ter-rain, as we was in a ravine, come to find out we was in the middle of one of their CP [Communist Party] camps. They came out, and there was four of us and I guess about six of them, and they had a machine gun, and two [of our] guys had a carbine, one guy had a .45. And the sergeant that was with us said, "Well, we don't have a chance against the guns," because one of [our] guys did load his carbine, he was getting ready to cut loose, but a carbine against an automatic weapon is no good, not when you're within twenty-five yards of each other. I knew I couldn't use my hand grenade then, 'cause I had more peoples with me, and believe it or not, I kept that hand grenade for about two days before they actually found it. They didn't search us as good as they should have when they took us in, because what they was doing, they was feeling me, mostly, be-cause I was something strange to them, they kept saying, "Ethiopee? Ethiopee?" And I kept saying, "No, American Negro. American Negro." 'Cause back then it wasn't, you know, "Black," it was "American Negro." And that was it, and they took us to this hut, and I come to find out they had more POWs in there. They had been watching us for quite a while.

I got captured in December 1950, the 2nd of December. So about the 5th is when they started the walking. And we walked from the 5th of December up until about the 25th of February. Just making moves at night. And it was snow-ing, and Christmas of '50 was one of the most beautiful nights I've seen, nothing but snow and the moon. But it was cold. The equipment that we had [with us at capture was] all we had . . . for about eight or nine months or so. I had combat boots when I got captured. And [when they] wore out, then they gave us ten-nis shoes. And that's all they gave us, sneakers. And tennis shoes in fifty-below-zero weather is rather uncomfortable. And lots of guys, they'd lose their toes or whatever; in fact, everybody did get frostbitten. The thirty-three months I was there, that's all I wore was sneakers. And the year after, our clothes was deteriorated, they gave us some real padded stuff, padded cloth. And we was hoping that eventually we'd get something from the Red Cross. Well, the first year they still counted me as MIA, and then after [my mother] did find out I was alive, it took eight months for a letter to get from the States to me, and the same thing for one to get back to her. And, as I say, I was hoping that they was gonna let the Red Cross in, but we never did see nothing from the Red Cross.

[I did try to escape once,] but that only lasted for maybe a couple hours or so, and they had us back in there. 'Cause after the [march north,] we had to rebuild this area that we was living at. And this particular area, when we was building it, we didn't make it too strong, because we was hoping that one night we could slip through it [and get away because we were] that close to the Yalu River. I guess we were gone about an hour or two hours, this particular time, and they knew. In fact, we looked up and there they were. The people in the villages had told on us, and you know, by being rather tall and big and Black compared to those peoples, we rather did stand out. So many thoughts was going through my mind, if I was going [to live]. Well, for some reason, we knew we wasn't gonna be shot, I don't know why, but torture, yes. Well, I was the only Black in this group when I did get captured, and the only thing I was worried about was [are] they going to try to skin me like some of those guys that we had found. That was about the only actual fear that I had then.

I had two kids [back home] then, and I was just determined to live. And [our captors] didn't have no medical care, and hot food that we was used to, and so we was eating millet and soybeans. Soybeans, I knew what it was, but millet I didn't. Trying to get the guys to eat was the biggest thing. We would make ourselves eat, because the stuff just didn't have no taste to it. And we just had to [survive, but] lots of the guys that I [was with didn't. There] was, about two thousand in this camp and only about fourteen came out. And most of them died due to the fact that [there was] no food and medical care, 'cause we had quite a few wounded with us.

During that time I was real, well, I wouldn't say real religious, but I was brought up in church, and I just prayed a lot. And for some reason, I don't know, I guess I'm the type I just figured I was gonna make it. It was gonna be done. And we figured that we weren't gonna be there long. Because every day when those planes would go north, come back, one would come over the camp, shake his wing, so we figured it wouldn't be long, but it turned out to be quite a while.

Well, I'm getting to be better now, [but] I never did talk about this Korean stuff much. And [now] I can talk about it a little bit long[er]. I mean, I was young, too, but I met lots of young people who died. I was twenty-five, but we had some guys that was fifteen and sixteen years old. They just didn't make it. And I think too many of us just died for nothing due to the fact those people just didn't have no food, no food and medical for us. But I said, I'm doing lots better though now. I can talk around other POWs. I guess because we know how each other feels, what stuff each other went through, and I found out that it's something that a man can do now, he can cry. I mean before, you know, mens didn't cry. And when I went to this class and I see lots of these World War II guys, [like] the ones in Germany [who were] older than I was, and they was crying, and so I mean, I didn't feel so bad, so I started talking, and they, they know how you feel.

They had a celebration and everything set up for me at home, and I didn't think I deserved it. I thought that I left the heroes over there, the ones that had died. I did feel that way when I came back, but now, I mean, I'm not ashamed that I was a POW. I'm just glad that I came out of it. But as I said, there's lots of them that didn't.

Samuel Farrow
Private 1st class, unit unknown
US Army
Interviewed October 7, 1993
Andersonville National Historic Site

ROBERT FLETCHER, ANN ARBOR, MICHIGAN

I served with an all-Black regiment, 24th Infantry Regiment, 25th Division, the last of the all-Black regiments in the United States Army, the Buffalo Soldiers. We were the oldest Black regiment; in fact, we were the oldest regiment, period, in the United States Army. We fought as an all-Black unit. We had white officers. A lot of the white officers would let you know they did not want to command, and some of them never stayed very long. We had this one officer from West Point. We got him in one day, and two days later he was gone. There were a few [Black officers,] but not on the large scale. You didn't find a lot of Black captains or colonels because that meant they commanded white officers. Uncle Sam wasn't ready to have that happen yet.

[Initially,] I went to Japan. I got ten, fifteen days of that good duty, which was great, [and] I was going to stay in the service forever. But I was only in Japan about ten or fifteen days when the Korean War broke out. When the war started, they told us that we were going over for a police action. I asked, "What's a police action?" They said, "Oh, we'll be back in two or three weeks. We'll just go over, rough up a few people, put them back in line, and that's it." So I said, "Hell, let's go. Shit, I'm in a hurry." B Company was the first unit out of the 24th to land in Korea. That was about July 11, 1950. My unit landed about the 12th or 13th. We sailed out of Sasebo, Japan, and they were rushing us out in a big hurry. When we landed in Pusan, they tried to load us on these little small-gauge trains, but they couldn't pull us. So a lot of us got off and got on trucks and we started north. E Company had already engaged the North Koreans while we were still on trucks moving up. You could hear the firing and smell the gun smoke. We said, "Boy, somebody's really raising hell over there." Then later that day our middle truck and last truck got hit by road mines. We dived out of the trucks and into some rice paddies, and we were in the war.

[But that] realization didn't dawn on me until probably my second or third day in combat, when I saw lots of my friends getting killed and I said, "Jesus, this shit could happen to me." You start to sweat and get nervous, and you get a little too protective. When your sergeant says, "Come on. We're moving out," you kind of think, "Oh, should I? A guy could kill me." But then the fear leaves and you figure, "Well, I'm only going to live here so long. If it's my turn, I'm going to get it, so let's go," and you move out.

We were just west of Yechon and I remember we moved back. There were two roads coming down into South Korea. One came down through Yechon and the other came down off the west coast. I remember we got to Yechon, and we were told to take a hill. We called the mountains "hills." They were just jagged rock. There was some cover, but not a tremendous amount like you would find in the Smokies, nothing like that. We didn't have names for them until later in the war. We'd just refer to the hills by their elevation: 1222, 2646, et cetera. You'd look at the map and say, "That one right there is the biggest one, we got to take it." Pork Chop Hill and all these others, I never heard of them until I came back from prison camp and someone said, "You know Pork Chop Hill?" "No, I never heard of Pork Chop Hill." "Were you in Korea?" "Yeah." Ninety percent of these places were mostly where white troops were because we never named hills. One hill we called Bloody Ridge, and that was down around in the [Gangwon] area. It was a mountain, and both sides of it turned red.

One of the worst things [was] we had no budget for Korea. People don't realize that. We fought Korea on what was left [over] from the Second World War. We went over there with the 2.3 sixes, and they just bounced off those Russian Tiger tanks. So then they brought us the .57s and 3.5-millimeter twenties. I was a gunner and [the] 3.5 was great as long as you had a side shot. If you had a front shot, against twelve, fourteen inches of steel, it would bounce off unless you were using high explosives. Then we got [the] .57s up. The .57s would penetrate them like mad, but you had no eye sights [at first], so you had to bore-sight them. You just sighted [along] the barrel, followed it, and fired. That's what we called bore-sight. Your assistant gunner would leave the breech open and they'd start moving and you'd say, "Right there." He'd put a shell in and you'd fire. [After] about two or three weeks, finally the sights caught up.

I can remember when our company almost got totally wiped out. This was down in the Pusan Perimeter. We had called in an air strike for that next morning, but we tried to take it back just before daybreak. But the air force didn't get [the order]. So I'm sitting in a foxhole and these jets come over. And I said, "Oh shit, these motherfuckers are going to strafe us." I dove in my hole, and the next thing you know arrrrrr, voom, voom, voom, voom, those cats were flying up in the air. And the F.O. [forward observer] got on the radio and got a hold of them. Then they had nerve enough to come over dip their wings at us.

I got there in July. I was there until November of 1950. Let me put it this way: We annihilated the North Korean army, but then the Chinese came in. We had gone up close to the Yalu River when Truman ordered us back. We sat down below the 38th Parallel just about the whole month of October, maybe fifteen, twenty days. Our spirits were high. We knew we were going back to Japan. Then we got orders to go up to the Yalu River. This was approximately November 10. We had gone up without any opposition. Then we became what they call Task Force Dolvin. We linked up with a company out of the 27th Wolfhounds [and] a company out of the 35th Cacti, which were all in our regiment. And there was one other company which was out of the 2nd Division. We'd gone up to the Yalu River and at night you could see all the tracers over there. We'd say, "Boy, some-body is really catching hell." But we had not run into any opposition because the Chinese were letting us come through. That evening we radioed back our grid coordinates and that we had no opposition.

We engaged the Chinese [on November] 22nd and fought until the 27th. We had these old Second World War radios, the great big ones, so if you were a mountain away, sometimes you could transmit and sometimes you couldn't. A Company was on our right, B Company was on our left. B Company got orders on the 21st [of November] to pull back five miles. We [in C Company] didn't get the word, and we kept trying to get in touch with the battalion com-mander. He says that he gave the order for everybody to withdraw five miles back. But we hadn't got anything on our radio, so we were still holding because that was our last order, and in the military you go by your last order. We fought for five days until November 27.

They did try two airdrops. But in the mountains you have all kinds of funny winds. They would start down, and they didn't use dead drops then like they do now because of the much better wrappings for protection. So they would come down [in] the parachute and . . . you would see them drift away, and all at once these Chinese would go out and drag them in, so the Chinese were get-ting our ammunition, food, and clothing. And by the 27th I had very little ammo left, maybe a clip, maybe a half a clip. Nobody had any ammo; we checked. The Chinese had maneuvered us to a little riverbed that ran in back of us. We had crossed it and the ice broke through, so a lot of us had wet feet. We got to this riverbed, and three mortar rounds went off in a tree. Well, Lieutenant Ikendorf, who was my platoon leader, and about ten or fifteen others went in another direction. They got out. We stayed together.

The company commander was wounded quite badly. He was hit in the left shoulder, arm, and leg. He called squad leaders and platoon leaders to come forward and told us to check how much ammo we had so we could fight our way out of there. We told him, "Well, sir, we don't have any." So he said, "I'm not going to make the decision. Ask the men what they want to do." Then he called the sergeants back. He was the only officer that I know who was alive at this point. The sergeants came back and he asked them, "What did the men say?" "Well, the majority of the men want to surrender. We stand a fifty-fifty chance of survival." He said, "We should stand a better chance than that." But he said, "Okay, we cannot fight." So we surrendered. He sent Sergeant McCullough out with a white flag on his rifle. Everything had stopped and got real quiet. I think they were letting us mull it over. Sergeant McCullough came back and said, "Field strip your pieces, break up your firing pins, and throw the breeches away." So we bent barrels around trees and destroyed what we could destroy. He said, "Now put your hands on your helmets; we're going out in a single file." So we started filing out. And 137 of us out of about 240 [we started with] got captured. So if you count the 20 or so that were with Lieutenant Ikendorf, that would have given us a 150-some people at that time. But the rest of the [company] had been killed.

I've never seen so many, as we call them, little people in my life. They came out of the bushes, the trees, the ground. I was captured five days before my eighteenth birthday. [Now remember,] September is when it [had] started to get cold. I never got winter clothes. Some guys got winter clothes, but I never got any. I had combat boots. I had my fatigues and a field jacket without a liner. [That's what I was wearing when] we got captured on November 27 when we ran out of ammunition. I spent thirty-three months in a prison camp.

That night they took me in for interrogation, and I gave them name, rank, and serial number. This officer kind of smiled, and he spoke English very well. He said, "You're from Company C, 24th Infantry Regiment, 25th Division. Your company commander is Captain Stanley, and your battalion commander is Colonel Miller." I gave him my name, rank, and serial number as I was told to do. He said, "Okay. Next." Then I asked, "Do you mind if I ask you a question?" He said, "It depends." I said, "It's kind of two questions: If we hadn't surrendered, what would have happened?" He said, "Our orders were to take no prisoners, so you had about five more minutes." I said, "Yeah, but how could you do it with just these few men?" He said, "There are approximately 30,000 troops here." And there were 121 of us. I told him, "Okay," and I never saw him again.

We stayed there until the next night. They fed us corn. That next night we started marching. We marched in different directions every night. It was in North Korea above the Chosin Reservoir. And we walked this way and that. They never took us in the same direction so we could never pinpoint where we were in case we escaped. We ended up in a little town called Pyoktong, in North Korea. It was right on the Yalu River. This was the largest prison camp; it was the first. Well, we didn't even go directly to the camp. We went to the mining town [first,] and that was about December 23 or 24. As we marched, we picked up more and more prisoners of war. It was cold, and when someone got sick, they would say, "Leave him. We will bring him up in a truck." We never saw any of our sick or wounded again. If you fell out of line, you were struck by the butt of a gun or you were bayonetted if you were far enough behind. So if a person got sick, we would put him in the middle of two guys and carry him. We knew that the guards would just kill them. We knew that, so we started carrying them along. You would hear, "No, no, no, no," and [they would] point at us to leave them. But we knew that would be the last time we'd see them, so we did everything we possibly could.

We huddled, even when we were walking, because the cold winds were so severe. I was told that the average temperature at night was forty-five degrees below zero. That was the worst winter North Korea had ever experienced. Daytime temperatures ran about thirty-five below zero. We had no covers or blankets. You'd go to sleep, and when you woke up, two or three guys would be frozen to death. The winters were just bitter. And they just jammed us into these small rooms. You would try to get in the middle, so everybody else piled on top of you in order to [stay] warm. That's survival. Crack corn was the main staple, and that was pretty much all we got. We got a handful of cracked corn, parched, boiled, stewed, fried. A lot of the North Koreans hadn't gotten their crops out of the ground before the winter, which had set in very quickly that year. So at night we'd steal turnips alongside the road.

I really doubt seriously if anyone escaped on the marches because we were heavily guarded. I just can't see it — they kept you so weak, it would have been almost physically impossible. They never gave you enough food. On the front line we got 3,400 to 3,800 calories a day. As a prisoner of war marching to the camps it was 300 to 800 calories. We were just on the verge of starvation all the time. One night we were walking, cold as hell, snow was blowing, and we stopped. All at once these three planes came down and we were going up into a draw between the mountains. Those lights lit up everything. It was the only time I saw those guards throw their god darn rifles aside and dive. You could hear noises like firing, but they were cameras, I'm sure. And they took off and [we] couldn't see them because once they turned their lights off, they were gone in the dark.

We finally got to Pyoktong . . . after New Year's, about January 11 or 12. One loses track of the days. They segregated us by race . . . once the camp was set up. When we first got there, no, but by that spring they started segregating us. I went into an all-Black unit. The officers were up on this hill, sergeants were over here on the hill, Turks were over there on the hill, British were down in the corner, whites were there, Spanish were over here — the Puerto Ricans, African Americans were here, just as you came through the main gate into camp.

I would say the Chinese guards were decent. I never ran into a mean, belligerent, or nasty Chinese guard. The North Koreans were mean. We called them mean sons of bitches. They'd just as soon kill you as look at you. That's one of the things that happened in the prison camps. Sometime between late February or early March, the North Koreans took us over, and when they did, approximately eighteen hundred men died. And the Chinese went, "Wow, shit." They came back and took the prison camps over. The North Koreans disappeared. The Chinese even said that if we all died, they couldn't face the world. No way would the world accept them as human beings, period. So they took us over, although the diet didn't change very much until they realized we could not survive on just rice and cracked corn.

By then the damage had been done to our bodies. I didn't realize it at the time. The Chinese brought in more cracked corn during the middle to late 1951. Then they started bringing in some rice and green vegetables like their cabbage. We didn't get any meat until 1952. But the cabbage was like celery. So you'd dice up one of those and you throw it in one of these huge Black pots and cook it up. If you got a piece of leaf, boy, you were happy. Before I got out I was already starting to put weight back on. I was around 150 pounds, but I had gone down to about 90 pounds. So the government told me, "Oh, I see you're almost to your exact weight of 169." I said, "Is that right? You should have been there in 1950 and '51. Then see what you would have said."

That spring they wanted us to go on wood detail for the winter. You'd go get your wood in the mountains and stack it up. They came to get us enlisted men, and we looked at the officers and they gave us a no sign, and so we just stood there. They threatened to bayonet us and everything else, but we just stood there. So they thought, "Something's wrong here." They got wise, and they shipped the officers off to another camp. They did not understand our chain of command. Officers leave, and sergeants take over. So they said, "Now you go on wood detail." We looked at the sergeants, and they shook their heads, and we just stood there. Same thing. So that fall they shipped all the sergeants out. They still didn't understand our chain of command. When the sergeants are gone, the corporals take over. I was a PFC. So they said, "Okay, you don't get any wood, then you can't cook your food. You'll just eat your food raw." So guys that were well enough said, "Fine, we'll go get wood for everybody; we can't eat raw food." It wasn't because we wanted to; it was because we were made to.

Once you went on these details, guys were volunteering to go. They could look for escape opportunities. They would also find garlic and wild onions. Then the guys from the cities found the marijuana. Oh, shit, it grew wild in Korea, bushes as high as this roof. I didn't know what it was. Guys I knew had used it as part of our camouflage in South Korea. Guys would say, "You've got a million dollars over your head." I would look up and say, "Where?" They would shake their head because they knew I didn't know what was going on. We would go out on wood detail, and some guys would come back with bulging pants. I would ask, "What you got, onions and stuff in there?" And they would say, "Oh, we got something better than that." I'd say, "What are you talking about; that's nothing but weed; you can't eat that stuff." "No you can't, but wooo, watch later on." I was still a dumb little country boy. I didn't know nothing about it.

Nobody [successfully] escaped from the permanent camps. Why? Number one is they wouldn't let you shave. Number two is the color of your skin. Koreans don't have heavy, bushy beards. They have just little old scraggly beards. If you escaped all somebody had to see was the beard. They'd call the Chinese, and they'd hunt you down. Oh, we had guys who were gone two or three days, but they'd bring them back and say, "You can't escape because of the villagers." A dog would bark at night and the owner [would] come call the Chinese guards, and they would start searching the area and finally they would find you. My platoon sergeant, Al Pough, tried to escape twice. The longest he was gone was a couple of days before they brought him back.

To heat our buildings you would make a fire outside, and it would go through this maze of flues under the floors. It would burn maybe a half a day and that would heat the floor, and that was what you used at night to keep yourself warm so you didn't need a lot of blankets. Well, we weren't used to this, so a lot of guys got pneumonia and a lot of other diseases as well. We were used to the central heat rather than a heat in the floor. I think the biggest disease was cholera from bad water. The well was just a pool . . . and the farm fields were [above it]. And there was human body waste up there. They would pour it on the fields, plow it in, it would rain, and it would run down. But we weren't even thinking about that. The Chinese kept telling us, "Lěngshuǐ, lěngshuǐ, lěngshuǐ," in other words, "Cold water. No good, no good!" They boiled all their water before drinking it. We could not see it until we lost eighteen hundred people. This was due in part to the lack of proper food. Dysentery was also just rampant. I don't know a pow who didn't have dysentery. You'd just come back from the latrine and off you'd go again.

But by the fall of '51 we were getting a little better diet. They were giving us a little rice. On Chinese holidays we'd get rice so we knew it was a holiday. We'd get maybe a little piece of pork. By 1952 I'm sure the Chinese realized they had to fatten us up. Peace talks were going and if we went home in this sorry condition, the world was going to frown on the Chinese. We knew how things were going [with the talks] by how they were treating us. When things were going great, they treated us like kings. When they broke off the peace talks, oh, they tightened the reins, they were nasty, and if somebody did something, they would punish him severely. The Chinese would not always punish the individual who supposedly had done something wrong. The Communistic way is to punish the person who is most liked. That punishes everybody. Oh, they were no fools. For example, this one guy tried to escape and killed a guard. The Chinese didn't bother the guy who did it; instead, they took this fellow, who was liked by everybody, and tied him on a tripod and threw cold water on him in thirty-five-below weather. Every hour they went out and threw a bucket of water on him until he froze to death. The Chinese then told the rest of us, "This could happen to you, and you, and you. Just keep it up, and that's what's going to happen."

By late 1951, more Chinese-speaking officers came in. We had a fellow by the name of Lin. He was there about two weeks, and he never said a word. He put his hands behind him and just walked around. Americans have a bad habit of calling people names. They would go up to Lin and call him a "tight-eyed son of a bitch." Then they'd smile and bow, and he would bow, and he would put his hands together and keep walking. One morning about two or three weeks later, everybody was in formation and Lin was standing there. Lin stepped forward and said, "Good morning, men." You could see some faces drop to the ground. He then told us, "I was educated in your country. I went to MIT and I went to the University of Michigan, and I finally got my doctorate . . . ." He said, "My friend came over to visit me and he was from Communist China, so they deported me back to China." He said, "I'm here to do a job, and I'm going to do a job." His job was to start our "reeducation," as they called it.

Every morning an instructor would start roll call. Lin or one of the other English-speaking instructors would give us a little lecture for about a half hour or forty-five minutes. Then you'd break up into groups of ten or so for what they called "study groups," where we were supposed to discuss what we had just heard. The instructors would compare Communism to capitalism, starting back in the Stone Age [to] Lenin and Engels versus the Rockefellers and Du Ponts. They would talk about when wars started, none of the rich go but always the poor people. So in the discussion groups you discussed the pros and cons. The Chinese always called me a "Reactionary" because I'd say, "Let's look at the Second World War." I'd tell them, "I can talk about that because I was a young man. In Russia, which is a Communist country, who fought the fucking wars there? There were no poor and no rich. Everybody was poor." They'd say, "Yes, you see, that was a different matter." And I'd say, "Yeah, it is always different when it's in your favor." So they said, "We need to punish you. You're not understanding what we're talking about." But I understood exactly [what] they were talking about.

I used to make the Chinese very angry at me. They would say to me, "Everybody works." And I'd say, "Chairman Mao gets out and works on the highways just like the peasants do?" And they'd just look at me. So I'd say, "Nobody serves him food? He cooks his own food?" Then they'd say, "You're a Reactionary." I just could not play their games with them. So finally they had me up to headquarters, and the commander was bitching and saying, "We should shoot you." I looked at him and said, "You know what you can do? Shoot me, fuck it," and I walked out of the building. He shouted, "We're not through talking!" I just kept on going, figuring any minute the guard would shoot me. Later the guards would come by and point at me and say, "He's crazy. Don't even bother him."

They said, "You do not have much education." Well, my platoon sergeant, Jerry Morgan, had told me, "Fletch, don't let these people know what you know or you're in trouble." So when they first started asking about name, rank, and serial number, and how much education I had, I put down name, rank, and serial number and sixth grade. They called me up to headquarters and said, "No, no, you have more than a sixth-grade education." I said, "Well, if you say so, I'll have whatever you want me to have." I said, "In my country white people won't let me go to school." "Oh yes, oh yes," because they were used to hearing the tales about down south, and they still believed it. So I said, "I had to quit to go to work. I had to do the mediocre jobs that white people didn't want to bother with, such as cleaning toilets and sweeping the streets." And they'd say, "Oh yes, yes." They never realized that I had almost finished high school. So when I wrote letters home, and they monitored those letters, I made a lot of mistakes. I'd spell "the" as "tha." I'd spell "that" as "tht." They monitored those letters, and a lot of them made it home. Later I looked at those letters, and I laughed. They are now all in the University of Michigan Archives.

In the educational sessions . . . they would remind me that I had said, "You know, white people will never let Black people accomplish anything in the United States." So they'd tell me, "They're always going to control the money, control the jobs, make sure their friends will always have a job, and Black people will just get so far. What you need to do is go back to your country and help start a revolution. Get the money out of their hands. Get the controls away from the warmongers." The Chinese did not like white people very much. So the Chinese knew the history of the United States very well, and they played the game with it.

The Chinese would tell you to write an article about what you disliked about the United States. And the majority of the Blacks wrote they disliked segregation, they disliked not being able to go to college and get a decent job. The Chinese would then take that one step further. They would edit that and put in the text they wanted and publish that in a Communist paper. "So and so says this," but you didn't say that. But your mind was not as sharp as theirs because they were eating vegetables and solid meat while you're getting a handful of cracked corn. So, your body is withering and your mind isn't sharp, and usually if they called you up to headquarters, they would have food around. They would say, "If you write this article, you can eat that. Just write that article. You don't have to write anything derogatory about your country, just what you don't like about it." So you'd write and they would give you the food—but that's the last you got. It wasn't that you got it every day. The article was not about how poor the United States was. It was about how you as an individual or as a race had been treated. You never saw the article, but I heard some people say, "Yeah, I saw it. It wasn't like you wrote it, buddy. When they got through [with] it, oh, you downed the United States." I never wrote any myself. I told them, "I can't write. If you people want to write it, go ahead and write it." But they wanted your handwriting so they could copy it.

There were three African American [POWs] that stayed [with the Chinese]: Adams, White, and Sullivan. If you notice, they were all from the South. Adams, White, and Sullivan were all from the South: Missouri, Kansas, and Memphis. I knew them very well. Adams and I slept in the same room; in fact, we slept head to toe to each other. But way before this ever happened we used to sit up at night and talk. I never understood the South. I never understood what Blacks went through in the South. He was from Memphis, Tennessee. He'd tell me, "I'm not going back to what I had to put up with." I told him, "Adams, I'm not going to put up with bullshit either. I'm not going back to the same crap." I had never faced prejudice in the sense that they had—where you're walking down the street and a white person says, "Get off the street." I just couldn't fathom this in my mind. History books never told you anything about this in high school. By never living in the South, I never knew anything about it. Adams used to tell me, "Fletch, if you were born and raised down south, you'd be dead." I looked at him and said, "Bullshit. I wouldn't be by myself. Whoever came after me, some of them would go, too." He said, "You just don't understand it, do you?" I said, "No, I don't understand it and never will understand it." I never really understood what southern Blacks went through. And even when the civil rights movement started, I didn't understand it. I said, "Why are they doing all this?"

And when we were getting ready to be repatriated, I said, "Well, Adams, I'll see you down in Freedom Village." He said, "Yeah." Then I was in Freedom Village and I kept waiting for Adams because he and I had been very close. So I asked, "What happened to Adams?" Someone said, "They've detained him; the

Chinese won't turn him lose." "What? For what reason?" And he said, "I don't know." Then we heard that twenty-one had actually decided to stay.

Adams stayed in China for about fifteen years, spoke Chinese fluently, graduated from a university there. Then he decided he had enough. He found out there was no difference between Communism and capitalism. The few and the rich were still in control and always will be in control. If you got bucks, you're going to make it. If you don't have bucks, you're nothing. That's Communism or capitalism. White and Sullivan came back first. Adams was the last African American to come back. White and Sullivan died. Both of them died here in the United States. They died within a short time after coming back. Clarence Adams lives in Memphis.[48] He owns a Chinese restaurant. He owns more than one. He is married to a Chinese lady and they have two kids. Doing real well. He was told when he came back that the University of Hawaii wanted him as an assistant professor to teach Chinese. But the United States government said, "If you do, we are not giving you a dime."

The United States government classified me as a security risk. They said I knew more than I was telling them. When we came back on the ship they asked me all these questions about different people. I told them, "You know we were all in prison camps; we all suffered the same goddamn thing. I didn't know anybody that got favors. Not Adams, not White, or Sullivan. If they got sick, 'There's no medicine.' They didn't get any medicine. So what are you trying pick out of me? That this guy got better treatment? Better treatment, bull." I said, "They'd call your ass up to headquarters; sometimes they wouldn't even speak to you; they'd give you a pack of cigarettes and tell you to go back. That was so the rest of the guys said, 'Oh, oh, he told them something.'" I said, "I don't know what occurred at headquarters with those guys. I know I was called up there two or three times. And one time they didn't even speak to me. But I was there for about an hour and they said, 'You can go back now.' It would be two or three o'clock in the morning when they'd do this. The guys would crack open their eyes and see you smoking a cigarette, so they figure you told them something." So these military investigators decided, "He knows more. If he stays in the service, we need to interrogate him more intensely." So they classified me as a security risk. I didn't know this at the time, of course, but you have to remember, this was during that McCarthy era. I don't think it was just me who was singled out for interrogation on board ship coming home. I think we were all classified as Communist until proven innocent.

[There was] a guy named Tiny who killed a guy over some food. He was going to be put on the ship, but he disappeared. We wanted him on the ship because he would have never made it to the States. We knew he couldn't swim the ocean, and that's where he was headed. But he disappeared. I can't even remember Tiny's name, but he never got sick in camp so he was taking advantage of all these guys who were sick. He'd take their money. They'd have scrip—we didn't have American money—so he had a bunch of scrip and watches and all this kind of stuff that he took from these guys. They'd get sick, and they would die, and he would take their food before they died and sell it to somebody else like it was his own food. People would buy it with all this scrip. I know this happened, and they asked me and I told them about it. But the last thing I heard, he was in Fort Leavenworth.

Many writers wrote stuff about the Korean War generation saying they had been pampered and were not made out of the same stuff as the guys were in other wars, [but] what dictates conduct are conditions more than anything else. If you are starving and about gone, all the niceties disappear. The army now says, "Resist until you cannot resist anymore; then it is not a shame to tell them what you know." They told us to say nothing but name, rank, and serial number. Even if you're starving, just name, rank, and serial number. Until the conditions got to be where you were starving, that's what you did. Then it became survival of the fittest. When you're dying, you want to live. I don't know anybody who collaborated.

It was amazing, but in prison camp we never looked at each other as Black and white. We never heard people say, "Oh, that's a white guy." Or, "That's a nigger or that's a Black guy." You never heard those words because their ass didn't have shit. And we depended on each other to make it. Sartillo was from Philadelphia. He was a young sixteen-year-old [white guy]. I was seventeen; shit, he and I had a lot in common. Those older guys he was with wished his ass was dead because he was a happy-go-lucky kid, and they had wives and kids, so they isolated him. Every evening he and I would talk about playing basketball and football and high school and girls. We'd just laugh and have a good time. I didn't know it, but at the time he was thinking about committing suicide. So after we get back to the States, [he] gets married, stays in the service, and retires as a master sergeant. I go to the second reunion the ex-POWs had in Louisville, Kentucky, and somebody calls out, "Fletch." And I said, "Sartillo, how are you doing?" We grabbed and hugged each other. And his wife comes over and gave me a kiss and said, "I've been knowing you all my life, and thank you." I asked, "For what?" She said, "You saved my husband's life." And I said, "Huh?" And he said, "Yeah, Fletch, I never told you, [but] before you and I started talking, I was thinking about committing suicide. Those guys didn't want me, they wouldn't to talk to me, they thought I was too young." We were both young, and had everything in common. And the guys I used to call old were twenty-two, twenty-four, twenty-five. Yeah, those sons of bitches were old.

Robert Fletcher
Private 1st class, 24th Infantry Regiment, 25th Division

US Army
Interviewed April 24, 1998
Andersonville National Historic Site

CHARLIE CODE SR., MACON, GEORGIA

I lived in Macon, Georgia, and my occupation was box maker. I [was drafted and] enlisted [on] August 7, 1952. My basic training was in Count [Camp] Breckinridge, Kentucky. . . . After four months of training in Count [Camp] Breckinridge, Kentucky, I was then sent to . . . Korea and I was assigned to the 31st Infantry Regiment, [7th Infantry Division].

What [is] a prisoner of war? It's someone that had been denied of all his privileges. He don't have no say-so of what he can and what he cannot do. He is completely controlled by someone else. That's my definition because that's the way I was treated. I didn't think for myself. They did all the thinking, you know.

[I was captured] somewhere around maybe March 23, 1953. We were on [an] observation post [on what] is known as Pork Chop Hill and my duty there was to let patrols in and out from the afternoon and then let them out through back in in the morning to go back. That's primarily what we were supposed to do. But on the 23rd or 24th of March, 1953, we was completely surrounded by the Chinese and our position was overrun. That's what led to my capture. I can't tell how long we had been [fighting off the Chinese advance] because in a situation like that I don't imagine time was too important — it's whether I would survive or not — but we had been [and] my M1 rifle jammed. I couldn't load it or get the clip out of it. So then I was stuck. I made several attempts to try to leave Pork Chop and try to escape down the hill, but to no avail. So the only thing I knew to do was to try to stay in this bunker. Maybe [by] morning they would draw back and I would have time to, you know, come out to my company. But luck wasn't for me that way.

I was captured in a bunker. I was by myself at the time of the capture, but before that, [there] was two of us fighting and I think this [other] guy got hit. I don't know whether he survived or not. But it was just two of us at that position at that one time. I was about twenty-two, between twenty-two and twenty-three [years old]. After I repatriated, I found out there was very few people that survived out of my company. I was in a little company. We had maybe three squads and most of those was killed, that was my understanding.

The Chinese came in . . . [and] they tried to shoot me at first, but there wasn't enough room in the trenches. Because I was in the bunker, it was so close they couldn't maneuver their rifles so they missed me. I don't know whether they didn't know about trenches, but they're so narrow and you don't have much maneuvering space [so] they missed [shooting] me. After they didn't hit me, then they motioned for me to come out and at that time I didn't know whether I'd be shot or not . . . because I couldn't understand [them]. They couldn't speak English of any kind. So after I came out, they motioned for me to throw my rifle down and then do it with the cartridge belt so I did away with all that.

Well, on Pork Chop, [there] was something like a command bunker and they had maybe three or four more prisoners [there] they had captured. They put us all in there for maybe . . . thirty minutes, forty-five minutes or so, what have you. Well, [I] thought . . . that they probably [would] interrogate you and after that they would probably kill you. Those are the things that were going through my mind, that I probably wouldn't ever make it back home anymore because this was probably the end. [But] after that they [took] us out and they marched us back downhill and across the line on the Chinese side of going into North Korea. When I was marched, I was marched maybe half a day . . . without any food, no water, until about maybe dark. We came to a first interrogation point. At that point, we was given water and a bowl of rice. They was persistent in moving [us]. I don't think at that point they would have just killed me, but it seemed like they were trying to walk me to death, the next day after I was captured. We went over a whole lot of mountains and there was times where I just completely gave up. I mean, it wasn't a matter of whether they would have killed me at that time or not because I was tired [out]. I hadn't had anything to eat. They was just trying to walk me to death. If a death march was any worse than that, I wouldn't have wanted to be in it. And I say I completely just gave up. They had been pushing me and they had been rushing me all day and I just completely stopped. Every time I would stop, they would keep pushing me in the back with those guns. They just kept pushing me with these guns. I started crawling. I was crawling and figured I wasn't walking no more. I was crawling. I was really, completely exhausted at times. They just kept pushing. I hadn't eat[ten] since the day [I was captured]. It was Tuesday afternoon when they hit and it was all day Tuesday afternoon from the time I ate to all day going on Wednesday going on toward night. And I still hadn't ate anything and I was doing all this walking and at times they would get on us to trot. Had I just been able to just get water. So you can imagine walking or running or what have you without water or food or anything like that all day. It was all day with very little stopping for breaks. It was all day from daybreak until dark. From somewhere I just got strength and I kept going until the day was gone and we wound up in this interrogation point.

I was there maybe about three to four days and I was interrogated mornings, afternoons, and sometimes late at night. I never did know what time it was, but late at night they would come and ask you the same questions over and over again that they had asked you that day or the day before. What they was really trying to find out was the strength of the company you was in and regiment or battalion or how many men or what have you and what weapons or whatever. They wanted to know what kind of firepower you had. That was most of what they were concerned about. And your weakest points so where they could strike. Their main subject was trying to find out your manpower.

They brought me into a room and they sat me down on the floor. Then they would sit around on, about three of them, on cushions. They would sit up on cushions but they had me sit down. It was three on one. They would always speak in Chinese and then let one speak in English and he would ask the questions. I never did get to prison camp. At that interrogation point, I stayed there maybe three or four days and I was moved from that interrogation point to another one. When I left the first interrogation camp, they told me they would be better [than] the next people I'd meet because they didn't believe anything I had told them. Well, [at the next interrogation point] they had all the information they was asking me in a big book this thick and they were asking me questions out of it. They had the answers. They wanted to hear what I had to say. They did interrogate about three or four of us: a pilot, me, and maybe two or three more. I stayed at that place about maybe over a month. It wasn't a camp. I don't know exactly. Once I left my life, I don't know where I was at. Only thing I knew was I was in North Korea. Somewhere in North Korea. I didn't know how far [north] but I never did get to a camp. I wound up in three [interrogation centers]. It was about six months in total from the 23rd up until I was repatriated. The third one, I stayed there until we were repatriated. I was in that one over three months. I always wanted to go [to a formal prison camp]. It was maybe about twenty-five or thirty of us that they didn't move. The next place would have been a camp but we was in between those two places.

Th[e] afternoon, before [the armistice was signed,] they made us all go to bed . . . early. I can remember aircraft flying, but they were flying real high and they hadn't ever did that before. They were flying real high. You could just hear them. But they never did come until that night. They woke us up at daybreak that next morning. They had us all come into this room right like this. That was their speech. After they went through all this other — I really didn't hear all this other, what they were talking about. I knew something had happened. I said either this is a full-scale war or we're going home because they wouldn't have woke us up just to tell us about how it is in China and all this other crap. Then, at the very end, they told us what had happened. Because they knew if they had told us at the beginning, we wouldn't have heard the rest of it. I wouldn't have. Because after they told us that, guys [were singing] and everything else. It was really good news. We were looking forward to going home. It was a joyous occasion. I was really glad to hear that.

I didn't throw away no clothes [like some guys did], I didn't have any to throw away. I noticed some of the guys had the whole army boots and coats, but the only thing I had was something like a pajama top and bottom. That's what we wore. I didn't have anything to throw away, but if I had had it, I would have thrown it away so I looked real good like the rest of them did. Then I started to have dreams about coming home. [But] they also told us that . . . until that day, until we was completely handed over, we were still under their command. We wasn't free to roam or do anything that month. It was just like the very first day from when we got there until we came through Freedom Village. They were still in charge of us until we did that. Even in that month, those were some joyous people. You should have seen them!

I think it was the last [day] in August [I was repatriated at] . . . Freedom Village by truck. They would be sending a truck and we would be sending one. I think we sent three to their one because we had that many. We had women, then men. We could see their truck going into North Korea. Then we had one or two going this way.

When we got to Freedom Village, they welcomed us there. They took down your name, rank, serial numbers. They welcomed us there. The only thing they had given me was liquids. And told me they would give me whatever I wanted to eat later. They wanted a doctor to kind of look at us before we ate any hard food. Find out what you say, how you feel. But we were checked out at Freedom Village. They had doctors on hand to take statements on how you felt and were you sick or have any wounds or anything like that. When I got captured I think I weighed about 160–62. When I got repatriated, I think I weighed about 140. I felt pretty good at that time.

They flew me from California, San Francisco. They told me, "Four to six days on a bus or a train," and I said, "No." So, they said, "Any way you want to go, we'll get you there." So, that's the way I chose to come, by flying. They had a parade of cars that was supposed to meet me at the airport, along with the mayor and those city officials, they had planned to do that. Because they had already had one POW come in about a week or two before I did and they had already had a parade for him. They was supposed to meet me at the airfield and from there all the way downtown to city hall, where the speech was supposed to be made. But the information they got [was] that I had been pulled off the ship and sent to the hospital. They sent them a telegram saying I wouldn't be coming in as planned, that I had to go for more tests. And when I got to the airport, there wasn't nobody there.

So I just [caught] a bus and went all the way to Robbins and back into Macon. And when I got into Macon, I called my brother and he came and picked me up. Everybody was disappointed when I got there. The people that had gotten ready for the parade and all that, my family and friends and neighbors, they had settled down and they was celebrating — to keep it from having been a complete flop, they decided to celebrate themselves. After my brother came and got me, people started coming from everywhere. They had already started celebrating, so the only thing I needed to do was join in. That's what I did. Helped them finish celebrating after I got there.

I was glad to be, and blessed, to be able to be repatriated. I don't know and I've never tried to figure that out yet, but for some reason I was spared. And I always said being captive was my only way out. After I look at it and look back over it, that was my only way out. Any other way out, I probably would have gotten killed. So, I'm just thankful for being here.

Charlie Code Sr.
Private 1st class, 31st Infantry Regiment, 7th Infantry Division
US Army
Interviewed November 6, 1993
Andersonville National Historic Site

CURTIS BOLTON, SAN DIEGO, CALIFORNIA

I was stationed in Japan prior to the war, and we left as a whole unit and left to go to Korea in July of 1950. [I was] twenty-one. We were on the front line for four and [a] half months, from July until November 26, 1950, the date of my capture.

We were moving north towards the Manchuria border, and the order was given that when we reached the border, people that had enough time, that had been on the line, were going to be rotated [out]. I qualified for that because I had been there for four and a half months. And we were hit in the morning of 26 November of 1950. Around 8 o'clock we began to receive fire and finally orders were given to return the fire and we commenced to firing. And people were getting hit and wounded and I got wounded, shot beneath the right eye, and [it] came out the back of my ear. After that they were trying to get people that were wounded back to where the helicopters were landing to try to get us taken out. And [we] were all surrounded and captured.

We [had] heard a lot about how the North Koreans were tying [prisoners'] hands behind them and shooting them, so we didn't know what was going to happen. Training [for possible capture in those days] was very limited, it was very routine. We had some basics, things like [only saying] name, rank, serial number, but it was very limited compare[d to] what it is today as we have learned from several wars between then and now. But we had a little training.

We were moved at a fast pace to try to get us on down the line, and as we moved along [we were joined by] little groups of men, then they started getting bigger, and eventually there was around 150. They tried to march us at night at a rapid pace behind the lines. That went on for several weeks it seemed like. We kept going round and round in circles, but we were going up the hills further and further north.

The ones that were injured, we had to carry them. The Chinese said that they would shoot them if we couldn't carry them, so we had one officer in the group, so he would help carry the wounded and I tried to help them, too, but I had a head wound. I didn't receive any medical treatment, they didn't have anywhere [to treat us]. So I had a big knot come into my eye from the wound, and it being exposed to the cold weather and when I reached the main camp is when it came up, and finally [I] took something like scissors and poked a hole in it and got the pus and put something like tissue or gauze in it to keep it on it for like ten days. By nature it healed up and over the years it kept getting smaller and smaller. [But] it affected my vision—from that point [on] my vision kept getting worse and worse.

First I was in a group that we called the Valley Camp. They had us between these huge mountains and you could see a little bit of the sun, and they kept us there from November to January, then they moved me to Camp 5 and I was in Camp 5 for the duration of the war. [During] an average day at Camp 5 we would get up at about six in the morning, then we would have to take head count, then we would go back and we would get this one bowl of chow, which was cracked corn and millet [and sometimes] seaweed. The first eight months or so everybody was so weak and a lot of people were dying so fast. A lot of people were dying of starvation because they couldn't survive on that little amount of food we were given. We would get that, then we would get a lecture. They would get us out on the field and the lectures were on the two forms of government, one being [the] socialistic type of government and [the other being] the capitalistic form of government and they were trying to point out the difference of the governments to us. The lecture on the field would be given in the Chinese language—not a single person in the camp spoke any [Chinese]—and it would take him perhaps two hours to give a lecture in Chinese. Then you would have a Chinese that could speak English and he would write it down and give it to us so we could understand it. Then we would go back to the huts and the compounds [and] we would have someone to be designated as the monitor and they would ask questions like, "Was the Americans justified in bombing the reservoirs?" and we would have to give our opinions on the question. And I would ask them on that particular question, "How do I know that they bombed the reservoirs?" And they would say, "We're telling you that they bombed it." And I would tell them that I have no opinion on this, you know, that is my answer, and they would say, "Why? You have to have an answer!"

They would consistently [make us] study, study, study. I guess they thought that we would be sympathetic to the cause. And they tell us that they were common people and we were just fighting for the war mommies back in the United States and they blamed the United States and not the United Nation we were fighting under, [they felt] the United States were the instigators [who had] started the war.

And sometimes we would do [work] detail and we were so weak that we couldn't do much detail in the first year. It was thirteen months before my name appeared on a list, so my mother found out thirteen months later that I was captured as a prisoner of war. I received in the thirty-two and a half months I was there sixteen letters and they were very important. It wasn't much but we would pass it around and others would pass theirs around and we would all read each other's letters. So, yeah, I thought about my family a lot. And when I wrote letters back home, they had some type of symbol on it, you couldn't really see it but some of the guys would hold it to the light and they could see some Communist symbol on the stationery. So we decided we wouldn't write. [Then] they gave [us] some literature on stationery so we started writing again, but letters wouldn't go through if you said you were starving and were dying. [So] if you wrote a letter you would have to think it out before you started to write it. I would write that "I am doing as well as expected" and that "I hope you have a nice Easter and this time next year I hope to see you," something like this so they would at least know that I was still alive and maybe the letter would go through. One time I wrote a little poem to my mother and some lines went something like "Thank God above for giving me a mother such as you," I can't remember, but I had to do something to make sure it got through. I couldn't just force my opining or how I really felt because it wouldn't get through.

[The worst part] I guess [was] just seeing the hardship of people dying. We were dying [in great numbers] the first eight months. You could just look at the head count and the people around you and you would just think how many days it would last. During my stay I was so sick I had to be admitted to the hospital but to get to the hospital you had to get clearance from the doctor. We had one American doctor working in the hospital and he tried to get as many people to the hospital as he could, but the Chinese had the last word on who went. The doctor told them that I needed to be in there, my breath was so short that I couldn't walk three steps before I had to stop. I went to the hospital for about twenty-six days and . . . the days went by [and] I started getting better. I would try to help the others by feeding them and things like that.

We made cards out of boxes, you know, playing cards, and we played pinochle and things of that sort [to keep our morale up]. And they had a library set up there [by] the Chinese, but most of it was Communist literature and nobody didn't want to read them. We played basketball when the guys started getting better as time went along. Then we started trying to have in the camp competition of sports and you know their company would come up and our company and we would play ball.

At first the Chinese philosophy was that they used the term "Respect the masters and conquer the nation," so what they thought they would do is divide us. So they came to the Black company and they told us how many people we had in Congress or in the Senate. They thought they could get the program over better [if they played the races against each other, and] we had little problems. We were thinking and the white company were thinking that some in the camp were getting more food than others, so we formed committees and they would go from company to company to see if we were getting the same food, and the consensus was that everyone was getting the same amount of food, no difference. But to get their program to go over better, [the Chinese] felt like they could work with us one way and the others another way and become successful.

They told us, sometime in July I guess, [that we'd be released] right after the armistice was signed. The Chinese, every time they would have formation, they would always say they have good news for us or something like that. And this day they came out and they had this nice formation and they said, "We have good news for you," so everybody was listening, thinking it was the same old thing. Then they went on about [how] the armistice was signed and we were going to be released, and everybody was elated and excited and overjoyed. Guys were laughing and jumping for joy, but some was wondering if this was true. Later on that evening, they had a PA system set up and everybody ran down to get close to it to see if their name was being called. We figured it would be in groups, so everyone was running down to see if they were in the first group. And I was thinking, what if they go in alphabetical order, then I would be in the first group. And then when we got down there and the names started being called, they started skipping all through the alphabet, everybody was listening for our names, the guys that were my close buddies were Claris Levert, C. L. Wright, Godfrey Jones, William Cox, and there was another one, I can't remember his name. And all of our names were called except for C. L. Wright. We're from the same town and we were trying to console him because his name was not in the first group.

[We] went back and everybody was happy and it seemed like it took days and weeks before we started moving out of the camps for processing. When leaving the camp we got on some little barges, then a place on the trucks along the rail. You could just see these big bomb craters where bombs were dropped. Then they finally got us there [and] we had other processing before you could leave to get to Panmunjom, the peace site. It seemed like we were there for months. It seemed like they called fifty guys [to] leave a day and you would run out and everybody was excited. When we got to the freedom site they had all these officers and people there to greet us and we're going through and guys were taking the [prison camp] caps and jackets off and it was like how kids feel on Christmas Day. Everyone was excited and everyone one was just filled up, and it's hard to describe how I felt.

August 8, 1953, was when I was released. [When] I got home, because my nerves were shaken up so badly, I went to volunteer at a hospital at Camp Breckenridge, Kentucky. I wanted to look strong for my family. So, when I got into the hospital they wanted to keep me in the hospital for a period of time. I talked to the doctors and told him that I was strong enough, I had been in here for five or six days and that I hadn't seen my family in four and a half years and I would like to go home. And he said that he would let me go under one condition, if you promise me that you will come back to the hospital when you return. And I told him that I will, [but] I didn't return.

[My family] asked a lot [of questions] but they were pretty lenient because we were kind of withdrawn. And the thing that kind of helped me out was this other guy, C. L. Wright. The only time we were happy was when we were together and our families just backed off because we were kind of different, we felt a little withdrawn. The press wanted to talk to us and I skipped out on them a lot.

It probably made me stronger because it took a lot out of my life, it took a lot out of everyone's life. When you go through an ordeal like that it changes you and it makes you try to hide it, but it is there. A lot of things that wouldn't bother most people — the stress and the hardship — [get to me]. And physically, some of the guys are worse than others, and it took a lot out of your life, being young and all. I wish [people] would try to understand [and] ask questions. Some of the guys that are withdrawn might not want to talk, but just ask them, contact them.

Curtis Bolton
Private 1st class, 24th Infantry Regiment, 25th Infantry Division
US Army
Interviewed by Alan Marsh, June 10, 2004
Andersonville National Historic Site

PRESTEE DAVIS, COLUMBUS, GEORGIA

[I am] Prestee Davis, I was living in Durham, North Carolina, and I played professional baseball. I spent two years at Fort Dix, New Jersey, and I was in the army [reserves up until early] 1950 and the war began in June of '50 and they called me back in August. I was a former reservist and I was supporting C Company, 1st Battalion, 24th Infantry [Regiment, 25th Infantry Division]. And the Chinese crossed the American lines on 26 November 1950, and the company that I was supporting was left back [on a] hill while the battalion moved back and we were captured. I was captured on the 26th of November 1950. I was twenty-two [and] I was an E5 [staff sergeant].

The day I was captured just about everybody had been killed or wounded so I was with the company that was left back. We hadn't eaten in four or five days and we had no ammunition and no medical supplies and everybody was wounded. And the company commander says, "Well, we will have to surrender. Anybody that wants to try and get out, get out and try to make it on your own." So two of us took off and tried to make it on our own. [We didn't get] very far and I looked up and didn't see nothing but Chinese with guns pointed at me, so I put my hands up, and a Chinese soldier told me to put my hands down because we will not harm you. I had seen prisoners that Koreans had captured and they had their hands tied behind them and then they shot them, so I didn't know what to expect. None of us knew what to expect.

[So] we all wound up at the same place, a Chinese staging area, [with] a lot of American soldiers. And like I said, we had not eaten and they gave us some food. What they did, see, they pushed [our] lines way back to Pusan and so they moved all the prisoners south by foot. We walked and it was the wintertime and it was cold, very cold. A lot of people would wind up with frostbite on fingers and ears. And then they moved us back north all the way to the Yalu River to the POW camp.

I was very sick in the early part of my capture. I went from 160 to 97 pounds because at that time we wouldn't get any food, any real food, just cracked corn and millet, and in this country they feed it to the cows, they don't feed it to humans. And it was full of rocks and our teeth were breaking off. We had some doctors that were captured but the Chinese didn't have any medicine so there was very little medicine. We had I think around eighteen hundred people that died in that camp from lack of medicine because American doctors couldn't do anything without medicine. [The main problems were] pneumonia and malnutrition. [There was a cemetery] somewhere in the mountains. I don't know where it was because I never went on [that] detail. Like I said, I was sick so I didn't have to go on the detail. A lot of the guys that went into the mountains, two days later they were dead because of the weather conditions and no medicine. You would get pneumonia and that was that. [To survive] I think was mind over matter. You had to make up your mind if you wanted to live and I know a lot of people who died because they said, "I can't eat this or can't do that," and if you can't do it you're not going to make it.

When we first got there we lived in the building they drove the Koreans out of. Then we built our own building out of wood and straw. Matter of fact, we built two buildings—one a recreational building and one we lived in. [I was held] from November of '50 to August of '53. Most of the buildings were heated through the floor, so we had . . . wood detail . . . to go in the mountains to cut down trees for the fire so we could heat the buildings. We had those combat suits they were wearing, but when we first [got] captured we wore what we were captured in.

[I was first interrogated] probably after we got to the regular POW camp in North Korea, Camp Number 5. [It was] just a basic camp, just a large area, and everybody was separated and segregated. They had all the Black soldiers in one company, all the white soldiers in one company, they had all the Turks in one company, they had the French and English and Puerto Ricans, the Spanish people, in another company. I can't say [if we were treated differently than whites] because we were all in the same camp but they were a distance from us, so I can't say how the Chinese treated them. The whole essence of the interrogation was how bad the American government was and how bad MacArthur was and how bad Truman was. They had what they called classes broken up into subjects [like] American government. And they would conduct classes on cotton and the gin and all this stuff—I forgot a lot of this stuff now.

I got into trouble because I refused to write a letter home, because in order to write letters home you had to say you were being treated nice [and that] we had good food and all. So I got into trouble with the camp commander because I refused to write. He called me into his office one night about two in the morning, him and a guard, and he asked me why I refused to write. I told him because I wasn't going to say all this stuff, and he got angry with me and spit in my face, and I wanted to kill him but the guard was standing there with the gun. But I wanted to hurt him.

That was early in our capture. In 1952, they started giving us halfway decent food. We started getting rice and chicken and dumplings. They had a building where the cooking was done and you just walked in there and got it. We had water out of the Yalu River but we had to boil it. We had a hot-water house. Things got a little better, people started getting into better shape and started building up. I contribute it to the peace talks were going good and the Chinese didn't want to send [us] back in the condition we were in so they started feeding us.

When we first got there they were doing all these [indoctrinations] and stuff. Later on there wasn't [much of that]. After '52, there were a lot of sports going on. We played within ourselves so we had something to do. We had softball, baseball, basketball, football, and we had track and field competitions between the companies. I participated in [these]. I coached the football team and the track and field team. I didn't have [much] to do with basketball but I coached the other teams. The Chinese [supplied the equipment]—we gave them a design for a football and they had it made in China.

We didn't have any problems with the guards because we were inside the fence and they were outside the fence, so we had very little contact with the guards. They didn't bother us, so we didn't bother them. They had a jail within a jail with cement blocks that they would put us in when we got out of line. I did something once that they marched me down to the Yalu River and made me take my shoes off and stand there on ice. [Escape was impossible because] we were on the Yalu River and there was nowhere for us to go unless there was a boat out there to pick us up.

I don't remember [the exact date of liberation] but it was August [and] the conflict ended so they released the prisoners. [But] they told me they were going to take me to China and put me in jail. They had shipped about [everyone out], all of the people in that camp were gone, and there was twelve of us left back there and we didn't get repatriated until about the last minute of the last day. You had to have a sense of humor. [Then] they just turned us over to the American troops. I think we stayed down there two days before they exchanged us. We went from Green Village to Inchon, then to the ship, [and] then we came home. Everybody was happy just to be back in the States.

[The POW experience] affected me by making me give respect to people who deserve [it] and it also made it hard for me to trust people, and it has been hard for me trying to change that. It changed my faith in human beings, too. [However,] I think it made me a better person. I think it made me understand people more than I did because I was young and I really didn't understand people, but I think I understand them now. Yeah, I am almost sure it made me a better person. [But] physically, I am in bad shape. I am 100 percent disabled now. Nightmares I had for three or four years, but I haven't had one in a while, but I had bad nightmares. I was always fighting somebody—the Indians, Chinese, or somebody—for the first three years, but that's all gone now. [Prestee Davis passed away on April 30, 2003, due to complications from his time in the service.]

Prestee Davis
Staff sergeant, 24th Infantry Regiment, 25th Infantry Division
US Army
Interviewed by Alan Marsh, August 3, 1996
Andersonville National Historic Site

III

The Battles Continue

7

From the Service to the Streets

Korean War Veterans and Social Change

Depending on where in the United States they returned, Black Korean War veterans sooner or later firmly reencountered Jim Crow; whether it was de jure segregation in the South or de facto elsewhere, segregation and other limitations to equality remained firmly entrenched on the home front. But when inequality was challenged, and freedom and equality were demanded, veterans—many fresh from service in Korea—where often on the front lines of this battle as well. Having experienced greater freedoms abroad, even if only haltingly or in some small measure, returning veterans would have nothing less once their boots were back on home soil.

The great degree of desegregation realized by the United States military during the Korean War, and the long struggle that led up to it, served as a galvanizing call to arms for civil rights activists, who now had a concrete example of success to point toward. In November 1951, the US Army acknowledged that desegregation in the Far East Command was still "an experiment" and that bringing integration home to the United States "will present problems of greater magnitude and variety than those encountered in Korea and Japan." This, however, did not stop Michael Straight, national chairman of the American Veterans' Committee, from declaring, "It is a mockery of democracy that colored and white soldiers who are fighting together in Korea should be kept apart here at home."[1] Some editorialists claimed by war's end that they could already see the beneficial effects of armed forces integration leaking into civilian life, for example, by modeling interracial friendships and socializing in off-base housing and beyond. "In many a small Southern Army post town," wrote one journalist, "Negro GIs can be seen drinking with their white comrades in bars where no Negro except the janitor had ever stepped foot before. . . . A subtle, yet definite encroachment has been made. And it took a war to do it." Indeed, by the end of 1953, the army reported that more than 90 percent of African American enlisted men served in integrated units. Desegregation was not complete, especially in the National Guard, which would remain nearly 99 percent white through the Vietnam War, but as historian Daniel Widener has written, "The armed forces were by 1954 unquestionably more mixed than any other single institution in civil society. Some argued that the U.S. military stood as the ultimate symbol of national possibility, while others lamented that dying seemed to be the primary thing that whites were willing to share with Blacks."[2] Nevertheless, in the years immediately following the war, the desegregation of the military continued to be invoked as a model for civilian life.

One sociologist concluded in 1955 that army desegregation provided a solid blueprint for school desegregation in that it showed that preconceived notions fell away when put to the test. "The success of Army integration," said Paul Foreman of the University of Alabama, "depended not so much on what people who had not tried it thought as it did on what happened when people did try it.'"[3] And although this book focuses on African Americans and the African American experience, the majority of those who served in the military during the Korean War years were white, and their experiences of segregation and desegregation must be given strong attention in understanding how, when, and why civil rights change was eventually achieved. Many of those white soldiers and sailors and flyers who served with Blacks as equals experienced some level of conversion that they brought home with them from the war. Charles Day of Panola, Texas, for example, later spoke of his experience as a white replacement brought in to desegregate the formerly all-Black A Battery of the 999th Field Artillery Battalion: "I said, 'My Lord, what [have] I got into?'" At first, Day was hesitant as to how his presence could possibly help. "To me, they could do a more efficient job between theirselves than having some white dude interfering with them. . . . Everything smoothed out, but it was rough there for two or three months." Soon, he found that the men learned to tolerate him, and he gained sudden new respect for them. "As a kid [in segregated Texas], I just thought, well, 'They're maybe not as good as me.' That opinion changed drastically . . . after a period. [Desegregation] changed some opinions — like it did me."[4]

For African Americans, the experiences during the Korean War era, and especially after the end of active hostilities in Korea, differed vastly. But the achievement of desegregation during the war, though not perhaps totally completed, was tremendously symbolic for a Black community that had long set its sights on military service as a lever with which to pry equality from a recalcitrant American society. And at a very personal level, individual Black soldiers, flyers, and sailors who experienced even a modicum of independence or responsibility or a brief relief from the yoke of segregation were profoundly altered. They returned to the

United States, some to civilian life, utterly changed. Many veterans, fresh from serving their country, many from serving in integrated units, knew the rights they had earned and bristled at being returned to the back of the bus. Transformed by the war, they found their lives back home little changed. But whereas they had once accepted that position as just the way things were, more and more they refused to accept the system as it stood. The changes they were part of, or that occurred around them, just after the war testify to the role their service played. On May 17, 1954, the Brown v. Board of Education *Supreme Court decision officially ended school segregation. In late August 1955, young civil rights movement activists were galvanized by the brutal lynching of Emmett Till in Mississippi, which along with the example of the Montgomery Bus Boycott of December 1955 would spark a movement that would spill into the nation's streets and lunch counters and energize a generation of activists from Martin Luther King Jr. to the young people of the Student Nonviolent Coordinating Committee, the Black Panther Party, and the Deacons for Defense and Justice, among many others. As historian Daniel Widener writes, "The unease, anxiety, and opposition generated between 1950 and 1953 produced lasting impressions among a critical swath of black Americans who would play critical roles" in the turbulent years following the Korean War.*[5]

Not every African American marched in the streets, though, and similarly, not every veteran turned into a civil rights activist. In fact, most veterans simply returned to their lives, whether continuing with military service or not. But action and resistance take many forms and even though most Korean war veterans weren't at the front of civil rights marches, many contributed to the movement, or resisted Jim Crow or inequality, in a myriad of other ways. The NAACP, as we saw, had vastly expanded during the drive for equal Black participation in the armed services, and it and an alphabet soup of allied civil rights organizations built on that momentum, and the change within the military, to use a combination of the courts, public protest, voter registration, and other means to turn civil rights struggles into a civil rights movement. Change, once started, gathered momentum, although it never came fast enough. Truman had issued Executive Order 9981 on July 26, 1948. The war in Korea began on June 25, 1950, and ended by armistice on July 27, 1953. Less than a year later, on May 27, 1954, the Supreme Court effectively ended school segregation when it heard five cases consolidated under the heading Brown v. Board of Education. On August 28, 1955, a fourteen-year-old Black boy from Chicago named Emmett Till was severely beaten and murdered by a white sheriff and others in Mississippi, with photos of his open-casket burial galvanizing a generation of Black youth. In December that same year, NAACP-trained activist Rosa Parks refused to accede to segregated seating on an Alabama bus, launching the yearlong Montgomery Bus Boycott that would propel a young preacher named Martin Luther King Jr.

to the forefront of the struggle, including a stirring experience at the March on Washington, August 28, 1963—the same March on Washington that had been started by A. Phillip Randolph thirty years and three wars earlier. And on and on, through the creation of the 1964 Civil Rights Act and the 1965 Voting Rights Act. The struggle would continue, still continues, but the desegregation of the military was a key milestone, and veterans were at the forefront of demanding and creating change, during the Korean War and after.

The list of African American Korean War veterans who participated in some key way in the Black freedom struggle and civil rights movement events of the 1950s and 1960s serves as further testament to the effects of military desegregation and of the veterans themselves. Among them are: Congressmen Charles Rangel and John Conyers and Virginia governor and Bronze Star recipient Douglas Wilder, who devoted their long political careers, in part, to achieving equality and justice for African Americans. Ivory Perry, who devoted his life to civil rights causes in the city of Saint Louis. Martyred civil rights activist Clyde Kennard, who tried unsuccessfully to integrate the University of Southern Mississippi. James Meredith, who needed the intervention of federal government protection in order finally to integrate the University of Mississippi. One of the six cofounders of the Black Panther Party, Elbert "Big Man" Howard. Civil rights activist and one-time director of the Student Nonviolent Coordinating Committee James Forman. Earnest "Chilly Willy" Thomas, founder of the armed self-defense group the Deacons for Defense and Justice. Black Power advocate and organizer Robert F. Williams. Longtime South Carolina activist and organizer William "Bill" Saunders. Charles Jones, aide to the Reverend Martin Luther King Jr. and author of the original draft of the "I Have a Dream" speech. African American poet, writer, activist, and cultural icon Amiri Baraka. All are African American veterans of the armed forces in the years just before, during, or after the Korean War.

They were among the great number of other African Americans returned from the war in Korea to a country that not only denied them freedom and equality but bombarded them with insults and hurts. The so-called bus incidents that tormented World War II veterans and inspired President Truman to desegregate the military continued long after his goal had been largely accomplished. In December 1953, for example, just months after the war's end, forty-eight Black soldiers were arrested after one of them sat beside a white female on a bus in Columbia, South Carolina. Local police claimed that when they boarded the bus to locate the soldier responsible, 2nd Lt. Austell Sherard, the ranking officer, "interfered." The policemen then ordered the bus driver to drive the whole group straight to the police station and arrested all fifty soldiers aboard, eventually charging forty-eight of them. Most of the men received a fine of $25.50, and Lieutenant Austell was fined $200, just under $2,000 in current dollars.[6]

Several months earlier, Lt. Thomas Williams, an air force pilot in training at Craig Air Force Base near Selma, Alabama, was arrested in Crestview, Florida, when he refused to sit in the segregated section of a Coastal Stages bus bound for Alabama. Even though the Supreme Court had found segregation on inter- state buses to be illegal, Williams was eventually drummed out of the air force for continuing to press for his rights.[7]

Indignity could also quickly move to violence, and not always off base, as Pvt. Euba C. McWilliams of the 87th Regiment, 10th Infantry Division, found in Fort Riley, Kansas, in June 1953, just as the war in Korea was drawing to an end. The NAACP office in Mobile encouraged the defense secretary to pursue an investi- gation of attempted murder after McWilliams was allegedly badly beaten and hospitalized by white members of his company who objected to an argument he had had several days earlier with a white soldier regarding "the race issue." A large group of white soldiers then "waylaid" him and "apparently were bent on killing" him. He said that his complaints to his company commander went un- heeded in a company where racism was condoned.[8] And in late October 1956, twenty-eight-year-old Korean War veteran James Mapp was "brutally whipped" by three policemen at his West Philadelphia diner who were responding to a noise complaint that the diner's jukebox was too loud. Mapp, known as Jimmie and with a two-month-old daughter, had already turned down the jukebox and returned to his chair on the street to take the summer breeze when the three police officers grabbed him, forced him back inside, and beat him, even at one point using his own chair as a weapon. A Philadelphia Tribune reporter would describe the officers as "apparently driven by motives of viciousness which would have made Hitler's Gestapo appear like Sunday school teachers." Mapp was later treated at Presbyterian Hospital for "at least thirteen cuts on the head" before being brought into the police station and charged with assault and bat- tery on a police officer, disorderly conduct, and resisting arrest. The case was so severe that it drew the attention of the Federal Bureau of Investigation on pos- sible civil rights abuses.[9]

In 1964, in a case that would galvanize the nation, three civil rights workers, two white and one Black, were murdered during Mississippi's Freedom Summer. Neshoba County sheriff and Ku Klux Klan member Lawrence Rainey was one of eighteen men indicted for the murders of James Chaney, Andrew Goodman, and Michael Schwerner. Although Rainey was acquitted, he admitted to killing Black Korean War veteran and former Chicagoan Luther Jackson during a traffic stop five years earlier. Pulled over while on his way to visit relatives, Jackson was alleged to have last said, according to his family, "What have I done wrong?" before Rainey "shot and killed him in cold blood." A fellow passenger who wit- nessed the killing later recounted that Rainey then returned to his squad car and made a call on his radio. Hattie Thomas said, "I heard him say, 'Come on down here. I think I just killed the nigger.'" Thomas was then pistol whipped and charged with drunkenness, assault and battery, and resisting arrest. No charges against Rainey were ever filed.[10]

Most Korean war veterans who got involved in politics and advancing civil rights efforts did so at the local level, so many of their names are not well known. One such example is Lucius Amerson, a veteran who, a year after the famous Selma March in Alabama, ran for sheriff of Macon County against two white opponents, including the incumbent. Amerson won by a two-to-one margin, becoming the first African American sheriff in Alabama since Reconstruction.[11] Another Black Korean War veteran, former paratrooper Leroy Stover, while not elected to office, nonetheless broke a major color bar when he was sworn in as the first Black policeman in Birmingham, desegregating what had been the country's largest all-white police force. The president of the Alabama NAACP said that the appointment "could be considered as a major break-through in the lily-white system of Birmingham."[12] As important as these events were, however, it must be noted that these veterans had been home from the war and a desegre-gated military for about thirteen years at that point. Again, change was coming, in part because of Black veterans, but it came slowly.

Even when there was tragedy, eventually it, too, came with signs of change. At the end of 1966 and into early 1967, several bombings targeted two local Black civil rights workers in Natchez, Mississippi, both of them workers at the town's Armstrong Tire and Rubber Company. George Metcalfe was seriously in-jured in August, while Wharlest Jackson, a thirty-seven-year-old veteran of the Korean War, leader in the local NAACP chapter, and father of five, was killed when his booby-trapped pickup truck exploded. Instead of glossing over the cases or ignoring them, however, city leaders, business officials, and private citizens quickly raised thirty-six thousand dollars in reward money for assistance in lo-cating the killers. Ten thousand dollars was pledged by the president of Arm-strong, even though his company was said to consistently hire "known Ku Klux Klan members." It was suspected that it was from this group of their coworkers that came the killers of the two Black civil rights activists. Again, the racial situa-tion was beginning to change in the South, but slowly and often painfully.[13]

The slow pace of change was not lost on the military or its Black servicemem-bers. In the summer of 1968, amid the country's next war in Asia, reporters for the New York Times conducted a monthlong nationwide survey of "Negro vet-erans." Black veterans, the paper reported, generally "had the feeling that the dramatic racial changes in military service, especially in Vietnam, would be re-flected in civilian life. 'You don't think about it in Vietnam, you just expect it,'" said veteran Richard Whitehurst of biracial cooperation and good race relations. "The brothers thought that because they fought and saw their buddies die, it would make a difference. But they came back to SOS—the same old stuff. It's business as usual in America, and business as usual means Black people are going to catch hell." Another veteran, a Black former infantry officer, said, "The Black veteran quickly gets to feeling like he has been 'seduced and abandoned' by the man. . . . This is why you won't find many Black vets as hawkish back home as they were in the Nam." Charles B. Howell Jr., a Korean War and Vietnam War air force veteran who had just retired after twenty-two years, was even sharper: "I wouldn't tell one of these kids around here that they should go into the service. . . . The way they treat you when you come back—you never get higher than [pushing] a broom as far as they're concerned. I think I'd shoot one of my kids before I let him fight for this country." Dozens of other veterans concurred, adding that they left highly specialized and responsible positions in the military only to be put back on the bottom rung in the civilian work force. "The rights we fought for somebody else just don't exist for us," said Arthur Caree, a former radar specialist and petty officer on an aircraft carrier.[14]

Opening opportunities in the military spelled inequality of a different sort for African Americans as well, one that would have been hard to imagine in 1948 or during the Korean War. Now, in 1968, although they composed only 10 percent of the national population and about an equal percentage of the servicemen in Vietnam, Blacks were inordinately deployed in the most dangerous specialties, making up 20 percent of the combat troops, over 25 percent of the paratroopers and other elite army units, and 25 percent of enlisted frontline supervisors. And African Americans counted for about 14.1 percent of those killed in action.[15] Was this high a price what A. Phillip Randolph and Harry Truman had in mind?

A number of Korean War veterans were involved in the Black Power movement of the civil rights movement as well. Black Power meant a number of things, foremost the achievement of Black economic and political power. But it also came to be associated with the notion of armed self-defense, in contrast to Martin Luther King Jr.'s tactic of nonviolent resistance and direct action. For some civil rights activists, the ability to represent oneself against armed foes with a like show of force was a key component of dignity and masculinity. Among the best-known proponents of armed self-defense was Robert F. Williams, who as the president of the NAACP chapter in Monroe, North Carolina, in the late 1950s, recruited a number of veterans like himself who believed in armed resistance to violent white supremacy, before going into exile in Cuba in 1962. Like Williams, a small group of African American men, many of them veterans of Korea and World War II, believed that there was an alternative to passive resistance and wished to meet the threat of arms with the threat of arms, forming the Deacons for Defense and Justice in Jonesboro, Louisiana, in 1964. Seeing their role primarily as protecting other civil rights workers, allowing them the ability to protest nonviolently, the Deacons' chapter in Bogalusa, Louisiana, came to national promise with their work against a bloody and vicious KKK terror campaign in their area. And of course, the Black Panther Party, although its main work consisted of supporting free meals and running health clinics and other "survival programs" in underserved Black communities, became most famous for their militant attitudes, military bearing, and long guns. Elbert "Big Man" Howard, one of the founders of the Black Panthers along with Bobby Seale, Huey P. Newton, and three others, was a Korean War veteran whose decision to arm himself and monitor abusive local police influenced a major piece of Panther strategy.

Robert F. Williams was born February 26, 1925, in Monroe, a town dominated by the Ku Klux Klan. When he was a boy, his grandmother, who had been born a slave, gave Williams his first gun, a rifle that had belonged to his grandfather and symbolized the family's refusal to bow to racial violence. Williams joined the US Army during World War II, mustering in at Fort Bragg, North Carolina, on July 12, 1945. Segregated and mistreated, Williams rankled against the conditions of the Jim Crow army, earning himself a three-month stint in the stockade for insubordination. "I told them that I was Black, and that prison did not scare me because Black men are born in prison. All they could do was put me in a smaller prison." He was proud of his resistance—"they would have preferred to have me as a nigger than locked up, but I preferred to be locked up than to be what they considered a nigger," he recalled. He was discharged after eighteen months for the "convenience of the government" and granted an honorable discharge, although it was noted in his FBI file that he had "caused considerable controversy" for disrespecting officers and refusing to obey orders. Despite his less-than-perfect fit with the US Army, Williams felt that military service had given him and most other Black veterans "some feeling of security and self-assurance. The Army [in]doctrination instilled in us what a virtue it was fight for democracy . . . and upholding the Constitution. But most of all they taught us to use arms."[16]

Williams returned to North Carolina, held a series of factory and other jobs, got involved in a labor union, briefly moved to Detroit, and then, desperate to bring a steady paycheck, signed up for a three-year stint in the Marine Corps. He joined up in 1954, just after the Korean War, with the hope that the Jim Crow military he had known a decade earlier was gone. He also had hopes of being assigned to information services, preparing him for a career in journalism. Instead, he found opportunities for Blacks still severely limited. He was made a supply sergeant, a typical so-called Black job and a position he bitterly resented, and he was told that there were no Black marines in information services. "If I had been in possession of a hydrogen bomb, at that moment, I would have sacrificed my life to explode it," he later wrote. He sent off a flurry of letters protesting his treatment by the corps, including one to the president of the United States in which he "expressed a desire to renounce his citizenship and live in a country which would not let his family starve." Coming under scrutiny from naval intelligence, he was first sent to the frozen plains of Nevada and then dishonorably discharged. His older brother John Williams recalled that his brother was incensed by his experience in the Marine Corps "and he became real militant."[17]

Once again Williams returned to Monroe, North Carolina, where the local NAACP chapter was down to its last handful of members and reached out to Williams to get involved, soon naming him president of the chapter. In truth, the bourgeois members were handing the organization to Williams to oversee its death, as they all quickly left. Undaunted, he scoured the bars and pool halls, rapidly gaining members and building a chapter based in the working classes, not the middle class, just about the only NAACP chapter of its kind. He also brought to the chapter a belief in the use of guns for protection, and when the chapter got into it with members of the local KKK, he formed armed squads to protect his community. "Most important," he later wrote, "we had a strong representation of veterans who were militant and didn't scare easily."[18]

The same could most certainly be said for the Deacons for Defense and Justice down in Louisiana, which initially formed during the Freedom Summer of 1964 to protect visiting activists from the nonviolent Congress of Racial Equality (CORE), as well as themselves, against Klan violence. Almost immediately after the two white and four Black CORE students arrived in Jonesboro to begin their summer work, white harassment and petty acts of violence began. The Black citizens of Jonesboro were at first hesitant. "They had never been confronted with the challenge of defending strangers in their midst." At first they proceeded with great caution, since "a reckless display of armed self-defense might provoke whites to retaliate with deadly force."[19] The Black community was deeply aware of a racial code, dating back to slavery and fear of slave rebellions, that forbade self-defense, but they felt that their responsibility to their guests left few alternatives. "Within a few days, a small number of local Black men began to quietly guard the CORE activists. Slowly they appeared, unarmed sentinels, silent and watchful." By day they guarded simply with their presence, but when nightfall brought the threat of marauders in white sheets, the guns came out. "The guards knew that a show of weapons would discourage Klan violence. So the night brought the moon, the stars, and the guns."[20] For their part, the CORE workers certainly appreciated the protection. After one incident in which two of them were violently attacked on the road by five local Klan members, they took shelter in a café only to see it quietly filled over the next few minutes by silent Black men with guns. "I'm sure many of these men were combat veterans," recalled one of the CORE students, "they certainly deployed themselves as such." And he added: "Up to that point, I embraced the concept of nonviolence. At that point I guess I said, 'Oh, I guess I'm not nonviolent anymore.'"[21]

Quickly emerging as the leader of this new defense squad was Earnest "Chilly Willy" Thomas, a short but powerfully built US Air Force veteran who had served during the Korean War, where "three years and eight months as an air-borne radio operator had afforded him brief and seductive glimpses of a world free of segregation." He also gained valuable tools, including leadership skills and "an appreciation for the power of disciplined collective action."[22] Many of the men who joined him were also veterans, of either World War II or Korea or both. Among these men were A. Z. Young, a World War II veteran who emerged as one of leaders in Bogalusa, and Henry Austin, a twenty-one-year-old from Bogalusa who had served two years in prison while in the air force for stabbing a white soldier who had called him a n——. Austin would become well known within the Deacons as the man who, attempting to rescue an innocent young girl and a fellow Deacon who had both been set upon by a white mob, fired his pistol into the chest of one of the attackers.[23]

Beginning in Jonesboro as a self-created Black police force and then defense force, the Deacons spread to Bogalusa and another local chapter before expanding into Mississippi; by the end of 1966 there were several hundred Deacons in twenty-one chapters in the two states. Later the Deacons would attempt to establish chapters in Chicago and the North.[24] Unlike Robert F. Williams in North Carolina, the Deacons drew from quiet but well-regarded middle- and working-class citizens, and they approached their work with a military precision and a quiet dignity that at times could blossom into passionate support of justice. But the military past of the majority of members cannot be overstated, and it was these experiences and what they had gained from them that made adherence to nonviolence not just difficult but anathema. As one of the CORE volunteers summarized it, "There was too much pride for that." And too much at stake as far as their own sense of themselves and as men. Historian Lance Hill concludes that "nonviolence required Black men to passively endure humiliation and physical abuse—a bitter elixir for a group struggling to overcome the southern white stereotype of Black men as servile and cowardly. For the Black men of Jonesboro, nonviolence appeared to ask them to sacrifice their manhood and honor in order to acquire it."[25]

Not so for James Forman, who held an abiding belief in the power of nonviolent direct action. Born in Chicago in 1928, Forman was raised by his grandmother in abject poverty in rural Marshall County, Mississippi. In 1947, after graduating high school, he was refused enlistment in the US Army due to racial quotas and enlisted instead in the air force, where his three-year stint would be extended to four by the Korean War. A cousin had told him that there was lots of downtime in the air force and that he'd have plenty of time to read. He didn't prepare Forman, though, for the segregation and racism he would meet. The difficulties began almost at once. His air force recruiter had promised the intellectual and ambitious young Forman that he would have access to a number of advanced training courses. But he soon found that the only schools open to

Blacks were welding, surveying (which meant you "ended up holding strings on hot hills all day"), cooking and baking, mechanics, typing, and welding. "I felt double-crossed by the Armed Forces," he later wrote, "a special kind of anger caused by . . . the feeling of having been taken." This was magnified by the fact that he felt he had already taken an enormous compromise by accepting "the contradictions of entering a segregated Army Air Force." But he had done so in the same way "I 'accepted' other types of segregation—in the sense of deciding not fight them each time they came up. How does a person survive psychologically in a society of all-pervasive racism? To fight it every time, all of the time, is to commit a kind of suicide."[26]

Forman would go on, however, to join the fight with everything he had and to do so constantly and continually. In 1961, he joined the Student Nonviolent Coordinating Committee, the largest student-led civil rights group that organized throughout the South, and rose to the position of executive secretary. He later worked with other groups and in 1969 famously interrupted service at New York's Riverside Church to deliver the "Black Manifesto," a demand for churches and synagogues to pay millions of dollars in reparations for the sin of slavery. On his death, the New York Times called Forman "a civil rights pioneer who brought a fiercely revolutionary vision and masterly organizational skills to nearly every major civil rights battleground in the 1960s."[27]

Forman's revolutionary vision was certainly sharpened during his time in the air force. He was outraged to be sent to a Jim Crow train car while traveling in full uniform and possessing a ticket for a private sleeping car. When he was sent to Okinawa with the 822nd Aviation Engineering Battalion, he discovered that "I had become an occupier. Here lived a brown people, and the white soldiers called them gooks just like they called me nigger. They had captured Okinawa; they had captured us too. But now I was with them."[28] Forman waded through his time in Okinawa as if in a bad dream that was slow to end. Eventually, he was shipped stateside, was discharged, and went to college. While studying at the University of Southern California, he was arrested by campus police on trumped-up charges and beaten while being kept for three days. It would affect him profoundly. Eventually, he finished his schooling at Roosevelt University and then went to graduate school at the University of Chicago. Looking back at his time in the military, Forman later wrote, "Today I would never volunteer for a segregated army, nor take a seat at the back of a bus or the front of a train. Those battles have been won; the struggle . . . now stands on a higher level. And I myself changed."[29]

Another activist who translated a negative experience in the US Air Force into a focused wave of energy to create change, was LeRoi Jones, later Amiri Baraka. Baraka joined the air force a year after the Korean War ended, attained the rank of sergeant while a gunner on a base in Puerto Rico, but found the post–Korean

War "Error Farce" still riddled with racism. He later described the experience to Essence magazine: "It was the worst period of my life. I finally found out what it was like to be disconnected from family and friends. I found out what it was like to be under the direct jurisdiction of people who hated Black people. I had never known that directly."[30] Hating the air force environment but being assigned to the base library, he retreated into its books, discovering a love for the Beat Poets and beginning to write poetry himself. He also read widely in philosophy, fiction, and history, a reading list that inspired someone to accuse him anonymously of Communism. This led to his reassignment to gardening duty and to his eventual dishonorable discharge. His time in the air force, he said later, was "racist, degrading, and intellectually paralyzing." His tone echoed that of Forman, who called the armed forces "a dehumanizing machine which destroys thought and creativity in order to preserve the economic system and the political myths of the United States."[31]

Clearly, not all veterans have positive experiences or memories of the US military, but whether their racial experiences in the armed forces were positive, uniformly negative, or, more likely, some combination, veterans took these experiences with them into the rest of their lives. Some made names for themselves by directly challenging the racial status quo in the years immediately after Korea; many more did the quiet work of living and, in so doing, also testified to their dignity and demands for equality. Whether or not veterans see themselves as having been actively involved in the pursuit of civil rights, they were, without question. To stand up in uniform as an African American man or woman during a time when basic human rights were denied them was undeniably a form of activism and an act of great dignity. Their stories are indeed an essential part of the Black freedom struggle and ongoing quest for civil rights in America.

8

Fighting the Back
of the Bus
Transforming the
Home Front

Whether they served in a desegregated circumstance or not, when Korean War veterans returned home, they often brought with them not just the experience and scars of war but an expectation of more equal treatment. The small hurts they had long endured were no longer easy to let slide, and the big hurts were unconscionable and demanded change. For many, though, it was the routine daily insults of a racially biased system that rankled and that they now determined to dismantle.

For those who decided to stay in and make the military a career, especially for officers, the post–Korean War road was certainly not easy but opened onto a great many more opportunities than previously. Julius Becton experienced just about everything in a long military career, from the worst of segregation to rising to lieutenant general. But even his road was hindered by obstacles. Why did he not rise even higher in rank? Why did he find his postmilitary career opportunities limited at first? His story is equal parts heroic, happy ending and cautionary tale.

JULIUS W. BECTON JR., SPRINGFIELD, VIRGINIA

Fast forward to Vietnam — I was battalion commander equivalent, squadron commander. There were five hundred soldiers in my squadron, of that, maybe four Blacks. Airborne squadron, all volunteers. I had people — once we got into combat — visit us, because there weren't that many Black commanders in Vietnam, just to see what kind of operation, how are they different from anyone else. One reporter from the *Chicago Defender* came to visit and he said, "I want to talk to your soldiers. Aren't you going to be with me?" "No, I don't care. Find somebody and talk to them. Let me know what you find out." He spent a little less than twenty-four hours. He thanked me and went away. We never saw one word printed about that unit. Because we didn't live up to the expectations of a lot of folk—we were good at what we did and that's not what people expected.

[Integration of the armed forces] certainly was [a significant event]. It was integration that gave support to the Black folks that they could complete, accomplish things, could make things happen. In World War II, we had one Black general, Beale [Benjamin] Davis Sr. He was in the IG [inspector general] office. We had a few Black colonels, none that I'm aware of that did all that great in battle. We had no role models that we could look to, who had done it before. And that's what we took into Korea, four years after World War II.

Move to 1967, '68, how many Black colonels did we have in combat? We had one, Freddy Davidson. He became the next Black general, '76 from 1945. Long time. It's important to know that, hey, they can do it.

How important was it? I was the sixth Black general in the United States Army. Today we have more than two hundred. Let me say it again. I was the sixth Black general; today we have more than two hundred. We have more than thirty on active duty right now. And we've had on active duty for a very long time, about that number. How important is that to the nation? It proved that it could be done. We now have American Express, AOL, Fannie Mae—I'm naming companies that happen to have Black CEOs. A lot of people don't know that. Proven that it can be done.

In the '60s when there was a lot of demonstrating, there was a lot of concern about the Blacks in the military. Were they going to join this group and be carrying placards? And you find that there was very little of that. And the reason for that, I think we're proving how good we are by just doing my job. We are making things happen. [I was] not opposed to those sitting in [and] supported them financially. [But] we felt that we had a chance to prove that we could do certain things. Yes, it did have significant impact on the rest of America [although] it wasn't that easy [to make a living after the military]. When I retired in 1983, I had a very hard time getting a job. When putting in my résumé, until people told me to change it, I would say the fact that at one time I had eighty-eight thousand soldiers under my control, twenty-seven thousand civilians' employees, a budget of 1.2 billion, and I would go on and on like that. "Becton, who the hell is going to hire you? No matter who hires you, you could do their job." Sure [I was] overqualified, but more important was the threat to other people who thought I was looking for their job. And I wasn't looking for their job, just wanted to survive. The first two jobs I had after I retired, I worked for the government. I was under dual compensation, so I could not draw retirement pay. That was typical of my peers as we tried to get employment. That's part of developing wealth; you have to have an opportunity to get in. Later I became a member of three corporate boards. How? It wasn't because the companies came to look for me. It was because somebody made a recommendation—a friend, a collogue, or somebody else. And then they brought about the idea that you need diversity and that's how we finally got through. One at a time, demonstrating that it could be done.

Julius W. Becton Jr.
Lieutenant general, 542nd Heavy Construction Company; 369th
*   Infantry Regiment, 93rd Infantry Division; K Company and*
*   L Company, 9th Infantry Regiment; 101st Airborne Division*
US Army Air Forces/Corps; US Army
Interviewed by Kate Ellis and Stephen Smith, February 2003, Springfield, VA
American RadioWorks, Minnesota Public Radio

MELVIN BOYKIN, MEMPHIS, TENNESSEE

The worst thing to happen to me while I was in the army [was] when I came back from Korea [and] they sent me to the army hospital in Fort Benning. I had braces on my legs, my wife then was in Atlanta, in school. We boarded a trolley outside the apartment where she lived, going to a movie, sitting about halfway up the trolley. This driver told us we gotta move, in the middle of downtown, because the car was filling up with whites. I was in full uniform, said I wouldn't move. He got off [and] went to get a cop to make me move. Cop asked me where we were going and then paid for a taxi for us to go to the movie. I said I wanted back my thirty-cent bus fare! But I was in full uniform, that's what pissed me off.

Melvin S. Boykin
Specialist 1st class, 187th Regimental Combat Team, 7th Division
US Army
Interviewed by Kate Ellis and Stephen Smith, September 5, 2002, Memphis, TN
American Radio Works, Minnesota Public Radio

JOHN B. JACKSON, HOUSTON, TEXAS

One of the incidents that [I recall was when] I came [back to the United States], to Houston. My wife and son were living in Freeport, Texas. I got into Houston, off the Greyhound bus from El Paso. I rode the bus to Andiron, Texas, which is about twenty-five miles from Houston, and I got off the bus about 11:30 at night and I walked the next fifteen miles to Freeport. I wanted to get to my wife and son. So I started out walking and I must have been three blocks from the bus station and the sheriff came up and he said, "Boy, where are you going?" I said,

"I'm going home. I just got back from Korea—I'm going home to my wife and son." And he said, "Well, boy, if I wasn't going on this emergency, I would take you to Freeport." But with me with the uniform on, that hurt. This hurt me. If he had had his emergency lights on when he came up and left with them on when he left me, I would say, "Okay, sure," but I say he was going to get a coffee break. Because he left me on the street there and luckily a driver came up and took me to Freeport. Now that was one of the things that hurt most as far as I was leaving integration. I left a segregated community, went into an integrated community, and I came back into the same thing from an official. That angered me and I often think about it. I fought for the Korean people and served my country and I had been back less than seventy-two hours and I was treated like this by a citizen of the US to a citizen of the US. That was one of my hurts.

And then the next morning I had to get up and go to the store and when I walk in I had to come back to that, "Yes, sir, no, sir," that I had [not] been exposed to for twenty-four months and I found out that we are people. We may have had different skin color, but we are people. And I had to come back to JB and [call him] Mr. JB and he's younger than I am. And President Harry Truman has sent me into the service to fight for our country. Here is this person who hasn't gone anywhere, hasn't done anything and yet I have to recognize him, for what I do not understand, but to keep peace, to live in this society, I had to abide by it, and it hurt. I really was hurt more going to a country fighting for democracy and then we had to come back to a democracy that was not there for us.

When I returned from Korea I went back to Dial Chemical and got my old job back and I worked there about five months, and working there I came in contact with almost a death situation—it was just an accidental thing, I got in the magnetic field—and I told my foreman, I went to Korea and didn't get killed so I'm not going to get killed in this plant, and so I quit that day. And I got home, and my wife said, "What are you gonna do?" And I said, "I don't know."

And I was looking for education because I knew I was going to go to college because I wanted a degree and my mother and father put that stress in us to get our education. That was our stepping-stone to improve ourselves. I came from Freeport, Texas, but [my wife's] sister taught at Texas Southern University and so I said, "Okay, I'll go to school." My wife and I enrolled at Texas Southern U and I went three and a half years in college there and I went into the civil service.

I accidentally was hired at the VA. I did not want to work at the hospital but carried someone out there to apply for a job and they enticed me because they needed mail workers at the VA in 1957 and so that's how I go[t] into civil service. And then I did 9.5 years at the VA and then went to the post office and then retired from the post office in 1986.

[In terms of civil rights,] things changed rather fast compared to what [they'd been] from 1952 back, but from 1958, '60, things started changing and they started changing real good because first my wife was able to get a job as a cashier at Wagner's Supermarket, one of the largest supermarket chains in Houston, because of the integration. She was the second African American to work the cashier because it was never heard of as far as a large chain store in Houston. So it did change fast and from then on it just started moving, rapidly improving. Everything was more acceptable. It was just integration: integration in schools, integration of jobs. It did move fast compared to before '52, but it took time.

As far as being a soldier, the experience of learning was the greatest thing that could have happened. I don't think I would have appreciated life if I had not gone in the type of service, whatever service it would have been, but after going in there, getting the training, working with people, it taught me a lot and I really carried that from October 1952 up to today.

[I've been] very involved in veterans' associations [since] 1991. Korean War veterans—Caucasians, African Americans, Spanish—we did not talk about our service connection. We might say, I was in the army, navy, marines during the Korean War, and that was all we said. We did not talk. [I'm] getting ready to celebrate my fiftieth wedding anniversary, and up until nine or ten years ago, my wife could say only, "JB was a Korean War veteran," and that's it, because I did not tell her anything. I did not talk in conversation even if I saw a picture on television with the Korean name on it. So, in 1991 I was reading in the paper about veterans [of] the Korean War, and I made a call to the telephone number and they invited me out for the first meeting, and we were organized, and I have been with that organization ever since. I started opening up and talking about [being] in the trenches and the training and buddies and all that and then meeting other Korean War veterans. And [then] Texas alone started a chapter of Korean War Veterans Associations, and I have been from the president down, and I have enjoyed working with what we wanted to accomplish and what we have accomplished as far as veterans are concerned.

[Young people] think democracy is on a platter for them—after you're born, democracy is there for you. It is not. It has been a fight for democracy since the beginning of Christ. Since the first book of the Bible, it talks about the struggle for democracy and what it has been. It's not nothing new if you go way back. But today young people do not want to discuss it, they do not want to get involved, they are against wars, which I am, too, but two people or three people cannot sit at a table and come [together], and so there are going to be some disagreements. And out of disagreements come war, but that's life, we have to deal with that. And they do not want to deal with it. They picketed everything and they have they're rights, but how did you get your democracy today? Because of World War I, World War II, because they fought, that's why we can sit today and talk about democracy in the United States because of other wars. So it is something that the young people need to understand. That's part of going with life. You're going to disagree, but you've got to sit at the table.

John B. Jackson
Platoon sergeant, 4.2 Mortar Company, 32nd Regiment, 2nd Division
US Army
Interviewed by David P. Cline, January 10, 2003, Houston, TX
American RadioWorks, Minnesota Public Radio

JESSIE BROWN, HARVEY, ILLINOIS

Over there, I didn't experience any racism on the front, in combat, [it] was when I got back home. That's what hit me so hard. On the way home, I stopped at a place called Carthage, Missouri. Myself and a white sergeant was together. I didn't know him, we were just traveling [together]. He was coming to Saint Louis and I was coming the same direction. This was [the] first racial thing that happened. He said, "Let's get a beer." So, okay, let's get a beer, go and get us a Pabst Blue Ribbon. We were at Camp Crowder so we left just nearby, went into a tavern in Carthage. We walk in together and sit down at the counter. Both of us [had] come back from Korea. Sit there a while [but] the bartender was down the counter with his apron on talking to some gentlemen at the counter there. So the white sergeant with me—I'm mentioning race here—he said, "Hey, bud." I wasn't about to speak out at [the bartender] because I knew better, [but the sergeant] said, "How about a couple beers down here?" We had been sitting there ten, fifteen minutes. So he looked down and he didn't say a word. So [the sergeant] said it again. And he looks down here and says, "You're not about to get anything in here, and you get up and get out of here and take that 'n——' with you." The chills went over me and I said, "Let's go, man. Let's get out of here." So we got up and walked out.

Went outside and he began to complain about it. I said, "Don't complain about it, I know what's going on." He kept saying, "America don't show me nothing. I should have stayed in the Far East." That's what he was saying. I said, "Don't worry about it. We'll get some beer. Let's not worry about it." We went on our way, and right around the corner was a restaurant there. It was high class. We walked on over there and he said, "Let's get something to eat." Walked in there, walked right straight through all the people eating, eating, [and] sit down at the table, just the two of us. White waitress came over—young girl—walk[s] over to us and said, "What you all going to have?" I like to have fainted. "What you going to have!?" He went on and ordered, I looked at the menu and I told her what I wanted. She went on back and brought it all back to the table. We ate, got up, and went out. Not an incident. I was amazed. It was so [different,] from that to this. It just shows that not everybody is thinking the same way.

One other incident: I was on the bus coming down from a place called Cape Girardeau, Missouri, to my home, Hayti, Missouri. [I was the] only one on the back of the bus. I was sitting back there, on the back seat. Had on my uniform, all my ribbons. This old [white] gentleman was sitting a couple seats up ahead of me and kept looking back at me, looking back. Finally he decided to say something to me and said, "Boy, you look mighty good sitting back there with that uniform on." I said, "Thank you, thank you." That was [an] incident.

Coming on, we got to Kansas City. We get to the train station, check our luggage in. There was two guys with me, two white boys, one from Arkansas and the other from Oklahoma. I didn't know [them but they were] soldiers, we met up and we were talking together. They didn't make no different with me. They said, "Let's go get something to eat." We checked our baggage in and left there and went up on the street [where] there was a restaurant. We walked in the restaurant and walked on through, went in and found a nice table. But we had to walk through a lot of tables with everybody sitting there at the tables, all white. We walked in and sit down. Three soldiers. Come back from Korea, all three of us. The waitress came over and we were sitting there, and I noticed people kept looking up and over. She says, "What are you all going to have?" [Just like the other time.] And we told her and she says to them, "I'm sorry, but I can't serve him." They say, "What do you mean?" "Well, I just can't serve *them*. It's not me, it's management." I said, "I understand, let her alone, let her alone."

Now, this will blow your mind. She said, "But I can do this: I can't serve you out here in the dining area, but I can serve you in the kitchen." And the [white soldiers] said, "Well, we're going to eat where he eat." And she took us up, and they followed me, and we went in the kitchen by the big stove and there was a little table. She sat me at the end and other guy at the side and the other guy at the end, served us out there. We got through eating and marched right on back through, right on back out to the street. That blew my mind. "Why did you take me in the kitchen and wouldn't serve me out where I could be seen?" That was amazing that she did that.

That didn't really bother [me] till I began to think back that I had just come from Korea. And there was a lot of incidents happened all along there, and all [of] them sound the same. One more, but there are many others: [I was] with another guy, a Black guy . . . from Denver. He [had] bought a car at Camp Crowder with his little money that he had. Didn't pay much for the car, didn't have a heater in it and this was in January. We left Camp Crowder on our way to Indianapolis, Indiana. We like to froze. He had an army blanket in the car, and I would cover up and warm awhile and sleep awhile while he drove. And when he got tired, I would drive. We were coming into Chicago from Camp Crowder to see a relative of his. We stopped in at a place called Quincy, Illinois.

We pulled into a trailer stop, and there was a little filling station where they served coffee, where there were trailer hitches all on the floor. We pull in there and he says, "Let's get some coffee." You could hear our bones crack, we were just that cold. Went in and sat at the counter, little stools. Lady came over and said, "What are you going to have?" We said, "Coffee." There was one white gentleman sitting there and looked like he was forty, forty-five years old, sitting there at the counter talking to her. We were shivering, we were cold in there. She got the coffee and the mugs and set them there, and she said to us, "But you can't drink it here." We said, "What are we going to do with the mugs? These are your mugs." She said, "You can drink it in here, but you gotta go over in the corner. You can't sit at the counter. Go in the corner and stand there and drink it."

This guy said, "What's with her?" I said, "Shut up and drink your coffee." I didn't say a word, [but] he started complaining. "What do you mean? We bought the coffee. How come we can't drink it?" And the guy down there said, "You heard what the lady said." I said to him, "Let's go and drink our coffee over here." There were trailer hitches in the corner. We went over and stood between all the trailer hitches that they were renting and drank our coffee. We got through and went over and gave her the cups back. Went out and got in the car and we left.

[Another time I was] home on furlough and [went] to the movies. The ticket agent at the movie, a white lady, was there. And this was in a little town where I was brought up at after I moved away from Tennessee. I was in my uniform and went in and bought my ticket. Well, we had to go up in the attic. We couldn't sit down[stairs]. On my way up, she said to me, "Are you just coming away from Korea?" I said, "Yeah." She said, "I heard about you boys. How well you were doing over there. How you held that perimeter." I said, "Sure." Those were the hot times in July in '50. What happened after that I don't know 'cause I was gone, I stayed out the months of July and August.

Anyway, I went up there and sat down. The movie got overcrowded downstairs where the big auditorium was with the whites. No Blacks [were allowed] down there. So she hollered on the loudspeaker, "Will you Blacks move back to the back of the theater?" So the excess whites just coming in . . . can come up there. But they had to have preference for the front of the balcony to look over, so we had to [move] to the back of the building. That's one time when I said, "No, I'm through with the movie. I've got to go." And I got up halfway through the movie and went down the steps, through the attic, had to bend down. Went down and got to the window where she was. She stopped me and she said, "Why are you leaving? Are you leaving because I told the other whites to come up where you were?" I said, "No, I've got to go." I didn't tell her the truth. I didn't tell her the truth 'cause if I had, I don't know what might have happened." So I said, "I'm leaving 'cause I've got to go, my time is up. I've got to go. I'll come back." She looked at me and I went on. I got out of there and went on my way.

Just so many experiences through life, you know. Not only in the armed forces, but before I went in the army, I had racial experiences. [I was] so used to [being] Jim Crowed until it was like, so what? That's the way it was. But being in uniform, once you look at it, it does bother you a little bit. I got many more details, but I don't care to bring them up.

Experiences like that is just where you went and where you stopped and who you come into contact with. I forgot about it while I was in the military. When I got out [of] the military, I began to look back on the military life and what I experienced, and I began to bring them up a lot. But there were many more incidents.

War is war. War is war. I left a lot of buddies over there and I think a lot about them. War is war. They do the same thing in one war as they do in another — kill. You can't do much more than that. And its humans being killed. Every war should be really legitimate. In a way [the Korean War was legitimate], I say yes, and, in a way, I say no. The reason I say no is, they say they were fighting Communists. They still didn't defeat it then. And they signed the armistice. They signed that and they just come away and the guys are still there. I came away and I've had nephews go into the army and go there and be on the Demilitarized Zone and be there as a soldier. I've had a couple of nephews in the armed forces and go to Korea. I've had a niece go in. My brother was there in Korea with me, [but] not in my outfit, he was an artilleryman. His daughter went in years later and went to Korea to serve. I don't think she'll ever know what he and I went through.

I hope [America doesn't] forget us. Here lately they've been coming out with different things. Now they've declared it was a war now. The first battle ever won in Korea was my outfit. The first one won. There was others fought, but they had to be withdrawn and they weren't won. It was a battle raging and defeated. It was my outfit. [The] War Department [records] show that. That's the experience I had in there no matter how short it was. It lasts a lifetime. I get to telling it, I get chilled all over, start to vibrate.

They told me I suffered from combat fatigue, [but] that's what it was. Locked me up when I came back the last time. I stayed in hospital [in Japan], in the annex. But I got out and got married six months after I was discharged and began to raise a family. Put it on the backburner, but . . . I guess it will always be there. I didn't go around any solders [for a long time]. I was completely away from all of them and raising my children and grandchildren. I've been [on] the edge. My wife's been trying to calm me down for forty-eight years now. We've been married forty-eight years. I get up in the morning and I say, "I've got to go, I've got to go, I've got to go." "Where you got to go?" I say, "I don't know." I say that just about every day. She say, "Just go then." I'll go to the store and get something and come back. And I'll begin to settle down. I used to drive there. I don't sleep no nights all these years. Last night I woke up [at] 3:00 in the morning. Some nights 4:30, 5:00, then I've got to go. I don't know when I've gotten a good night's sleep. I don't remember.

I thought I had this thing licked, but when I began to see TV and all the things going on in [the war in Iraq], I got this inner rage come over me and I start[ed] shouting and screaming at the TV, hollering at the president. War is not good. Why go there? I find myself screaming and hollering. Now eleven years later, I found myself running through the house saying that again. War is not good, not good. Go if you will, but it's not a good sight to see. I don't know. I guess it's something that happens to some of us, some get over it, some don't. I start talking about it and sometimes I just have to stop.

Jessie Brown
Private 1st class, Company 2, 2nd Battalion, 24th Regiment, 25th Division
US Army
Interviewed by Stephen Smith, January 7, 2003, Chicago, IL
American RadioWorks, Minnesota Public Radio

ISAAC GARDNER JR., CHICAGO, ILLINOIS

[The Korean War] didn't [change race relations]; President Truman did it, when he integrated the military. That made it better. [But] after I got out of the hospital, they put me down there [at Fort Benning, Georgia]. I think it was the 22nd Infantry Regiment. We were training recruits to go to Germany. Everything was going along real good, but in about July or August, the ROTC young white boys from universities came in for training, and during their spare time they played golf. And they wanted us to shag balls for them. And I told them, I ain't shagging balls for nobody. That's when it came to a head. I said, "I ain't gonna shag no balls." And so the commander said, "Soldier, are you disobeying a direct order?" And I said, "No." And he said, "Well, you better rephrase that."

We had a Black sergeant who winked at me. When we got on the bus to go to Columbus for a weekend, you sit anywhere you want to sit, as long as you're on military property. But at the city limits, the bus driver would stop. "Now you white boys gotta come to the front and you Black soldiers you all gotta go to the back." "Man, let's go." A lot of the white guys, they were from Massachusetts. And all we wanted to do was get there, get some beers, and kiss some girls if we can. So, we had a problem, and it got so bad that the post commander had a meeting with the mayor and told the mayor if those white policemen didn't leave those Black officers alone, he would put Columbus, Georgia, off the map and run the bus every weekend to Atlanta, Georgia, and Birmingham, Alabama.

What really changed was that it was much worse in Georgia than it was in Kentucky. Had I gone back to Fort Knox or Fort Bragg, I probably would've finished. Georgia was just a low-down state. If guys went into town and messed up, they'd go to jail, and Monday morning they'd have them out on the work farm. They'd have to go help Mr. So-and-So get his crop. The commander would have to go out to get them. The commander said, "If you don't leave them alone, we're gonna put it off-limits," and they don't want to lose all that money for the economy of the city.

I couldn't see the logic in [treating us like that]. It made me realize that what I'd done [in the war], it was for naught. I tried to get transferred from Fort Benning, but they said, "No, we need you here." Old Sarge saw that I was going to get in a lot of trouble, and he said, "Why don't you go on to the hospital and have them look at your feet. Maybe after you've stayed back for a while, they'll send you somewhere else." I said, "Doc, my feet are hurting me all the time." I said, "I want to get the hell out of the army; I want to get out of Georgia." They put it in my file, so now they know I want to get out.

I can recall that doggone captain's name who saved my life. He said, "You wanna get out of the army?" And I said, "I want to get out of Georgia, and if getting out of the army will get me out of Georgia, let me out of the army." He said, "Well maybe we can get you an honorable discharge stating that you just can't adjust to military life." I said, "That's fine by me." So I go back to the hospital and go before the board. They gave me a 20 percent pension. About two weeks after I got home, I got a letter stating [that] due to the findings, they could only give me 10 percent. According to the record, the frostbite on my hands wasn't bad enough. But if you come back to Georgia, there's a chance we can give you the 20 percent. [I said,] "Uh, uh. Give me the 10, and let me outta here." And then that was it. Wasn't nothing to get bitter about, because that's just the way it was and how it's going to be.

Even when I was in the hospital, I met a guy from Minnesota who told me he had never seen a Black person before. We started mixing, we started playing cards together, eating chow a little together. At the end of World War II, we did a complete turnaround. Japan was our enemy, and at the end of the war they became our friend. If the powers that be wanted to resolve the racial problem, they could do it overnight. We're 13 percent of the population. It's economics. But it's geared that way, if I can be candid. If a person has been your footstool, he's been your subordinate, and a hundred, hundred fifty years later he's gonna come up and be equal to you. No, you've done him too bad. No, he can't have the same stick I got. It's easier for the suppressor to forget than the suppressed. [White folks are] just empire builders — and I don't say that in a derogatory fashion — they just take it.

[The 24th Infantry] did not [get the recognition it deserved,] no doubt. No sense talking about that. We don't get a fair shake anywhere we go. We can get in a race, but you can't win. They let you finish in the money sometime. The sooner people accept that, the better off they'll be. The way I've gotten through life, I don't care who is driving the bus, as long as I'm riding. [If the 24th had been all white,] they would've gotten [the attention] the 1st Cavalry got, or the 7th. Let's face it, Europeans are conquerors, get real about it. That's all. Empire builders. You know it and I know it. If I had been born into it, I'd support it, too. There's never going to be any fairness. If the Europeans went down and the Asians took over, you wouldn't get it from them. And if the Africans were to get lucky — uh, uh. Kids can come from the same womb and not be treated equally. So, what do you expect with different races? Ain't no way in the world I could treat you the same [as] I treat a Black girl, unless you were a friend and I knew you. But if you come in and a Black girl comes in, you're both hungry, and I have one piece of bread, I'm gonna give it to the one who looks like me. That's just human nature. Am I right or wrong?

In my opinion, Koreans are decent people, they're nice people, but America seems to think that her almighty dollar can solve all of her problems, but it just can't do it. You can't just give people money and then treat them like they're less than human. Those rich men who make war, if they're gonna start a war, they got to finish it. Too many of our boys died to finish at a stalemate. If you gonna fight it, fight it to win. Don't be in there half-stepping. Fight it to win. And throw everything you got at it and get it over with quick as possible.

Isaac Gardner
Rank unknown, Company L, 3rd Battalion, 24th Infantry
  Regiment, 25th Infantry Division
US Army
Interviewed by Kate Ellis, September 2002, Chicago, IL
American RadioWorks, Minnesota Public Radio

GEORGE CUREAUX JR., GARYVILLE, LOUISIANA

I have never had any problem racially with white or Black at no time. But again, where I was brought up, my neighbors on both sides were white. I was going to one school and my neighbor, [who] was white, was going to another school. So we are playing one day, and he asked me, he said, "Why are we going to separate schools?" We were about in second grade at that time. I said, "Heck, I don't know." I didn't, he didn't know, you know. We are still neighbors. Our kids grew up playing with one another, you know. And our grandkids would have, [except] my grandkids are off, but his grandkids are there [and] we get along like one big, happy family. We never had any problems.

I have never had any problems [being light skinned]. Now, it may be my personality. I have the type of personality that gets along with people. But I have never had any problems through school, from elementary school on. And the darker Black guys, I never had a minute's problem with them. [I did pass for white sometimes], going into some of the joints in South Carolina. The guys that I was with, the white guys that I may have been with, they knew how it was. [So] when [we went] in a joint, they just wouldn't say anything [about me being Black] 'cause nine times out of ten, they would have gotten in a fight because the [place] wouldn't have want[ed] me in there.

I remember, well, this was way after, after I was out of the service and I was on vacation in Mobile, my wife and I and my two kids. It was raining hard that night and my wife said she wanted something to drink. So I went into [a] bar and got a drink for her, and there were two white guys sitting on one end of the bar, four whites sitting on the other end of the bar. Well, I stopped right by these two whites, and one of them started talking with me. And well, these two were drunk. So I got the drink, getting ready to leave. One of them said, "Well, look, why don't you stay and have a beer with us?" Alright, I wasn't in a rush. I said, "Okay." We started talking. One of them looked down the bar, the one that invited [me] to drink, he looked down the bar, he said, "Look at the guys over there. See, they don't like us talking to you. Let's go over there and get in a fight with them." Now, I said, "I will see you. I am leaving." I am the only Black guy in there. If the cops come, who is going to get arrested? Me. They are not going to ask any other question. I started the fight. See, I am the only Black one there, I started the fight regardless, I am getting arrested. So, I moved out of there. Usually, that's how I would handle myself when I was with any of those guys. But as I said, I never had any problems as such.

The [Black soldiers] look at it this way: this was our country. We were fighting for our country, although we were considered second-class citizen[s], we were still fighting for our country, and that never came up as to what we were doing and why we were doing it.

[Integration] basically started with the military, with Truman integrating the services. There was one guy that I knew that was, that belongs to my VFW now, [a] Black guy, he was in the navy during World War II. And in the navy, the only thing a Black person or a Puerto Rican could do was to be a cook or a servant to the officers, that was their duty. And he was asked one day, we were having luncheon and one of the white guys asked him, "Henry," he said, "you were in the navy. You were a cook, weren't you?" He said, "Yeah. I didn't want to be a cook, but I was a cook." You know, there is a difference: whether you want to or not. "But I was a cook; not that I wanted to be," which means he wasn't a cook now.

But I was fortunate in a way that my parents had seen that I had an education. I dropped out of school because I wanted to drop out of school. But I guess I am satisfied with my life as it has turned out. I enjoyed the service while I was there. I tell most people now, young people, that I didn't want to go when I went. But now I am glad that I went, because there is experience you can get in the service that you can't get anywhere else. The type of people you meet and the things that you do, and you can't get that in just ordinary life. You miss all kinds of experience there.

George Cureaux Jr.
Sergeant, 999th Armored Field Artillery Battalion, X Corps
US Army
Interviewed by Kate Ellis and Stephen Smith, August 2002, Little Rock, AR
American RadioWorks, Minnesota Public Radio

WALTER LEE DOWDY JR., CHATTANOOGA, TENNESSEE

And then I get out of the hospital, and I was taking shots and stuff, and then they shipped me from there to Fort Sam Houston, Brooke Army Hospital. I stayed there eleven months. Shrapnel went in my left eye, took the lid off, went across my nose and messed up my sinuses, and messed this right eye up. This eye was turned down, and I still got the shrapnel in [my] head now. They wouldn't take it out because it would have paralyzed me if they would take it out. So what they did, they made me a new eyelid, [and] they tied the two nerves together. My records say the medial rectus and superior oblique, they tethered those together. Now my eye will move left and right but won't move up or down vertically, but horizontally, so that's why I got to wear two pair of glasses to read or to think. I remember in the hospital I had headaches. Oh, man, I was going through headaches. They put me in straitjackets, because I was thrashing, thrashing, thrashing, thrashing, thrashing. They gave me shots to calm me down because the shrapnel was, oh, it was killing me.

And my parents came down to see me from Michigan. They came down to San Antonio to see me. I came home for the holidays, for Christmas, in December 1951. And I had got the train out of San Antonio, Texas. Now, I'm in uniform. I always kept myself neat. When I got on the train, a Black porter put me behind a curtain. Yes, I rolled behind a curtain from San Antonio, Texas, to Saint Louis, Missouri. I'm not kidding you. And I got off of the train to get a train coming to Chicago, and the MPs were walking around in the station. They wrote me a citation because I was clean. The other guys got wrote up because they were raggedy and crumpled up. I kept myself neat all the time. But see now, they really hurt me because now I'm hurt, I was looking like this from fighting a war, and I was sitting behind a curtain.

But I didn't get angry. I could have been a radical, a what you want to call it, and marched all around and give all vitriolic speeches, but I didn't do that. I went back to school and made sure I got what was due me. And I got what was due me by what the Lord had me to do, get my education. We were taught to do your best, be your best. Treat other folks nice, and you'll be treated nice, you know. We wasn't taught to hate or what [not,] we wasn't taught that from my parents. There were injustices. We knew they were there. We didn't hide our head from them. We knew. But we knew that our character would take us where we wanted to go.

But, still, there is a difference between being bitter and just really resenting. I mean, you have to resent [the injustice]. Hey, when I'm saying bitter, I mean bitter like those guys in the '50s and '60s, H. Rap Brown, or Muhammad Ali, he's a big boxer, and he's a bitter man. When you listen to Al Sharpton, he's a bitter man. I'm naming names. When you listen to Jesse Jackson, he's a bitter man, or [Louis] Farrakhan. These are bitter folks, you see. I'm not bitter, but I resent it greatly. Okay. But I said my character, my individual character, will carry me. Case in point: when I finished college in Michigan, I couldn't get a job in my field. They wasn't hiring Black folks. In Kalamazoo, Michigan, they weren't hiring. So I took a job at Fort Custer State Home for the mentally retarded. Okay. When I took the test for the civil service in Michigan, I passed it. They didn't hire me. They said I'm physically handicapped. Okay. So what I did, I appealed. I went to Lansing on an appeal, and it just so happened that my appointment in Lansing was during the week of hiring the handicapped week! So I went up there. They looked at me, and my wife was pregnant. They looked right at me, and they said, "Okay, we'll get you a job at the home for the mentally retarded, work for the home for the mentally ill, . . . on account of your blind side." So they gave me a job there. Then in Kalamazoo they had a[n] opening for a job at the juvenile detention home, a superintendent. The superintendent, a white man, didn't have his degree. I'm degreed. So they didn't hire me for that, [but] I quit my job at the state home to take a job at the juvenile home as an attendant. Then that job come up for a superintendent. I applied for that. And the board for the juvenile detention home had put in the paper: a white male. Okay. This is '55, '56, '57. And so I said, I got my credentials. And the NAACP during those days was marching and everything, [but] I didn't go [to] the NAACP. I got my credentials. I made an appointment with the probate judge, Judge Ivan Wheeler. I made an appointment with him, I talked to him, I said, "Judge, I want the job down there at the juvenile home. You have an opening there for a superintendent. Man, I want that job, and I'm qualified." He said, "Oh, are you?" I said, "Yes," and I reached in my pocket, gave him my credentials. He got up and walked around his desk and looked out the window. I said, "Man, the job says a white man. Man, that's not right. I'm not going to stand for that, Judge, and I'm going to tell you straight up." He said, "Well, Walt, the job is yours."

Walter Lee Dowdy Jr.
Corporal, 24th Infantry Regiment, 25th Division
US Army
Interviewed by Michael Willie, February 18, 2004, Chattanooga, TN
Walter Dowdy Jr. Collection (AFC/2001/001/20008), Veterans History
    Project, American Folklife Center, Library of Congress

Ernest Shaw was a Silver Star winner and went on to a successful agricultural career as a county agent in Texas. He felt that he had earned equal treatment, but he also took an attitude of not expecting too much and felt that the army had given him the skills to better survive tough times. Not all veterans would be so patient.

ERNEST K. SHAW, HOUSTON, TEXAS

When I arrived in Saint Louis, we came back into the southern area where it was legally segregated. When I got back to Virginia, it was Saturday. I'm a 2nd lieutenant. The conductor came and asked me if I wanted to move. And I said, "No." He said, "A lot of your people are getting on board, you can get on that coach if you choose." It was a local coach. I said, "I'm okay," and used the whole seat comfortably and rode until an Anglo lieutenant got on and we chatted all the way there. It was okay. We did what was expected, and so it went.

[We] started to have more opportunities, African Americans, even though I didn't experience any plausible discrimination that I could express, I'm sure some was there. I think it was October 1, 1951, that last Black unit was integrated. I felt good about it. If you prepare yourself, do the right thing and don't expect too much, you'll be okay. [But] I felt like I deserved what every other person deserved [and] made every effort to take advantage of opportunity. I find people very responsive without regard to [race] if you conduct yourself civilly. I've had a good career that I've enjoyed. I was able to get into field position with [the] Texas A&M system as a county agent, and that put me out with the people. And having been trained in agriculture, I knew both theory and practice of agriculture. I just carried on and did what had to be done. Being a county agent, first [Black county agent] in the state of Texas and working in five rural counties that are more conservative, whatever that means, I knew [that] in order to do my job properly, I would have to adapt to the folklore of the place, which I found sometimes not too tasteful, but sometimes not too distasteful. Some of the people, when they went to eat, would choose to go to where they could be with their peers. Interacting with them was my job so I would go and join them, but I was not forced by law to be there with them. I also trained African students out in the field. This was a little condescending [for me because as foreigners] they could go places where the law didn't permit me to go. So [if I] drive up to the window, and he could go and get the cheeseburger, but I'm training him. So that was unique, but you laugh and keep going. What I try and do with the young people is to make them aware of the opportunity that America offers. Our country is the greatest country on earth.

[War] was awesome. It was okay, but it was awesome. I had some traumatic experiences, I was traumatized. I didn't know that until later. This was before the PTSD [post-traumatic stress disorder] was declared or made part of the physiological system. I was having some experiences that were unique to me. My wife observed it as well but said, "It will pass." I had literally buried some things that needed to be exposed, some of my episodes from the war. Bottom line is: that experience took a toll. I didn't anticipate what I experienced until it came upon me. It was a defining moment in my life. I don't regret it, but it was costly. But it left me with the knowledge that I could persevere, that I could function. I've done okay. I have a counseling certificate. I am certified today. I was trying to get to the bottom of what was going on. Later, I had some counseling through the VA. I realized that when you are traumatized over time, it can be devastating, but you keep going until you move through it, but then it's not totally gone. I don't know if it ever totally leaves, but that doesn't mean you're a weak person, just that you had some experiences that exceeded the level of human endurance that you possess. The first response is to be as quiet as you can and almost hide. But as the old Negro spiritual goes, "They ain't no hiding down here," so you keep going. The other part was I was able to be in an environment where I was out in the open, [could] keep my own peace. I had superiors and advisers who respected me and who gave me every opportunity to succeed. And whether they knew I was having a little difficult[y], they never made a thing of it. I'm grateful to have been treated in such a way. I enjoy working. Anyone who's had a bad experience, don't give up, just pray and keep on going. That's it.

Ernest K. Shaw
First lieutenant, 1st Battalion, 31st Regiment, 7th Division
US Army
Interviewed by David P. Cline, January 10, 2003, Houston, TX
American RadioWorks, Minnesota Public Radio

Like the men above, Bill Saunders was rudely reintroduced to Jim Crow on his return to civilian life. But unlike many who kept things on a quiet and personal level, Saunders translated his anger into a drive for change, working with a number of well-known civil rights figures, including Esau Jenkins in South Carolina, Martin Luther King Jr., the community organizer and teacher Septima Clark, and the skilled grassroots organizer Myles Horton of the legendary Highlander Center in Tennessee. The household names of the civil rights movement are relatively few; many more deeply involved activists are like Saunders—very well known and well respected in their local communities, if not beyond them. Saunders has spent seventy years dedicated to the labor and civil rights of the people of South Carolina, building on his experiences in the US military, not all of them positive.

For John Conyers, his path to activism was through a political career that eventually led to Congress. But as a local politician in the years before that, he was in the thick of the civil rights struggle, which in some cases turned into violent expressions of frustration at inequality, abuse at the hands of the police, and the slow pace of change.

Clarence Jones had even more central, though more hidden, role at the center of the struggle, as a young Black attorney on Martin Luther King's staff, and most important, as the author of the original draft of what would become the "I Have a Dream" speech. Jones was drafted a month after the Korean War ended and already had a sharp legal mind and clear understanding of justice and injustice. He managed to parlay that into an honorable discharge, legal training, and a place in the cabinet of the nation's major leader of nonviolent civil rights resistance.

WILLIAM "BILL" SAUNDERS, CHARLESTON, SOUTH CAROLINA

[When I got out of the army,] I got paid, got about five hundred dollars, which was a monumental amount of money back in those days. And we went into Columbia, South Carolina, and I ran into the Greyhound bus station. My buddy kept the bags, and I ran into the Greyhound bus station. And a cop came to me with his gun pushed down and said, "Boy, what's wrong with you? You know you don't belong in here!" And I never knew that I didn't belong in a Greyhound bus station, because I'd never been off of Johns Island to go through that kind of segregation. I said, "No, officer, I didn't know I didn't belong here. Where do I belong?" And he showed me the back of the bus station where Blacks bought their tickets outside. And when the bus comes, whites loaded in the bus, and any seats that are left in the back, we had access to those seats.

My bitterness really began at that time, really hard. I just didn't understand it. And I used to call all whites racists at that point, because here are some guys that I was with for a year, and yet not one of them said, "Well, Bill, let me get the ticket for you," or, "Let him get his ticket." Nobody. Everyone—all of my white "friends"—just dropped their heads. Nobody said anything. You know, the only place that I've ever *really* been an American was basically in Hawaii, a little bit there, and Korea and in Japan. I've never been an American in America. I've always been a second-class citizen in America.

[When I got out,] I was about nineteen then, eighteen, nineteen, but I was still trying to be a man and I wanted to do some stuff to prove that I was. So, when I got [out] they sent me back to Fort Lewis, Washington, to Tacoma, and I went to administrative school. I took typing and all kinds of administrative stuff. I end up being company clerk and I was able to make sergeant before I got discharged. I was in charge of sending out people to get promoted, so I was in charge of who at least got to be eligible to be put in. So a lot of friends came back as sergeants. I end up making sergeant down in Fort Lewis.

And what I wanted to do—I felt like I could make a difference. I wanted to be a man—not a *Black* man, it would be years before I got the whole Black thing—but I wanted to be a man. I wanted to prove that I was good enough and that I could compete. So, when I came back out of the army, I joined with Esau Jenkins [legendary community organizer and civil rights activist in Johns Island, South Carolina].

During that period of time, Blacks had to read a part of the Constitution to register to vote. I used to teach people how to read and write those things. But a lot of the folk that we had from Johns Island, you couldn't teach them to read, but they would memorize the Constitution and they would go and take the test and pass it. And then, [the registrar] would [say], "God, this old lady reads so well." But she memorized it the whole time!

But, you know, I did a lot of things at that point just to prove [we were equal]. We had the Progressive Club, Esau Jenkins had an adult education school there. I got to be business manager of the Progressive Club. Dr. King came over and stayed with us. [And] in 1959, I went to Highlander Research Center, the Highlander Folk School in Monteagle, Tennessee. Esau Jenkins was the one in charge, but what they were doing, they had brought people from all over the South to go to Highlander, just to sit and talk to each other. Because so many of the times, we thought we had the worst problem, and other people had different problems. So, I'm meeting with people from Appalachia, poor whites that [were dealing with] the strip mining and all of that stuff. We got a chance to see how poor people were being treated, not Black people or Indian, but it was about poor people. It still took a while before I got all the way where I needed to go with that, but I started looking at people and started looking at our country as a class system and not a race system. It gets to be race at the bottom, but most of the time it's not racial—it's class.

Myles Horton, who was the director [at Highlander], was just a brilliant guy. He was able to work through the union and everything that was changing. He was a part of change. And he used to say to us, "I've got a little problem of my own now," what he had then. But he said, "You can't help people to do things. Then you want to tell them what to do. You've got to let them do what they think is best after you've helped them to get to where they need to start from." And he did a good job on that.

And they raided the place while I was there, and they arrested Septima Clark. I mean, they really physically abused her and arrested her. She and Guy Carawan was taken off to jail, and they took all of their property that they had. They had said Septima Clark was selling beer, breaking the law. They had beer and sodas and crackers and stuff, and they had it out on a table, and you could get anything you wanted, and if you wanted to leave a donation, you could. But they lost all of their property for that.

My bitterness continued, right from the military, [had] continued to build. [The police] wanted to search all of the cars [at Highlander,] and I refused to give them the keys. Esau Jenkins and DeQuincey Newman, they were there, they came and made me give the guy the keys, because I was going to make [the police] break it open. Again, I said, "This nonviolent thing is not for me. I've got to get out of this." And I left that in '59. I went back to Highlander again, but I really decided at that point the nonviolent thing, getting beat up for no reason at all, was not going to work for me. And I started searching then, and I heard about Malcolm X and then Stokely Carmichael, and some of these folks end up coming to Johns Island to see me.

I don't like the term "nonviolent," in that sense, because most of us that was in there because you had to be violent or nonviolent, when we believed in nonviolence. We just didn't believe in people beating you up for nothing, and I couldn't take [that]. Folk talk about turning your cheek; I only had one cheek, so I couldn't turn it. [Esau Jenkins] was really, really strong in that area. He and Dr. King and all, they really believed. It was not a fad or anything. They really believed in that. And so, I supported [them]. I did all of the work that they needed done for the nonviolent movement. I just didn't march. I just didn't do the other stuff. But the paperwork, the food, where we had it on Johns Island, wherever—I did the supportive background stuff for that. But I couldn't go out and get beat up.

All of these people came and stayed on Johns Island. We had Fannie Lou

Hamer, [who] told stories [to] us at [the] Progressive Club, that she would be marching and didn't get beat up as often, because she would say, "Hit me, motherfucker, I'll kill you! Hit me, motherfucker, I'll kill you!" And so, she would just keep on walking around and doing that, and the cop would just look at her and say, "That woman is crazy; ain't messing with that woman." There were a lot of tactics that folk used not to get beat up.

William Saunders
Staff sergeant, unit unknown
US Army
Interviewed by Kieran Taylor, June 9, 2011, Charleston, SC
Civil Rights History Project
Interview completed by the Southern Oral History Program under
    contract to the Smithsonian Institution's National Museum of African
    American History and Culture and the Library of Congress, 2011

JOHN CONYERS, WASHINGTON, DC

There was the major riot—the biggest civil unrest race riot in America—in 1967 in Detroit. And I know what set that off because I got a call that morning and they said, "Please get over here right away." There was an afterhours place [on 12th Street] that had been paying the police to operate, and for some reason the police decided they were going to raid this place anyway. And oh, boy, the word was that a woman had been thrown down the steps and severely injured. And it was all unnecessary because of police violence, and people were so angry. They've got a picture—they captured this picture of me on the top of a flatbed truck with a speaker trying to calm everybody down. And forty-three [were] killed, hundreds and hundreds injured, thousands arrested—they created a temporary prison holding center. They just built the place and locked everybody up. And the police were all on the side, all against the blocks. It was ugly.

The tensions, the racial tensions, were really being created by the Detroit police "Big Four." There was a lot of racial discrimination, of course. But they had this tactical cruiser in which four police [sat] —and they'd pull up and they'd harass young Black men on the corners—and frequently beat them up just right on the spot or arrest them or did anything they want. It was just constant. Then, though, it began to spread to all Black adults, period. I mean they were pulling doctors, Black doctors, out of cars. It was just raw, ugly, racial police violence. And it was being condoned by the city leaders. The mayor of the city, Louis C. Miriani then, was obviously—they all knew it. It was always in the papers, and we all knew what was going on. And so what happened that night on 12th Street set it off. But then the rioting turned into looting and burning. And they were indiscriminate. I mean, a whim comes along, everybody gets [it] — they don't [just] select white houses and white businesses. And so pretty soon, it was happening to everybody.

John Conyers
US representative, 13th District of Michigan
Michigan National Guard
2nd lieutenant, 1279th Combat Engineers
US Army Corps of Engineers
Interviewed by Renee Poussaint, August 20, 2007, Washington, DC
National Visionary Leadership Project
Interviewed by Louis Jones, September 19, 2003, Detroit, MI
Detroit Oral History Project

CLARENCE B. JONES, PALO ALTO, CALIFORNIA

The Korean War broke out June 25th, 1950. I was a student. As a fully enrolled student, I was entitled to a student deferment. I was scheduled to graduate in '53. In order to sustain your exemption, your student deferment, you either had to graduate or you had to be full time in school, and if you were nearing graduation, you had to have made an application to a graduate school. And if you didn't have either of those things, you were not entitled to be exempt from the draft. So, my draft board snatched me because I was in this space [between college and graduate school]. I was drafted on August 12th, 1953 [just after the armistice]. I was angry. In my draft board in Mount Holly, New Jersey, there were very few college students. And I still to this day believe that this prejudiced Mount Holly draft board said, "Well, we'll send this Negro. We'll draft him. Who does he think he is?" I mean, I think if I had been white, I don't think I would have been drafted. I think they would say, "Oh, he's enrolled in Columbia College [and] his mother [just] died." [But] they didn't care. So, I was bitter.

I had also become politicized in college. I had met Paul Robeson in New York, an extraordinary man. I went to see him in something with Uta Hagen on Broadway. My uncle had become friends with him. At this time, he was being summoned before the House Un-American Activities Committee, and I watched him on television. When Paul Robeson was being asked to be sworn in as a witness by the chairman, he stands up, six foot four, he says, "You!" He points his finger at him. "You, Mr. Eastland! You are unconstitutionally seated in that chair. You don't have the authority, the constitutional authority, to ask me any questions whatsoever, because you are illegally sitting in this Congress. You were illegally seated because of the mass exclusion of my people in voting. You have no authority whatsoever to ask me any questions!" Meanwhile, they're saying, "Shut the witness! Shut the witness up!" I said, "Wow!" I said, "That was a bad dude!" I mean, that influenced me, okay?

So, my mother dies, [there's the] influence of Paul Robeson, [and] my anger [at] not getting exempted, so . . . the night before I was to report for induction, I sat down and wrote a handwritten note, as to why I was *reporting* for induction but why I was not going to *serve* in the army. And, in the course of the note, I said, in effect: "I'm willing to go and serve and give my life for my country as a member of the United States Army when my country treats me as a first-class citizen. I'm not willing to put my life on the line in a war that I have lots of questions about, the Korean War, I'm not willing to do that. And so, therefore, I'm reporting for induction." And I wasn't a lawyer, I didn't know anything, [but] I cited the First, the Fifth, the Fourteenth, and Fifteenth Amendments to the Constitution as the reason I was not [willing to serve].

So, I'm in Whitehall Street in New York. I report for duty August 13th, early in the morning. Now, if you've seen some of these military pictures, when you report to duty, the first thing the noncommissioned officer says, and it was a Negro noncommissioned officer, and he says, "All right, sissies! You raise your hand, you're being inducted into the army!" Well, I didn't raise my hand, because I figured I didn't consent to this. And then Sergeant Somebody, he says, "Well, what's with you? What's with you, soldier?" And I said, "There's nothing. I'm here. I'm reporting." "Well, what are you, some kind of kook or conscientious objector?" And I said, "No," and then I gave him my statement to read. And he read it, he said, "What are you, some kind of Commie?" I said, "No." He said, "Well, get out of line!" [Also,] I didn't sign the loyalty oath. As part of the various series of papers you sign, consenting to being in the army, there's . . . a loyalty oath for four hundred organizations that the then–attorney general Herbert Brownell determined were either Communist or Communist-run organizations, including a lot of organizations I *knew* were not Communist. The Young Progressives of America, they were not a Communist organization, but they were there. And so, I didn't sign it.

So, he puts me out of line, and then a captain, a white officer, comes over and says, "What's the problem, Mr. Jones?" I said, "Well, I realize I'm here because I want to show up, but these are my reasons why I don't want to serve, sir. I think I'm being unfairly treated. I don't want to serve." He read it. And that's when he says, "Oh?" He said, "Well, you better come over here." And they had some kind of conference for about two hours. Oh, yeah, they decided they were going to put me on the bus to Fort Dix. I go to Fort Dix. And somebody at Fort Dix had been alerted that I was on the bus and coming. Now, at Fort Dix, that's when they get serious, because that's when they want you to sign up for your insurance, you sign that you're going to get paid, they issue your clothes. And so, they kept saying to me, "If you don't sign this, you're not going to get any money." I said, "I don't care. I'm not signing anything." "Well, if you can't sign, you're not going to have any insurance, you're not going to get any paycheck, you're not going to get anything!" I said, "I don't care. I'm not signing anything." So, they issue me standard things and . . . before they process me, I take placement examinations. So, about three or four days after I take the placement examination, I find that they're putting me in a group that's scheduled to go to someplace in Maryland, because we're going to be part of some Special Forces intelligence team. So, I said, "Well, I think there must be some mistake."

I remember going to one of these orientation things, and I'm listening. And they're talking about how we're going to be trained as this special unit. Some of us may go to California to the army language school to learn Russian or Polish, principally that, . . . [or] to Fort Jackson to paratroopers' school. The bottom line is that they were being trained to be special officers who would jump at night behind enemy lines in the Soviet Union and pull on to Czechoslovakia. So, I laugh when I find out. "Now, let's assume that I go through all of this, and I'm fluent in Russian. How am I going to explain this Black face of mine as I show up in the Russian countryside or Polish countryside? This is crazy!" Crazy, right? I mean, that's how insane the military was at this point.

So I'm [now] in [a] holdover [status] and I was bitter, angry over the death of my mother, and I was influenced by Paul Robeson and I was trying to find a way of getting out, not doing it. So, I was in Company D, 47th Regiment, at Fort Dix. I remember it being about 40 percent Black maybe, or more. My company commander was from Mississippi, [a] captain. The noncommissioned officers were virtually all Negro at that time. I develop some close friends [and] once word spreads that I'm going to be here indefinitely, I am not going to be shipped overseas after basic training, guys came up and [said], "Well, tell me how you did this," because they wanted to be in the holdover status [too], they didn't want to be shipped out.

[I stayed] at Fort Dix for twenty-one months. I was trained in telecommunications, army signal communications, teaching me the intricacies of how to operate signal equipment in the field and so forth, map reading. I went through the whole basic training. I went through everything that you go [through], bivouacs, marches with twenty-six pounds, I did the whole thing. But [after] twenty-one months, I'm in my barracks one morning, getting ready to go to what I normally do, and two MPs come in, and one of them says, "Are you Private Jones?" I said, "Yes." And they hand me this paper, and it's like a summons and complaint. It's a notice that they're bringing me up for court-martial as a security risk, with this whole series of allegations. One allegation [was] that I had refused to sign the loyalty oath, [and] the other allegation being that since 1938 up until the present, I'm a member of the Communist Party. Well, of course,

I was only seven years old in 1938. [Another] was that I had lived in a housing development that was run by the ILU, International Labor Union, one of the labor unions that was deemed to be a Communist front. [That] was true, after my mother died, my last year in college, that's where I lived. And the other [allegation] was that I had maintained a very close friend[ship], which was true, with a doctor—he's retired, a doctor at Stanford University—who at the time had been a vice-president of the International Union of Students. Been a member of the Communist Party since I was eight, didn't sign a loyalty oath, lived in the Allerton Houses in the Bronx, and that was it.

And so I'm assigned a defense counsel, and they have this field board of inquiry at Fort Dix. And my commanding officer is called. The principal evidence they put in are the allegations! And we rebut the allegations. He said, "[He's] not a member of the Communist Party. Yes, it is true, he did live there. Yes, it is true, he knows so-and-so. Yes, it is true, he didn't sign the loyalty oath." And even my adjutant general lawyer said, "Well, these are all [B.S.]."

He put my commanding officer on the stand, he said, to testify to whether I was a good soldier or not. "Bottom line, if you could have Clarence Jones in your company, [would you]?" He said, "He was the number one soldier. I would be honored to have him serve at any time. I have heard nothing but glowing remarks." Plus, I had been chosen as soldier of the month. And as a result of that, I was given the good conduct medal. So, I was chosen as soldier of the month, given a good conduct medal, and a special three-day leave, and all this is in the record. And I'm being court-martialed.

The verdict comes down the very next day. I have been found to be an undesirable, a national security risk to the United States government and to the United States military, at which point two MPs took me back to my barracks. They supervised me packing up all of my things, put them in a duffle bag, put me in a jeep, with a one-way ticket to Port Authority, and they . . . escorted me to the gate of Fort Dix under armed guard and put me on the bus under armed guard. I was given an undesirable discharge on August 13th, 1955. I was [sent out] on August 14th.

So I'm riding in on the bus, I'm smoldering, and I'm thinking, "They don't know what they've got on their hands." I discussed it with my uncle, and my uncle says, "Well, I think you ought to go see the American Civil Liberties Union." So, I go down to see the American Civil Liberties Union and I tell them my story. And they have me meet with a lawyer named Stanley Faulkner, God rest his soul, Stanley Faulkner. We filed an appeal.

It was the first time I went into the Pentagon. The Pentagon has something called the Army Services Discharge Review Board. It [is] like the Supreme Court, all of the uniformed services are sitting there, the navy, the marines, the coast guard, the air force, they're all sitting there, military officers. And it's like the court of appeals. To make a long story short, as a result of the appeal, they awarded me a general discharge. They moved up my discharge one notch. Stanley Faulkner says, "No, that's not satisfactory. He's entitled to an honorable discharge."

And I wasn't thinking about what I was going to do, but I decided I wanted to go to law school at that time. I went up to talk to the Columbia Law School and I told them the problem I had. They discouraged me because they said that, "I think you ought to get this problem solved before you consider entering law school. You're not going to be able to be a lawyer if you have this thing hanging over your head."

Meanwhile, I had become friendly with Judge Hubert Delaney and some other lawyers, and they suggested I go and talk to Boston University Law School. So, I talked to Boston University Law School and I told them the issue. And they said, "Well, listen, if you want a legal education, we'll give you a legal education. You decide whether you're going to ever practice, but we'll admit you. You'll get your papers. The mere fact that you have currently an undesirable discharge, in general, and you don't know how it's going to go in appeal, that's not going to stop you, so you're welcome to come."

But the key thing, of course, I needed an honorable discharge because, as an honorable discharge, I qualified for the Korean GI Bill. So, Stanley Faulkner [and I] sued. He brought a writ of mandamus, I believe. A writ of mandamus, for those people who are not familiar, it's an administrative proceeding that's brought against an officer of the government agency to compel that person to perform the duties that he or she is required to do, according to the statute. So, Stanley Faulkner's thesis was that the secretary of the army had a *constitutional* duty, was *compelled* by the nature of the authority, to issue me an honorable discharge.

I'm at Boston University Law School. I'm registering, knowing full well that maybe I'll win the case and maybe I won't win the case. But I haven't completed registering in law school, hadn't gotten my books, when I got this urgent message to call Stanley Faulkner. So, I called and he said, "We won! You've just been issued an honorable discharge. I'm going to get in touch with the Veterans Administration office in Boston and tell them that we're going to have your copy of your order and so forth, so that you can get your benefits." That's what happened, the Veterans Administration was notified I had a honorable discharge. The VA then notified the bursar of Boston University, and they then activated me as being going to school and getting my tuition under the Korean GI Bill. And, lo and behold, I got a check for, I don't know, several thousand dollars, it may have been about twelve thousand dollars, or maybe about thirteen thousand dollars, or something, for all the back pay.

[After law school], I went to California to go to work in [entertainment law], just starting out. I was thinking about what I was going to do [next] when I get a call in February of 1960 from Judge Huey Delaney. Dr. [Martin Luther] King had been indicted by the state of Alabama for tax evasion, for perjury, lying on his income tax return. Judge Hubert Delaney, a Negro judge, lawyer, was the chief defense counsel, along with three other lawyers. Two of the lawyers were from Chicago, very elite tax attorneys. The other lawyer was a local lawyer by the name of Fred Gray, [a] civil rights lawyer. He was a local person. But they needed a law clerk, a clerk who would go down and coordinate. I had never met [King] before. I had vaguely heard of him. I tell everybody: I was in law school from 1956 to 1959, I didn't know anything. I mean, I knew about the Montgomery Bus Boycott, but I was *studying*. I didn't have time to follow a little Negro preacher, what he was doing. I mean, I was really not focused on that. That was on a Thursday night. On Friday morning, I get another call from the judge, and he says, "Clarence, I did not know it at the time of our conversation, but Dr. King is on his way to California right now. I told him he has to find a way of meeting and talking to you." So, Friday night, doorbell rings. Martin King comes to my home in Altadena, California. So, he sits down and he says, "Mr. Jones, we have lots of white lawyers who help us in the movement. But what we need are young Negro lawyers."

Saturday morning, I get another call. "My name is Dora McDonald. Mr. Jones, Dr. King enjoyed so much his visit with you and Mrs. Jones. But, Mr. Jones, he forgot to invite you to be his guest at a church tomorrow in Baldwin Hills. He's going to be the guest preacher, and he would so like for you and Mrs. Jones to join him." So, I go to the church. And I had never heard Dr. King speak before, never heard him.

I was one-third from the front of the pulpit. And he gets up and he says, "Ladies and gentlemen, brothers and sisters, the text of my sermon today is the role and responsibility of the Negro professional in aiding our less fortunate brothers and sisters struggling for freedom in the South." So, I said, "One smart dude." Then, he begins to speak and he begins to describe what he's doing in much more detail and texture. I had never heard or seen him speak before. More accurately, I had never heard another human being walking on two legs on this earth speak that way before. It was mesmerizing! It was like, you could hear a pin drop. He was so intense, melodious.

And then he pauses during the course of his sermon. And he says, "For example, there's a young man sitting in this church today. My friends in New York who are lawyers, for whom I have *great* respect, my friends in New York tell me that this young man's brain has been touched by Jesus! They tell me that when this young man, a lawyer, does any legal research, he goes all the way back to the time of 1066, William the Conqueror and the Magna Carta. And then, my friends in New York, for whom I have *great* respect, tell me that when he writes down what he finds in the law library, the words are so compelling they just *jump* off the page." So, I'm thinking to myself, "Hey, he's not looking at me, [it's] inconceivable he could be talking about me." I'm thinking to myself—I'm a little bit of an opportunist, I want to find out who that man is, since I need to network. I'm not at Universal Pictures anymore. I need to network and find out, because this brother, this person is going to help me if he's that good. And then, he continues. He says, "But I had a chance to visit with this man in his home the other night in Altadena." And I said, "Oh, my Lord!" He'd started talking about me, never looking at me! And then, he took poetic license. The poet Langston Hughes has a poem called "Mother to Son." And the lyrics in that poem talk about a washerwoman, a domestic. She's washing the stairs, and she pauses on the landing and says, "I'm doing this for you, son. Don't you give up. Life ain't been no crystal stair. Don't you give up." Dr. King changes the lyrics and puts my mother as the actor in the poem, instead of the washerwoman, at which point I begin to cry. I began to recognize how much she loved me, how much she had sacrificed, and she didn't see any of the things [I achieved]. She didn't see me graduate from college, didn't see me graduate from law school, didn't see her grandchildren, didn't see any of that. So, I was moved by that. Sermon's over. Dr. King is a celebrity, so he's out signing autographs on the steps of the pulpit. As I walk over to him, he says, "You know, I never mentioned your name, Mr. Jones. I never mentioned your name."

I just walked up to him, took his hand in my right hand, my right hand in his right hand, and I grabbed his shoulder like this, and I said, "Dr. King, when do you want me to go to Alabama?" That was a major turning point in my life.

The bottom line was that the success in Birmingham became the spark that ignited a prairie fire of nonviolent protest across the country. Between May and late August of 1963, there were over thirteen hundred demonstrations, two hundred cities, thirty-six states. We recognized that something qualitatively had happened, was happening to the country. So, when the civil rights organizations announced at the Roosevelt Hotel in June that they were going to hold a March on Washington, I was surprised. And one of the reasons I was surprised is because I knew that Dr. King had been exhausted. He had been in jail for eight days in Birmingham. Then he had a big rally in Detroit, Michigan. And I was surprised that he would so readily consent.

Some people think that Dr. King came to Washington, sat down, and [was] just going to write this speech. He was at the Willard Hotel, working on his speech, but . . . I provided him with information that he could use if he chose to in the speech that he was preparing. I did not know until I was standing fifty feet behind him, and he actually spoke, and I listened very carefully, that as he began speaking, the first opening six or seven paragraphs or more were the draft paragraphs, which I put in summary form for him to use. Whether he was tired, whether he liked it, or whether he just was pressed for time [I don't know], but he didn't change a sentence, not a word, a paragraph, or a comma. He spoke verbatim what I had prepared. But what I had prepared was a summary of what we had discussed several times about the kind of things that he should say.

I just used a certain degree of drama, because I had had the problem of raising bail money [for protestors]. And I remember going to the Chase Manhattan Bank to raise some bail money, coming up to New York and going in and seeing money from floor to ceiling. And so, when I drafted the suggested paragraph, the language, I said I can't believe that, "We have assembled here today to redeem the promissory note to which the signers of the Declaration of Independence all fall heir. And which the present generation is an heir to this promissory note. I cannot believe that in the vaults of justice in the United States that there are insufficient funds."

So, he's speaking. That's the first time I had any idea that he was going to incorporate the actual suggested language, had no idea until then. The normal process: he didn't use *everything*, he didn't use *all* of the paragraphs. But he used the first six or seven of the paragraphs, and then he added his own paragraphs. And then, as he is speaking from this written prepared text, his favorite gospel singer, Mahalia Jackson, shouts out to him—she had performed earlier on the program—"Tell them about the dream, Martin! Tell them about the dream!"

And I'm watching him. In real time, he acknowledges her. But then, he takes the prepared written text and moves it to the left side of the lectern, and grabs the left side of the lectern, and starts to speak. And I turn to the person standing next to me, whoever that person was, [and] I said, "These people don't know it, but they are about ready to go to church." And I said that because I saw Dr. King's body language change. So that, the part of the speech, that speech that the nation and the world celebrates, the so-called "I Have a Dream" speech, was completely spontaneous, was completely extemporaneous. And but for the last part, where he's looking at notes in the end, he was quoting a poem about "free at last, free at last," which is from a hymn from a Protestant clergyman many years earlier. Everything else is spontaneous. Everything!

Now, I heard Martin speak many times. I'm not suggesting—well, whatever your belief, whatever your religious belief, if any, whatever your belief in spirituality or transcendentalism, if any—I can only tell you what I experienced and what I saw. And what I experienced and what I saw, I had never, I had never heard Dr. King speak that way before. It is as if some cosmic, powerful force came down and took over his body. There was this same body I was looking at, but something had taken it over! Because the *words*, the way he said [them], was so powerful! And I think it was the combination of the beauty of the day, two or three o'clock in the afternoon, the beauty of the day, the site, the Lincoln Memorial, the more than 250,000 people. You have to remember, at that time, no place in America had that many people ever assembled in one place at one time, peacefully, 25 percent of whom were white—no place! And something happened in the interaction between what Martin was saying and that audience. So that never, ever again, never, ever again in his lifetime had I heard him speak that way. But the power of his simple message, because he was calling for America, he was summoning America's conscience so that the nation could be as good as it was intended to be.

The genius of Martin Luther King Jr., the political genius, was that he knew and we knew that no matter how compelling or how fair the case for ending racial segregation was on its merits, there was no way that 12 percent of the population was going to *impose* that point of view, no matter how fair and compelling on the merits, on 88 percent of the population. The genius of Martin Luther King was that he would summon the conscience of America through peaceful nonviolent confrontation with racial segregation, so that the conscience of the 88 percent of the country would be forced to see the contradiction between the way in which it treated 12 percent of its people, people of color, and the commandments in the Declaration of Independence and our Constitution. To Dr. King, it wasn't a constitutional or legal question for America. It was a moral question. And he raised the level, raised the level of the 88 percent, raised the question in their minds, as [to] whether this is the kind of nation they want to be. Is it morally right to deny 12 percent of the population full access to equal protection of the laws, equal opportunity to vote, solely based on the color of their skin? That was his political genius.

Clarence B. Jones
Private, Company D, 47th Infantry Regiment, 9th Infantry Division
US Army
Interviewed by David P. Cline, April 15 and April 16, 2013, Palo Alto, CA
American RadioWorks, Minnesota Public Radio

African American veterans who got involved in the pursuit of greater civil rights did so in any number of ways and at any number of levels. James Gilliam is a good representative of those who got involved in a local civil rights organization, in this case the National Urban League, but focused his work mostly on individual growth and handling the everyday realities of a racially conflicted society. But still, he's keeping an eye open for the storm he thinks is inevitably on the horizon.

I guess, if I had to say what problems I had as a military person, the problem was I had two wars to fight. I had the traditional war to fight as a soldier would, and then I had the race war, which was very, very interesting [and] built [into] kind of a motivational thing to me. I think it's the thing that motivated me to want to be a founder of an Urban League here. And as I reflect back on it now and compare the two experiences, my experience in World War II and my experience in the Korean War [were] quite different, but still in many ways very similar. In the Korean War, when I went in it was 1950, and patterns of segregation still existed. So much so that when I got out of the military [after] the Korean War and I went back to Baltimore, I was then a member of the National Guard. This was in 1953. And the adjutant general of the state of Maryland at that time was a guy by the name of Record, General [Milton A.] Record, and he refused—even though the army said that there would be no more segregation—to integrate the Maryland National Guard. I wouldn't join the National Guard anymore, and I just boycotted it and called the preliminary officers to have a strike, which we did. And it was shortly after that that the Maryland National Guard became integrated. But I just wouldn't want to do it. And one thing that was for sure at that time, because I resigned my commission as a tactic, they couldn't put me in jail. They couldn't court-martial me.

And, I think, in spite of the pain that existed at that time, as I reflect back on things, it actually made me stronger. It didn't make me weaker. It made me stronger. And, in other words, I developed an "I ain't gonna let the bastards get me down" type of attitude, and it's paid off for me. I have found that it's better sometimes to have [people's] respect than for people necessarily to like you. That's the way I am, and that's the way I'm going to be all the time.

I think the message here is that it's very important that there be equity. That all people ought to be treated alike and be left to rise to whatever heights their capacity tells them to. And don't block anybody. Don't block anybody. I personally refused to be blocked. You know, I'm not going to take it. Unfortunately, I detect among the young people a kind of a "me first" syndrome. And this seems to be especially true in the white community, and it can work to everybody's disadvantage and, in particular, their disadvantage. In other words, they're not going to go any further in doing the things that needs to be done unless they pull somebody else along. That was one of the reasons why I became very interested in forming an Urban League, was that these kind of disparaging situations in education were too pronounced on a racial basis. And I said, it ain't gonna be this way. And the only thing I know how to do is [be ready to answer] the question, what did *you* do about it? Well, I got some pretty good examples of that [with] the fair housing thing, some pretty good examples [in] the Urban League with what it's trying to do. And I feel so much the better for having done these things. And I hope that the clock doesn't run out before I get a couple of more under my belt.

And I'm going to tell you something, and this might be a harsh way to put it. But the white community better wake up, because it ain't gonna be too long where they're not going to be the majority, if you stop and think about the Hispanic community. And the thing that I really hope is that this bond between the Hispanic community and the Black community become[s] very real. And if that happens, some changes are going to be made. And I hope I live long enough to be a part of it.

James H. Gilliam Sr.
Captain, 365th Infantry Regiment, 92nd Infantry Division
US Army
Interviewed by Thomas Healy, October 16, 2006, Wilmington, DE
James H. Gilliam Sr. Collection (AFC/2001/001/48906), Veterans
*   History Project, American Folklife Center, Library of Congress*

For others who took personal lessons from their military experience and trans-
lated them into their everyday lives, that could also mean seeking and enjoying
harmonious race relations. Despite the challenges, such experiences could be
readily available and deeply rewarding. For many others, experiences were de-
cidedly mixed, from ongoing racial challenges to being stonewalled by the US
Army and Veterans Administration.

CHARLES DAVENPORT, WASHINGTON, PENNSYLVANIA

The friendships [I had with white marines] were the same as any friendship I've ever developed in life. You don't take to anybody, just, right away—the friendship develops in a feeling of having something in common with somebody, or working with them side by side, and discussing things back and forth, and seeing similarities in one another, and so forth. But the friendships developed as we went along.

And one good friend there in 1950, 1952, was from South Carolina, [and] he told me how prejudiced he had been, and how prejudiced his family, mother and father still were. He said, "I'm working on them. I changed my attitude about Blacks in World War II." He [was on] several of the beaches that they had to take, and he saw that red blood was red blood. He didn't look at the color of the face, he said, "If a man was bleeding, he was a comrade," and, they were working together, fighting together. And he said he started to change his attitudes then, and I don't think I had a better friend than Sam Wells at that time. And the rest of them, it was the same way.

One of my very best friends was a [white] sergeant major from Texas, who was with me in Korea, and he is the one that helped me to fight against the Marine Corps in January 1957, when they got me an interview in Headquarters Marine Corps, to fight against the discrimination and segregation that was still going on in 1957. He'd been stationed at Headquarters Marine Corps, he saw all of the facts and attitudes and letters and orders that we didn't get to see in the field. And he sent me copies, he made the appointment for me, and the second day of January 1957, I was at Headquarters Marine Corps, and I was attacking the corps on their discriminatory practices that they were still pursuing after we had had fifteen years to prove ourselves in the Marine Corps.

When people look at you with some pride in you, and admiration, it makes you feel good that you were a part of that period that we went through, and won the battle of the races, you might say, the battle of who was the better marine and such. [I'm proud of] the absolute camaraderie that [Montford Point marines] developed in that we all were there for the same reason, suffering the same conditions, fighting and winning every battle that we were in, to gain recognition as United States marines, colored, Black, there's a camaraderie there that continues to this day. And at that time, during the war, any place you went, on the train, on the bus on the airplane, any place you went, and you saw a Black man in a green uniform, you knew he was from Montford Point, a Black marine, serving there with you. You knew you found a friend. You didn't know his name, he didn't know your name, but you were Black, he was Black, he had the globe and anchor, so did I, you had a friend.

I'm still proud I went into the Marine Corps. I met a lot of wonderful people, all over the world, and naturally, something comes up every once in a while, and the service enters into the conversation: "Well, I was in the marines." "I was, too." Right away, you have a friend. When you saw another marine, he could be Mexican, he could be Chinese, Japanese, Black, whatever, he's a marine, you're a marine, you have a friend. Once a marine, always a marine. He either trained at San Diego, Parris Island, or Montford Point, those three areas, [and that] tells you, you have a common bond. And having been a Montford Point marine, it's more important, 'cause even a white marine would say, "I remember when you guys were in the service, I hated what I saw." When someone says, "I think you guys did a lot to prove what you were," and so forth, [they say it with a] kind of admiration 'cause they know what we went through, and we all like to see somebody that has succeeded at something.

Charles Davenport
Gunnery sergeant/acting master sergeant, 7th Marines, 1st Division

US Marine Corps
Interviewed June 29, 2005, Washington, PA
Montford Point Marines Project
Copyright © 2004 Randall Library, University of North Carolina at Wilmington

JOHNNIE GIVIAN, JACKSONVILLE, NORTH CAROLINA

[When I returned from Korea,] I got orders to go to Albany, Georgia—they just had built a new supply center down there and I was transferred down there. I went on leave for thirty days, and after that I reported into [the] Albany, Georgia, supply center. [In all,] I was in the Marine Corps nineteen years and eleven months and about fifteen days. I'm about fifteen days shy of twenty [years]. I left the Marine Corps [when] I was stationed in Korea [as] one of the advisers for the South Korean offices over there at the time, [while the] Vietnam War was going real hot. I was over there and training the South Korean officers. And my wife was pregnant with the last child and . . . I wanted to be there when she had this baby. I had, I think thirteen days [left when] I flew to San Francisco, and then I went on leave from there, . . . but when I got home the baby didn't come. This sergeant major told me the only way you can stay in the States and [w]on't get in trouble is that you retire. Finally, I made my mind I'm just gonna go ahead and retire, and [I] did. Incidentally, the baby came two days later!

I went out the next day [and] . . . I found a job . . . making plywood in Jacksonville, [North Carolina]. With the children we had, I got to do something, so I got a job. It was a low-paying job, but I took it, and three or four months later I made supervisor out there. And I worked out [at] this plywood [company] for sixteen and a half years with an early retirement. I stayed out of work maybe a year and a half, and then I got another job . . . [at] a store up here in Jacksonville, and I worked there ten years. And then I retired for good. After that, [I helped] . . . develop a church system that we have, [growing it] from a church to a district of churches—we call it Assembly of Churches—and right now there's five of them, and I'm the bishop of all these five churches. One of them [is] located in Tuscaloosa, Alabama, one in East Dover, South Carolina, one up in Beulaville, North Carolina, Richlands and Jacksonville, and we got another one that we been working with out in Medford, Tennessee. So since that day [I retired], we been working [in] church life [with our] friends and relatives.

The fact is that something talked to me, inside of me, when I was fifteen years old that if I didn't make a change, I was gonna be destroyed or something bad was gonna happen. And that's why I joined the Marine Corps. I got in the Marine Corps, the Marine Corps had a great deal [of influence] on me, I mean it changed me. War [also] changed me and my wife changed me. If I had not went in the Marine Corps I probably would have been [lost]. I was just loose out there and I was afraid. And then I got in the Marine Corps and they just changed my disposition altogether. I got in war and it made me mature and, and then I got in the church and the church brought out the love, the compassion, that I was missing, that I had but I wasn't using. And my children, there's twelve children, and I was able to raise them good as we did because of the training I had in the Marine Corps. But my life was changed and this is the way it was. I wouldn't trade nothing for those twenty years I spent in the Marine Corps.

I think about it all the time, I dream about it. Being a Montford Point marine, it gave me some knowledge that I never would have had towards hate, prejudice, difference in peoples. I understand different things because of [having gone to] Montford Point [instead of] Parris Island, South Carolina, or somewhere down there. I wouldn't have got what I got up at Montford Point. I got to know how it is. If you were Black and I were white, I'd know how to treat you now. I would know how to deal with you now. I learned how . . . people try to prove themselves. And we had a lot of that at Montford Point. These people that were over me, they wanted [us to learn that we could do it as well as whites]. "I can do it. If I had to kill this guy, I can do it." And, brother, I was glad that they did because now I can understand better.

[This] December, I'll have been out of the Marine Corps forty years, I retired forty years ago and I'm still in training, so to speak. [It's been] forty years, [but] if I had the opportunity to go down to that post office again and go through all that I went through that changed me from the inside out, and I know this is gonna sound silly, but I would choose the same route. I would have Montford Point set up in the same [racially segregated] predicament, the same system, so I could go through it again. The Korean War was ridiculous, but I would want to go through that. The church is troubled now, but I would want it to be so I could go through it to prove who I am on the inside. I gained a lot at Montford Point—I dumped out a lot, but I gained a lot. And I don't think there's a Black marine that ever went through that place and didn't think himself better when he came out of that.

I was talking to a [white] gunnery sergeant. He and I just met [one day] and we just sat down and started talking. He was about twenty years younger than I was, probably, and . . . he wanted to express something within himself about the racial differences. And I mean he didn't say that, but as we talked, I picked up on that's what he was trying to do. In other words, [it was an] apologetic type of conversation. And as it went, I was able to sit there and tell him about this little place [called] Montford Point, and I could tell him that [I know that] inside of me, I'm the same as you, you're the same as me. And [Montford Point] just made me, I believe, who God would want me to be. I was talking to that Caucasian man and there was no difference, there was no nothing; I mean it was just like me and him were twins. Montford Point taught me this. The Chinese and Korea only taught me how to duck. But Montford Point taught me how to do this, how to feel this way, how to be this way. And now that's what I share with people everywhere I go, I share this with people, what I got from Montford Point.

Johnnie Givian
Corporal, 3rd Company, 5th Batch, 5th Battalion
US Marines
Interviewed August 17, 2005, Jacksonville, NC
Montford Point Marines Project

MARK BRADY HANNAH JR., HOUSTON, TEXAS

My fifty some years that began with the army is in every day of my life. Every day of my life, I still have sweats, I bathe [once] or more a day—I used to get in trouble for using up all the water. Because it's the blood. See, in Korea, we had helicopters, but we had to get [the wounded and killed] back there. We had to get them off patrols. We left nobody—bloody, dead, whatever. And there was quite a few [that were] just blood, blood. And still to this day I don't take baths because it's like bathing in blood. And I just discovered this last year that all these years I've been showering with my eyes shut. It just becomes part of your deal. [But] I'm having a hard time getting [a PTSD diagnosis] because this is where [they] always respond with, "He has three degrees, he studied psychology," and things like that, and so it's a battle.

Sometimes [my sons] check on me, my mother. Even when I was [working] in the Dallas school district I used to go buy a case of beer when I was getting off of work on a Friday, and then Saturday morning I was going and getting another case of beer, and my mother sent the police out to my place many times because I didn't answer the phone. My sons will say, "Well, Dad, when you get ready, you give me a call," so they just know. When I visit them, I have to stay a week and it's very hard. I'm good for about two or three days, [then] I'm ready to be back home. I don't like crowds. I like the school teaching, and working with the kids, and I go on weekends and tutor, but I don't let people get too close to me. Not even my sons. And yet we give big old hugs. They tell me what to do and how to do it. And I like that.

It took me fifty-one years to get my medals. They said they lost my records. Congressman John Culberson, he got my medals for me. He did so much for me. [He and] his assistant Ms. Hodges have worked with me over a year [on getting] the Purple Heart since [I was] burned in the leg. I have twelve or so different medals, but here in the regional office they said that I was not in combat. They were thinking about the cook, truck driver stuff. [But I managed to get my documents that said] "exemplary performance of ground combat," and [when] I was shipped out of the mortar company, [a document that] tells you that Mark Hannah was reassigned. [But] it's sickening [to be fighting for my medals fifty years later]. I almost wanted to take my medals and throw them in the river. I can't listen to the news with our president talking about another war and sending our young guys over there. It breaks my heart. It's very depressing. Yesterday and today is really the first day that I've been out of my place in about a month. Today is very hard.

Mark Brady Hannah Jr.
Platoon sergeant, 224th Regiment, 40th Infantry Division
US Army
Interviewed by David P. Cline, January 10, 2003, Houston, TX
American RadioWorks, Minnesota Public Radio

LAURENCE "LARRY" HOGAN, BOSTON, MASSACHUSETTS

Memories, memories, emotions, emotions. It never changes. [War is] just amazing. It's life, it's life. I'll tell you this: it's the realest thing I've ever done. I heard a guy say that the other day, I've read that over the years in various ways. That's why people go out, that's why you get all these wars and stuff like that. People get hung up on that stuff and start doin' it. It's [like] nothin' else. It's better than drinkin'. It's better than any high. Because if you come that close [to death], you know, and then to come [out] of it [alive], you can't turn it off, you never forget it. I met a lot of people over the years who say, "My father didn't talk about it." I say, "Man, go home and talk to your father." But you can't forget it. And the older I get, I think about all the people [who died] at such a young age, and I've lived a long time now, this is fifty years later, I've lived a long time, good guys, guys had wives and kids and shit. I was seventeen, eighteen.

When I was in Korea, [ready to cycle out], they said, "You want to make another strike? All you have to do is go down here to French Indochina, all you have to do is get some guys and train them." I said, "No, when I leave this land, I leave it!" A couple of guys I know, they went down there. This was way before Vietnam, that stupid thing. I did thirty-six months [and] when I came back I still had nineteen months to go. I went back to Fort Dix [and] I was in charge of the firing ranges, I was one of the [cadre] there. A lot of people are asking me, "You want to get an early out?" "You want to make another strike?" I said, "I don't need [it], I'm a hard sergeant." So, I came out, got out, got married, went into business, and after twenty-two years I still like the military and everything. So one day I'm talking to a guy I know, and he's like, "Why don't you join the National Guard for one year, because we need guys?" I said okay, joined for a year, and wound up doing another seventeen years in the National Guard. I ended up being the aide to Brigadier General John Carson, who was the assistant AG of the Massachusetts National Guard. I spent the last eight years with him, and it was really great. He was a good general, a good man. I retired in 1994 and I was, at the time, the oldest combat veteran to retire. So I have [had] a pretty interesting career as far as the military.

I always talk about the guys that are gone because I won't be silent about it. I think that's a disservice. I lived! [But] how the hell are you going to know about this other guy? How are you going to know that people made sacrifices so you could sit here and do what you're doing? I did my part of it, but I'm doing alright. What about the guy that's not doing alright? That's the reason you're here! Because he stood up there! And this is in all the wars! People talk about we're war mongers . . . let me tell you something, from what I see in this country, this is the best country on the face of the earth. You can do more here than you can anywhere else. You got freedom here. You got free minds. Nobody tells you: "Don't write that." I know this, the people that write history make history. And that's why I go out and speak. Tell my poem or [talk] a little about the war, try to be good PR for the military. Because they need it, they don't make much money, and what they do is a hell of a lot more than a fireman, I'm tellin' you. Many people don't see it. They say many are called and few are chosen, but people don't see what they do. Them guys are out there, they're out there, they're puttin' a lot out. It's a big sacrifice.

Laurence "Larry" Hogan
Sergeant 1st class, 31st Infantry Regiment, 7th Infantry Division
US Army
Interviewed by David P. Cline, October 25, 2002, Boston, MA
American RadioWorks, Minnesota Public Radio

Like Clarence Jones, a number of important activists in the civil rights struggle spent their time in the US military just after the Korean War ended on July 27, 1953. The final two men here each demanded serious change from their country and were unwilling to take anything less. James Meredith famously and courageously desegregated the University of Mississippi. And Elbert "Big Man" Howard was one of the six young students who created the Black Panther Party. Like the poet and cultural critic Amiri Baraka, they were veterans of the US Air Force in the mid- to late 1950s and took those experiences into the shaping of conceptions of Black Power and change on their own terms. Howard recalled, in a self-published memoir years later, that when he was sent to Knoxville, Tennessee, in

1956, three or more years after the Korean War supposedly eliminated segregation in the military, Black recruits could not be put up in the same hotel as white
recruits and were instead housed "in this old Black gentleman's house" near the
bus station. "That's where they put the Blacks up for the night. I thought that
was kind of racist." The next day, in Atlanta on his way to San Antonio, Texas,
a taxi driver refused to take him to a local movie theater. "The taxi driver [said,]
'Yeah, there's a movie [theater] but no niggers allowed. That nigger can't go.' I'm
enlisted in the Air Force to probably fight for this fat, white bastard and he's up
here talking about 'nigger can't go to the movie.'"[1] While overt Jim Crow may
have receded into the past, many of the other problems of systematic racism that
Howard and other identified and the solutions they suggested remain stunningly
relevant in the age of the Black Lives Matter movement, some fifty years later.

JAMES MEREDITH, JACKSON, MISSISSIPPI

The only thing that was really important to me [in the air force was] I could
see [the notion of white superiority] was all manmade, and if it was manmade,
I thought I was smart enough to unmake it. So that was what was important.
But more important was 1957, when Eisenhower sent troops to Little Rock. And
I had always known that power—I had calculated that the only way to defeat
Mississippi was to get a greater armed force on my side, and I knew I'd have to
force the federal government into assisting me to do that.

Well, now, whether it's true or not [that I would be able to change the sys-
tem], I was in the military nine years. I was only a sergeant, but I ran every outfit
I was in. I mean, I maneuvered and [got] whatever I wanted done. I was efficient. Every commander wanted to look best, and I could make that happen.
So that gave me a power, and it's very important. You know, when you get old,
you can think how foolish you were at some earlier periods of time, but I always
somehow felt that it was going to go my way. I ain't never had the feeling it
wasn't, and I also know that that impacted a whole lot of folks. You see my picture [from the University of Mississippi]—that just might look innocent, but
that's twenty years of practice, how you look like that. There's a reason why I
looked like that. One of those great old historians wrote about the pope the last
time his troops conquered Rome, and how he looked when he walked. He had
his troops stop at the edge of the city, and he walked alone into the heart of the
city, and he looked a certain way, and it was to have an impact. My intent, and it
worked, was to scare the life out of everybody that was around me, and it happened. I mean, they would be shaking like leaves on a tree.

So then all I had to do was figure out how to now go back to Mississippi and
get this force, this powerful force, on my side, and there was a lot of luck involved. This is something that is very little known: I got out of the military and

came back to Mississippi to restore the power and the glory to my bloodline, but I quickly found out that the timing wasn't right [with Eisenhower as president]. See, I selected my station to launch my war. I came to Mississippi to conduct a war against white supremacy, and to me, it didn't have nothing to do with education and all that good stuff. It was strictly [about civil rights].

As a ploy, [President John F.] Kennedy toyed with . . . [a] civil rights plan. He not only got it in, but it elected him. So now it was a matter of time, and the day Kennedy took the oath of office, that same day, I dropped my letter in the mail to Ole Miss. Because I wanted to put pressure. You see, the civil rights plan was a political position and ploy, and it had been little talked about since [the primaries]. I wanted to force the Kennedys to either live up to it or be immediately criticized for not doing what they said they would do.

Well, first of all, naturally, I didn't tell them I was Black, and they sent me a letter of admission, told me when to report, and then, by the way, included an application, which had a photo spot on it. When I sent the application back with the photo, they immediately recognized what they had, and they sent me a telegram, telling me not to appear, that they had to discontinue considering applications the day before they received mine. Then, within a couple of days, I wrote the Kennedys, and the letter that I wrote Kennedy is now on display in Boston in the Kennedy Library and on Robert Kennedy's desk, which is the only thing in the rotunda in the Justice Department in Washington, and my letter is right in the center of his desk. [In it,] I said that I'm a citizen, and if I'm a citizen, the government is supposed to support my right to citizenship, and I implied that if it didn't, I was going to go to war.

James Meredith
Staff sergeant, unit unknown
US Air Force
Interviewed by Renee Poussaint, June 27, 2006, Jackson, MS
National Visionary Leadership Project, Library of Congress

ELBERT "BIG MAN" HOWARD, SANTA ROSA, CALIFORNIA

Ready? Okay, my name is Elbert "Big Man" Howard, and I'm a native of Chattanooga, Tennessee, but a longtime resident of California, Northern California specifically. And I wound up in Northern California after military service, spending four years in the air force. I decided I wanted to be discharged in California because I loved it here. I loved the people, and being a young man, I was trying to find my way, and so I ventured into Oakland and started my formal education in Oakland at Merritt College.

Growing up, I don't know if it was typical or not, but my father died [and] I never knew him. All I knew was my mother and aunts and cousins, and I think that I was pretty much raised up by women, the aunts, my mother's sisters. And then my cousins were, I guess you could say, my brothers and sisters really. I attended school and high school . . . and I think long about 1954, they began to talk about integrating schools, and you know, I heard about that and I told myself, I have no problems going to school with white kids. I have my own set of friends and, living in my own set of society, so I'm not up for that, but if it happens, it happens. But I had teachers who I thought were concerned about me, who tried to teach me things that I needed to know to survive in a hostile world. So, I had no problem not wanting to integrate, or anything like that.

I went through to the eleventh grade, and my mother, being a single parent and everything, I got to growing up and becoming an adult. I figured one of the best ways for me to help support her and to develop myself was to join the military, the air force. After conversing with a lot of my friends who had been through basic training and all of that and come back—I picked their brains as to what it was all about—I made my selection to choose the air force. That was right [about] 1956, I think I went in. I missed [the Korean War, but] I had some relatives that had been to war and stuff like that, and they advised me to stay away from the army, for one thing. Because the army was the catapult to going into combat. And what I could find out about the air force is: you go in, you go through your basic training and everything, and after that it was like a job. You went to work, you did what you were told, and you had three meals a day, a decent place to live, and you had freedom to explore the places that they sent you to. So I felt very fortunate to be sent to Europe. I got to know Paris and Stockholm and Copenhagen.

I visited all those places and met different people, and to me it was a revelation and eye-opening to meet people of other cultures, and realize that even though the people were Caucasian or white, if you want to give it a color, they were very different than the whites that I had a great fear of in the South, that I grew up with. So that was a revelation and a learning experience, and to immerse myself and learn about their cultures, learn how to drink wine and go to art museums and be taught stuff, that was a good part of maturity, maturing, to me.

[There were still] little nuances of segregation and even in France, which is a different environment, you had the Blacks hanging together because, I don't know, our cultural similarities or whatever. And you got along with the whites, but again, when it comes to stuff like economics, when it comes to promotions and stuff like that, you were looked over or screwed over, and so you just let it go by and enjoy yourself, you know? And learn what you wanted to learn, and survive, [and] to a great extent, be happy without having to look over your shoulder all the time.

At the time [I enlisted,] I thought it was kind of a way out, to learn something different and at the same time to support my mother, through an allotment. She got a check every month, and I had food and shelter and everything for myself, and to me it was a pretty good deal. I just had to put up with whatever I had to put up with, and it wasn't all that strenuous. Just abide by the rules and the routines and do what you were told, and as long as you were there in the camp or whatever, or when you got your free time, you had a chance to get out and explore and pretty much have a good time, you know? Go to jazz clubs and converse with jazz musicians who had left the US for the freedom of Europe, to be able to practice their art, and so forth. [It] became an adventure, for me.

[And when] I was still in the service on the air base in Northern California, I used to go into town in Oakland, and that's where I met a lot of people [and learned], you know, the very rich culture. You had blues and jazz and great soul food and friendly people, and they took me under their wing, so to speak, as a young trooper, and showed me around, and I enjoyed that. So when I got my discharge, I decided to take it here in Northern California, and hang out in Oakland. And not really having any focus as to what I really wanted to do, I looked for a job, and at that time they were very hard to come by, pretty much as they are today.

I had educational benefits from the air force, so I decided to enter into City College in Oakland, and draw on my GI Bill, use that to sustain me until I found some type of employment and all that. And in the meantime, well, I began to study Black history and stuff like that, and I didn't have any real academic ambitions, but I always thought that I wanted to be able to write, and express myself clearly, so I took some courses in writing in school to try to develop writing skills. Nothing professional, just my own, when I wanted to convey something, to be able to do it.

And enrolling in Merritt College, I began to associate with other students who had similar interests, and that's where I met Bobby Seale and Huey Newton. After our classes, we'd have rap sessions and talk about these things, and talk about ways of dealing with them, because we had repression going on in Oakland. Police repression—people getting killed by cops every week. And we would kick around ways of dealing with that, try to figure out a different way of approaching it as opposed to the Civil Rights [Movement] and the nonviolence, and all that sort of stuff. Because we knew what that was about, but we were trying to develop a new approach, something progressive and revolutionary, if you will. Bobby Seale said, "I want you to meet Huey, and we're thinking of starting a new organization," and they started to develop the Ten-Point Platform and Program, which was the mandate that would differentiate us from other organizations. Because [there were] other organizations that dealt with culture, Swahili camps, learning the language, and stuff like that. We were more interested in trying to deal with combating the ills in the community on a progressive and a revolutionary level.

We want[ed] freedom. We want[ed] the power to determine our destiny, which was number one on the list, and we felt we were occupied by police forces doing the bidding of the rich politicians. So, we began to study things like the writings of Che Guevara and Mao Zedong, [and] of course, Malcolm X and all the revolutionary people around the world. And we started to cherry-pick some of their philosophies and ways of thinking and apply it to what we wanted to do. Because we fully realized that we were not in China, we were not in Cuba, and we could emulate anything that those people did, but we had to come up with our own approach, utilizing what we could from these great people. That's where we got a lot of our philosophy.

Bobby [Seale], I hung more with him than with Huey [Newton]. Huey was always in and out, so to speak, but he was, to me, very knowledgeable about the justice system because he had been through it, and whenever I had a case or some problem with the police, I could usually go to Huey and say, "How should I approach this?" And going to court, and stuff like that, too, he knew how I should do that, and so I got some advice from him. But we never hung together, except for having meetings as the organization began to come together and grow, you know. I saw more of him then, but Bobby, to me, had a great skill for organizing. He had great ideas and at the time, early on, a lot of them seemed very far-fetched to me, but I've always been a listener—[I] try to internalize what I'm hearing and put it in the locker for later references.

But we would get together with other kids on campus and we'd sit down, and we would go back and forth about approaches, and ways of solving problems, and so forth, and in the meantime, Bobby said, "We're starting a new organization," and then we began to work on that Ten-Point Platform and Program. And Richard Aoki, who was an Asian who pretty much grew up—after he got out of that damn camp [Topaz War Relocation Center in Utah] that they put his family in—he began to live and associate with the other poor and oppressed people in Oakland. I mean Black people. So, he used to hang. He would work with Bobby on that Ten-Point Platform and Program, and it started to come together, our ideas and so forth. And we began to talk more and more with more and more people, and they'd say, "Yes, I can relate to these ideas," and so forth. "What do we do next?" [It came] together pretty much like that.

As I said, I enjoyed going out to Oakland to the blues and jazz clubs and so on, and one night I was out at a club, and Don Barksdale was the guy that run the club, a Black ex-basketball player, and I think it was Lou Rawls, when he was first coming on and getting popular, [we] went out to see his show, me and my date. And when it was over, we were leaving, and it was drizzling outside, so I told my date, "Wait here, I'm going to go and get my vehicle, and I'll come back and pick you up right here in front of the club." So I pull up in front of the club, waiting for her to come out, and the cops come up and start writing tickets. Well, they wrote me a ticket. And I looked behind me, they didn't write the guy behind me one, and the person ahead of me. I took offense, because I had a brand-new red pickup truck. I protested. I asked them, "Why the hell am I getting a ticket and you didn't write these other people any?" And they said something smart, and I said, "Well, fuck this, I'm taking off," so I got in my truck and took off, and then here comes the gang. Box me in, and took me and my pickup to jail.

So, from then on, I said, "Well, I got to get involved with something that combats this kind of crap." And this is what Huey and Bobby were talking about, ... and I asked Huey to advise me. And he went to court with me, and the judge says, well, something that offended me, something like, "He's probably guilty, but I'm going to dismiss it." In the meantime, the cops were sitting there in the court laughing and shit. I got highly pissed off about that. Anyway, they dismissed the case. After that [incident] I [was] very angry, and I took to driving around in my pickup, where I had a rack put in the back of it, and I put a legal shotgun in the back of it. So I rode around and I'd say, "Well, I'm as good as some of these rednecks that ride around like this, and if I'm ever confronted, I'm going to defend myself, period." So luckily, nothing happened, and I didn't have to do that, but I continued to [drive around]. As I joined the [Black Panther] Party, I continued to do that. On the way to take Huey home after the court date, I [had] asked him about the legalities of carrying a weapon in a car, and he schooled me on that. That's why I was able to do that. I knew that it was perfectly legal, and it was a twelve-gauge shotgun that I purchased, and went from there.

A little bit later on, when we began to get more members and we began to acquire more firearms and stuff, and once again, consulting with Huey—he knew the law and knew that we could do that legally—we began to do that at night, on the weekends, when we knew cops were patrolling our community. And so we decided that we would get out and patrol them, and not to confront them, necessarily, and engage in any battle, but to teach people in the community that they had rights. And we would advise people when they were stopped by the cops. We'd get out and observe the cops so-called performing their duty. We were on the scene [so that] they were not abusing people, [but] they became more concerned with these young Black people with guns! So we would advise people that are being arrested, "Go ahead and take the arrest, don't resist, and we're going to follow you down to the courthouse and we're going to bail you out." And we did that, and people began to wonder, who are these guys? Why would they be doing that? As a result, they'd drop around to the Panther office to find out more about it, and we began to gain recruits, more people to join the party, ... [and] that was building up the organization, with people coming in.

The attitude of many young people coming in was that [they thought] the emphasis on the Black Panther Party [was just] that we would confront cops and be ready to deal with shootouts and so forth. But when they'd come in, we'd say, "No, we' re going to have political education class, it's on such-and-such a night." If we hadn't scheduled one, [we'd say,] "Give us your phone number and we'll call you and tell you when we're going to hold it," and we began to teach revolutionary principles. [That was] more what we were about, and it went from there. We weren't in the business of getting anybody killed at that point, but at the same time, we were determined to defend ourselves no matter what. We were determined, [if] any of our members [were] arrested, if they went to jail, we were going to do everything we could to get them out as quick as possible. And so, of course, that pissed the authorities off, too. If you're not creating animosity or hate, then you're not doing very much against the system or the people that propagate the repression.

I learned a lot from Bobby in terms of dealing with the ills of the community—like the Denzil Dowell incident in Richmond [California]. Denzil Dowell's family wasn't getting any answers from the authorities, . . . [who said] that they were justified in shooting this kid in the back as he ran and tried to climb a fence. And his mother knew . . . that he couldn't possibly jump a fence because he had some injury. People . . . had taken notice of the Black Panther Party [and they came to us], and so we exposed that as a lie. And we had a demonstration in front of the Richmond courthouse to protest that. . . . So, that was one of the first organized rallies that we had. By the way, we were armed when we went to that rally, and that, of course, drew the attention of the police and all that, but it was part of the growing process.

The symbolic power [of being armed] was that the people in the community saw that, and they saw that we weren't rushed or put upon by the authorities because we were there ready to defend ourselves and, in essence, to defend the community if necessary. So, we had a demonstrated determination to do that, and the people saw that, and so that, once again, drew people to us. We began to get more requests of support, whatever, and whenever we would call a rally, bunches and bunches of people would show up without fear, and with enthusiasm. [They were] willing to help, and help us in whatever endeavor we were getting into, donations for this, that, and the other. We needed an office, and we had to pay rent for an office to have a focus in the community where people could relate to, rather than just [be a] roaming group of young men with guns—[to] have a place for people to come if they wanted to join, or to come and give us a small donation, what have you. So, we were in the community. We were visible in the community, so it kind of started there.

Bobby Seale said something when we were at the [first] rally, said, "We need our own organ, we need our own news facilities," so we come up with a [newspaper] we were going to mimeograph, and then I did the text to it and Bobby Seale did the graphics, drew the panther on it, and all of that. We gave that out and that was really the beginning of our news outlet. We were all young and feeling our way, as I said, . . . [but] I had written little quips for different little radical publications in the community, and Bobby said, "Well, you can be our first editor. You can be editor of the paper, and we're going to do some progressive moves and develop this thing, and you can be the editor," and I would say, "Well, I don't know much about being an editor." But [I had] that fierce determination to do whatever was necessary, [so] I said, "Well, I'll do it." So, it started out and people [would] write articles, and I would read them [and edit them so] that it would be more readable and so forth when we printed it. It kind of started there — I said, "Well, okay, I'll do whatever's necessary." Eventually, Eldridge Cleaver got out of prison, and he was a best-selling author with his book, *Soul on Ice*, and we said, "Well, we're going to make Eldridge the editor — I said, 'fine' — and he'll be the minister of information and you be the deputy minister of information." Whatever.

[Giving speeches,] that came later. We needed a steady stream of information going out, so I would write some articles, Bobby would write some articles, and other people. We did what we thought was right, to put out some cohesive information to the community. So, from there, speeches came later as more of the main speakers went to jail, and all of that. Other people had to step up, and I had never considered myself a public speaker or anything, but once again, that old hard-nosed determination said I was going to do whatever the hell it took to advance this vehicle we got going, so I took a shot at it and [it] turned out all right. The more you do it, the more coherent, I guess, I was. I had a billion things to do. We had other people step in, because Eldridge, he would write an article now and then, but he became a popular spokesman, and so he was always somewhere doing his thing.

I had people come in and take responsibility for the paper. I had other things to do, because as many members started to get busted across the country and going to jail and everything, I was selected, if you will, to go and deal with that. I began to crisscross the country going to different penitentiaries and jails to see about party members, to see if they had any needs, and also see what the legal situation was, and see how I could help with their legal defense, talk to lawyers. [I would] also talk to people in the particular community, wherever these people were in jail, and begin to try to organize defense committees in the community to deal with getting that person out of jail. I was quite busy with that for a long, long time. That was my job for a long time, and I would go from Denver to New Orleans, wherever we had people locked up. Some of the big issues came up when they were framing Bobby Seale and all, and Ericka [Huggins], and all those people in New Haven [Connecticut]. I had to pick up and move to New Haven, and work on those issues. [It] wasn't public knowledge what I did, in newspapers and all that stuff, and that was fine with me because I had my hands full dodging the authorities and sidestepping traps that they might be setting for me, and moving and doing what I needed to do.

But that's the way that started. But I never gave too much importance to a title. I just wanted to do the work. I just wanted to make [a difference], do something, to stick a fucking fork in the system.

Elbert "Big Man" Howard
Rank and unit unknown
US Air Force
Interviewed by David P. Cline, June 30, 2016, Santa Rosa, CA
American RadioWorks, Minnesota Public Radio

Conclusion
Remembering

Heroes come in different forms, and the African Americans who served during the Korean War era provided many examples. Courtney L. Stanley certainly fit the expected description—a Black private from Louisiana, he was just nineteen years old and seeing his very first combat with L Company of the 9th Infantry Regiment, 2nd Division, when they came under heavy fire from two Chinese regiments. His commanding officer, Harry A. Clark from Columbus, Georgia, led the replacement platoon under heavy fire, stopping only when the third of three wounds took out the use of his legs. Stanley and a fellow soldier helped Clark into a bunker, and then Stanley stood in a trench out front, fighting off the enemy and defending the bunker single-handedly for three and a half hours.[1] He fought off an encroaching group of some fifteen Chinese soldiers, firing his BAR until it jammed, then grabbed an M1, killing at least eight of the enemy and saving the lieutenant colonel.[2] One line officer recounted that Stanley "stood over his commanding officer and killed [the enemy] left and right," and Stanley's commanding officer later described the private as the "bravest man I ever saw."[3] Of the 150 men in Stanley's company, 134 were killed or wounded.[4]

A week later, both Stanley and Clark received the Silver Star from Maj. Gen. James C. Fry. Stanley was also told he'd be receiving the Distinguished Service Cross, and he then returned immediately to the front line.[5] Clark would eventually return to his native Georgia, where Jim Crow still stood strong and even military integration was opposed.

Clyde Kennard's name is little said now, but he should also be considered an American hero. Kennard also has one of the most heartbreaking stories of African American veterans, a proud veteran who just wanted an education and was instead broken by the system and essentially murdered by his own government. Kennard was born in Hattiesburg, Mississippi, in 1927 but moved to Chicago to help care for an older sister. He joined the US Army in 1945 at the age of eighteen and served for seven years, including as a paratrooper during the first two years of the Korean War. He earned the Korean Service and United

Nations Service Medals, a Good Conduct Medal, and the Bronze Service Star. While stationed in Fort Bragg, North Carolina, he took classes at Fayetteville State Teachers College. After leaving the military, he transferred to the University of Chicago. In 1955, as Kennard was finishing his junior year, his stepfather died, and he returned home to Mississippi to help his mother on her chicken farm.[6] Soon after returning to Hattiesburg, he contacted Mississippi Southern College, now the University of Southern Mississippi, to inquire about finishing his education there. Knowing full well that it was a segregated white institution, Kennard eventually met with the college's president and registrar, who said that all of his application materials were in order except the requirement to provide five letters of recommendation from alumni living in his home county of Forrest. University officials, however, refused to give Kennard the names of alumni, and his application was rejected. He applied two more times, in 1958 and 1959, and on September 15, 1959, he drove to campus to register, where he was again turned away. Knowing that he was coming, campus police intercepted him as he was sitting in his car on campus and charged him with speeding and possession of five pints of whiskey and other liquor bottles, allegedly hidden under his front seat and forbidden in a dry county. Although his car was parked at the time he was allegedly speeding, he did not drink, and he had no liquor, he was found guilty on both charges and fined six hundred dollars.[7]

Kennard appealed the charges, which were thrown out by the state supreme court, but Hattiesburg police arrested him again in mid-November 1960, this time for allegedly inducing a nineteen-year-old local African American man to steal five bags of chicken feed, valued at twenty-five dollars. He was sentenced to seven years' hard labor at the Mississippi State Penitentiary at Parchman Farm. Kennard's friend and NAACP activist and fellow army veteran Medgar Evers broke down in tears at a rally after the sentencing, decrying it as a "mockery of justice." The comedian and activist Dick Gregory hired investigators at his own expense to discover the truth and found the boy who had actually committed the theft, but he was unwilling to testify for Kennard out of fear of retaliation against his family.[8]

After serving about a year in prison, Kennard was diagnosed with colon cancer and was treated at the University of Mississippi Hospital by doctors who pleaded with prison officials to release him, turn him over to their care, or at the very least allow him regular clinical visits. Instead, Kennard was returned to Parchman and forced to work six days a week in the cotton fields as his condition rapidly deteriorated over the next eighteen months.[9] Only after the intervention of Martin Luther King Jr., Medgar Evers, and others who accused Governor Ross Barnett of murder was Kennard's sentence suspended and he was allowed to seek surgery at Billings Hospital in Chicago. It was too late to save him, however, and he died on Independence Day, July 4, 1963, less than a month after

Evers was assassinated in Mississippi. Dr. Andrew L. Thomas, a Black physician and civil rights activist in Chicago, proclaimed a few days later that "the Mississippi prison people murdered Clyde by inaction," since the cancer had been eminently treatable when first discovered. "With proper follow-up, no doubt Clyde's situation would have resulted in a longer life. Prison officials murdered him through negligence." Trying to see some hope in the Korean War veteran's life and unnecessary death, Thomas concluded, "His death is one of the most heroic in the civil rights struggle and should serve as a beacon for more people to get involved in destroying the kind of evil forces that murdered him."[10] However, Mississippi civil rights historian John Dittmer would come to a different conclusion about the martyrdom of Clyde Kennard: "It was the saddest story of the whole movement."[11] In 2005, more than forty years later, Johnny Lee Roberts, the chicken feed thief whose testimony had convicted Kennard, told a reporter that Kennard had nothing to do with the planned theft and had been arrested and convicted "not because of the feed but because he was trying to go to Southern." Roberts wanted to set the record straight because he "always felt bad about what happened to Clyde."[12] On May 16, 2006, in the same courtroom in which he had been tried, Kennard's conviction was overturned, and he was declared not guilty.[13]

Kennard had dared to challenge the status quo in Mississippi, regarded by the NAACP as "the worst state" in the country when it came to the treatment of Black people, and he paid dearly for it. It is impossible to know exactly why he determined to take on the state's Jim Crow laws, especially since those who knew him described him as "extremely polite and soft-spoken" and "just as nice a person as you wanted to meet, . . . just a Christian, but some have seen clues in his military background."[14] Historians Timothy Minchin and John Salmond cite Kennard as one of the instances in which "military service was . . . crucial in motivating a generation of southern Black men to fight for their civil rights at home" after having gone "'overseas to protect my country, try to fight for my country, and then come back and be a second-class citizen."[15] And as the Reverend Malcolm Boyd, a civil rights and gay rights activist, noted after Kennard's death, "He believed. This alone could account for his ordeal. He believed in his right to be a human being in this life on this earth." Boyd concluded, "Freedom cannot exist without, from time to time, the blood of martyrs. Clyde Kennard is a saint of freedom."[16]

There is much in our present world that could benefit from the lessons hard learned by Black veterans of the Korean War. As their generation reaches the end of their long and many battles, it is time that we remember, that we remember at last.

Acknowledgments

Most history books come about from the work of far more people than the name on the cover and result from perhaps far more time than one had wished, and what you hold in your hand is proof of that to an exponential extent. The African American men and women who served in the US military during the Korean War era did so seventy years ago or more; first and foremost, I want to acknowledge my admiration and gratitude for their service overseas during the particularly fraught years in which the Cold War and Jim Crow bitterly and sometimes brutally overlapped. And I wish to thank all those, some gathered here and many more elsewhere, who shared their important stories, without which we would have a far poorer idea of that pivotal era. Time after time I was welcomed into homes, VFW halls, and library meeting rooms by folks who entrusted their sacred recollections to a stranger and made a friend for life. Each time I read through these stories, stories I myself have now lived with for decades, is always a humbling journey of discovery. We are honored to have been gifted these words. I also thank all of those who had the foresight to listen and to gather these stories. Although I have had the great good fortune and pleasure of interviewing a number of Korean War veterans, I have also relied heavily on the work of others, especially those ordinary Americans who have contributed thousands of recordings to the Veterans Oral History Project at the Library of Congress. My thanks to them and to the tireless staff at the VOHP, especially Megan Harris.

I first began work on this project in 2002—yikes—as an intern with American RadioWorks at Minnesota Public Radio, working on the documentary "Korea: The Unfinished War." I am indebted to Professors Marla Miller and David Glassberg at the University of Massachusetts at Amherst, who have created a truly exemplary Public History program, and to Deborah George, Stephen Smith, Kate Ellis, John Biewen, and Sasha Aslanian at ARW and Minneapolis Public Radio for welcoming me onto the project and for their years of producing important and compelling audio.

I would also like to thank the Harry S. Truman Library and Museum, Independence, Missouri, and the College of Liberal Arts and Human Sciences at Virginia Tech, Blacksburg, Virginia, for research support and much appreciated time for writing. The librarians there and at the University of Hawai'i at Manoa, Joanie Schwarz-Wetter at the Marine Corps Recruit Depot Museum in San Diego, and Rebecca Baugnon, Special Collections Librarian at the William M. Randall Library at the University North Carolina Wilmington, all provided wonderful research support.

Thanks, too, are owed my former colleagues in the History Department at Virginia Tech, and especially Chair Mark Barrow, for reading drafts, encouraging me to write "a real book," and providing support on the project and a fantastic intellectual community for several years. Peter Wallenstein, who has been a mentor and is a generally outstanding example of a human being, deserves special mention as always. And thanks to the members of the Team Awesome digital history research group, who made my years in Blacksburg a heck of a lot more fun.

My colleagues on the Civil Rights History Project of the Library of Congress and the Smithsonian's Museum of African American History and Culture were always generous with their time and support and good humor, and tolerant of my constant attempts to bring the Korean War into the historiography of the civil rights movement. One could not ask for a better team than John Bishop, Seth Kotch, and, above all, gentleman scholar Guha Shankar of the American Folk Life Center of the Library of Congress. Thank you to all of his generous colleagues at the AFLC and to Elaine Nichols at the National Museum of African American History and Culture.

The History Department at the University of Hawai'i at Manoa, with Chairs David Hanlon and Shana Brown and Dean Peter Arnade, kindly gave me an office, with blessed air conditioning, library privileges, and much appreciated aloha kindness during the spring of 2018 as I worked on the key central chapters of this book.

My colleagues in the History Department at San Diego State University have been incredibly welcoming and supportive in my return to California after thirty years away. Chair Andy Weise made a welcome home for me in the department, and Ed Beasley has kept the tradition going and has laid the foundations for our two new centers, the Center for War and Society and the Center for Public and Oral History. Dr. Greg Daddis, director of the Center for War and Society, immediately became a cherished colleague and friend. Thank you especially to the SDSU College of Arts and Letters for time away from the classroom in order to, after two decades, complete this work. And thanks to Deans Glen McClish, Monica Casper, Patrick McCarthy, and Scott Walter for their support of the San Diego State University Center for Public and Oral History.

And much gratitude to my partners at the center, the fabulous Gloria Rhodes of SDSU Library and Todd Kennedy of SDSU's Veterans and Military Programs. I also owe much of my happiness here in California to the cabal of surfing professors who welcomed a kook into their mix with shocking good humor and plenty of craft beer—Mike "Rogers" Roberts, Jess "Kiwi" Pontig, and David "Van Beethoven" Kamper. Thanks, guys.

Importantly, a heartfelt thank-you to Mark Simpson-Vos, editorial director at UNC Press, who first expressed interest in this project a decade ago, and to my absolutely terrific editor—twice over now—Brandon Proia, for his patience, guidance, patience, suggestions, encouragement, and patience. Without Brandon, I might still be futzing over the manuscript ten years from now. I honestly couldn't imagine a better editorial team to have in my corner.

And even though I thanked them at the start of this, I wish to thank again the veterans who were so generous with their time and memories. To them I give great admiration and gratitude, while begging their forgiveness for taking approximately seven times longer than the Korean War lasted to get their words on the page.

Last, I wish to thank my daughter, Genevieve, my family, the lovely Penny, and those friends and confidantes who traveled some of the many parts of this long journey along with me.

Notes

PREFACE

1. Charles M. Bussey, *Firefight at Yechon: Courage and Racism in the Korean War* (Lincoln: University of Nebraska Press, 2002), 1.

2. Adriane Lentz-Smith, *Freedom Struggles: African Americans and World War I* (Cambridge, MA: Harvard University Press, 2009), Kindle.

3. Todd J. Moye, *Freedom Flyers: The Tuskegee Airmen of World War II* (New York: Oxford University Press, 2010).

4. Martin Luther King Jr., *A Testament of Hope: The Essential Writings and Speeches*, ed. James M. Washington (New York: HarperOne, 1986), 118.

5. Richard Hooker, *M*A*S*H* (1968; repr., New York: Pocket Books, 1969), 126, 129–30.

6. Leo Bogart, ed., *Project Clear: Social Research and the Desegregation of the United States Army* (1969; repr., New Brunswick, NJ: Transaction Publishers, 1992).

7. C. D. Halliburton, "South of the Mason-Dixon: By-Product of Army Integration," *Philadelphia Tribune*, Sept. 11, 1951, 4.

8. *Steel Helmet*, written, directed, and produced by Samuel Fuller (Deputy Corp., 1951), 84 mins. The character of the Black medic calmly responded, "You're right I'm in the back of the bus, but one day I might be in the middle."

9. Korean War 50th Anniversary website fact sheet, archived at http://jackiewhiting .net/ushistory/coldwar/afamkorea.htm.

10. John B. Jackson, 4.2 Mortar Company, 22nd Regiment, 2nd Division, US Army, interview by author, Jan. 10, 2003, Houston, TX, author's collection.

11. "National Grapevine: Give Us Eyes to See," *Chicago Defender*, July 29, 1950, 6.

12. James Forman, *The Making of Black Revolutionaries* (Seattle: University of Washington Press, 1972), 63.

INTRODUCTION

1. Legislation passed in 1866 and 1869 required the US Army to maintain the four all-Black regiments that had come out of the Civil War era. In 1867, by federal statute, Blacks were able to participate in militias, and a number of states integrated their state militias. As in civilian life, Blacks in the military could participate, but only if they remained separate; this doctrine of "separate but equal" was eventually made national racial policy by the Supreme Court's *Plessy v. Ferguson* decision in 1896. The army attempted to apply the

principals of *Plessy* to its four Black regiments, with Black soldiers separated from whites but receiving training and pay equal to that of their white counterparts and adhering to the same regulations. For good general overviews of Black military service, see bibliography.

2. Sherie Mershon and Steven Schlossman, *Foxholes and Color Lines: Desegregating the U.S. Armed Forces* (Baltimore: Johns Hopkins University Press, 2002), 6.

3. Adriane Lentz-Smith, *Freedom Struggles: African Americans and World War I* (Cambridge, MA: Harvard University Press, 2009), 60.

4. "In Our Opinion: The Brownsville Affray," *Chicago Daily Defender*, Oct. 7, 1972, 8.

5. W. E. B. Du Bois, "The Reward," *Crisis*, September 1918, 217.

6. James Jeffrey, "Remembering the Black Soldiers Executed after Houston's 1917 Race Riot," *The World*, Feb. 1, 2018, https://www.pri.org/stories/2018-02-01/remembering -black-soldiers-executed-after-houstons-1917-race-riot.

7. Lentz-Smith, *Freedom Struggles*, 60.

8. Maj. Gen. Tasker Bliss to Secretary of War, Aug. 24, 1917, in *Blacks in the United States Armed Forces: Basic Documents*, vol. 4, *Segregation Entrenched, 1917–1940*, ed. Morris J. MacGregor and Bernard C. Nalty (Wilmington, DE: Scholarly Resources, 1977), item 5.

9. Mershon and Schlossman, *Foxholes and Color Lines*, 7.

10. Mershon and Schlossman, 5–6, as published in L. Albert Scipio, *Last of the Black Regulars: A History of the 24th Infantry Regiment, 1869–1951* (Silver Spring, MD: Roman Publications, 1983), 135.

11. William T. Bowers, William M. Hammond, and George L. MacGarrigle, *Black Soldier, White Army: The 24th Infantry Regiment in Korea* (Honolulu: University of Hawai'i Press, 2005), 16–17.

12. Bowers, Hammond, and MacGarrigle, 19, quoting Du Bois, *Crisis*, September 1925, 218–19.

13. Mershon and Schlossman, *Foxholes and Color Lines*, 8.

14. Richard M. Dalfiume, *Desegregation of the U.S. Armed Forces: Fighting on Two Fronts, 1939–1953* (Columbia: University of Missouri Press, 1969), 40.

15. Bowers, Hammond, and MacGarrigle, *Black Soldier*, 19.

16. Herbert Garfinkel, *When Negroes March: The March on Washington Movement in the Organizational Politics for FEPC* (1959; repr., New York: Atheneum, 1969), 34.

17. "No Longer Forgotten: African American Service Women during the Korean War Era," Military Women's Memorial, https://womensmemorial.org.

18. Robert B. Edgerton, *Hidden Heroism: Black Soldiers in America's Wars* (Boulder, CO: Westview Press, 2001), 134.

19. Henry Stimson quoted in Michael Lee Lanning, *The African-American Soldier: From Crispus Attucks to Colin Powell* (Secaucus, NJ: Birch Lane Press, 1997), 164.

20. Between 1943 and 1945, 50 percent of Blacks and 30 percent of whites were rejected by the Selective Service System for failing to meet health and literacy standards. Bowers, Hammond, and MacGarrigle, *Black Soldier*, 19.

21. Stimson quoted in Edgerton, *Hidden Heroism*, 134.

22. Edgerton, 135.

23. Cathy D. Knepper, ed., *Dear Mrs. Roosevelt: Letters to Eleanor Roosevelt through Depression and War* (New York: Carroll and Graf, 2004), 215.

24. Mershon and Schlossman, *Foxholes and Color Lines*, 94.

25. *Atlantic World* quoted in Rawn James Jr., *The Double V: How Wars, Protest, and Harry Truman Desegregated America's Military* (New York: Bloomsbury Press, 2012), Kindle.

26. "Still Cannon Fodder," *Baltimore Afro-American*, Apr. 20, 1940.

27. *Pittsburgh Courier* quoted in James, *Double V*, and on http://hennessyhistory.wiki spaces.com/Double+Victory+Campaign-1, accessed Mar. 14, 2013, no longer active.

28. Quoted in Phillip McGuire, *He, Too, Spoke for Democracy: Judge Hastie, World War II, and the Black Soldier* (New York: Praeger, 1988), 55.

29. Mershon and Schlossman, *Foxholes and Color Lines*, 136–38.

30. Mershon and Schlossman, 142–43.

31. Morris J. MacGregor Jr., *Integration of the Armed Forces: 1940–1965* (Washington, DC: Center of Military History, United States Army, 1981).

32. Mershon and Schlossman, *Foxholes and Color Lines*, 150, 157.

33. Bernard Jackson, NAACP Youth Council, Boston, to civilian aide to Assistant Secretary of War, Apr. 4, 1946, and *Pittsburgh Courier*, May 11, 1946, as quoted in MacGregor, *Integration of the Armed Forces*.

34. *Pittsburgh Post-Gazette*, Dec. 19, 1946, as noted in MacGregor, *Integration of the Armed Forces*, 186n48.

35. Mershon and Schlossman, *Foxholes and Color Lines*, 81.

36. *Lynching in America: Targeting Black Veterans* (Montgomery, AL: Equal Justice Initiative, 2017), https://eji.org/reports/targeting-black-veterans/.

37. Steven F. Lawson, ed., *To Secure These Rights: The Report of President Harry S Truman's Committee on Civil Rights* (Boston: Bedford/St. Martin's, 2004), 4.

38. Langston Hughes, "Here to Yonder: Hey Doc! I Got Jim Crow Shock!," *Chicago Defender*, Feb. 26, 1944, 12.

39. So, too, was the perceived new behavior of returning veterans. In Georgia in 1946, Black World War II veteran Roger Malcolm was accused of stabbing his white employer after the man made a sexual advance on Malcolm's wife. Following Malcolm's release from jail, he and his wife, her sister, and the sister's husband were all murdered by the Ku Klux Klan, who regarded Malcolm, according to author James Lawson, as one of the "'bad Negro' veterans who returned from war and were 'getting out of place.'" Quoted in Christopher S. Parker, *Fighting for Democracy: Black Veterans and the Struggle against White Supremacy in the Postwar South* (Princeton, NJ: Princeton University Press, 2009), 47.

40. "The Story of Jim Crow Travel," *Chicago Defender*, Apr. 12, 1952, 10.

41. Mershon and Schlossman, *Foxholes and Color Lines*, 82.

42. Bowers, Hammond, and MacGarrigle, *Black Soldier*, 20.

43. "White MPs Beat Negro Sailor on Alabama Train," *Chicago Defender*, June 2, 1945, 8.

44. Bayard Rustin, oral history interview by Ed Edwin, Sept. 12, 1985, Columbia University Oral History Collection.

45. "Negro Rights: They Will Come When the White South's Fear Is Divided into Rational Parts," *Life*, Apr. 24, 1944.

46. "German Jim Crow," *Baltimore Afro-American*, Jan. 27, 1940.

47. Gunnar Myrdal, *An American Dilemma: The Negro Problem and Modern Democracy* (New York: Harper & Brothers, 1944), 75.

48. Editorial, *Nation*, July 3, 1943.

49. Quoted in Jon E. Taylor, *Freedom to Serve: Truman, Civil Rights, and Executive Order 9981* (New York: Routledge, 2013), 72.

50. Quoted in Philip M. Klinkner and Rogers M. Smith, *The Unsteady March: The Rise and Decline of Racial Equality in America* (Chicago: University of Chicago Press, 1999), 199, 204.

51. Bowers, Hammond, and MacGarrigle, *Black Soldier*, 36; Truman quote in David McCullough, *Truman* (New York: Simon and Schuster, 1992), 588.

52. "No Defense for Jim Crow, Vets' Bigwig Admits," *Chicago Defender*, Nov. 10, 1945.

53. For an excellent overview of the historiography dealing with Truman's civil rights record, see Taylor, *Freedom to Serve*, 120–33.

54. Quoted in James, *Double V*, 217.

55. Quoted in James, 217.

56. Quoted in Taylor, *Freedom to Serve*, 72–73.

57. "Presses for Rights," *Chicago Defender*, July 27, 1948; Alfred E. Smith, "Adventures in Race Relations," *Chicago Defender*, July 17, 1948; Daniel Widener, "Soul City Sue and the Bugout Blues: Black American Narratives of the Forgotten War," in *Afro Asia: Revolutionary Political and Cultural Connections Between African Americans and Asian Americans*, ed. Fred Ho and Bill V. Mullen (Durham, NC: Duke University Press, 2008), 56.

58. Harry S. Truman, Executive Order 9981, July 26, 1948, Harry S. Truman Library and Museum, https://www.trumanlibrary.gov/library/executive-orders/9981/executive-order-9981.

59. *New York Times*, July 27, 1948; *Los Angeles Times*, July 27, 1948.

60. *Chicago Defender*, July 31, 1950, 1; "President Truman Wipes Out Segregation in Armed Forces," *Chicago Defender*, July 31, 1948; "Truman Army Order Means No Segregation," *Chicago Defender*, Aug. 7, 1948.

61. As quoted in MacGregor, *Integration of the Armed Forces*.

62. "Randolph, League Not Satisfied by Truman's Order," *Chicago Defender*, Aug. 7, 1948, 5.

63. "Offer 7-Point Plan to Overcome Jim Crow in U.S. Armed Forces," *Chicago Defender*, Sept. 18, 1948, 1.

64. "Brass Tacks," *Chicago Defender*, Oct. 9, 1948.

65. "Non-Violent League to Bolt Draft Despite Randolph," *Chicago Defender*, Aug. 28, 1948, 1.

66. "Civil Disobedience," *Chicago Defender*, Sept. 25, 1948, 14.

67. Mark Slagle, "Mightier Than the Sword? The Black Press and the End of Racial Segregation in the U.S. Military, 1948–1954" (PhD diss., University of North Carolina at Chapel Hill, 2010), 99–102.

68. Quoted in Martin Duberman, *Paul Robeson* (New York: New Press, 1996), 341–42.

69. Vance H. Marchbanks Sr., "What the People Say: Why Truman Won," *Chicago Defender*, Nov. 20, 1948, 6.

70. Omar Bradley, op-ed, *Washington Post*, July 28, 1948.

71. "Retain Race Line in Army: Gen. Bradley," *Chicago Defender*, July 28, 1948, 1; "Bradley Makes Himself Clear," *Chicago Defender*, Sept. 4, 1948, 3. Baldwin quoted in MacGregor, *Integration of the Armed Forces*.

72. James L. Hicks, "Army Still Setting Up Jim Crow Units," *Cleveland Call and Post*, Mar. 15, 1952, 1A.

CHAPTER 1

1. "The Story of Jim Crow Travel," *Chicago Defender*, Apr. 12, 1952, 10.

2. "48 Soldiers Defy Jim Crow Law; Get $1,573 Fine," *Chicago Defender*, Dec. 5, 1953, 1.

3. "48 Soldiers Defy Jim Crow Law"; "Seat Row Revises Bus Issue," *Chicago Defender*, Aug. 1, 1953, 1.

4. "Speaking of Travel," *Chicago Defender*, May 22, 1954, 2.

5. James A. Wiggins, sergeant 1st class, 24th Infantry Regiment, 25th Infantry Division, US Army, interview by Hattie Lowry, Apr. 8, 2003, Augusta, GA, Veterans History Project.

6. John Biewen and Stephen Smith, *Korea: The Unfinished War*, American RadioWorks, Minnesota Public Radio, June 2003, http://americanradioworks.publicradio.org/features /korea/.

CHAPTER 2

1. Civil Rights Congress, *We Charge Genocide: The Historic Petition to the United Nations for Relief from a Crime of the United States Government against the Negro People* (New York: Civil Rights Congress, 1951), 173.

2. "Army to Send All Inductees to Dixie Camp: Soldiers Must Go to One of the 'Worst Posts'; Airmen to Go to the Coast." *New York Amsterdam News*, Jan. 25, 1947, 1.

3. James L. Hicks, "Army Sends Wounded Korea Vets to Benning, Jim Crow," *Afro-American*, June 16, 1951, 5.

4. James L. Hicks, "Benning CO's Orders to Mix Are Ignored: General Fresh from Korea Fights Alone," *Afro-American*, June 16, 1951, 1.

5. Hicks, 1.

6. The semiofficial book on the history of Fort Benning, Peggy A. Stelpflug and Richard Hyatt, *Home of the Infantry: The History of Fort Benning* (Macon, GA: Mercer University Press, 2007), skips over the period of segregation and pays scant attention to diversity or equality on the base.

7. "Say Army Schools Use Jim Crow," *Philadelphia Tribune*, Oct. 7, 1952, 16.

8. James L. Hicks, "Civilian Personnel Segregated at Fort Belvoir," *Atlanta Daily World*, Jan. 4, 1952, 5.

9. James L. Hicks, "Mixed Marine School Proves That Truman Order Works: Major 'Sugar Ray' Robinson Runs Camp Lejeune Show, Integration Success at N.C. Camp Is Proof That It Could Work at Ft. Belvoir Also," *Afro-American*, Mar. 29, 1952, 22.

10. "Fort Belvoir Still Tense after MPs Slay Innocent Soldier," *Pittsburgh Courier*, Sept. 10, 1949, 3.

11. Hicks, "Civilian Personnel."

12. Hicks, "Mixed Marine School."

13. Hicks, "Civilian Personnel."

14. James L. Hicks, "Camp Pickett, Va. Sings a 'Symphony of Integration,'" *Atlanta Daily World*, Aug. 21, 1951, 1.

15. James. L. Hicks, "Integration Working at Virginia Army Camp," *Atlanta Daily World*, Sept. 27, 1951, 1.

16. "Jim Crow as Usual at Army's Fort Knox," *Cleveland Call and Post*, Aug. 19, 1950, 1-A; Ralph Matthews, "Jim Crow Riding High in the 'Land of Aloha,'" *New York Amsterdam News*, Aug. 11, 1951, 28.

17. James L. Hicks, "Inductees Separated on Arrival; Colonel Defends Jim Crowism," *Cleveland Call and Post*, Jan. 5, 1951, 1B.

18. James L. Hicks, "Integration Working Well at Camp Hood in Texas: Texas Is Amazed It Works So Well," *Baltimore Afro-American*, June 30, 1951, 5.

19. James L. Hicks, "Camp Rucker General Defies President Truman's Order to

Integrate Group: 406th Brigade Only Unit Not Obeying Order," *Afro-American*, June 23, 1951, 3.

20. "Miss. Segregation Laws Hit Oriental War Brides," *Chicago Defender*, May 31, 1952, 1.

21. "S.C. Shipyard Takes 1st Step to End Bias," *New York Amsterdam News*, Sept. 5, 1953, 20.

22. "End of Segregated Army Basic Training Requested by Delegation from Minn.," *Afro-American*, Mar. 10, 1951, 12.

23. James L. Hicks, "Camp Edwards in Mass. 'Disgrace' Worse Than Dixie," *Afro-American*, Aug. 18, 1951, 1.

24. B. K. Thorne, "Mixed Races Train Well in Air Force," *New York Times*, Sept. 18, 1949, 53; Otto McClarrin, "Langley Air Base Policy on Negro Pilots Lauded," *Pittsburgh Courier*, Mar. 4, 1950, 6.

25. James Hicks, "Courageous General Chases Jim-Crow from Georgia Air Base," *Cleveland Call and Post*, June 16, 1951, 1A.

26. "Maxwell Field Airmen Given Jim Crow Dose," *Atlanta Daily World*, July 3, 1949, 1.

27. Collins C. George, "Segregated Unit Sore Spot at Maxwell Field," *Pittsburgh Courier*, Apr. 14, 1951, 8.

28. George, 8.

29. Morris J. MacGregor Jr., *Integration of the Armed Forces: 1940–1965* (Washington, DC: Center of Military History, United States Army, 1981), 460.

30. Hicks, "Mixed Marine School."

31. Collins C. George, "13 Officers Railroaded: Courier Bares Vicious Move at Camp McCoy," *Pittsburgh Courier*, Oct. 6, 1951, 1.

32. George, 1.

33. George, 1.

34. Collins C. George, "Army Whitewashes Bias Charges at Camp McCoy: Unit Held Up at Port of Embarkation," *Pittsburgh Courier*, Oct. 27, 1951, 1.

35. George, 1.

36. "Army Removes Bustin' Col: Ex-McCoy Officer Ousted," *Pittsburgh Courier*, Apr. 5, 1952, 1.

37. "Army Removes Bustin' Col.," 1.

38. "Army Removes Bustin' Col.," 1.

39. "Army Removes Bustin' Col.," 1.

40. George, "Army Whitewashes Bias Charges."

CHAPTER 3

1. "A Dreamer's Holiday," words by Kim Gannon, music by Mabel Wayne, copyright 1949, Skidmore Music Company, New York. As used in John Biewen and Stephen Smith, *Korea: The Unfinished War*, American RadioWorks, Minnesota Public Radio, June 2003, http://americanradioworks.publicradio.org/features/korea/.

2. Bruce Cumings, *The Korean War: A History* (New York: Modern Library, 2010), xvi.

3. Cumings, 4.

4. Cumings, xvi; Richard Peters and Xiaobing Li, *Voices from the Korean War: Personal Stories of American, Korean, and Chinese Soldiers* (Frankfort: University Press of Kentucky, 2005), 3.

5. As quoted in Peters and Li, *Voices from the Korean War*, 4.

6. Peters and Li, 5.

7. Peters and Li, 5.

8. Peters and Li, 5–6.

9. Peters and Li, 4, 6.

10. Peters and Li, 4.

11. Peters and Li, 7.

12. Peters and Li, 4.

13. Peters and Li, 7–8.

14. Peters and Li, 8–9.

15. Peters and Li, 9–10.

16. Cumings, *Korean War*, 5, 6.

17. Biewen and Smith, *Korea*.

18. Peters and Li, *Voices from the Korean War*, 11, 13.

19. As quoted in Sergei N. Goncharov, John W. Lewis, and Xue Litai, *Uncertain Partners: Stalin, Mao, and the Korean War* (Stanford, CA: Stanford University Press, 1993), 145.

20. Peters and Li, *Voices from the Korean War*, 13–14.

21. Cumings, *Korean War*, 6.

22. Cumings, 11.

23. Cumings, 12–13.

24. Peters and Li, *Voices from the Korean War*, 15; Cumings, *Korean War*, 13. The marines also had an additional 75,370.

25. Charles M. Bussey, *Firefight at Yechon: Courage and Racism in the Korean War.* (Lincoln: University of Nebraska Press, 2002), 41–42.

26. Cumings, *Korean War*, 14–15.

27. Bussey, *Firefight at Yechon*, 41–42.

28. Kimberley L. Phillips, *War! What Is It Good For? Black Freedom Struggles and the U.S. Military from World War II to Iraq* (Chapel Hill: University of North Carolina Press, 2012), 130–31.

29. "Tan GIs Go into Action!," *Chicago Defender*, July 8, 1950, 1.

30. "Eyewitness Tells How Negro GIs Won First U.S. Victory in Korea: 24th Takes City," *Pittsburgh Courier*, July 29, 1950, 1.

31. "U.S. Hails Tan Warriors: 24th Infantry Victory May Turn Tide of Battle," *Chicago Defender*, July 29, 1950, 1.

32. "U.S. Hails Tan Warriors."

33. "Truman Praises Negro Soldier," *Los Angeles Times*, Sept. 12, 1950, 4.

34. "Holding That Line," *Chicago Defender*, Aug. 5, 1950, 6.

35. "24th Hit Hard: 24th Fights in Tatters; Hicks Says Casualties STAGGERING!!" *Baltimore Afro-American*, Aug. 19, 1950, 1.

36. "24th Company Ambushed; Heavy Losses," *Pittsburgh Courier*, Aug. 19, 1950, 1; "24th Soldiers Do Impossible: Pay Terrific Price to 'Hold That Line,'" *Afro-American*, Aug. 12, 1950, 1.

37. "24th Hit Hard."

38. "Officers in Scrap on Korea Front," *Chicago Defender*, Aug. 26, 1950, 1.

39. Peters and Li, *Voices from the Korean War*, 17–19.

40. "Here's How the 24th Bested White Rivals: Bussey's Engineers Beat Path to Sea," *Afro-American*, Dec. 9, 1950, 7.

41. Editorial, "Abolish 'Negro' Units," *Pittsburgh Courier*, Sept. 9, 1950.

42. "Color Line Falls in Korea as Army Mixes Combat Units," *Chicago Defender*, Sept. 23, 1950, 7.

43. "End Jim Crow Everywhere, NAACP Executives Demand: Home Front Color Line a Disgrace," *New York Amsterdam News*, Sept. 15, 1950, 3.

44. Mary L. Dudziak, *Cold War Civil Rights: Race and the Image of American Democracy* (Princeton, NJ: Princeton University Press, 2000), 13.

45. "Color Line Falls in Korea."

46. Biewen and Smith, *Korea*.

47. "Negro Unit Hailed on Hungnam Stand: Platoon Led by Bronx Officer Staved Off Most Serious Threat to Beachhead," *New York Times*, Dec. 22, 1950, 3.

48. "Town's First War Dead Are Negro," *Chicago Defender*, Sept. 23, 1950, 11.

49. "Bravery of Negro Troops Praised in Senate by Lehman," *Philadelphia Tribune*, Aug. 29, 1950, 2.

50. Charles Lucas, "Civil Rights Watch Dog: End of the 24th Infantry," *Cleveland Call and Post*, Aug. 4, 1951, 2B.

51. Lucas.

52. Sherie Mershon and Steven Schlossman, *Foxholes and Color Lines: Desegregating the U.S. Armed Forces* (Baltimore: Johns Hopkins University Press, 2002), 218–19; Daniel Widener, "Soul City Sue and the Bugout Blues: Black American Narratives of the Forgotten War," in *Afro Asia: Revolutionary Political and Cultural Connections Between African Americans and Asian Americans*, ed. Fred Ho and Bill V. Mullen (Durham, NC: Duke University Press, 2008), 59.

53. As quoted in Leo Bogart, ed., *Project Clear: Social Research and the Desegregation of the United States Army* (1969; repr. New Brunswick, NJ: Transaction Publishers, 1992), 16, 18–19.

54. "Along the Korean War Front: Southern Whites, Negroes Give Jim Crow Hard Time in Mixed Tank Group," *Chicago Defender*, Sept. 2, 1950, 4.

55. Mershon and Schlossman, *Foxholes and Color Lines*, 224.

56. "Clevelander Home, Safe from War: Says Army Integration in Korea Lifts Morale," *Cleveland Call and Post*, Oct. 6, 1951, 3B.

57. Mershon and Schlossman, *Foxholes and Color Lines*, 227.

58. "Fire Gen. Jim Crow," *Chicago Defender*, Apr. 28, 1951, 1.

59. Mershon and Schlossman, *Foxholes and Color Lines*, 228–29.

60. Ralph Hockley, oral history interview by author, Jan. 13, 2003, Houston, TX, author's collection; Biewen and Smith, *Korea*.

61. "Army's Abolition of Segregation Brings Better Fighting in Korea," *Chicago Defender*, Jan. 31, 1953, 7.

62. "AFRO Writer Finds Peace in Korea," *Afro-American*, May 16, 1953, 22L.

63. "G.I. Integration Decried by Clark: General Says He Still Feels Mixing of White and Negro Soldiers Was a Mistake," *New York Times*, Apr. 28, 1956, 25.

64. Mershon and Schlossman, *Foxholes and Color Lines*, 230–48; MacGregor, *Integration of the Armed Forces*, 473.

65. Mershon and Schlossman, *Foxholes and Color Lines*, 248–49.

66. "Integration in Marine Corps: Expert Rifleman Lone Representative in Co.," *Afro-American*, Dec. 2, 1950, 13.

67. "Marine Laud Negro Troops for Aid: Men Turn Skepticism to Praise," *Chicago Defender*, Oct. 21, 1950, 4.

68. "Marines Sent into Battle: Tan Marines Land in Korea," *Afro-American*, Aug. 12, 1950, 12.

69. Mershon and Schlossman, *Foxholes and Color Lines*, 249.

70. "Mixed Races Train Well in Air Force, White and Negro Recruits Are Harmonious in Relations at Texas Base, Says Head," *New York Times*, Sept. 18, 1949, 53.

71. "Air Force Men Find Conditions at Maxwell Field Difficult," *Philadelphia Tribune*, July 9, 1949, 4; "Air Force Backing Dixie Bias Charge," *Philadelphia Tribune*, Nov. 24, 1953, 1.

72. "Tan Fliers Battle Reds: Tan Airmen Engaged in Air Battle," *Pittsburgh Courier*, July 15, 1950, 1.

73. Mershon and Schlossman, *Foxholes and Color Lines*, 193–97; "698 Reassigned to Integrated Air Force: Officers, Enlisted Men, WAFs of 332nd Approved by Board, *Chicago Courier*, Aug. 6, 1949, 2.

74. "Air Force's Negro Combat Leader Commands 400 White Airmen," *Philadelphia Tribune*, Feb. 26, 1955, 3.

75. "Gen. Davis Inspiration to Negro Air Crews: Chicagoan Fulfills Army's Faith," *Chicago Daily Tribune*, Jan. 2, 1955, W6.

76. "Ensign Charles Teale Is Second Negro Commissioned by U.S. Navy," *Chicago Defender*, Nov. 8, 1947, 1.

77. Mershon and Schlossberg, *Foxholes and Color Lines*, 198–203.

78. "Ohio State U. Grad First Negro Navy Ace," *Cleveland Call and Post*, Oct. 21, 1950, 3A.

79. "Navy's Negro Pilot Dies in Flames," *Cleveland Call and Post*, Dec. 16, 1950, 1A.

80. "Tan Sailors Raid Korea: Wilson Hears Admiral Laud Negro Crewmen," *Chicago Defender*, Sept. 2, 1950, 1.

81. "Tan Sailors Raid Korea," 1.

82. Most women who served in and during the Korean War did so as nurses. Melinda L. Pash, *In the Shadow of the Greatest Generation: The Americans Who Fought the Korean War* (New York: New York University Press, 2012), 163–65; Linda Witt, Judith Bellafaire, Britta Granrud, and Mary Jo Blinker, *"A Defense Weapon Known to be of Value": Servicewomen of the Korea War Era* (Hanover, NH: University Press of New England, 2005), 2.

83. Witt et al., *"Defense Weapon,"* 32, 49.

84. Witt et al., 49–51.

85. Witt et al., 50.

86. "Tokyo Hospital Now Has Four Negro Nurses," *Atlanta Daily World*, Mar. 15, 1951, 6.

87. "Queen for 13 Days on Ship: Army Nurse Home after Eight Months in Korea," *Afro-American*, Oct. 27, 1951, 22J.

88. "War Effort Needs Nurses, Our Girls Claim Refusals," *Pittsburgh Courier*, July 29, 1950, 1.

89. Witt et al., *"Defense Weapon,"* 151–52.

CHAPTER 4

1. "2-Way Integration of Negro, White Soldiers Praised by Army General," *Chicago Defender*, Sept. 16, 1950, 1.

2. Christine Knauer, *Let Us Fight as Free Men: Black Soldiers and Civil Rights* (Philadelphia: University of Pennsylvania Press, 2014), 206–7.

3. William T. Bowers, William M. Hammond, and George L. MacGarrigle, *Black Soldier, White Army: The 24th Infantry Regiment in Korea* (Honolulu: University of Hawai'i Press, 2005), 216.

4. Kimberley L. Phillips, *War! What Is It Good For? Black Freedom Struggles and the U.S. Military from World War II to Iraq* (Chapel Hill: University of North Carolina Press, 2012), 139.

5. See William T. Bowers, William M. Hammond, and George L. MacGarrigle, *Black Soldier, White Army: The 24th Infantry Regiment in Korea* (Honolulu: University of Hawaii Press, 2005).

6. Phillips, *War! What Is It Good For?*, 135–36.

7. Sherie Mershon and Steven Schlossman, *Foxholes and Color Lines: Desegregating the U.S. Armed Forces* (Baltimore: Johns Hopkins University Press, 2002), 222–23. See also "Marshall Blasts Army's Court Martial Proceedings in Korea: NAACP Attorney Blames Army for Hasty Action," *Atlanta Daily World*, Feb. 18, 1951, 1; "Courts Martial Hasty— Marshall," *Afro-American*, Feb. 24, 1951, 1; "Army Policy Blamed for Korea Trials," *Afro-American*, Mar. 17, 1951, 6.

8. Phillips, *War! What Is It Good For?*, 136.

9. As quoted in Knauer, *Let Us Fight as Free Men*, 210.

10. "24th Regiment Rates High in Honors in Korean War," *Atlanta Daily World*, Feb. 14, 1951, 4.

11. "Was 24th Used as a Scapegoat?" *Pittsburgh Courier*, Sept. 23, 1950, 1; "Tears, Cheers Greet 'Taps' for Famed 24th: Mingled Emotions Hail Deactivation," *Cleveland Call and Post*, Nov. 3, 1951, 1B.

12. "Hero Points Out Flaws in Army Integration," *Chicago Defender*, Oct. 13, 1951, 2.

13. Flori Meeks, "Ernest Shaw Helps Other Veterans," *Houston Chronicle*, Nov. 7, 2007, updated Aug. 10, 2011, https://www.chron.com/news/article/Ernest-Shaw-helps-other -veterans-1825891.php.

14. From "At that point" to "bitter ever since" is taken from the Southern Oral History Project interview by Kieran Taylor and Jennifer Dixon, June 17, 2008.

CHAPTER 5

1. Bobby A. Wintermute and David J. Ulbrich, *Race and Gender in Modern Western Warfare* (Berlin: De Gruyter, 2018), 279; Daniel Widener, "Soul City Sue and the Bugout Blues: Black American Narratives of the Forgotten War," in *Afro Asia: Revolutionary Political and Cultural Connections Between African Americans and Asian Americans*, ed. Fred Ho and Bill V. Mullen (Durham, NC: Duke University Press, 2008), 57.

2. Sherie Mershon and Steven Schlossman, *Foxholes and Color Lines: Desegregating the U.S. Armed Forces* (Baltimore: Johns Hopkins University Press, 2002), 249.

3. Mershon and Schlossman, 249.

CHAPTER 6

1. Raymond B. Lech, *Broken Soldiers* (Urbana: University of Illinois Press, 2000), 2–3; Lewis H. Carlson, *Remembered Prisoners of a Forgotten War: An Oral History of Korean War POWs* (New York: St. Martin's Press, 2002), 2–3.

2. Melinda L. Pash, *In the Shadow of the Greatest Generation: The Americans Who Fought the Korean War* (New York: New York University Press, 2012), 142–45.

3. Pash, 145.

4. Pash, 147–48, 151.

5. Pash, 155.

6. "Tales of POWS," *Lubbock (TX) Morning Avalanche*, Aug. 10, 1953, 8.

7. Lech, *Broken Soldiers*, 4–5.

8. "'Klan' Operated in Red Prison Camps," *Philadelphia Tribune*, Aug. 18, 1953, 1; "Army Probes 21 POWs to See Why They Turned Red," *Chicago Daily Tribune*, Jan. 28, 1954, 6; Daniel Widener, "Soul City Sue and the Bugout Blues: Black American Narratives of the Forgotten War," in *Afro Asia: Revolutionary Political and Cultural Connections Between African Americans and Asian Americans*, ed. Fred Ho and Bill V. Mullen (Durham, NC: Duke University Press, 2008), 68. One of the Reactionary groups called itself the KKK, and while to this day it is disputed whether this was just a name or was a reference to the Klan, it seems unlikely to have been a benign reference.

9. "Freed War Prisoners Say Reds Played Race vs. Race," *Chicago Defender*, Aug. 15, 1953, 1; "Brave GIs Defied Red Captors," *Philadelphia Tribune*, Aug. 29, 1953, 1.

10. "Some POWs Desert 'Land of Jim Crow,'" *Afro-American*, Aug. 15, 1953, 1.

11. "Brave GIs Defied Red Captors," *Philadelphia Tribune*, Aug. 29, 1953, 1.

12. "Freed War Prisoners."

13. "Brave GIs Defied Red Captors."

14. "Brave GIs Defied Red Captors."

15. "POW Relates Beatings Received from Reds," *Atlanta Daily World*, Oct. 3, 1954, 1; "Former POW Reflects on Life in Captivity," *Red Rover* (Naval Hospital Oakland) 4, no. 1 (January 1992).

16. *Jet*, Sept. 3, 1953, 32.

17. "Former POW Reflects on Life in Captivity."

18. "Some POWs Desert 'Land of Jim Crow,'" *Afro-American*, Aug. 15, 1953, 1.

19. "Inter-Camp Olympics" (program), Pyuktong, DPRK, 1952. Courtesy of Korean War: Weapons and History, http://www.koreanwaronline.com/arms/.

20. "Inter-Camp Olympics."

21. Lynn Niedermeier, "The POW Olympics," WKU Libraries Blog, Apr. 23, 2014, https://library.blog.wku.edu/tag/korean-war/.

22. Clarence Adams, *An American Dream: The Life of an African American Soldier and POW Who Spent 12 Years in Communist China* (Amherst: University of Massachusetts Press, 2007), 62.

23. "Former POW Reflects on Life in Captivity."

24. "21 Americans Tell Why They Joined Reds," *Los Angeles Times*, Jan. 27, 1954, 1.

25. "2 Ex-POWs Called 'Squealers,'" *Afro-American*, Feb. 6, 1954, 1.

26. "Army Probes 21 POWs to See Why They Turned Red," *Chicago Daily Tribune*, Jan. 28, 1954, 6.

27. "Negro Deserters Blast Segregation in America: Recall Head-Whippings by Cops," *Pittsburgh Courier*, Feb. 6, 1954.

28. "21 Americans Tell Why They Joined Reds."

29. "Revolution in U.S.!," *Chicago Daily Tribune*, Oct. 26, 1953, 1.

30. "Army Probes 21 POWs."

31. As quoted in Knauer, *Let Us Fight as Free Men*, 214.

32. As quoted in Knauer, 215.

33. "Reds Made Overtures to Negro Prisoners," *Philadelphia Tribune*, Aug. 11, 1953, 1.

34. "Ex-POWs Agree Negroes Nixed Red Propaganda," *Cleveland Call and Post*, Aug. 22, 1953, 1.

35. "POW's Two Years Later: The Other Side of the Coin," *Afro-American*, Mar. 12, 1955, A10.

36. "Ex-POW in China Tells Shirley: 'I Know I'm Doing the Right Thing,'" *Pittsburgh Courier*, Apr. 25, 1959, B1.

37. "Bare Red Plans to Use 3 Negro POWs to Carry on Sabotage in U.S.," *Chicago Defender*, May 8, 1954, 3.

38. "Bare Red Plans."

39. "Korean War Defector, as 'Voice' of Hanoi, Bids G.I.'s Get Out," *New York Times*, Aug. 15, 1965, 3.

40. "Ex-POW in China."

41. Adams, *American Dream*.

42. "Tales of POWs," *Lubbock (TX) Morning Avalanche*, Aug. 10, 1953, 8.

43. Lech, *Broken Soldiers*, 216.

44. Lech, 51–57; "Took Food of P.W.'s: Witness Tells of Cruelties," *Kansas City (MO) Times*, Feb. 17, 1954, 29; "P.W. Case Is Cut Down: One Murder Charge and Larceny Count Are Dropped," *Kansas City (MO) Times*, Feb. 19, 1954, 27; "Ex-POW Testifies against Soldier: Says He Saw Sick Captive Slide to His Death from Back of Rothwell B. Floyd," *Joplin (MO) Globe*, Feb. 13, 1954, 5.

45. Lech, *Broken Soldiers*, 55.

46. Lech, 265; "Ex-PW Freed of Murder, 'Guilty' of Slapping Alabama Colonel," *Atlanta Daily World*, Apr. 2, 1954, 1; "P.O.W. Conviction Upheld," *New York Times*, Mar. 31, 1955, 5.

47. "Freed Prisoners Tell of Tortures," *Courier*, Aug. 15, 1953, 3.

48. Adams died in 1999.

CHAPTER 7

1. "Army Integration Depends on Korea," *Afro-American*, Nov. 24, 1951, 14.

2. "Integration: A Beneficial By-Product," *Chicago Defender*, Aug. 15, 1953, 11; Daniel Widener, "Soul City Sue and the Bugout Blues: Black American Narratives of the Forgotten War," in *Afro Asia: Revolutionary Political and Cultural Connections Between African Americans and Asian Americans*, ed. Fred Ho and Bill V. Mullen (Durham, NC: Duke University Press, 2008), 60.

3. "Army Integration Offers Guide for Desegregation in Schools," *Afro-American*, Apr. 23, 1955, 14.

4. Charles Day quoted in John Biewen and Stephen Smith, *Korea: The Unfinished War*, American RadioWorks, Minnesota Public Radio, June 2003, http://americanradioworks .publicradio.org/features/korea/.

5. Widener, "Soul City Sue," 56.

6. "48 Soldiers Defy Jim Crow Law; Get $1,573 Fine," *Chicago Defender*, Dec. 5, 1953, 1.

7. "Seat Row Revives Bus Issue," *Chicago Defender*, Aug. 1, 1953, 1; "Speaking of Travel," *Chicago Defender*, May 22, 1954, 2.

8. "Ft. Riley GI Beaten, U.S. Quiz Asked," *Chicago Defender*, June 13, 1953, 3.

9. "Head-Whipping Cops Sued for $25,000: 13 Stitches Used to Sew Up Wounds in Veteran's Skull," *Philadelphia Tribune*, Oct. 30, 1956, 1.

10. "Indicted Mississippi Sherriff Shot and Killed Chicago Man in 1959," *Chicago Daily Defender*, Oct. 6, 1964, 2.

11. "Selma Rejects Bid by Sheriff Clark," *New York Times*, Nov. 10, 1966, 30.

12. "Birmingham's First Colored Policeman 'Proud, Honored,'" *Afro-American*, Apr. 9, 1966, 13.

13. "Offer $26,000 Reward after Bomb Killing," *Chicago Tribune*, Mar. 1, 1967, B8.

14. Thomas A. Johnson, "Negro Veteran Is Confused and Bitter," *New York Times*, July 29, 1968, 1, 14.

15. "Negro Veteran Is Confused and Bitter," 14.

16. Timothy B. Tyson, *Radio Free Dixie: Robert F. Williams and the Roots of Black Power* (Chapel Hill: University of North Carolina Press, 1999), 46–48.

17. Tyson, 72–73.

18. Tyson, 79–89.

19. Lance Hill, *The Deacons for Defense: Armed Resistance and the Civil Rights Movement* (Chapel Hill: University of North Carolina Press, 2004), 24.

20. Hill, 26.

21. Lance Hill, "The Deacons for Defense: Armed Resistance and the Civil Rights Movement" (PhD diss., Tulane University, 1997), 140.

22. Hill, *Deacons for Defense*, 25.

23. Hill, "Deacons for Defense," 141–42.

24. Hill, *Deacons for Defense*, 2.

25. Hill, 27.

26. James Forman, *The Making of Black Revolutionaries* (Seattle: University of Washington Press, 1972), 64.

27. "James Forman Dies at 76: Was Pioneer in Civil Rights," *New York Times*, Jan. 12, 2005.

28. Forman, *Making of Black Revolutionaries*, 67.

29. Forman, 59.

30. "Amiri Baraka, Polarizing Poet and Playwright, Dies at 79," *New York Times*, Jan. 10, 2014, https://www.nytimes.com/2014/01/10/arts/amiri-baraka-polarizing-poet-and -playwright-dies-at-79.html.

31. "Amiri Baraka"; Forman, *Making of Black Revolutionaries*, 64.

CHAPTER 8

1. Elbert "Big Man" Howard, *Panther on the Prowl* (Baltimore: BCP Digital, 2002), 15–16.

CONCLUSION

1. "Top Medal Urged for 2: Korean Heroism of White Officer and Negro Private Cited," *New York Times*, Mar. 23, 1953, 3.

2. "Soldier, 19, Saves Officers from Red Fury," *Los Angeles Sentinel*, Mar. 19, 1953, A1.

3. "Tan GI Saves Wounded Colonel from Korea Reds," *Pittsburgh Courier*, Mar. 21, 1953, 1; "American GI Kills Eight, Rescues CO," *Pittsburgh Courier*, Mar. 19, 1953, 1.

4. "Naselle Student Project Discovers Forgotten Hero," *Chinook Observer* (Long Beach, WA), May 2, 2011.

5. "Stanley Gets Silver Star," *Atlanta Daily World*, Mar. 24, 1953, 1; "Fast-Shooting GI Called 'Bravest' by Man He Saved," *Philadelphia Tribune*, Mar. 21, 1953, 1.

6. Robert Shetterly, "Clyde Kennard," Americans Who Tell the Truth, https://www .americanswhotellthetruth.org/portraits/clyde-kennard (accessed July 4, 2013); "Civil Rights Trailblazer Clyde Kennard Remembered," *Clarion-Ledger* (Jackson, MS), July 5, 2013.

7. Dernoral Davis, "Clyde Kennard," *Mississippi Encyclopedia*, updated Apr. 14, 2018, https://mississippiencyclopedia.org/entries/clyde-kennard/; Shetterly, "Clyde Kennard."

8. Tom Dent, "Portrait of Three Heroes," *Freedomways*, Second Quarter, 1965, 257.

9. "Clyde Kennard Died as a Martyr," *Chicago Daily Defender*, July 8, 1963, 4.

10. "Clyde Kennard Died as a Martyr."

11. John Dittmer, *Local People: The Struggle for Civil Rights in Mississippi* (Urbana: University of Illinois Press, 1995), 79–83.

12. Timothy J. Minchin and John A. Salmond, "'The Saddest Story of the Whole Movement': The Clyde Kennard Case and the Search for Racial Reconciliation in Mississippi, 1955–2007," *Journal of Mississippi History* 71 (2009): 191–234.

13. Shetterly, "Clyde Kennard."

14. Dent, "Portrait of Three Heroes," 257; Minchin and Salmond, "'Saddest Story,'" 197.

15. Minchin and Salmond, "'Saddest Story,'" 197.

16. Reverend Malcolm Boyd, "Blind No More," *Pittsburgh Courier*, Aug. 17, 1963.

Bibliography

MANUSCRIPT AND ORAL HISTORY COLLECTIONS

All oral histories were conducted by the author unless otherwise indicated.

American *RadioWorks,* Korea: The Unfinished War *interviews,*
   Minnesota Public Radio, St. Paul, Minnesota
   Gerald L. Bailey Jr., interview by Tina Tennessen, August 3, 2002
   Billy J. Baines, January 10, 2003
   Julius W. Becton Jr., interview by Kate Ellis and Stephen Smith, February 2003
   Reamer C. Bell, interview by Kate Ellis and Stephen Smith, August 23, 2002
   Dorothy M. (Phillips) Boyd, October 20, 2002
   Melvin S. Boykin, interview by Kate Ellis and Stephen Smith, September 5, 2002
   Jessie Brown, interview by Stephen Smith, January 7, 2003
   William Cooke, October 23, 2002
   George Cureaux Jr., interview by Kate Ellis and Stephen Smith, August 2002
   Aden R. Darity Jr., October 25, 2002
   Isaac Gardner, interview by Kate Ellis, September 2002
   Hansel C. Hall, interview by Stephen Smith and Tina Tennessen, July 22, 2002
   Mark Brady Hannah Jr., January 10, 2003
   Ralph Hockley, January 13, 2003, Houston
   Laurence "Larry" Hogan, October 25, 2002
   Clentell Jackson, interview by Tina Tennessen, September 10, 2002
   John B. Jackson, January 10, 2003
   William L. Jackson, interview by Kate Ellis and Stephen Smith, August 23, 2002
   Samuel King, interview by Kate Ellis and Stephen Smith, August 24, 2002
   James H. Lacy, interview by Stephen Smith and Gerald Early, January 8, 2003
   Larry "Len" Lockley, October 29, 2002
   Isham McClenney, interview by Stephen Smith, January 7, 2003
   Alan Nelson, October 20, 2002
   Edward L. Posey, interview by Kate Ellis and Stephen Smith, August 5, 2002
   Ernest K. Shaw, January 10, 2003
   Stanley Perry Stone, interview by Tina Tennessen, August 19, 2002
   Joe Tamayo, interview by Ellen Guettler, November 23, 2002
   Manual "Manny" Texeiras, October 22, 2002

Harry Townsend, interview by Stephen Smith, March 7, 2003

Harold Woodman, interview by Kate Ellis and Stephen Smith, September 6, 2002

Eddie Wright, October 14, 2002

Andersonville National History Site Oral History Project, Andersonville, Georgia

Curtis Bolton, interview by Alan Marsh, June 10, 2004

Charlie Code Sr., November 6, 1993

Prestee Davis, interview by Alan Marsh, August 3, 1996

Samuel Farrow, October 7, 1993

Robert Fletcher, April 24, 1998

Civil Rights History Project, American Folklife Center, Library of Congress, Washington, DC

Elbert "Big Man" Howard, June 30, 2016

Clarence B. Jones, April 15 and April 16, 2013

William "Bill" Saunders, interview by Kieran Taylor, June 9, 2011

Columbia University Oral History Collection

Bayard Rustin, interview by Ed Edwin, September 12, 1985

Detroit Oral History Project, Detroit, Michigan

Interview by Louis Jones, September 19, 2003

Montford Point Marines Project, University of North Carolina–
Wilmington, Wilmington, North Carolina

Fred Ash, December 17, 2004

Adner Batts, June 29, 2005

Calvin Elijah Brown, May 17, 2004

Fannie Keyes Coleman, August 17, 2005

Thomas E. Cork Sr., July 23, 2004

Charles Davenport, June 29, 2005

Johnnie Givian, August 17, 2005

Paul Hagan, May 25, 2004

Ruben Lemuel Hines, May 17, 2004

National Visionary Leadership Project, American Folklife Center,
Library of Congress, Washington, DC

Congressman John Conyers, interview by Renee Poussaint, August 20, 2007

James Meredith, interview by Renee Poussaint, June 27, 2006

Southern Oral History Project, University of North Carolina–
Chapel Hill, Chapel Hill, North Carolina.

William "Bill" Saunders, interview by Kieran Taylor and Jennifer Dixon, June 17, 2008

Veterans History Project, American Folklife Center, Library of Congress, Washington, DC

Jeanne L. Beasley, interview by William L. Browne, August 7, 2009

Charles Earnest Berry, interview by Michael Willie, February 13, 2003

Rutherford Vincent "Jack" Brice, interview by Frederick Wallace, April 22, 2003

Walter Lee Dowdy Jr., interview by Michael Willie, February 18, 2004

Charles Walter Dryden, interview by Myers Brown, February 28, 2002

Maurice Garth, interview by Courtney Thompson, n.d.

James H. Gilliam Sr., interview by Thomas Healy, October 16, 2006

Clarence Johnson, interview by Theodore Gardner, n.d.

Odell Gregory Love Sr., interview by Edward Duling and Joy Leibbrandt, n.d.

James A. "Jack" Lucas Jr., interview by David Vassar Taylor
and Rachanice Tate, November 3, 2017

Congressman Charles Bernard Rangel, interview by Col. Robert Patrick, June 20, 2013

Bertran F. Wallace, interview by Brenda Breter and Jason Caros, April 9, 2007

James A. Wiggins, interview by Hattie Lowry, April 8, 2003

NEWSPAPERS AND MAGAZINES

Atlantic Daily World
Baltimore Afro-American
Chicago Daily Defender
Chicago Defender
Chicago Daily Tribune
Chicago Tribune
Chinook Observer (Long Beach, WA)
Clarion-Ledger (Jackson, MS)
Cleveland Call and Post
Crisis
Freedomways
Houston Chronicle
Jet
Joplin (MO) Globe

Kansas City (MO) Times
Life
Los Angeles Sentinel
Los Angeles Times
Lubbock (TX) Morning Avalanche
Nation
New York Amsterdam News
New York Times
Philadelphia Tribune
Pittsburgh Courier
Pittsburgh Post-Gazette
Pittsburgh Tribune
Red Rover (Naval Hospital Oakland)
Washington Post

SONG

"A Dreamer's Holiday." Lyrics by Kim Gannon, music by Mabel Wayne. Copyright 1949, Skidmore Music Company, New York.

FILMS

M*A*S*H. Written by Richard Hooker and Ring Lardner Jr. Directed by Robert Altman. 20th Century Fox, 1970, 116 min.

Steel Helmet. Written, directed, and produced by Samuel Fuller. Deputy Corp., 1951, 84 min.

RADIO

Biewen, John, and Stephen Smith. Korea: The Unfinished War. American RadioWorks, Minnesota Public Radio, June 2003. http://americanradioworks.publicradio.org /features/korea/.

WEBSITES

Davis, Dernoral. "Clyde Kennard." Mississippi Encyclopedia. Updated Apr. 14, 2018, https://mississippiencyclopedia.org/entries/clyde-kennard/.

"Inter-Camp Olympics" (program). Pyuktong, DPRK, 1952. Courtesy of Korean War: Weapons and History. http://www.koreanwaronline.com/arms/.

Jeffrey, James. "Remembering the Black Soldiers Executed after Houston's 1917 Race

Riot." The World, February 1, 2018. https://www.pri.org/stories/2018-02-01/remem
bering-black-soldiers-executed-after-houstons-1917-race-riot

Korean War 50th Anniversary website fact sheet, archived at http://jackiewhiting.net
/ushistory/coldwar/afamkorea.htm.

Lynching in America: Targeting Black Veterans. Montgomery, AL: Equal Justice Initiative,
2017. https://eji.org/reports/targeting-black-veterans/.

Niedermeier, Lynn. "The POW Olympics." WKU Libraries Blog, April 23, 2014. https://
library.blog.wku.edu/tag/korean-war/.

"No Longer Forgotten: African American Service Women during the Korean War Era."
Military Women's Memorial. https://womensmemorial.org.

Shetterly, Robert. "Clyde Kennard." Americans Who Tell the Truth. Accessed July 4, 2013.
https://www.americanswhotellthetruth.org/portraits/clyde-kennard.

Truman, Harry S. "Executive Order 9981." July 26, 1948. Harry S. Truman Library and
Museum. https://www.trumanlibrary.gov/library/executive-orders/9981/executive
-order-9981.

BOOKS

Adams, Clarence. *An American Dream: The Life of an African American Soldier and POW Who
Spent 12 Years in Communist China.* Amherst: University of Massachusetts Press, 2007.

Astor, Gerald. *The Right to Fight: A History of African Americans in the Military.* Cambridge,
MA: Da Capo Press, 2001.

Baldovi, Louis, ed. *A Foxhole View: Personal Accounts of Hawaii's Korean War Veterans.*
Honolulu: University of Hawai'i Press, 2002.

Becton, Julius W., Jr. *Becton: Autobiography of a Soldier and Public Servant.* Annapolis:
Naval Institute Press, 2008.

Biondi, Martha. *To Stand and Fight: The Struggle for Civil Rights in Postwar New York City.*
Cambridge, MA: Harvard University Press, 2003.

Bogart, Leo, ed., *Project Clear: Social Research and the Desegregation of the United States
Army.* 1969. Reprint, New Brunswick, NJ: Transaction Publishers, 1992.

Borstelmann, Thomas. *The Cold War and the Color Line: American Race Relations in the
Global Arena.* Cambridge, MA: Harvard University Press, 2001.

Bowers, William T., William M. Hammond, and George L. MacGarrigle. *Black Soldier,
White Army: The 24th Infantry Regiment in Korea.* Honolulu: University of Hawai'i Press,
2005.

Bristol, Douglas Walter, Jr., and Heather Marie Stur, eds. *Integrating the US Military: Race,
Gender, and Sexual Orientation since World War II.* Baltimore: Johns Hopkins University
Press, 2017.

Buckley, Gail. *American Patriots: The Story of Blacks in the Military from the Revolution to
Desert Storm.* New York: Random House, 2002.

Bussey, Charles M. *Firefight at Yechon: Courage and Racism in the Korean War.* Lincoln:
University of Nebraska Press, 2002.

Bynum, Cornelius L. *A. Philip Randolph and the Struggle for Civil Rights.* Urbana:
University of Illinois Press, 2010.

Carlson, Lewis H. *Remembered Prisoners of a Forgotten War: An Oral History of Korean
War POWs.* New York: St. Martin's Press, 2002.

Civil Rights Congress. *We Charge Genocide: The Historic Petition to the United Nations for*

Relief from a Crime of the United States Government against the Negro People. New York: Civil Rights Congress, 1951.
Cumings, Bruce. *The Korean War: A History.* New York: Modern Library, 2010.
Dalfiume, Richard M. *Desegregation of the U.S. Armed Forces: Fighting on Two Fronts, 1939–1953.* Columbia: University of Missouri Press, 1969.
Diggs, Louis S. *Forgotten Road Warriors.* Self-published, 2005.
Dittmer, John. *Local People: The Struggle for Civil Rights in Mississippi.* Urbana: University of Illinois Press, 1995.
Duberman, Martin. *Paul Robeson.* New York: New Press, 1996.
Dudziak, Mary L. *Cold War Civil Rights: Race and the Image of American Democracy.* Princeton, NJ: Princeton University Press, 2000.
Edgerton, Robert B. *Hidden Heroism: Black Soldiers in America's Wars.* Boulder, CO: Westview Press, 2001.
Forman, James. *The Making of Black Revolutionaries.* Seattle: University of Washington Press, 1997.
Garfinkel, Herbert. *When Negroes March: The March on Washington Movement in the Organizational Politics for FEPC.* 1959. Reprint, New York: Atheneum, 1969.
Gates, Henry Louis, Jr., and Nellie Y. McKay, eds. *The Norton Anthology of African American Literature.* 2 vols. New York: W. W. Norton, 2014.
Geselbracht, Raymond H., ed. *The Civil Rights Legacy of Harry S. Truman.* Independence, MO: Truman State University Press, 2007.
Gibson, Truman K., Jr., with Steve Huntley. *Knocking Down Barriers: My Fight for Black America.* Evanston, IL: Northwestern University Press, 2005.
Goncharov, Sergei N., John W. Lewis, and Xue Litai. *Uncertain Partners: Stalin, Mao, and the Korean War.* Stanford, CA: Stanford University Press, 1993.
Green, Michael Cullen. *Black Yanks in the Pacific: Race in the Making of American Military Empire after World War II.* Ithaca, NY: Cornell University Press, 2010.
Halberstam, David. *The Coldest Winter: America and the Korean War.* New York: Hyperion, 2007.
Hampton, Isaac, II. *The Black Officer Corps: A History of Black Military Advancement from Integration Through Vietnam.* New York: Routledge, 2013.
Hill, Lance. *The Deacons for Defense: Armed Resistance and the Civil Rights Movement.* Chapel Hill: University of North Carolina Press, 2004.
Ho, Fred, and Bill V. Mullen, eds. *Afro Asia: Revolutionary Political and Cultural Connections Between African Americans and Asian Americans.* Durham, NC: Duke University Press, 2008.
Holway, John B. *Bloody Ground: Black Rifles in Korea.* McLean, VA: Miniver Press, 2014.
Hooker, Richard. *M*A*S*H.* 1968. Reprint, New York: Pocket Books, 1969.
Howard, Elbert "Big Man." *Panther on the Prowl.* Baltimore: BCP Digital, 2002.
Jager, Sheila Miyoshi. *Brothers at War: The Unending Conflict in Korea.* New York: W. W. Norton, 2013.
James, Rawn, Jr. *The Double V: How Wars, Protest, and Harry Truman Desegregated America's Military.* New York: Bloomsbury Press, 2012. Kindle.
Jolidan, Laurence. *Last Seen Alive: The Search for Missing POWs from the Korean War.* Austin: Ink-Slinger Press, 1995.
King, Martin Luther, Jr. *A Testament of Hope: The Essential Writings and Speeches.* Edited by James M. Washington. New York: HarperOne, 1986.

Klinkner, Philip M., and Rogers M. Smith. *The Unsteady March: The Rise and Decline of Racial Equality in America.* Chicago: University of Chicago Press, 1999.

Knauer, Christine. *Let Us Fight as Free Men: Black Soldiers and Civil Rights.* Philadelphia: University of Pennsylvania Press, 2014.

Knepper, Cathy D., ed. *Dear Mrs. Roosevelt: Letters to Eleanor Roosevelt through Depression and War.* New York: Carroll and Graf, 2004.

Lanning, Michael Lee. *The African-American Soldier: From Crispus Attucks to Colin Powell.* Secaucus, NJ: Birch Lane Press, 1997.

Lawson, Steven F., ed. *To Secure These Rights: The Report of President Harry S Truman's Committee on Civil Rights.* Boston: Bedford/St. Martin's, 2004.

Lech, Raymond B. *Broken Soldiers.* Urbana: University of Illinois Press, 2000.

Lentz-Smith, Adriane. *Freedom Struggles: African Americans and World War I.* Cambridge, MA: Harvard University Press, 2009. Kindle.

Lipsitz, George. *A Life in the Struggle: Ivory Perry and the Culture of Opposition.* Philadelphia, PA: Temple University Press, 1988.

MacGregor, Morris J., Jr., *Integration of the Armed Forces: 1940–1965.* Washington, DC: Center of Military History, 1981.

MacGregor, Morris J., Jr., and Bernard C. Nalty. *Blacks in the United States Armed Forces: Basic Documents.* Wilmington, DE: Scholarly Resources, 1977.

Malkasian, Carter. *The Korean War, 1950–1953.* Westminster, MD: Osprey Publishing, 2001.

Marshall, Samuel L. A. *The River and the Gauntlet: Defeat of the Eighth Army by the Chinese Communist Forces, November, 1950, in the Battle of Chongchon River, Korea.* Nashville: Battery Press, 1970.

Maxwell, Jeremy P. *Brotherhood in Combat: How African Americans Found Equality in Korea and Vietnam.* Norman: University of Oklahoma Press, 2018.

McCullough, David. *Truman.* New York: Simon and Schuster, 1992.

McGuire, Phillip. *He, Too, Spoke for Democracy: Judge Hastie, World War II, and the Black Soldier.* New York: Praeger, 1988.

Mershon, Sherie, and Steven Schlossman. *Foxholes and Color Lines: Desegregating the U.S. Armed Forces.* Baltimore: Johns Hopkins University Press, 2002.

Morrow, Curtis James. *What's a Commie Ever Done to Black People? A Korean War Memoir of Fighting in the U.S. Army's Last All Negro Unit.* Jefferson, NC: McFarland, 1997.

Moye, J. Todd. *Freedom Flyers: The Tuskegee Airmen of World War II.* New York: Oxford University Press, 2010.

Myrdal, Gunnar. *An American Dilemma: The Negro Problem and Modern Democracy.* New York: Harper & Brothers, 1944.

Nalty, Bernard C. *Strength for the Fight: A History of Black Americans in the Military.* New York: Free Press, 1986.

Parker, Christopher S. *Fighting for Democracy: Black Veterans and the Struggle against White Supremacy in the Postwar South.* Princeton, NJ: Princeton University Press, 2009.

Pash, Melinda L. *In the Shadow of the Greatest Generation: The Americans Who Fought the Korean War.* New York: New York University Press, 2012.

Peters, Richard and Xiaobing Li. *Voices from the Korean War: Personal Stories of American, Korean, and Chinese Soldiers.* Frankfort: University Press of Kentucky, 2005.

Phillips, Kimberley L. *War! What Is It Good For? Black Freedom Struggles and the U.S. Military from World War II to Iraq.* Chapel Hill: University of North Carolina Press, 2012.

Plummer, Brenda Gayle. *Rising Wind: Black Americans and U.S. Foreign Affairs, 1935–1960.* Chapel Hill: University of North Carolina Press, 1996.

Posey, Edward L. *The US Army's First, Last, and Only All-Black Rangers: The 2d Ranger Infantry Company (Airborne) in the Korean War, 1950–1951.* New York: Savas Beatie, 2009.

Rangel, Charles B., with Leon Wynter. *And I Haven't Had a Bad Day Since: From the Streets of Harlem to the Halls of Congress.* New York: Thomas Dunne Books, 2007.

Rishell, Lyle. *With a Black Platoon in Combat: A Year in Korea.* College Station: Texas A&M University Press, 1993.

Rosenberg, Jonathan. *How Far the Promised Land? World Affairs and the American Civil Rights Movement from the First World War to Vietnam.* Princeton, NJ: Princeton University Press, 2006.

Scipio, L. Albert. *Last of the Black Regulars: A History of the 24th Infantry Regiment, 1869–1951.* Silver Spring, MD: Roman Publications, 1983.

Spring, Vickie. *Voices Almost Lost: Korea, the Forgotten War. True Stories Told by Soldiers Themselves.* Bloomington, IL: AuthorHouse, 2011.

Stelpflug, Peggy A., and Richard Hyatt. *Home of the Infantry: The History of Fort Benning.* Macon, GA: Mercer University Press, 2007.

Stur, Heather. *The U.S. Military and Civil Rights Since World War II.* Santa Barbara, CA: Praeger, 2019.

Taylor, Jon E. *Freedom to Serve: Truman, Civil Rights, and Executive Order 9981.* New York: Routledge, 2013.

Tyson, Timothy B. *Radio Free Dixie: Robert F. Williams and the Roots of Black Power.* Chapel Hill: University of North Carolina Press, 1999.

Wendt, Simon. *The Spirit and the Shotgun: Armed Resistance and the Struggle for Civil Rights.* Gainesville: University Press of Florida, 2007.

Wintermute, Bobby A., and David J. Ulbrich. *Race and Gender in Modern Western Warfare.* Berlin: De Gruyter, 2018.

Witt, Linda, Judith Bellafaire, Britta Granrud, and Mary Jo Blinker, eds. *"A Defense Weapon Known to be of Value": Servicewomen of the Korea War Era.* Hanover, NH: University Press of New England, 2005.

Young, Charles S. *Name, Rank, and Serial Number: Exploiting Korean War POWS at Home and Abroad.* New York: Oxford University Press, 2014.

DISSERTATIONS

Hill, Lance. "The Deacons for Defense: Armed Resistance and the Civil Rights Movement." PhD diss., Tulane University, 1997.

Slagle, Mark "Mightier Than the Sword? The Black Press and the End of Racial Segregation in the U.S. Military, 1948–1954." PhD diss., University of North Carolina at Chapel Hill, 2010.

Index

Aberdeen Proving Ground (Maryland), 66, 175

"acceptance," xv–xvi

Acheson, Dean, 120

Adams, Clarence Cecil (veteran), 249–52, 265–66

Advisory Commission on Universal Training, 16

African American military personnel: awards received by, 125, 142, 145–46, 161, 166–68, 178, 186, 243; "bugout blues" (retreat) alleged of, 142–43, 148, 153, 160, 161; combat roles denied to, 2, 4, 10; courts-martial of, disproportionate, xiv, 3, 12, 103, 126, 143; and entertainment, 62–63, 223–24, 336; as "second-class" citizens, xiv, 155, 172, 188, 194–95, 202, 221, 228–29, 231, 246, 288–89, 307, 308–9, 312–13, 345; families of, 33, 49, 81–82, 143, 207–8; and judicial hearings on incompetency allegations, 103–4, 107–9; northern soldiers in South, 23, 26–27, 36–38, 44–45, 53, 54, 86–88; quotas limiting military participation, 2–3, 9–11, 18, 20, 28–29, 127, 132, 135, 209, 292. *See also* civilian life after military service; officers, African American; prisoners of war; women in armed forces, African American

African American military personnel, assignments of: artillery positions, 10, 49–50, 71, 88, 96, 103–4, 132, 161, 170, 176, 192; cooks, 24, 43, 47, 75, 94, 133, 189, 191, 205, 219, 240–41, 242, 307–8; engineer companies, xiv, 33, 35, 50, 81, 103–4, 241;

for leadership, 137–38; nurses, 62–63, 135–36, 209–10; paratroopers, 49, 50, 77, 90, 121, 125, 181; pilots, 24, 26, 49, 133–34, 206, 216, 286; radio operators, 94–95, 139, 182; stewards, 9–10, 43, 60, 83, 131–35, 205–6, 240–42; truck drivers, 43, 75, 137, 145–46, 330. *See also* officers, African American

Afro-American, 19

air drops, 123, 157–58, 165, 231, 258

Air Force, US, xv, 9, 24, 82, 205, 335; all-Japanese administrative unit, 208; battlefield experiences, 206–15; "Breakthrough on the Color Front" report, 131; continued segregation after Korean War, 332–33; and Dixiecrat senators, 132; integration of, 74–76, 98; racism in, 292–94; tactical air controllers, 206; women in, 44, 53, 136, 213–15

Air Force, US, units: 3rd Strategic Support Squadron, 74; 4th Fighter Wing Headquarters, 74, 75; 5th Air Force, 502nd Tactical Control Group, 209; 5th Air Force Command, 133; 332nd Fighter Wing, 133; 437th Interceptor Squadron, 133; Mosquitoes, 206

Alameda, California, 58

Almond, Mark (lieutenant general), 128

Almond, Ned (lieutenant general), 139

American Civil Liberties Union, 319

American Dilemma (Myrdal), 14

American Veterans' Committee, 283

Amerson, Lucius (veteran), 288

Aoki, Richard, 337

apartheid, South Africa, 169

armed forces: decommissioning of African American units, 4–5, 43, 79, 126–27, 129, 140, 159–62, 227; as dehumanizing machine, xv, 294; efficiency concerns of, 7–8; enlistment and reenlistment rates of, 1950, 127–28; firepower of, 155; loyalty oath by, 317–19; and quotas for Black military participation, 2–3, 9–11, 18, 20, 28–29, 127, 132, 135, 209, 292; resistance of, to desegregation, 9–10, 11, 19–20, 71–72, 81, 128, 138; segregated units in, ix, xiv, 24, 31, 49, 77–78, 82, 85, 92, 137–38, 154–55, 220–30; Steward Branches in, 9–10, 132–35, 205–6, 240–42; white supremacist policies in, 4–7, 11–12, 19. *See also* Air Force, US; Army, US; Coast Guard, US; Marine Corps, US; National Guard; Navy, US

Armstrong, Louis, 63

Army, US: 4th Army area, 42; assignments in Asia, Europe, and United States, 203–4; battlefield experiences of, 137–204; Black combat units in, 4, 50, 351n1; Black leadership in, 137–38; competition between regiments, 124; courts-martial, 160–61; desegregation of, 129; integrated units in battle, 178–204; integration of, 44–45, 49–50, 53, 65–66, 69–70, 77, 105, 159–62, 310; in Japan, 121; and lack of preparedness, 123, 137, 140–41, 158–59, 160, 171; as largest employer of Blacks, 2, 5; quotas limiting enlistment, 10, 135; reduction of Black forces after World War I, 4–5; reduction of forces after World War II, 120, 140–41; resistance to desegregation, 9–10, 71–72; segregated units, ix, xiv, 1–2, 24, 49, 71–72; segregated units in battle, 137–78; Special Forces, 192; Taegu (Daegu) regional headquarters, 139; World War I service, 4

Army, US, 25th Infantry Division, 24th Infantry Regiment of, xiv, 2, 3–5, 20, 24, 33, 49, 71, 93, 120, 137, 146–62, 184–85; 2nd Battalion, 33, 141–44, 148; 77th Combat Engineer Company, 124; 573rd Engineers Pontoon Bridge Company, 128; Global Communication, 203–4; integration of, 105, 159–62; lack of equipment, 123;

as last all-Black unit in US Army, 20; as oldest army regiment, 256; press coverage of, 121–23, 159–60; Puerto Rican 65th Infantry Regiment, 170; reputation of under attack, 105, 142–43, 146–47, 148, 153, 156, 159, 211, 306; Task Force Dolvin, 258

Army, US, units: 1st Armored Division, 81; 1st Cavalry Division, 120, 121, 128, 160, 306; 2nd Armored Division, 81; 2nd Infantry Division, xiv, 81, 99, 121, 129, 145, 160, 180, 192–94, 197–99, 252, 254, 258; 9th Infantry Regiment, 26, 88, 128, 137–44, 146, 343; 3rd Battalion, 130, 137–38; 503rd Field Artillery, 71–72, 161–62, 247, 249; 32nd Regiment, 99; 2nd Team Major Support (Yokohama, Japan), 96; 3rd Infantry Division, 176; 15th Infantry Regiment, 125, 138; 23rd Infantry Regiment, 192–94; 30th Infantry Regiment, 79; 41st Signal Construction Battalion, 54, 88; 555th Parachute Infantry Battalion (Triple Nickel), 49, 50, 77, 90, 121, 125, 181; 999th Field Artillery, 96, 170–78, 284; ; 7th Infantry Division, 84, 120, 145, 199; 2nd Ranger Infantry Company, 166–69; 2nd Ranger Infantry Company (Airborne), 80; 31st Infantry Regiment, 39, 51, 178, 268; 34th Infantry Regiment, 178–84; 187th Regiment, 76; 10th Cavalry (Buffalo Soldiers), 121; 10th Infantry Division, 87th Regiment, 287; 11th Airborne Division, 91–92; 24th Infantry Division: 21st Infantry Regiment, 121; 25th Regiment, 121, 147, 185; 25th Infantry Division (*see also* Army, US, 25th Infantry Division, 24th Infantry Regiment of); 27th Infantry Regiment (Wolfhounds), 142, 153, 258; 35th Infantry Regiment, 258; 187th Airborne Regimental Combat Team, 90, 287; 73rd Engineer Combat Battalion, 33; 82nd Airborne Division, 90–91, 121; 82nd Infantry Regiment, 3rd Battalion of 505th Division, 50; 87th Anti-Aircraft Battalion, 129–30; 88th Airborne, 77; 89th Medium Tank Battalion, 127; 92nd Infantry

336; northern African American views of, 265

Civil Rights Watchdog, 126

Civil War, US, 1, 3, 351n1 (intro.)

Clark, Harry A. (soldier), 343

Clark, Mark (general), 131, 179–80

Clark, Septima, 312, 314

class issues, 313–14

Cleaver, Eldridge, 340

Cleveland Call and Post, 81, 251

Cleveland Indians, first African American members of, 17

Cloud, Colonel, 240

Coast Guard, US, 43

Code, Charlie, Sr. (veteran), 268–72

Cold War, xii, 113, 115, 124–25

Coleman, Fannie Keyes (veteran), 62–63

Colmar (France), 170

colonial people, African Americans as, 19

Columbus, South Carolina, "bus incident" (1953), 23, 286

combat fatigue, 303–4

Command and General Staff College, 94

Committee Against Jim Crow in Military Service and Training, 16

Communism, 169; accusations of lead to discharge, 294, 318–20; and repatriation issue, 250–52

Communist Party, Korea, 117

Communist Party USA, 19

Como, Perry, 113

complexion, 225–26, 228–29, 307

Confederate army, 80

Congressional Medal of Honor (CMH), 168

Congress of Racial Equality (CORE), 290

Congress of the Partisans of World Peace, 19

Connally Air Force Base (Texas), 74

Constitution, US, 15, 313, 317, 324

Conyers, John (veteran, US representative), 34–36, 105–6, 286, 312, 315–16

Cooke, William (veteran), 36, 38–39, 44, 102–4, 107–9

Cork, Thomas E., Sr. (veteran), 63–65, 232–36

Corley, John T. (lieutenant colonel), 123

courts-martial: African American counsel, 210–11; discriminatory, xiv, 2–3, 103, 126, 143; and Houston incident (1918), 3; of Jackie Robinson, 12; NAACP investigation of, 160–61; of POWs, 252–53; and loyalty oath, 318–19

Covington, Clarence B. (veteran), 248

Craig Air Force Base (Alabama), 287

Cree, Arthur (veteran), 289

Crisis (NAACP journal), 3, 4

Croix de Guerre, 4

Cureaux, George, Jr. (veteran), 306–8

Dantzler, Earl (veteran), 247–48, 249

Darity, Aden R., Jr. (veteran), 175–76

Davenport, Charles (veteran), 67, 326–28

Davidson, Frederic E. (general), 296

Davis, Benjamin O. (brigadier general), 5, 133, 174, 209, 226, 296

Davis, Benjamin Oliver, Jr. (general), 133, 174, 226

Davis, Prestee (veteran), 247, 249, 276–79

Day, Charles (veteran), 284

Deacons for Defense and Justice, 286, 289–90, 291

Dean, William F. (major general), 79

Declaration of Independence, 324

dehumanization, xv, 12, 294

Delaney, Hubert (judge), 320–21

Demilitarized Zone (DMZ), 114–15, 238, 303

democracy, x, 8, 11, 16, 125, 128, 213; military personnel as "second-class" citizens at home, xiv, 155, 172, 188, 194–95, 202, 221, 228–29, 231, 246, 288–89, 307, 308–9, 312–13, 345

Democratic Party Dixiecrats, 16

Derflinger (sergeant), 196, 197

desegregation of armed forces: resistance to, 9–10, 11, 19–20, 71–72, 81, 128, 138; on battlefield, 79, 178–204; civilian life of military personnel, effect on, 283–86, 296, 298–99, 304, 307, 332–33; civil rights movement, effect on, xi–xiii, 278–79, 284–94; Cold War influence on, xii, 124–25; and experimental integrated units, 18; Korean War as impetus for, 113–36; psychological impact of, 128; symbolic